D0803432

PRAISE FOR
MARCH OF THE
MODERATES

March of the Moderates is a clear, informed and informative account of the ways in which Bill Clinton's 'New Democrats' and Tony Blair's 'New Labour' were able to build successful political movements of the centre left. It has much to consider for British and American audiences alike – and offers insights into both the policies and the personalities.

CHARLES CLARKE, *former British Home Secretary and distinguished visiting fellow at the Price School of Public Policy, University of Southern California.*

March of the Moderates is a well-researched, illuminating analysis of the realignment of progressive politics in the US and UK. Anyone looking to understand how Bill Clinton and the New Democrats and Tony Blair and New Labour regained their electorates' trust and, ultimately, managed to change their countries for the better would do well to read it.

AL FROM, *founder of the Democratic Leadership Council and author of* The New Democrats and the Return to Power.

An engrossing account of the journey to power for inspirational leaders on both sides of the Atlantic. It shows how they crafted a new future for their countries, charting both the successes and the failures. This readable book brings it home that vision and courage are needed to unlock opportunity for those who are so frequently overlooked. A timely reminder that progressive politics is about building opportunity for all, and that there is no crime in aspiration.'

BARONESS HELEN LIDDELL, *former Secretary of State for Scotland.*

'At a time when trust in politics and hope for a better future is ebbing away, this book shows it is worth a trip back to the 1990s to remind ourselves how the New Democrats and New Labour built up that trust, won five elections between them and then used that power to build a more optimistic and equal society. Of course, mistakes were made – and we should learn from them – but Blair and Clinton were the most successful centre-left leaders since FDR in the US and Attlee in the UK.'

RACHEL REEVES MP, *Chair of the Business, Energy and Industrial Strategy Committee, and author of Women of Westminster.*

MARCH OF THE MODERATES

MARCH OF THE MODERATES

Bill Clinton, Tony Blair, and the
Rebirth of Progressive Politics

Richard Carr

I.B.TAURIS

LONDON • NEW YORK • OXFORD • NEW DELHI • SYDNEY

I.B. TAURIS
Bloomsbury Publishing Plc
50 Bedford Square, London, WC1B 3DP, UK
1385 Broadway, New York, NY 10018, USA

BLOOMSBURY, I.B. TAURIS and the I.B. Tauris logo are trademarks of
Bloomsbury Publishing Plc

First published in Great Britain 2019

Copyright © Richard Carr, 2019

Richard Carr has asserted his right under the Copyright, Designs and Patents
Act, 1988, to be identified as Author of this work.

For legal purposes the Acknowledgements on pp. xiii–xiv constitute an extension
of this copyright page.

Cover design: Adriana Brioso
Cover illustration by Alice Marwick based on image by Spencer Platt/Getty Images

All rights reserved. No part of this publication may be reproduced or transmitted
in any form or by any means, electronic or mechanical, including photocopying,
recording, or any information storage or retrieval system, without prior permission
in writing from the publishers.

Bloomsbury Publishing Plc does not have any control over, or responsibility for,
any third-party websites referred to or in this book. All internet addresses given
in this book were correct at the time of going to press. The author and publisher
regret any inconvenience caused if addresses have changed or sites have
ceased to exist, but can accept no responsibility for any such changes.

A catalogue record for this book is available from the British Library.

A catalog record for this book is available from the Library of Congress.

ISBN: HB: 978-1-7883-1734-4
        ePDF: 978-1-7867-3622-2
        eBook: 978-1-7867-2616-2

Typeset by RefineCatch Limited, Bungay, Suffolk
Printed and bound in Great Britain

To find out more about our authors and books visit www.bloomsbury.com
and sign up for our newsletters.

CONTENTS

LIST OF ILLUSTRATIONS

ACKNOWLEDGEMENTS

F irst, I should thank all the interviewees who contributed their time and expertise to the research process for this book. On top of those listed in the bibliography, conversations with Lord John Eatwell, Morris Fiorina, Stan Greenberg and Mike Kenny undoubtedly helped spark some of the better ideas and eliminate some of my poorer ones. Charles Clarke was particularly kind in meeting for various coffees, whilst Nick Garland, Rachel Reeves and Dan Sleat lent a hand in welcome logistical ways. My colleagues past and present at Anglia Ruskin University – in particular, Alison Ainley, Lucy Bland, Luke Cooper, Jonathan Davis, Susan Flavin, Sean Lang, Rohan McWilliam and Will Tullett – have been great throughout the writing of this. Participants at the 2018 conference I convened at ARU on the Third Way equally provided many useful conversations. One such conference participant, Bradley Hart, took time out of researching and promoting his stellar work on *Hitler's American Friends* to assist in various ways. The usual rules about the content representing solely my own views apply.

Secondly, this project owes much to various institutions and their diligent staff. Spending time at the Hoover Institution as part of their Political Economy Workshop in the summer of 2017 was a formative experience – and Jennifer Burns was instrumental in making this possible. Stacy Davis at the Gerald R Ford Presidential Library was likewise incredibly helpful and my thanks to the Gerald R Ford Presidential Foundation for a Research Travel Grant. A Theodore C Sorensen Fellowship at the John F Kennedy Presidential Library was vital in accessing the views of JK Galbraith and particular thanks to Stephen Plotkin for this. Winning a Bordin-Gillette Fellowship at the Bentley Historical Library, University of Michigan provided valuable time to research the politics of the rust belt – my gratitude is owed to Meg McKenzie and Nancy Bartlett here. As for other archives, I must thank Herbert Ragan and all at the Clinton Presidential Library in Little Rock. Heidi Egginton, Allen Packwood and Andrew Riley at the Churchill

Archives Centre were as great as ever. To everyone who answered my overly detailed e-mails asking them to go on various archive catalogue goose chases, my apologetic thanks. On the publishing side, Olivia Dellow and all the staff at IB Tauris have been a pleasure to work with. From the planning stage to the editing process, Jo Godfrey has been brilliant throughout.

Lastly, Larry and Molly apart, some personal thanks are sorely needed. In the course of my writing this book, Sarah became as wonderful a mother as she has been a wife. The unusual hours of academia probably allow me to spend more time working from home than most, but anything parental I've done pales into insignificance by comparison. I've also been lucky for my own mother's babysitting duties helping get this thing across the line. And, finally, to baby Maeve herself – born, appropriately, in a hospital vastly upgraded under New Labour. I don't know what current celebrity will be president by the time you are of an age to read this. But one thing I can guarantee is that the joy you've brought to our lives is felt by your mum and I each and every day.

INTRODUCTION

In early 1995, the then little-known Vermont Congressman Bernie Sanders published his verdict on the incumbent President, Bill Clinton. Two decades before seeking the Democratic nomination against Clinton's wife Hillary, Sanders at least had the good grace to acknowledge that Bill was a better president than his immediate Republican predecessors, Ronald Reagan and George HW Bush. But, for the self-identified socialist, this was a pretty low bar. After all, Sanders asked, 'have [Clinton's] policies begun to seriously address the enormous problems facing our nation? No. Has he tried to build a political movement that would empower working people so they could make real improvements in their lives? Absolutely not'. Instead, mid-way through Clinton's first term, Sanders thundered that the White House needed to raise the minimum wage to '$5.50 an hour immediately'. He demanded that the president should 'put Americans back to work' and declared that he must 'press Congress for significant decreases in military spending'.

Faced with a new Republican congress emboldened by their stunning gains at the 1994 midterms, Clinton could well have metaphorically thrown such ideas in the bin. Certainly, this would fit the image of the 'Democrat in Name Only' that figures on his party's left would attempt to pin on him. But the reality was quite different. In the coming years, Clinton preceded to get a $5.15 minimum wage past the Republican Congress, oversaw unemployment falling from 5.6 per cent at the time of Sanders' column to 4.2 per cent when the president left office and reduced the defence budget from 4.3 per cent to 3.5 per cent as a percentage of GDP (including an overall reduction in nominal spending). Clinton did much to appeal to Republican sentiment too, including welfare reform, but he was always a leader who placed ends above means. And therein lay the difference between Sanders' wing of American progressivism and Bill Clinton's. The hard left brought forward its collective shopping lists and, when it came to contesting major elections, lost. The centre-left not only won power, it then delivered.[1]

Clinton's two election victories in 1992 and 1996 gave him eight years in office. In doing so, he became the first Democrat to be re-elected to the White House since Franklin Delano Roosevelt. But, astonishingly, New Labour's record in the UK of three victories (1997, 2001 and 2005) and 13 years in power was even better. In over a century of existence, only Tony Blair has ever won three successive terms for the British Labour Party and he remains the only leader to have a won a stable parliamentary majority for the left since 1966. As such, it was only in the era of New Labour and the New Democrats that the two self-proclaimed parties 'of the people' secured their trust on a regular basis. It does not seem unreasonable to suggest that there may be some lessons here.

As it is, the perception and record of both political forces have rather come undone. When critics like the left-leaning journalist Owen Jones argues that New Labour's appeal was always owed 'to, frankly, despair: the idea that socialist policies were electoral poison and offering them to the British people would invite only landslide Tory victories', he perhaps overlooks not only their radical agenda, but what happened to a small chunk of the British electorate under Tony Blair and Gordon Brown. Such exceptional cases include millions of the low paid bolstered with an historic National Minimum Wage, parents and children who benefitted from upgraded state school facilities, new Sure Start Centres or a government-funded Child Trust Fund, any father wanting paternity leave, any citizen in need of an improved hospital or doctor's surgery, the hundreds of thousands of pensioners lifted out of poverty through a new Winter Fuel Allowance, the virtual elimination of street homelessness, the end of state-enabled discrimination against homosexuals, the long-term unemployed helped back into work using the proceeds of a windfall tax on big corporates and the citizens of Northern Ireland gaining a peaceable province for the first time in decades. This was a pretty long list for a movement of 'despair'. One might even call it progressive.

The point of this book, therefore, is that the moderate centre-left was a largely successful project in *both* the UK and US because of the dialogue *between* thinkers and politicians in both countries. As such, the *March of the Moderates* involved a concrete set of proposals that, though modified for national circumstances, showed a remarkable coherence. Encouraging a buoyant private sector to generate the tax receipts necessary for transformational change. Introducing and/or increasing the minimum wage. Radical redistribution through the tax credit system. Greater autonomy away from state or local authority control for frontline public services. A general suspicion of monopoly and vested interests within the public sector. Record investment in education and health, to be matched by reforms within the system. Aid to the poorest parts of the globe. The use of the military to overthrow or destabilise dictatorial regimes. Whatever one makes of this combined agenda – and it had numerous benefits – it was hardly the valueless PR exercise its opponents assert. Nor, again, was it without meaningful effect. As the economist JK Galbraith noted, 'the Clinton Years, as they must be called, were clearly the best since those of FDR'.[2]

For the avoidance of any doubt, this is unashamedly a top-down study. It utilises both newly opened archives of major figures on both sides of the Atlantic and interviews by the author. As such, for those seeking a blow-by-blow account of local constituency or party machinery intrigue, John Golding, Dianne Hayter and Jeff Bloodworth have done it more extensively. Likewise, for a philosophical take on 'The Third Way' – that renewal of social democracy outlined in the late 1990s by the sociologist Tony Giddens – there is more 'academic' literature to digest, not least, of course, by Giddens himself. This book is a study of some key politicians and their interconnections. The context in which they operated is important, but, for upfront readability, some sacrifices must be made. I intend to return to such issues in the coming years.

This book therefore makes its case over nine chapters. The first two detail the twists and turns of the left from the New Deal era to the machinations of the 1980s – in short, taking in the historic achievements of both Labour and the Democrats, but also how progressive forces began to lose their way. Chapters three and four then outline the rise of the Third Way in a staggeringly difficult political climate and the protagonists who helped Clinton into office in 1992. Five and six then discuss Clinton's first term, both in terms of its contemporary outcomes for American citizens, but also how the British centre-left absorbed its lessons. Our final three chapters then discuss the era of Blair and Brown – the impact they had in the UK, their continued dialogue with the US Democrats and, finally, the controversies of Third Way foreign policy. Throughout, differences in national histories and contexts are acknowledged – but there is a combined story here worth telling.

This is not an uncritical account. In the lead up to the economic crash and, indeed, the Third Way's adherence to an increasingly unpopular brand of identity politics, there are lessons to be learned for modern progressives. Moderates were rightly critical of the left's doctrinal faith in the power of government, but they did not always apply such a sufficiently critical lens to monopolistic, or generally damaging, activities in the financial sector. Likewise, former British Cabinet Minister Charles Clarke is sage to assert that 'whatever the economic successes of "globalization" in the round, it did not answer widespread concerns of [particular] individuals and communities . . . Nor did it address worries about control of the immigration which was a significant side-effect'.[3] To be sure, with a combined two decades of governance, if one seeks errors during the New Labour and New Democrat years, you will not come up short.

But, equally, if we are unable to highlight the good that centre-left politics can do then, frankly, we deserve the politicians we have got of late. The *March of the Moderates* is a tale of political bravery and significant achievement. At the very least, this era deserves to be seen not as the last vestige of self-serving machine politicians before the authentic truth tellers took over, but a decent, progressive period we should look to replicate the successes of, rather than relentlessly tear down. After all, the alternatives have become all too obvious.

Notes

1 See Sanders' article. Available at: http://inthesetimes.com/article/18889/bernie-sanders-president-bill-clinton-1995. Stats via US Bureau of Labor: www.usgovernmentspending.com.

2 Galbraith open letter, 31 August 2004, ARC/JFK/JKG/78.

3 COR/Clarke.

1 TOO TIED TO MYTH; TOO ROOTED IN THE PAST

In June 1983 an assorted group of Labour Party activists held a gathering in the northern English town of Spennymoor. Promisingly entitled 'Lessons from Defeat', this occasion was to be addressed by an eclectic line up including several trade union delegates, the left-wing parliamentarian Dennis Skinner and, playing the pantomime villain, their newly elected local MP, Tony Blair. Since those attending had been promised 'the most frank debate', this was precisely what the future Prime Minister intended to give them. In this seemingly low-key affair, years before he shook the hand of Bill Clinton, won power or became embroiled in the controversies over the war in Iraq, Blair would seek to earn his political stripes by speaking the truth to Labour's then establishment. There was not yet a codified theory of what moderates like Blair thought was the answer to the left's woes, nor any labels like 'the Third Way' or 'New Labour' to encapsulate it, but the problem, at least, was clear. For the 30-year-old barrister, whose well-spoken timbre seemed to somehow defy a precise geographic hinterland, the 'thumping great annihilation' just received at the polls – Labour's lowest number of seats since 1935 and its lowest share of the vote since 1918 – was demonstrable proof that 'Labour had lost touch'. For Blair, the party had 'failed to spot how society had changed', held attitudes 'from the era of black and white TV' and its activists and leaders alike had grown too comfortable 'simply repeating old adages learned on your grandparents' knees'. Thatcher had just won, certainly, but she had not done so because voters were somehow unaware of what Labour was offering. Rather, they had taken a good hard look and, on polling day, willingly put their cross in the Conservative box.

This message did not go down well. Many, it seemed, did not want to face this new reality. Around the same time, a few hundred miles to the south, the newly elected MP for Islington North, Jeremy Corbyn, was declaring to allies that this wasn't time for 'a binge of recrimination'. After all, 'the campaign had started well and then everything had been fudged'. The problem was an 'incompetent party machine' that had put out leaflets that were, in Corbyn's words, 'bland crap', not Labour's actual offer. This was the echo chamber to end all echo chambers. Two days before polling day, after all, even the liberal-leaning *Guardian* had declared Labour's manifesto to be 'in the most despairing sense, an internal party document'. 'The left, who believe that their policies are blazingly right and, therefore, if put and implemented *must* automatically command success' were to be greeted by an electorate that didn't 'always agree with Mrs Thatcher' but had come 'to admire her'.[1] The people's party and the people themselves had come apart.

Choosing to believe the soothing notion that all was well, when Blair addressed them, the majority of the Spennymoor audience 'folded their arms, in unison, their faces grimacing as if a thousand lemons had been forced down their throats'. After all, this was solid Labour country. Spennymoor was in the Sedgefield constituency which had returned a Labour MP at every election since 1935 (a record that still stands at the time of writing) and had a long and proud history of coal mining and the trade union activism that had gone with it. Little surprise, then, that just as the audience had greeted Blair so coolly, so too would their faces begin to break into a collective smirk in anticipation of the reply from his more experienced fellow MP, the former coal miner, Dennis Skinner. As Blair later recalled, 'they knew what was coming, I didn't'.

A powerful orator who would harangue successive Prime Ministers for decades, Skinner began by the *ad hominem* technique of mocking the young man's background. In his earthy Derbyshire accent, he referred the audience to 'your new MP, supposed to be a *Labour* MP, whose experience in *Labour* politics up to now includes [the private] Durham Choir School [and] Fettes College, Edinburgh – the Eton of Scotland I'm told, not that I'd know'. Moving through Blair's spell at Oxford University – 'said', as Blair recalled, 'with an especial sneer' – Skinner derided his having been called to the Bar – 'and that's not the one you buy a pint in'. But Skinner's playing for laughs was just the preamble. He soon thundered that 'your new Labour MP thinks our grandparents didn't know what they were talking about; that it's time we disowned them; that now's the moment when we tell them ... that they don't belong in Thatcher's Britain'. By now the audience was already baying for Blair's blood. Reaching his conclusion, Skinner pointedly used the new MP's full name, 'Anthony Charles Lynton Blair: my grandparents were poor, it's true, [they] were humble folk, I admit it; [they] were I dare say, a little old fashioned in their principles of loyalty and solidarity; but THEY WERE DECENT PEOPLE AND PROUD OF BEING WORKING CLASS'. The crowd erupted in applause to a degree 'that fairly lifted the roof off the place' and were promptly rewarded with further folksy tales from union delegates of 'how entire mining communities had been on the brink of destruction until rescued by some miraculous intervention of grandma or granddad'. Blair had to be virtually smuggled out of the building.[2]

Such institutional conservatism – doffing the progressive cap to interest groups like the trade unions and ideas like blanket nationalisation – was far from rare in both Britain and America during the 1980s and formed the citadel that the moderates of this book would need to break down. As such, thousands of miles away from Spennymoor and after Walter Mondale's crushing defeat against Ronald Reagan in 1984, the 38-year-old Governor of Arkansas, William Jefferson Clinton, sat down to discuss the future of the US Democrats with the strategy consultant David Osborne. Clinton, like Blair, was furious with the direction his party had drifted. 'If all we do is talk about particular programs and how we don't want this or that or the other thing undone', he told Osborne, 'then our fundamental message doesn't come across'. To Clinton, 'one of the real things that Reagan stuck on us was, he said, "They are the party of government and we are the party of the people."' Indeed, being 'seen to defend the status quo in a time of change' was electoral poison and the party had been rightly defeated. Thus, whilst Clinton would eventually win the Presidency in 1992 alongside the refrain of Fleetwood Mac's 'Don't Stop Thinking About Tomorrow', the truth was that for much of the previous two decades, many US Democrats had been as obsessed with the struggles of the past as their British counterparts. Voices like the Reverend Jesse Jackson, who argued that there was 'a progressive wing of the Democratic Party that can take us to victory ... *if we believe it*' continued to hold sway, even when the electorate was repeatedly rejecting their offer.[3]

In essence, this ideological civil war was waged over history – how much the past mattered and how far it should continue to shape the left even in the face of thumping electoral defeats. In later years, the term 'modernisation' – frequently used with reference to Tony Blair, Gordon Brown, Peter Mandelson and other reformers – would come to be viewed by critics as a vacuous public relations exercise put forward by ambitious figures who somehow 'weren't really Labour'. Quite why any ambitious pseudo-conservative would choose to join the British Labour Party in the early 1980s remains a mystery. It certainly didn't pay: becoming an MP in 1983 saw Blair swap an £80,000 salary in the legal profession for a pay packet of less than £20,000. But, as this book argues, it was vital such moderates stepped up to the plate.

Before we get to the 1980s, then, we need to understand the history and the place that the twentieth century played in shaping the myths that the Anglo-American left lived by. Not all these myths were false, nor was the past without significant achievement. But the point was that the past of both the Democrats and Labour could be interpreted in vastly different ways and, to many activists, doubling down on decades-old rhetoric would come to trump any attempts to forge a new path amidst changing global circumstances.

There were four crucial periods here:

- The New Deal and the New Jerusalem of the 1930s and 1940s.
- The limits of liberalism of the 1960s.
- The dilemmas of defence and disorder of the Vietnam era.
- The British disease and bunker mentality of the 1970s.

Experiences in Britain and America were not uniform. But as Philip Gould, New Labour's most famous pollster, would later write: for much of the twentieth century the left in both countries had been 'too tied to myth; too rooted in the past'.[4] To understand the mountain the moderates of this work were up against we need to analyse each of these eras in turn and the protagonists' collective understanding of them. The road from Spennymoor to Downing Street, and Little Rock to the White House, would be long and arduous.

The New Deal and New Jerusalem

In January 1993, just before a triumphant Bill Clinton took the oath of office, *Rolling Stone* ran an article by the economist William Greider. Around this time, Clinton, a boyish-looking Democrat promising great technological change allied to the spirit of renewed national service, was often compared to John F Kennedy. But though such claims held a superficial truth, they were always of limited currency. Just as the journalist EJ Dionne would declare Clinton to be a new Teddy Roosevelt – who likewise wanted to 'forge new rules to realize a new era's potential while containing its threats' in the early 1900s – the references to JFK obscured as much as they illuminated. Instead, Greider's readers were therefore told that 'the ghosts that cast a large shadow across Clinton's path are not those of Kennedy and [Jimmy] Carter but of two other Democratic presidents, Lyndon B Johnson and Franklin D Roosevelt. Both men presided over eras of great reform, just as Clinton hopes to and both produced important breakthroughs toward greater equity. But they governed in very different ways and produced dramatically different results. Clinton will have to choose between these two models'. Though such comparisons were not without some foundation, in fact, Clinton's project and that of the transnational Third Way per se, would involve superseding both these Democratic icons.[5]

To begin with the first, whilst there has been much debate about the results of Roosevelt's New Deal, its symbolism and impact on the direction of travel for the left can scarcely be questioned. For future Clinton pollster Stan Greenberg, in the 1930s 'the New Deal represented *a turn to government* to provide relief and lead America out of the Depression'. This occurred on a broad front: 'market controls in agriculture, bank regulation, standards in the workplace, labor-management relations, minimum wage, unemployment insurance, social security, public works, electrification and expanded credit and investment'.[6] In a recession, the state 'proved impatient with market outcomes' and decisively stepped in to pick up the slack. Fannie Mae, the Securities and Exchange Commission and the Federal Housing Administration would be but three of the famous legacies of this period. As such, from FDR onwards the left had its answer to economic chaos and that answer was *universal*. In the more prosperous 1940s and 1950s the two main parties would compete to fill in the missing gaps of the Roosevelt era, but the general map of economic prosperity producing benefit for *all* was set.

Whilst nationalisation experiments had begun under Roosevelt, the post-war era saw several examples of further state intervention. The 1944 GI Bill provided $500 a year for college tuition (enough for fees at even Harvard) and subsidised rates of borrowing for former soldiers to acquire a mortgage or to start a new business. The 1946 Employment Act then placed a statutory responsibility on government to maximise employment and, though President Truman could not get much of his so-called 'fair deal' including national health insurance through Congress, his fight to extend state power is still viewed sympathetically across the American left. Aid to Dependent Children (later Aid to Families with Dependent Children – AFDC) a policy which gave federal assistance to families on low or no income, had been launched under FDR but again expanded under Truman. The New Deal got a lot done and much was universalist and statist, in nature.

This all came with a corollary, however. From the New Deal onwards, the Democrats would believe and be identified as the party that believed that *big government* was the way forward. As moderate Senator Chuck Robb would note in 1989, 'in the 19th century, Democrats generally saw government as a threat to equal opportunity and sought to limit its reach'. The party's origins most certainly lay in Thomas Jefferson's opposition to an overly powerful executive and a desire to boost states' rights. But, as Robb noted, 'in the 20th century, Democrats have seen government as a means to restore opportunity by … providing a stable framework for economic growth'.[7] By the 1980s, he continued, 'far too many Americans have come to believe that our party is more interested in expanding government for the benefit of special interests' and this 'narrow outlook has become entrenched as national party orthodoxy, enforced by activists and interest groups who exercise disproportionate influence over the party's nominating process'. Big government that delivered for all was broadly palatable – but an administration that one could perceive as intrusive, incompetent and for 'others', not so much.

The British experience was not dissimilar. Whereas Roosevelt backed state intervention as a means of arresting the Great Depression in America, in the 1930s Britain had been governed by a Conservative-dominated National Government, which broadly argued that the market would self-correct if politicians stayed out of things. With unemployment reaching record levels and a massive regional divergence between a relatively prosperous Conservative south and a decimated north (Labour's heartland), for many on the left it became clear that the state would need to intervene to secure prosperity for all. Some looked to Roosevelt, others to the *New Civilization* supposedly inaugurated in the Soviet Union and a few even to the big infrastructure projects of Benito Mussolini. But the broad lesson was clear: interventionist economists like

John Maynard Keynes were right; the era of laissez-faire was over and, should it ever gain power again, Labour would be the vehicle of big government, too.

Since 1918, Clause IV of the party's constitution had promised to 'secure for the workers ... the common ownership of the means of production, distribution and exchange'. For friend and foe alike, this was generally taken to mean government ownership or 'nationalisation' of vast tranches of the economy. In this regard, the 1945 Labour Government, which won a landslide majority, would assume a virtually untouchable place in the aeons of the party's history. It would truly deliver a 'New Jerusalem' – as leader Clement Attlee had called for during the election campaign. Under his government, the railways, telephone, steel industry and gas supplies were all brought into public ownership – as was the central bank, the Bank of England. Most emblematically, 1948 saw the launch of Britain's new National Health Service – which socialised medicine from the local doctor to the big hospital. This new institution was funded by general taxation and was free at the point of delivery, a pattern that holds, for the most part, to this day. The achievements here

FIGURE 1 Harry Truman and Clement Attlee led their parties to major election victories, but, within two decades of their losing power, the New Deal-New Jerusalem consensus was fracturing in both the US and UK (Abbie Rowe, National Park Service, Harry S. Truman Library and Museum).

were obvious and rightly lauded, particularly compared to the long-term quagmire on healthcare of its American cousins.

Though the moderates of this book would come to challenge the idea that the state should hold a monopoly on all public services, they were not without veneration for the NHS. When probed about the issue in a 1993 CSPAN interview conducted alongside Gordon Brown, Tony Blair told the watching US public that 'we're both big supporters of the National Health Service. And that's on practical rather than simply ideological grounds. Although there have been problems ... the idea that my generation has grown up with in Britain that if you are sick you will be cared for, irrespective of your wealth, is now a basic belief that underpins our society'. Both shadow ministers believed 'that it yields efficiency as well because you are pooling resources and you don't get these big vested interests – doctors, insurance companies and so forth within the system – who end up subverting it for their own purposes'. By implication, the American system was not delivering in that regard.

Such adoration was not driven by mere electoral calculation, either. After suffering a stroke in 1964, Tony Blair's father Leo had been barely able to speak for three years and required constant care from his wife to be nursed back to health. Twelve years later, his mother Hazel would die of throat cancer. Coupled with the operation which saved Gordon Brown's sight in his right eye after a rugby injury and the fact that Peter Mandelson's grandfather, Herbert Morrison, had served as Deputy Prime Minister in the 1945 government, the Third Way in its British incarnation would be determined to funnel record sums into such services. Brown's famous allusion to 'prudence with a purpose' belay a deep commitment amidst the centre left to the preservation and modernisation of the services people needed the most. Modernisation would not be about ridding Labour of its values but updating them for changing circumstance. They would, however, need to win power to do just that.

The New Deal–New Jerusalem era has thus, perhaps understandably, assumed biblical status for Anglo-American progressives, with its various policy offerings akin to scripture. But it was always dependent on levels of taxation which were and remain politically difficult. To balance the budget in the wake of the Wall Street Crash, the Republican President Herbert Hoover had raised the top rate of federal income tax to 63 per cent (from just 25%) in 1932. Under FDR, the combined threat of a new recession and involvement in a second world war saw this increased to 79 per cent in 1936 and 94 per cent by 1944. The British trends were similar – with Churchill permitting a 99.25 per cent top rate to help fund the conflict against the Axis Powers. As such, the dial had moved to a degree unimaginable in times of economic or military normality. With domestic policy after the Second World War very much proving a reaction to perceived errors after the first – in Britain the inter-war notion that homes had *not* been delivered for 'heroes to live in' – there was also a natural stickiness to government spending and the combined debts of two world wars had to be serviced somehow.

Such revenues were also notably spent on an element of the Attlee and Truman era which some on the left would later wish to down play: defence. Having laid out a significant programme of Marshall Aid to boost ailing western economies like the UK and, more famously, those eastern European states under threat of communist advance, Truman helped co-ordinate the North Atlantic Treaty Organisation (NATO) which pledged democratic states in Europe and North America to resist Soviet aggression. Ernest Bevin, the trade unionist turned virulently anti-Communist British Foreign Secretary, had gladly signed the treaty and, concurrently, when it came to developing a British nuclear bomb, commented that 'we've got to have this thing over here whatever it costs ... We've got to have the bloody Union Jack flying on top of it'. During this era, as Anglo-American involvement in the Korean War illustrated, the left was demonstrably willing to defend the country at home and the concept of democracy abroad. As such, even as late as 1970, when Harold Wilson left office having kept Britain out of Vietnam, his Labour Government was still spending over 4.5 per cent of GDP on defence. Part of the post-war Vital Center – the state-regulated free market hypothesised by the historian and Kennedy ally Arthur Schlesinger Jr – was that the left should not only deliver a better world for its citizens at home, it should, where necessary, be prepared to fight for liberty overseas. The consequences of allowing totalitarian despots to enslave their populations were, after all, clear.

The limits of liberalism

Though the left would eventually lose power, it looked like the New Deal and the New Jerusalem had defined politics for a generation. In 1951 and 1953 Attlee and Truman left office, to be replaced by moderate centre-right administrations. Dwight Eisenhower ran in 1952 more as a national hero than archetypal Republican politician and he broadly accepted both the New Deal and increased social security vision of the Roosevelt–Truman era. Trade union collective bargaining was generally praised, whilst the Republicans pledged themselves to 'relentlessly protect our free enterprise system against monopolistic and unfair trade practices'. Likewise, from the party's 1947 Industrial Charter onward, reforming British Conservative MPs like Harold Macmillan and 'Rab' Butler managed to keep a lid on Churchill's more rabid right-wing leanings and anchor their party to the centre ground. As Labour moderates Peter Mandelson and Roger Liddle have since argued, 'since the war the Conservatives ... thoroughly reinvented themselves twice over' – first through Butler dragging 'the Conservatives into acceptance of the modern welfare state and the commitment to full employment' and then through the reforms of the Thatcher years. 'Labour, on the other hand, was more resistant to change.'[8]

This was demonstrably true, even in the wake of three successive election losses for the British left in the 1950s. On the economy, Attlee's moderate successor as Labour leader, Hugh Gaitskell, attempted to replace the old pro-nationalisation Clause IV, but was defeated by his party's radical wing who preferred to dream of an ever-expanding state. Meanwhile, when it came to foreign policy, influential figures like Aneurin Bevan – the Health Secretary who had founded the NHS – campaigned for unilateral nuclear disarmament in a world where the Soviets now had the bomb. Such internal debates put Labour out of step with the voting public and occurred at a point where the party's image remained one of post-war austerity, controls and rationing, whilst the Conservative government rolled back restrictions on food and freed the private sector to build more houses. In the full employment economy of the 1950s, Labour's very rationale of tackling economic injustice was also on the wane. Academics and policy wonks began to speak of so-called *embourgoisement* – what would the left do if, as it seemed at the time, capitalism was beginning to rid the west of the kind of grinding poverty of the inter-war years. To whom would it appeal?

Part of the answer seemed to come when, in November 1960, America elected Senator John F Kennedy as its thirty-fifth president. Like Roosevelt before him, Kennedy's symbolism remains clear enough: hope, optimism and a turn from government embodied by asking Americans 'not what your country can do for you', but 'what you can do for your country'. As Gordon Brown later noted, 'growing up, I like others witnessed the power of the idea of change with John F Kennedy – 'the torch has passed to a new generation' – and, [later] as an MP, with Bill Clinton's summons to 'make change our friend and not our enemy'. As Prime Minister, Brown would take notice of a piece of moon rock gifted to Downing Street many years earlier and 'often highlighted Kennedy's visit to what is now called the Kennedy Space Center in Florida, where he asked everyone there what they did. He talked to an engineer, a research scientist, a manager and several astronauts. Then he came to a lady who happened to be the cleaner. He asked her what she did. "I'm helping put a man on the moon", she proudly replied. She had been captivated by a strong sense of what a group of people could achieve by working together'.[9] In truth, however, though his administration delivered strong economic growth, much of Kennedy's domestic agenda – including Medicare and mass transit – was held up in Congress as Lee Harvey Oswald entered the Texas book depository. Even the tax cuts outlined in his 1963 State of the Union would not be enacted until after his death.

Instead, as Stan Greenberg notes, it was really 'the fury of the political debate' between 1964 and 1968 'that redefined America and the American dream'.[10] During this period, Kennedy's successor, Lyndon Johnson, would enact his Great Society agenda that sought to reconfigure the Democratic Party, shift its electoral base and thereby remake the left. This involved some bold policy making, fought at every turn, which served as a powerful part of the president's legacy. The Civil Rights and Voting Rights Acts passed through 1964 and 1965 collectively banned racial segregation in public facilities and places of work and stopped southern states from gerrymandering qualifications to deliberately exclude African Americans from the franchise. Then, in 1967, anti-miscegenation laws were declared un-constitutional by the Supreme Court, thus making inter-racial union legal across the country. This was a new order which improved life opportunities for millions of Americans.

But the Great Society also involved a series of trade-offs that, as America's economic position became less certain, began to bite. In this regard, it was the War on Poverty that most symbolised the new bind this had placed the Democrats in. Lyndon Johnson's flagship programme – which included the full-scale introduction of food stamps in 1964 and increased health insurance through Medicare (for the over 65s) and Medicaid (matched federal funding for low-income families) a year later – saw overall poverty rates drop significantly. But it shifted the US welfare system in a number of ways. First, many of the programmes, including food stamps, Medicaid and subsidised housing, were means tested – thus chipping away at the principle of universalism that had marked much of American welfare under the New Deal. Secondly, the establishment of various interventionist projects in inner cities saw the War on Poverty assume a heavily racialised dimension. Having claimed that 'Negro poverty is not white poverty' and constituted a unique 'American failure', Johnson's creation of Community Action Agencies (local bodies charged with spending devolved federal monies) 'in effect [created] for the poor separate social welfare institutions whose client base was half minority'.[11] As *social security for all* morphed in sections of the public mind into *welfare for some*, the Democratic dream to speak for *all* the forgotten men and women seemed distant. Between 1964 and 1972 Democratic support amongst the lower middle class, manual workers and Catholics tumbled.

To be sure, there was much to commend about the War on Poverty and it proved formative in the lives of many future New Democrats. One such figure was Al From, later to work for Jimmy Carter and who went on to form the Clinton-backing Democratic Leadership Council. Employed in 1966 by the Office of Economic Opportunity (the federal body that co-ordinated Johnson's 'War') From visited government projects in both Mississippi and Alabama. There, he noted, the dispersal of federal funds to community groups decisively 'changed the power arrangements'. 'Now disenfranchised blacks were empowered with a piece of the antipoverty program pie and that became a platform to drive further social and economic change.'[12]

The trick, as Bill Clinton would come to argue, was to couch such programmes in a discourse the electorate would wear; in a time of great upheaval, this was not easy. In 1970, the US was over 87 per cent white (roughly equivalent to the UK in the 2010s). Voters needed change that was sold in the language of mutual benefit for all and where working Americans – white or black – could plausibly connect the taxes they were paying with the services the state was delivering. But, for many, this was demonstrably no longer the case. Indeed, between 1964 and 1969 the number of Americans believing that the level of federal income tax they were paying was too high rose from 56% to 69% despite almost no change in the rates paid by the average family.[13]

At the beginning of the 1960s the Democrats had been associated with a universal form of liberalism: one where, broadly, a rising economic tide would lift all boats. This was always somewhat imagined and relied on eliding questions of race but, save Eisenhower, it had secured every Presidential election from 1932 to 1964. By the end of the 1960s, however, as Clinton aide Sidney Blumenthal has argued, the party was easily portrayed by the Republicans as 'soft on racial quotas, crime and the abuses of welfare'. For many, things seemed to be going backward rather than forward. Some of this was undeniably inflamed by the left's opponents, but it was also not merely the product of blind prejudice. Between 1965 and 1970 levels of violent felonies, murders, rapes and assaults in the US more than doubled. Meanwhile, from 1965 to the election of Bill Clinton in 1992, the number of recipients of Aid to Families with Dependent Children trebled. Thus, by 1967 two-thirds of the American public were telling pollsters that Johnson's administration had gone 'too far' in its Great Society vision. The Democrats were, in short, no longer 'the party to define the American nation'.[14]

Clearly, not everyone agreed with the progressive changes of the sixties. Barry Goldwater's 1964 run for president had energised a conservative base within the Republican Party that, as more and more liberal acts passed Congress, would only grow. With the future Governor of California Ronald Reagan performing well on the Goldwater campaign trail, the conservative academic George Nash would later write that 'if I were a Hegelian, I might say that the 1964 election created a thesis, the Great Society and an antithesis, Ronald Reagan, who, as president, [would attempt] to curb the excesses which the Great Society has wrought'. There was much in that. And, indeed, nor was the phenomenon uniquely American. As Harold Wilson's Labour Government passed legislation decriminalising homosexuality, legalising abortion and banning racial discrimination in public and private realms, politicians had to some degree marched ahead of British public opinion. This was brave, necessary policy making, but it also served as an agenda not without electoral trade-offs.[15]

Defence and disorder

For Nixon advisor Kevin Phillips, 'as liberalism metamorphosed from an economic populist stance – supporting farm, highway, education and pension expenditures against conservative budget cutting – into a credo of social engineering, it lost the support of poor whites'. Yet the turn from the New Deal to the Great Society was not just divisive in terms of domestic policy. When Johnson escalated the war in Vietnam soon after the 1964 election, he did so against voices like Senator William Fulbright, whose staff included a young Bill Clinton. During that controversial conflict, 58,220 Americans would be killed, including 592 from Clinton's home state of Arkansas. In the wake of military setback, between January and July 1967 the number of Americans disproving of the president's handling of Vietnam increased from 43 to 60 per cent. Protests erupted in college campuses and city centres across the country. On top of his controversial Great Society initiatives, Johnson was now in trouble – as were the Democrats.[16]

As Al From notes, 'in the late 1960s and 1970s many life-long Democrats believed their party that had once symbolized prosperity, expanding opportunity and unambiguous opposition to communist totalitarianism had become identified with Hippies and the drug culture, a breakdown of discipline and passivity towards crime, alternative lifestyles and fervent denunciations of the use of U.S. power abroad'.[17] The decision of Lyndon Johnson not to seek the Democratic nomination for the 1968 election in the wake of the quagmire in Vietnam then proved decisive. With Johnson's authority more or less gone, the party would spend the rest of the year divided between local and national machineries, the Eugene McCarthy (and later George McGovern) inspired student protestors against the war, the Catholics, African Americans and Hispanics who had largely been behind Robert Kennedy and segregationist white southerners, most of whom would back the third party candidacy of George Wallace. This led to the utter chaos of the August 1968 Democratic Convention in Chicago – which saw mass anti-Vietnam protests outside the hall, whilst inside several southern states challenged who would form their presidential voting delegates, with particular anger at the prospect of enfranchising African Americans with such power. When this was settled Hubert Humphrey, the sitting Vice President, would take the nomination, but not before several attempts had been made to strong-arm Ted Kennedy into standing.

In place of a broad, unified message which knew what it was for and knew what it was against, as under Roosevelt and Truman, the Democrats had splintered in a number of directions. Whilst FDR had experimented with different policies, his chief aim to tackle unemployment and industrial injustice was at least clear. Under Truman, most Americans could assume that their president was for *them* and was certainly prepared to defend the country. Now it was not clear what the Democrats were all about. Watching the 1968 convention on the TV of a hotel room in

Louisiana, where Clinton was taking a trip to get to know his mother's new boyfriend, the 22-year-old future president was profoundly glum. Whilst he objected to the heavy-handed tactics of the police in putting down the anti-war protestors, Clinton was 'heartsick that my party and its progressive causes were disintegrating before my eyes'. As he later wrote, 'growing up in Arkansas had given me an appreciation for the struggle of ordinary people who do their duty every day and a deep scepticism about self-righteousness on the right or the left'. Whilst 'the fleeting fanaticism of the left had not yet played itself out ... it had already unleashed a radical reaction on the right ... one more resourceful, more addicted to power and far more skilled at getting it and keeping it'. As Richard Scammon and Ben Wattenberg would write, to the archetypal American voter – they hypothesised a housewife in Dayton, Ohio – the protests outside the 1968 convention symbolised the 'ideal of confrontation politics, of confusing cops with pigs, of justifying riots, of sympathy for muggers and rapists, of support for the drug culture'. In too many people's eyes, that was now the Democratic Party.[18] The silent majority increasingly looked elsewhere.

As Tony Blair reflected in, of all things, a 1995 speech delivered on Rupert Murdoch's private island, 'during the sixties and seventies the left developed, almost in substitution for its economic prescriptions, which by then were failing, a type of social individualism that confused, at points at least, liberation from prejudice with a disregard for moral structures. It fought for racial and sexual equality, which was entirely right. It appeared indifferent to the family and individual responsibility, which was wrong'. In doing so, 'there was a real danger, occasionally realized, that single-issue pressure groups moved into the vacuum. Women's groups wrote the women's policy. Environmental groups wrote the environmental policy and so on'. Later, Blair remembered 'a telling intervention of a speaker at the Republican Convention of 1984 in the US asking rhetorically, "When was the last time you heard a Democrat say *no?*" It was too close to the truth for comfort'.[19] The left looked a toxic combination of weak and disorderly.

Once Richard Nixon won the Presidency in November 1968 on a mixture of economic moderation and a 'southern strategy' which undoubtedly inflamed racial tensions, this reached something of a nadir. As historian Jeff Bloodworth has ably chronicled, 'energized by their opposition to the Vietnam War, New Politics liberals gained control of the Democratic Party during the 1970s'. This new brand of

'New Politics liberals differed from their New Deal or Vital Center brethren'. They were 'predominantly young, educated and middle-class' and 'largely indifferent to the issues of working-class Democrats'. As Sidney Blumenthal writes, in the late 1960s and early 1970s, 'the Democrats were perceived as a centrifugal party of identity politics', not the concerns of most ordinary Americans. After significant reforms were made to democratise the primary process, in 1972 New Politics liberals managed to secure the nomination for George McGovern, who was destroyed by 49 states to 1 by Nixon. There was no rainbow coalition of middle-class liberals, women and ethnic minorities that was going to get the job done for the left. Even if judged on the narrow terms of the New Politics coalition, McGovern won 87 per cent of non-whites in 1972, but lost women (62–38%) and college graduates (63%–37%). The Nixon campaign strategy of 'monopolizing the center and shoving McGovern to the left' had indeed worked. As such, although moderate Democratic Senators such as Edmund Muskie and Representatives like Jim Wright would spend the 1970s forlornly, as Republican advisors noted, 'caught between the radicals in [their] party and a desire to act responsibly', the party itself was floundering. Until the Democrats could tell a truly national story, one which included a hard-headed pragmatism on questions of war and peace, they would find power difficult to attain, much less keep.[20]

British Disease, Bunker Mentality

The 1964–1970 Labour Government kept Britain out of Vietnam, but, like America, it was not immune from a far wider and certainly longer-term, problem: economic globalisation. In truth, the effects of globalisation, ever more competitive markets in areas Britain had previously dominated, was the backdrop to almost everything British politicians touched from the latter half of the nineteenth century onwards. As the former Labour MP David Marquand would write, 'at some point between the depression of the 1870s and the First World War, the astonishing surge of social, technological and economic change which had made Britain the first industrial society in history and the British people the richest in the world, began to lose momentum'.[21] Increased productivity from Germany, America and Japan begat lesser British market share not only in domestic markets, but across the globe. Imperial preference was briefly attempted – tariffs against the rest of the world, free trade for the empire – but the impending loss of Britain's colonies soon put paid to that. A new economic model was needed.

This was a pattern repeated across the Atlantic a few decades later. From the 1950s to the 1970s, as Clinton's future Labor Secretary Robert Reich notes, 'Americans were to discover that foreigners could undertake *high-volume* production of standard goods – cars, televisions, household appliances, steel [and] textiles – and sell them in the United States more cheaply (and sometimes at higher quality) than America's core corporations'. This changed the rules of the game to a degree that soon shook the political spectrum. Where both the post-war left and post-war right had been united was in the general expectation that the old norms of capitalism could be restored after the recent global conflict. Certainly, they prioritised different things – Conservatives and Republicans tended to oppose inflation (as they were more likely to represent lenders and savers), whilst Labour and the Democrats rallied against increased unemployment. But what each took years to comprehend was the idea that the old national bargain between labour and capital could no longer hold. As late as 1960, for instance, America was still a largely self-sufficient economy. In that year only 4 per cent of cars Americans purchased were built overseas, less than 6 per cent of televisions and only 3 per cent of machine tools. This created an implicit deal: 'Big Business, Big Labor and the public at large would subsidize high-volume production in order to gain greater efficiencies of scale which, in turn, would employ a growing middle class of Americans.' The same was true, more or less, for post-war British corporatism: a period of relative harmony when the interests of the industry, the state and the workers seemed – more or less – to converge.[22]

But with growing global competition this mutually beneficial relationship no longer held. Thanks to rising mechanisation levels in developing economies and the lower cost of shipping, American and British consumers increasingly bought goods cheaply made abroad (or which contained foreign-made components). Previous assumptions now had to be cast aside as dollars and pounds flowed overseas rather than into domestic profits and, indirectly, worker's wages. This was a game changer and initially politicians of all stripes would fumble around for answers. Introducing major new tariffs would be anathema to the 1947 General Agreement on Tariffs and Trade (GATT) and, even where they could be applied, were only a stop-gap. British and American business simply could not pay the low wages of the developing world, thus meaning a price war was only going to end one way in the long run. Meanwhile, attempts by big western conglomerates to diversify through merger and subsequent re-sale, or to achieve tax advantages via leveraged buyouts of competitors, either did not work or only had limited gains. For Reich, the big solution was obvious – a shift from *high volume* to *high value* production (those goods and, increasingly, services, in which the west had a competitive, technical advantage). But for several years it was not clear that many shared his vision, nor were they prepared to take on the vested interests which would oppose it every step of the way.

The 1970s then saw a series of further shocks. Nixon's decision to end the convertibility of the dollar into gold effectively ended the era of fixed exchange rates and by 1973 the major currencies, including UK sterling, were all free floating. The same year the British joined the European Economic Community, later the European Union, acknowledging its dependence on the global (or at least regional) economy – but thereby creating a series of debates about its international role that have lasted until the present day. And when the Arab members of OPEC imposed an oil embargo after American support for Israel in the Yom Kippur war, the subsequent quadrupling of the price of oil (and thereby energy for domestic and commercial use) produced dramatic consequences across the west. As the former British Prime Minister Harold Macmillan put it, 'in the 20th century we've started a new thing. We made one mistake that our predecessors didn't make. They at least made a society based upon the raw material which they controlled: coal. We made one – a society – based on a raw material which isn't in our control: oil. And we're paying a heavy price now'.[23]

By the early 1970s, the halcyon post-war 'old bargain' days of unions, business and government planning long-term prosperity seemed a world away when the first two were at loggerheads and the third found it impossible to broker an acceptable share of the proceeds of inconsistent growth. Control, order and stability seemed to have passed the west by. In the UK, after Harold Wilson had given way to Ted Heath's Conservative administration, 23 million days were lost to strike action in 1972, including coalminers working for the state-owned National Coal Board, as the trade unions attempted to turn the screw on government and business alike. With perceived public weariness at Heath's attempt to implement pay restraints to curb inflation and the opportunity presented by the Yom Kippur oil shock, British coal miners stopped working overtime in late 1973. This led to the imposition of the so-called 'three-day week' in early 1974 which drastically restricted commercial use of electricity and, eventually, more strikes. The striking miners were eventually bought off with inflation-busting pay rises, though this did not help Heath, who was defeated in the two General Elections of 1974. The Tories had been unable to cope with buffeting conditions abroad and industrial unrest at home.

Labour then came back into office but faced many of the same problems. As such, the inability of both Britain's left *and* right to deal with militant trade unions and increasingly competitive global markets became something of a psychosis. To borrow the title of a November 1976 episode of *CBS' 60 Minutes*, many American thinkers were even beginning to ask, 'will there always be an England?' As one Wall Street technology firm was briefing to US senators at the time: 'developments in the past have suggested that trends in the United Kingdom tend to be transplanted across the Atlantic with only a brief delay'. Such terrifying British trends in 1976 included undermining 'the effective operation of the free enterprise system', the existence of 'political instability and gross government mismanagement' and 'militant union or communist interference with the capitalist process and investment stagnation'. These symptoms were even given a sobriquet, 'the British disease', supposed to denote a society in crisis and one which successive administrations had done little to address. The implication was that if America was not careful it would soon be going the same way.[24]

This typified the morbid fascination American intelligentsia had with the decline of Great Britain during the 1970s. On the conservative side of the fence, William F Buckley's *Firing Line* – a public affairs programme watched by the great and the good – interviewed a range of British politicians on subjects as upbeat as 'the British Crisis' (February 1974) and 'the Crisis of British Trade Unions' (February 1979). During the 1970s, guests included Tony Benn, Margaret Thatcher, Enoch Powell and Keith Joseph, who did little to buck this collective picture of chaos. In July 1977 Buckley would ask Thatcher 'What Have We Learned from the Failure of British Socialism?' The new Tory leader would praise 'the very different' nature of American politics which, unlike Britain, had 'two parties based on a free society, or free enterprise and economic freedom'.

The two major problems here were sky-high inflation and growth that at best was only managed by government stimulus and, at worst, not there at all. The combination of these two phenomena would become known as 'stagflation' a technical term for a phenomenon that was acutely felt in factories and homes across the west. As to the first, British inflation was about four times its average level in the 1970s than it had been in the previous decade, whilst America enjoyed a scarcely better threefold increase. In 1975, inflation reached over 24 per cent in the UK, with the US figure hitting 12.4 per cent in 1980. Prices were therefore rising dramatically, but economic productivity was not keeping pace. Indeed, growth was inconsistent at best – with the middle of the 1970s even seeing negative growth in both countries. Even where growth could be secured, this was largely through substantial and increasingly unsustainable governmental deficits. As Alan Greenspan advised President Ford, 'the British economy appears to be at the point where they must accelerate the amount of government stimulus just to stand still' and this 'should give' all American policymakers 'considerable pause' for thought.

The need to borrow 'to stand still' meant that the UK moved from an annual governmental surplus of £900 million in 1969/1970 to a deficit of £7.7 billion in 1975/1976. Meanwhile, in the US, a 1969 budgetary surplus of $3.2 billion was converted into a $79 billion deficit by 1981. This could not go on forever and it became burned into the minds of young New Labourites at the time. As such, in his first conference speech after New Labour won the 1997 election Gordon Brown would come, in the words of one key revisionist, to 'slag off' the 1974 administration 'for committing itself to injudicious public spending increases that it could not finance'. For such modernisers, there was nothing necessarily virtuous about spending going up and up, not least because the poorest paid the highest proportion of their income in tax to fund such largesse.[25]

That was all a world away, however. Back in the 1970s British and American politics had forked into two potential solutions to the crisis of globalisation: New Right and Old Left. For the New Right, the answer lay in supply-side economics. In a 1980 submission to British politicians, the economist Milton Friedman laid out the reasons why he thought only a 'supply-side' vision could succeed. He began by noting that 'Britain, like the U.S. and many other countries, faces two different though related problems: inflation and slow growth'. As for the latter, 'the retardation of growth in the UK and the US in recent years reflects primarily ... an earlier explosion of government spending and government intervention in the economy, which has impaired incentives to work, save, invest and innovate'. For Friedman, although matters 'had been made worse by the energy crisis ... both problems preceded [it]'. The general issue was 'too big and too intrusive a government'.[26] The state was the enemy to employment, a free market and a generally healthy economy. If the right could cut taxes and limit the power of government, it could free the people from the shackles of stagflation. Business would figure things out in the long run. And, more or less, hang the short-term consequences.

Whilst the New Right prepared their theory, the Old Left had to deal with the realities of office. It was not all doom and gloom, but Labour's relative success in pulling inflation down was obscured by two phenomena. The first was that, as sterling tumbled in early 1976, the UK Government was forced to go to the International Monetary Fund for a loan of $3.9 billion. To facilitate this, the IMF demanded significant annual governmental spending cuts. When parcelled together with the so-called 'banker's ramp' view of the collapse of the Labour Government in 1931, this suggested to many on the left that Labour had 'succumbed to the pressure of the international financial community and hardliners in the United States'.[27] In his speech at the 1976 Labour Party conference, the new Prime Minister Jim Callaghan formally ended the Keynesian era by telling delegates that the 'option' to 'spend your way out of recession and increase employment by boosting government spending ... no longer exists'.

This ideological shift, embodied by the decision to take the IMF loan, split the Labour cabinet and ultimately the British left, down the middle: between the social democrats led by Callaghan and a hard left, whose figurehead became Tony Benn, then Secretary of State for Energy. As Benn told his colleagues, accepting the loan 'would involve cuts into public services so deep as to endanger their basic function and cuts in social benefits that put at the risk the Social Contract'. Instead, he proposed an 'Alternate Strategy' for economic recovery which would shape the views of Labour's hard left for years to come. This amounted to a siege economy flying in the face of a newly globalising world. Quotas should be introduced for imports, exchange controls should be introduced on sterling and a Capital Issues Committee should help channel investment into areas of 'national priority'.[28] As we will see, proponents of this course continued to make its case well into the 1980s.

The left's second major problem, as Benn's comments hinted, was that it could no longer adequately manage 'the Social Contract'. As the moderate MP Giles Radice later put it, 'Heath's Conservative government had foundered on its inability to "get on" with unions and Labour's "social contract" approach appeared likely to offer a more successful alternative'. In sum, 'the social contract was based on a compact with the unions and was an ambitious attempt to link together social welfare, tax policy, output, employment and incomes into a coherent whole'.[29] In essence, the British electorate, having grown weary of corporatist cooperation in the late 1960s, was willing to give it one last shot in the 1970s. Like many a broken relationship, however, there was no going back.

A snapshot of the dysfunction this produced can be seen in the memoirs of Peter Mandelson, often regarded as the 'Third Man' of New Labour. By virtue of his Oxford tutor, the historian Alan Bullock, Mandelson had taken a job in the late 1970s with the economic department of Britain's Trade Union Congress. Recalling the site of his new job, Mandelson notes that 'Congress House in Great Russell Street was more than just a union headquarters and the economic department was more than a policy talking shop'. Hearing his bosses '*demand* to talk with this Labour Cabinet Minister or that, or acting as a designated notetaker in an endless series of bargaining meetings … I had a crash course in how power was then wielded inside Labour'. This 'left an indelible impression … a lesson in how not to run the country'. For Mandelson, 'Great Russell Street virtually shared sovereignty with Downing Street'.[30]

There was much in this. Emboldened by the movements' early 1970s militancy and late 1970s power sharing, by 1979 there were 13.2 million British trade union members – an increase of 3 million in just ten years. Moreover, the unions had been instrumental in the foundation of the Labour Party, played a key role in the selection of its parliamentary candidates and in elections to internal positions of influence within the party. Their job was to advocate for better pay and conditions for their workers and they had secured significant historic advances, not least the legal right to strike and the imposition of an eight-hour working day for the majority of workers. Given the unrest seen in 1970s western capitalism, it was entirely reasonable for individual workers to seek an economic life raft.

But, as Mandelson knew, by the late 1970s there was widespread evidence that union bosses were overplaying their hand. The apogee of this was the 'Winter of Discontent' – the moment the British Disease became a full-on epidemic. Under the Social Contract, Labour had negotiated successive national pay rise caps with the TUC to provide an 'attack on inflation'. Up to 1978 this policy broadly worked. However, in

July that year Chancellor Denis Healey proposed to take the policy a stage further and deliver a 5 per cent limit for both government employees and those private sector companies who wished to receive governmental contracts. Crucially, one such affected business was the Ford Motor Company. Ford had achieved huge profits in 1978 but, since it was a government contractor, chose to make its workforce an offer within the prescribed 5 per cent. By way of response, 15,000 Ford workers went on strike which, after sympathetic action from the Transport and General Workers Union, increased nationwide to 57,000 strikers. Ford eventually climbed down and ceded a 17 per cent pay offer – rendering the government's proposed pay cap as meaningless. The left could no longer broker a harmonious relationship between industry and labour and with inflation still relatively high, looked like it was losing control. Business wasn't listening. The unions weren't listening. And the government was collapsing.

Looking across the Atlantic, things were scarcely any better. Working as Deputy Advisor for inflation in the White House, the future Clintonian Al From saw all this first hand. The Carter administration would collapse in several areas and was not helped by its uneasy relationship with Congress. Though the president managed to pass a National Energy Act which incentivised a greener America, it would be oil that would come to undermine his authority, as it had with Ted Heath in the UK. As gas companies jacked up their prices when price controls imposed under Nixon were lifted, From urged the president to call them out. He did not. Then, in 1979, the ongoing Iranian revolution caused commodity-hoarding, price-hiking panic from the markets, leading to shortages of gas which saw just 5 per cent of New York pumps remaining open. Seeing their own wages undermined by the rising cost of gas, 60 per cent of the nation's independent truckers then went on strike, helping tip the economy into recession. Carter's response was broadly Keynesian and in their attempted re-election platform, From recalls, 'every economic plank was a public jobs plank'.[31] Loose monetary policy at the Fed and then the doubling of the price of crude oil by OPEC, brought the return of significant inflation in Carter's last two years in office. Like Labour, the American left looked unimaginative, incompetent and tired. 1930s 'national' solutions were being tried in a truly globalised 1970s. The British Disease had arrived Stateside.

The Carter administration also looked fundamentally unable to solve the question of welfare. In 1976, Ronald Reagan's failed campaign for the

Republican nomination had pushed the idea of 'welfare queens' to the forefront of the debate, whilst, partly in response, Carter himself had consistently vowed to deliver reform. In a pledge which both Blair and Clinton would come to honour the spirit of two decades later, Carter promised on the stump that if welfare recipients refused employment on completion of a training programme, he would 'not pay them any more benefits'.[32] After some dithering in the early months of his administration, however, the Program for Better Jobs and Income (PBJI) eventually put before Congress would prove a mish-mash of New Deal liberalism's commitment to full employment and New Politics liberalism's emphasis on a guaranteed income for all. The PBJI sought to combine a universal negative income tax payment (ie payout) for those not expected to work – which included all single mothers with children under six – with a massive stimulus to create 1.4 million public service jobs at minimum wage level. Whereas Clinton and Blair would come to emphasise the time-limited nature of welfare and the requirement to work, Carter would ditch this language once in office and still fail to pass a meaningful bill. He would lose decisively to Ronald Reagan in November 1980, 18 months after Labour had given way to Thatcher in Britain.

By the time it left office in both countries therefore, the left had presided over double-digit inflation and rates of income tax that were taking a third of earnings at the lower end and four-fifths at the upper. It was associated with a divisive trade union movement and had backed nationalised industries that seemed to be inefficient at best and a drain on resources at worst. Even though it had opposed controversial conflicts abroad, it had reaped little electoral reward for doing so and was increasingly viewed as a movement of protest, even when in actual power. It was for minorities, but not the majority. This combined reputation was not totally representative of reality, but it had become deeply ingrained. By contrast, the New Right at least had a plan (massive tax cuts and rolling back government on the one hand, attacks on the trade unions on the other) and, whatever their downsides, possessed two leaders the electorate viewed as decisive. It was a bad place from which to begin the *March of the Moderates*.

The Start of the Moderates

The broad outline of this work is the path centre-left moderates took from obscurity within their own parties in the 1980s through to the exercise of power from the 1990s onwards. But Messrs Blair, Brown, Clinton and others did not appear from nowhere – they had lived the majority of the preceding tale firsthand and, as hinted at, had gained particular insights from it. As Sidney Blumenthal notes, 'they were generational peers, had the same reference points, shared the same Transatlantic outlook and the same innovative, liberal social democratic politics'.[33]

To begin with then, even though they were all baby boomers, the Depression clearly weighed heavy. Tony Blair's father Leo had been a foster child brought up in a very poor part of Glasgow between the wars. In 1938, Leo became Secretary of the Scottish Young Communist League, served as a copy boy for *The Daily Worker* and then, as his son later remarked, was 'virtually the only person I have come across who went off to serve in the [Second World War] as a confirmed socialist and came out the other end as a Conservative in 1945'. When reviewing Blair's memoirs, Bill Clinton touched on this point: 'if you want to see how Tony . . . came to this [Third Way] position, there is an incredibly moving passage in the beginning of his book where he talks about his father and how he came out of a hard scrabbling poor background and how he became a member of the Conservative Party in the UK because he thought that once you had made it you had to be there. [And this was] because the purpose of the Labour Party essentially was to build the big state, to redistribute income'. Henceforth, Blair's radar was always attuned to the sense that the Tories were the natural party of government and Labour would have to operate within their consensus.[34]

When young Tony (born 1953) was only 19 months old, the family emigrated to Adelaide, Australia where Leo taught law at the local university. Five years later, the family returned to the UK when Leo became a lecturer at Durham, a few miles away from the Spennymoor Town Hall in which his son would run into such trouble in 1983. Only his aforementioned stroke prevented Blair senior from completing his political trajectory by entering parliament as a Conservative – having secured a safe northern seat ahead of the 1964 General Election. Although Leo's condition impacted the Blairs' income significantly, they had built up enough savings to send young Tony to the private Fettes School which Dennis Skinner would so ruthlessly mock decades later. The idea that one should aspire to better your family's lot – rather than being a class traitor for doing so – would fundamentally divide Blair from his later left-wing opponents.

Blair's roots, then, were both conservative and mobile – but this was not true for all such modernisers. Two years older than his friend and rival, Gordon Brown would grow up in the Labour stronghold of 1950s Kirkcaldy on the northern shore of the Firth of Forth. With his father a minister in the Church of Scotland, Brown spent his childhood in a house that was 'as much an advice and drop-in centre as a family home'.[35] An exceptionally bright youngster, Brown was rapidly advanced through the state school system to the point where he was accepted to read history at the University of Edinburgh at just 16. After suffering the rugby injury which left him permanently blind in one eye, Brown doggedly persevered and graduated with first-class honours. Like Bill Clinton at Oxford, Brown would become a student activist and, from his position as a student magazine editor, regularly criticised his university's decision to invest in companies with links to the Apartheid regime in South Africa.

British voters would come to see Brown as somewhat haughty when in power, but this belied more revolutionary interests. His doctoral thesis would be written on James Maxton, the Red Clydesider who had opposed British intervention in the First World War and been a radical leftist parliamentarian between the wars. When Brown re-released a book on the subject in 2002, at a time when his own leadership ambitions were strongly mooted, it was commented by sympathetic voices that 'this indicated his greater understanding of Labour's past and values' than Blair. The pragmatist in Brown would lead him to a different form of politics to Maxton, but he was always rooted in Labour's history, tradition and its institutions. He saw the burning injustices of British life and sought to tackle them, not with the grandstanding of his student days but with practical, deliverable action. Not everyone on the left made such a decisive transition. As Steve Richards argues, 'like Maxton [Brown] was in politics above all to help people fulfil their potential and he associated education, training and work as the way in which this would be brought about'.[36]

Five years before Brown entered the world, Bill Clinton had been 'born in a little town called Hope, Arkansas'. In 1992, his campaign ads would make much of this ordinary background, though, in reality, there was much that was atypical about his youth. His father had been killed in an automobile accident three months before the then Bill Blythe was born in 1946 and, when his mother moved to Louisiana to take a nursing course, the young boy moved in with his grandparents. Like Blair and Brown,

Clinton's parents – mother Virginia and stepfather Roger (from whom Clinton took his new surname) – had been raised during the era of inter-war economic uncertainty. One of Clinton's earliest memories was of Virginia's 'tale of a Depression Good Friday when my grandfather came home from work and broke down and cried as he told her he just couldn't afford the Dollar or so it would cost him to buy her an Easter dress'. She never forgot it and 'every year I had a new Easter outfit whether I wanted it or not'.[37]

With his mother away Bill spent a lot of time at his grandfather's grocery store which provided an interesting experience of the post-war south. As Clinton noted, 'a lot of my grandfather's customers were black' and 'it was rare to find an uneducated rural southerner without a racist bone in his body'. But 'that's exactly what my grandfather was. I could see that black people looked different, but because he treated them like everybody else, asking after their children and about their work, I thought they were just like me'. Toni Morrison's comment that Clinton was 'the first black president' would be much debated, particularly when the president declined to move on drug law reform that would have established greater racial parity in sentencing, but his affinity with African Americans was undoubtedly not merely confected for political gain. Meanwhile, time spent around the dinner table with his extended family not only saw a lack of racism, but also meant that Clinton grew up around 'meals, conversation and storytelling'. His famous patter was learned from an early age and, when Roger Clinton took the family to live on a Hot Springs farm with an outhouse, a homespun 'log-cabin' image – akin to Andrew Jackson – was also cemented.[38]

His views on race were not those of many of his contemporaries. Indeed, Clinton's Arkansas was part of the 'solid south' which voted Democratic in every Presidential election from 1876 to 1964. Southern Democrats were generally opposed to Roosevelt's shift towards economic interventionism, any limits on states' power and certainly to greater civil rights for African Americans. Such an uneasy relationship occasionally boiled over. During Clinton's youth, the Supreme Court had declared the segregation of schools to be unconstitutional and, in 1957, nine black children attempted to enrol at Little Rock Central High School. Governor Orval Faubus, a segregationist Arkansas Democrat, promptly called on the National Guard to prevent integration – only to be met by Eisenhower using the 101st Airborne to protect the students from the massed protestors. As part of his reply to the president, Faubus shut down Little

Rock's High Schools for the entire 1958–1959 academic year. The incident brought great global controversy but, in a sign of the times, the Governor was successfully re-elected four more times. Faubus would go on to run against Clinton himself in 1986 (receiving a credible 34 per cent in the Democratic primary), but during the 1950s and 1960s he merely represented 'the scars of Little Rock and the stains of cronyism'.[39]

Britain in the 1950s and 1960s had its share of racial unrest – the 1958 Notting Hill riots not least – but the country's vastly different demographics meant that race would not form as strong a part of the Blair–Brown youth or their political makeup. Blair did not recall seeing a black man until he was ten and thus his concern was more that in the post-war period 'Labour lost touch with its basic purpose'. For the future leader, 'that purpose was always, at heart, about the individual'. Things like 'a more powerful state, unions, social action, collective bargaining – all these were a means to an end: to help the individual gain opportunity'. But with the economic successes of the 1950s, 'the problem for all progressive parties was that by the 1960s, the first generation of those helped had [already] been liberated'. In place of the man or woman in Whitehall telling them what to do, these newly empowered voters 'wanted choice, [the] freedom to earn more money and to spend it'.[40]

Blair would later read the most famous example of this view, Anthony Crosland's *The Future of Socialism*, which he saw as 'a magnificent essay in bringing Labour to the reality of life in the 1950s', even if the party 'only really imbided it and digested it by the late 1980s'. That landmark text tried to shake Labour out of their addiction to nationalisation and argued for a 'society in which ownership is thoroughly mixed up – a society with diverse ... patterns of ownership, with the State, the nationalised industries, the Co-operatives ... pension funds, foundations and millions of private families all participating'. Quoting Keynes, Crosland urged Labour to start 'valu[ing] ends above means'.[41] Or, in later Blairite parlance, to move to a position from the doctrinal veneration of big government to 'whatever works'. The strategic use of government to deliver record levels of housing construction through both public and private sources in the 1950s and 1960s would prove one such admirably bipartisan example of this tendency, as would corporatist bodies such as the National Economic Development Councils.

Whilst Blair and Brown spent the 1960s in school or university exam halls, seeing such political developments at several steps removed, it would serve as the decade where Bill Clinton achieved true political maturity. On 28 August 1963, the teenage Clinton sat alone in the big reclining chair in the den of his house, watching 'the greatest speech of my lifetime, as Martin Luther King Jr stood in front of the Lincoln Memorial and spoke of his dream for America'. Just a few months earlier, Clinton had shaken President Kennedy's hand at the White House as part of a Boys Nation trip – footage that proved very useful on the campaign trail in 1992. This was a time of liberal icons when change was most certainly in the air. Clinton, who worked for Senator Fulbright after choosing to study at Georgetown, saw the broad course of the civil rights struggle at both national and local levels.

In the summer of 1966, he would campaign for Frank Holt, seeking to win the Democratic nomination for Arkansas Governor after Faubus had elected to stand down. But, for all Clinton's assistance, the 'honest and decent' Holt was unable to defeat Jim Johnson, a candidate who won the backing of 'people upset with federal activism in civil rights, scared by the Watts riots and other racial disturbances, convinced the War on Poverty was socialist welfare for blacks and frustrated with their own economic conditions'. Though he lost to the Republican candidate in 1966, Johnson would go on to resurface 26 years later, heavily criticising Clinton and declaring his dismay that America had elected 'a president of the United States who is a queer-mongering, whore-hopping adulterer; a baby-killing, draft-dodging, dope-tolerating, lying, two-faced, treasonous activist'. Arkansans could bear a grudge. But, for Clinton, the wider lesson would be to walk a path between Lyndon Johnson's unpopularity and Jim Johnson's heinousness.[42]

In any event, Clinton's canvas and his imagination were always wider than the machinations of his home state. Armed with a reference from Senator Fulbright, Clinton successfully applied for a Rhodes Scholarship to attend Oxford University in 1968. Socially, Oxford would give Clinton many things, including his first taste of alcohol and raiding college kitchens for late night snacks. Though not a big drinker, he would enjoy the odd pint in the Turf Tavern (where a few years earlier, future Australian Prime Minister Bob Hawke had set a world record for consuming a yard of ale in 11 seconds) and devoured several English breakfasts at Oxford's covered market – the closest thing he could find to good old southern food.[43] In an issue regularly raised during his run for the Presidency – his time overseas also reduced the likelihood he would have to serve in Vietnam.

If he did not see any of 1960s Asia, he would, however, see much of Europe. Harold Wilson's 1967 devaluation of the pound had increased

Clinton's relative dollar purchasing power dramatically and, like many American students at Oxford, he used this additional money to travel the European continent. On New Year's Eve 1969 Clinton thereby found himself boarding a train to Moscow from inside Finland. When the train arrived at the Russian border, 'I met my first real life Communist, a pudgy, cherubic-looking guard'. Looking at Clinton's bags suspiciously, the future president 'expected him to check for drugs'. Instead, he asked in heavily accented English, 'Dirty books? Dirty books? Got any dirty books?' Laughing, Clinton could only show him some Tolstoy, Dostoevsky and Turgenev. More seriously, the experience of travelling through eastern Europe left Clinton with 'renewed faith in America and democracy. For all its faults, I had discovered that my country was still a beacon of light to people chafing under communism'.[44]

When it came to the UK, Clinton was not just another example of a Yank 'overpaid, over sexed and over here'. He seems to have thrown himself into British life through rugby, various bus trips and the odd bit of militant student activism. That said, at times it appears that the ostentatious intellectualism of Oxford got to Clinton. After a seminar on 'pluralism as a concept of democratic theory' – which Clinton found 'boring' – he wrote in his diary that it was just another attempt 'to explain in more complex (therefore, more meaningful, of course) . . . terms what is going on before our own eyes'. At this time, he was keener to soak up knowledge than make big political statements, with one former girlfriend later telling the Conservative MP Giles Brandreth that she couldn't remember any great ideological statements from the man whilst at Oxford (he was, however, 'absolutely gorgeous'). But outside the university he saw much of the country – from Wales to Manchester and Derby – and enjoyed giving basic talks to British school children about the American political scene. All in all, during his two years at Oxford, Clinton 'travelled a lot and loved it. I had also ventured into the far reaches of my mind and heart, struggling with my draft situation, my ambivalence about my ambition and my inability to have anything other than brief relationships with women'.[45]

There were many around his Cabinet table with whom he would be able to share stories of British days. Madeline Albright, Clinton's second Secretary of State, was Czech by birth and had spent the Second World War living in London (her father was a member of Benes' wartime government in exile). Bob Rubin, Secretary of the Treasury between 1995 and 1999, attended the LSE in the early 1960s – as did his successor, Larry

Summers, as a visiting academic in the late 1980s. The Arizonan Bruce Babbitt (Secretary of the State for the Interior throughout Clinton's term in office) had attended Newcastle University on a Marshall Scholarship and the president had encountered his future Secretary of Labor, Robert Reich, as a fellow Rhodes Scholar at Oxford (Reich had also previously been on a date with the then Hillary Rodham when both were at Dartmouth). British politics was not an abstract notion for these politicians and the New Democrat world view was always tilted towards its Anglophone cousins. There was a lineage, an interconnected set of figures born from the mid-1940s to the mid-1960s who viewed the world in Anglo-American terms and were keen to transmit solutions across the Atlantic Ocean. By the time of Clinton's victory in 1992, Robin Renwick, the UK's Ambassador to Washington, was therefore able to chide those 'British correspondents [engaging] in their usual masochistic desire to declare the "special relationship" dead'. For, as he noted in a memo to the Foreign Office in London, 'this is a bit bizarre when applied to an administration which looks likely to be stuffed with Rhodes scholars'.[46]

Even though it was less exotic, Oxford was profound for Blair too. Whilst studying law from 1972, Blair was influenced by both the Anglican priest Peter Thomson – a 'deep socialist' – and Geoff Gallop, later Premier of Western Australia, who taught Blair 'all the right terms and phrases of leftist politics at the time and [who] was a member of the Internationalist Marxist Group'. The first political book Blair would read was Isaac Deutsch's trilogy of Trotsky (lent by Gallop) which 'opened a new world to me, full of extraordinary causes and injustices and here's this guy Trotsky who set out to change the world. It was like a light going on'. Blair's infatuation with Trotsky would be 'reasonably brief' but would allow him to 'really understand *that politics* . . . and to come finally to the conclusion that it wasn't right'. When a jejune Blair loftily forwarded the 'usual Marxist line' that 'the state had to take over from the interests of capitalism, which only cared for profit', he was soon corrected by an Indian student, Anmol Vellani. 'It isn't as simple as that', said Vellani, 'the state too, can be a vested interest [which] isn't the same as the public interest . . . not in practice at least'. To Blair's protests that 'it should be', Vellani patiently replied, 'should be and is are two very different things, my friend'.[47]

Whereas Blair spent significant chunks of time on acting and music at Oxford, Gordon Brown was always more immersed in the practicalities of left-wing politics when at Edinburgh. In 1970, he had canvassed for the

24-year-old Robin Cook, later Foreign Secretary under Blair, but then unsuccessfully fighting the seat of Edinburgh North. Brown also became chair of the University Labour Club in 1971 and, in something of a precursor to later events, attempted to engineer a revival of its fortunes by separating it from the International Marxist and Trotskyist factions. In 1974, Brown had the opportunity to work for Cook again, in his now successful bid to enter parliament and, later, went on to throw himself into the debate for a new Scottish devolved assembly – another policy eventually enacted by New Labour. Compared to Blair, who had spent a gap year before Oxford promoting his rock band Ugly Rumours and then worked as a barman in Paris, this was all deeply political and deeply Labour. Brown would go on to work in Scottish television journalism, whilst Blair eventually entered the bar in London.

FIGURE 2 Gordon Brown was a student politician *par excellence*. Here, in 1972, he successfully campaigned to become Rector of the University of Edinburgh (Trinity Mirror/Mirrrorpix/Alamy Stock Photo).

Certainly, Bill Clinton's early political activities more closely mirrored Brown than Blair. Still, there were other significant milestones around this time. Attending Yale Law School upon his return from Oxford in 1971, Clinton first laid eyes on a woman with 'thick dark blond hair [who] wore eyeglasses with no makeup, but . . . conveyed a sense of strength and self-possession I have rarely seen in anyone, man or woman'. This was his fellow Law School student Hillary Rodham who, having broken with her early Republican leanings after perceiving racism in the GOP's 1968 campaign, had just worked for Walter Mondale's Senate Committee looking into the conditions of migrant labour. She was confident, competent and politically malleable – a good match for her would-be suitor. After seeing Bill stare at her, Hillary walked the length of the library, looked him in the eye and said, 'If you're going to keep staring at me and I'm going to keep staring back, we ought to at least know each other's names.' Four years later, after several rebuffed proposals from Bill, they would be married.[48]

At the time America's future first couple met, the 1972 Presidential campaign was more or less underway. Nixon's opponent would end up being the left-wing Senator from South Dakota, George McGovern – who offered Clinton the job as his southern states co-ordinator ahead of the Democratic Primaries. As Clinton later chuckled, this was in part 'affirmative action: they had to have at least one southerner in a responsible position'. After some humming and hawing – he did not want to be too far from Hillary, who had taken on a legal position in San Francisco – Clinton firmed up a role on McGovern's national staff in late 1971, with an eye to turning Arkansas and South Carolina's delegates towards his nomination. Although McGovern's New Politics platform proved deeply unelectable, Clinton made 'some good friends who shared my passion for politics' and the experience taught the Arkansas native much 'more about the mechanics of electioneering'. He also learned that 'winning as a progressive requires great care and discipline in crafting and presenting a message and a program that gives people the confidence to change course'.[49]

As Clinton would note, 'our society can absorb only so much change at a time and when we move forward, we must do it in a way that reaffirms our core convictions of opportunity and responsibility, work and family'. Most people, for sure, 'don't think about government policy as much as liberals do'. 'They have a lot of common sense and a desire to understand the larger forces shaping their lives but can't be expected to abandon the values and social arrangements that at least enable them to survive and feel good about themselves'. Though not directly commenting on McGovern, Tony Blair had a similar view. Blair wanted to 'take the good bits of the Labour Party in the 1970s and 1980s – proper progressive attitudes such as equality for women, gays, blacks and Asians – and ally them to normality, bring them into the mainstream and out of the suffocating strictures of political correctness'. The McGoverns weren't the types to effect this transition.[50]

This wider sense that the left had lost its way dogged the moderates through the 1970s. Clinton had elected to run for an Arkansas seat in Congress in 1974 against a Republican incumbent and, in the wake of Watergate, only marginally failed to be elected in a previously safe district for the GOP. Though it did not take him to DC, the run gave him a voice and a platform. Speaking to the Arkansas State Democratic Convention in Hot Springs in September 1974, a few weeks after Nixon had resigned the Presidency, Clinton called for a reinvention of government that went far beyond the machinations of a crooked leader. 'We do not want the federal government to give up its attempts to protect our national security and promote domestic wellbeing. But we *do* want to cut back on wasteful spending and bloated bureaucracies. These middlemen of government meddle with our lives without increasing the common good.' For Clinton, 'in short, in the words of a friend of mine who works on the Scott County Road Crew: "the people want a hand up, not a hand out"'.[51] These words would mark the Third Way strongly thereafter. Though Clinton lost in 1974, he was now an established Democratic star in a small state and became Attorney General two years later, before winning the Governorship in 1978.

Even when one could win an election, however, this was hardly the optimum time to enter progressive politics. Reviewing the British Labour performance in the 1970s, Peter Mandelson and Roger Liddle noted that the government had 'based its public spending on optimistic forecasts of economic growth that failed to materialise'. This meant taxes needed to be raised, which squeezed incomes and thus, in turn, made the government's attempts at pay restraint more difficult. The overarching issues were a 'failure to provide a stable macro-economic framework', an inadequate industrial strategy to address 'fundamental weaknesses of competitiveness', the decision to genuflect to the trade unions whilst leaving them unreformed and, more generally, the left's inability to challenge the 'deep-seated institutional and interest group resistance to modernisation'.[52]

If the left did not reform itself, the young Third Wayers realised, the electorate would look elsewhere. There needed to be change – at both a cosmetic and substantial level. In a landmark speech at the 1980 Democratic Party Convention in New York, therefore, Bill Clinton told his party that Americans could no longer 'be moved by the symbols and accomplishments of the Democratic Party of the past'. Even though 'we have proved that our party is more sensitive than the Republicans to equality and justice' it was time to 'offer more in the way of creative and realistic solutions' and show 'that we have a vision that can withstand the erosion of special interest politics that is gripping our land'. For ten years, 'through Democratic and Republican administrations alike, [the] economic system has been breaking down'. Even if the American people did not believe everything Ronald Reagan was then selling, 'they do not know what our vision is and whether it will make any difference if our president and our party are returned to the White House'. By the time Clinton spoke, after all, that reality was only a few months away. And things were about to get even worse.

Notes

1   *Guardian*, 7 June 1983.

2   Blair 1/45–47.

3   Jackson speech, 11 June 1984, ARC/HDC/19/7.

4   Gould/24.

5   *Rolling Stone*, January 1993, Dionne/11.

6   Greenberg 2/81.

7   Robb speech, 13 November 1989, ARC/HOV/TED/104.

8   7 July 1952 Republican platform; Mandelson and Liddle/19.

9   Brown 1/28, 8–9.

10 Greenberg 2/97.

11 Greenberg 2/110.

12 From/17.

13 Gallup data at https://news.gallup.com/poll/1714/taxes.aspx.

14 Bloodworth/39; Blumenthal/12.

15 George H. Nash, 'The Historical Roots of Contemporary American Conservatism', September 1981, ARC/HOV/ABE/99; 'The Family in America', June 1987, ARC/LOC/MOY/2423/8; *New York Times*, 16 September 1990.

16 Phillips/206; Roper Center data. Available at: https://ropercenter.cornell.edu/public-support-vietnam-1967/.

17 From/12.

18 Clinton/131, 133; *New Republic*, 15 August 1970.

19 *The Atlantic*, June 1996.

20 Bloodworth/4–5; Gallup Exit Polling 1972; Haldeman memo, 8 August 1972, ARC/FORD/RT/65; Loen memo, 10 January 1975, ARC/FORD/MFD/6.

21 Marquand/115.

22 Reich 1/62–69.

23 24 November 1980, ARC/HOV/FLBR.

24 'European Technology Comments', 29 October 1976, ARC/SHS/TEL/4362.

25 Office for National Statistics: Economic Trends, 204 (2004), 38–46; US Bureau of Labor Statistics. Available at: https://data.bls.gov/pdq/SurveyOutputServlet; House of Commons Briefing Paper No 05745; OMB. Available at: www.whitehouse.gov/omb/budget/Historicals; Greenspan to Ford, ARC/FORD/PHF/7; Radice 1/396.

26 Friedman submission, 10 June 1980, ARC/HOV/MFR/61/14.

27 Radice 2/22.

28 Benn memo, 29 November 1976, ARC/KEW/CAB/129/193/7.

29 Radice 2/21.

30 Mandelson/60.

31 From/38.

32 Bloodworth/118.

33 COR/Blumenthal.

34 Reflections with Peter Hennessy, 10 August 2017, BBC Radio 4; National Constitution Center Debate, 10 September 2010.

35 Radice 4/16.

36 Richards/45.

37 Clinton/11.

38 Clinton/11–12.

39 Clinton/82.

40 Blair 1/90.

41 Crosland/384–85, 409.

42 Clinton/64, 84.

43 Levin/68.

44 Clinton/169–70.

45 Clinton/148, 173; Brandreth/127.

46 Renwick memorandum, 2 November 1992, ARC/KEW/PREM 19/4496.

47 Blair 1/80.

48 Clinton/181.

49 Clinton/184.

50 Clinton/200; Blair 1/90.

51 Levin/111.

52 Mandelson and Liddle/10–11.

2 'UNCONVINCING, UNINFORMED AND TIRED'

The left in the 1980s

In March 1985, pollster Stan Greenberg travelled to Macomb County, Michigan to take the temperature of the average American voter. In later years, Greenberg would serve as a major figure in Bill Clinton's famous 'War Room' during the 1992 campaign and then, after somewhat falling out of favour with the White House, assisted Tony Blair in New Labour's rise in the UK. But in the mid-1980s, in the cold rust belt, he was a world away from the corridors of power. Initially fictionalised as 'Greene County' in internal memoranda to preserve anonymity, Greenberg's focus on Macomb would become synonymous with the idea of the 'Reagan Democrat'. Located on the northern edge of Detroit, in 1960 Macomb had been the most Democratic suburb in America. Having given John F Kennedy 63 per cent of their vote, Macomb then voted 74 per cent in favour of Lyndon Johnson in 1964. But over the next 20 years something clearly shifted, for in 1984, 67 per cent of Macomb residents backed the very different offer provided by Ronald Reagan. Greenberg's task was to work out why this area had turned so dramatically away from the Democrats at a national level even when local elections and the fact that four in ten households were members of a union, indicated lingering sympathy towards the left.

Greenberg would detail the gist of his findings in his 1995 book, *Middle Class Dreams*, but his original report is worth quoting at length. He had set out to interview 37 people who were all 'blue-collar workers who traditionally voted Democratic [but], in 1984, voted mostly for Republican candidates.'[1] Such conversations took place in 'small, comfortable settings like a hotel room or the back of a restaurant where like-minded people would feel free to open up and speak their minds'. Greenberg wanted to cut through what such voters *thought* they should tell pollsters and get a real sense of the everyday conversations going in in bars, sports stadia and workplaces across America. Some of this was uncomfortable, yet it was vital work. For all the Gores and the Clintons would seek to produce the Third Way in government, it was arguably these 37 (all white, mostly male) individuals who were most influential in shaping its early mood music. Such was the strategy of the modernisers. As Bill Clinton once remarked, 'there is no one more powerful than a member of a focus group'.[2] Future New Labour analysts like Philip Gould would come to see them as of equally vital importance and Labour's Shadow Communications Agency, set up by Gould around the same time, would make much use of the tool.

Greenberg's 'Report on Democratic Defection' began by noting his focus group's contention that 'the Democratic Party no longer responded with genuine feeling to the vulnerabilities and burdens of the average middle-class person; instead the party and the government were preoccupied with the needs of minorities and [inner city areas like] Detroit'. This problem was both about presentation and policy. On the image side, 'the Democratic Party under Jimmy Carter and Walter Mondale ... proved weak, chaotic and vacillating'. As for policy, 'they advanced spending programs that offered no appreciable or visible benefit for those who supported the government with their votes and taxes'.

These fears took the form we discussed in Chapter 1: the world was growing more competitive, historically powerful nations such as the United States were seeing their market share under threat and consequently large chunks of their workforce felt insecure. In industrial Michigan the continual fear of 'plants ... threatening to "split" and leave people with nothing' was particularly acute. As global capital took chunks of American companies, including heavy manufacturing, 'workers fe[lt] they will be subject to decision centers that are even more remote and inaccessible'. More broadly, 'these workers feel threatened ... by computers and robotics'. The computer was felt to take 'a lot of jobs away' and created 'opportunities that these workers, because of their backgrounds, feel they have no access to'. The continual refrain was to ask, 'how can today's worker gain access to those jobs?' The left's answer here – a siege economy and extensive government planning – was hardly going down well.

There was a vicious cycle here and worker pessimism was more even acute for their children than it was for them. 'Young people, they believe, are having a particularly hard time. They need computer skills, yet their school system can barely afford to buy computers.' Cutbacks in 'college loan eligibility made an impression' too and the idea that a college-educated elite would be running the country for time immemorial was firmly set. There was, then, a distinctly public service argument that voters might buy, but only if the fundamentals of policy making could be got right. The left would struggle to outdo the right on tax cuts, nor were voters enamoured with its traditional offer: the big state. Progressives would need to be smarter.

Self-identity was a major part of the contemporary malaise and this was reflected in economic and ethnic dimensions. The general notion was that 'the average person' is 'supporting both ends' of the spectrum: 'you have the extremely rich who pay very low tax and you have the poor who are paying none.' 'The minorities and the poor . . . do not have to pay for anything and do not pay taxes.' As Greenberg summarised, 'these workers now see themselves as members of a new minority class that is ignored by the government but forced to support social programs what do not benefit them'. Because of 'all the taxes', one 'can't save for a down payment' on a house or car and there was 'no linkage in their minds between their taxes and some visible and valued public spending'. This was what New Labour thinkers would later call 'the squeezed middle' – not economically secure enough to feel comfortable, but not poor enough to receive welfare.

In 1980s Macomb there was also a significantly racial dimension. As Greenberg recorded, 'for these white suburban residents, the terms "blacks" and Detroit are interchangeable: Detroit is just "one big ghetto" . . . [and] for them, blacks mean "crime," above all, but also "dirty" and "corrupt."' Reading out an old statement from Robert Kennedy that called on people to honour a special obligation to African Americans who were burdened by the legacy of slavery and widespread racial discrimination, replies included 'that's bullshit' and 'no wonder they killed him'. More calm responses included the notion that 'I don't think anybody should have any preference because he is black or green or purple' and 'this happened years ago. And they talk to you about it as if it was happening right now'.

This cut across the redistributive agenda of the left and the notion of quotas or special exemptions was particularly frowned upon – something Bill Clinton would pick up on. It was also a product of a lived experience over and above intellectual theory. One participant noted that 'my son, he passed the test and went through all the qualifications [for an unknown job], but they, at that time, had to hire the minorities. He lost out'. This was especially the case for federal positions where 'if you apply for a job at the post office, a *federal* job, you might as well take the application and tear it up' because 'there are 20 blacks behind you, they will get the job'. Since the Great Society, the state and the perceived favoured treatment of ethnic minorities had become intertwined, leaving the left viewed not as the liberator of the oppressed, but the defender of particular vested interests that, certainly in areas that were 99 per cent white, were abstract to some.[3]

Such debates did not completely obscure old rivalries, but they allowed candidates like Reagan to float above them. Although the Republican party was still viewed suspiciously by blue collar audiences in the 1980s, the President had clearly performed well. Reagan's foreign policy seemed to restore a sense of national vigour, as opposed to the 'mouse' Jimmy Carter who 'fiddled around' like a 'mother hen'. Whilst 'many of these Democratic defectors differ on Reagan on specific policy questions . . . the power of this imagery overrides the reservations'. This imagery included his being as 'straight as an arrow, [like] John Wayne'. Nor was this unique. Elsewhere, Republican focus groups were criticising the 'wishy-washy' Mondale and praising Reagan's 'strength of character'.[4] Whilst many of Greenberg's trade union respondents were angry about 'the smashing of PATCO, [they] nonetheless made allowances'. As one put it, 'I have been out of work for five years and I still voted for him'. This voter 'didn't hold it against [Reagan] that I am out of a job 'cause I feel it was all the giveaway plans for the Democrats that created the problem that I got laid off with'.

This was a toxic cocktail. In a decade where a dictatorial Soviet Union possessed nuclear weapons, capitalism appeared inexorably on the march in the west and, crucially, the British and American electorates consistently voted for right-wing governments, the leadership of both Labour and the Democrats would become obsessed with a series of issues at times abstract and, when it came to anti-Semitism or an overly pacifist defence policy, offensive. Macomb and areas, like it, deserted in droves. In 1980, Jimmy Carter had lost to Ronald Reagan heavily and in 1984, his former Vice President Walter Mondale would go on to repeat McGovern's 1972 record of a 49 states to 1 defeat. Likewise, between 1979 and 1983, the hard left of the British Labour Party, managed, as Tony Blair later noted, 'the political equivalent of a conjuring trick'. They 'convinced the Labour Party that the real reason we had lost in 1979 to Margaret Thatcher was because Jim Callaghan, the Labour Prime Minister, had been too right wing'. Under Michael Foot's leadership from 1980, Labour therefore 'moved sharply left and advocated pulling out of Europe and wholesale nationalisation'. This was certainly due to the leader, but also owed much to the 'charisma and persuasive power' of Tony Benn who continually stressed the need to be ideologically 'pure'. 'With Reagan and Thatcher in power', Benn wrote in November 1980, 'the polarisation and the choice for British electors, will be clearer'. It was indeed so, though the outcome was far from what Benn expected.[5]

Actually, Tony Blair could have extended his critical analysis a little further. When he and Gordon Brown reached parliament for the first time in 1983 – elected, ironically, on Michael Foot's manifesto with which they largely disagreed – they soon saw that even Labour's worst result in decades was not enough to shake the cobwebs. During a post-election debate of the Parliamentary Labour Party, Foot declared that moderates were being 'complacent by suggesting that the election result justified their views'. For the soon to be ex-leader, 'the party could not jettison the [1983] manifesto' and 'it would be a disgrace if it did'. If Blair was present at that meeting it has not made the record. But his new parliamentary office mate, Dave Nellist, certainly threw himself into such discussions. Whoever had allocated the offices to new MPs was either ignorant of the men's politics or playing an amusing joke. Nellist was a hard-left MP who offered unwavering backing for the Militant tendency. At a similar meeting of the PLP, a week prior to Foot's comments, Nellist told his new colleagues that although the House of Commons was important, 'to the needy in this country it meant nothing'. Instead, 'the party had to come across as a wing of the Labour Movement; fully integrated with the TUC and the Unions'. He thundered that MPs 'should be there on picket lines giving every help to comrades in the struggles against the Tories'.[6] Perhaps wisely, Blair soon sought a new office – and began sharing with Gordon Brown.

So started a partnership that would shape global politics, but things began slowly. Since Blair would become father to three children in the 1980s and Brown did not yet have a family, the two did not tend to socialise much outside of work. As Cherie Blair later reflected, during the 1980s Gordon 'fell into the category of people who weren't used to the constant pressure of small children'. That said, the Scot was less comfortable with London life all told. Between his election as an MP and becoming Chancellor in 1997, Brown did not spend a full weekend in Britain's capital city. He would arrive in parliament on a Monday or a Tuesday and promptly head north after parliamentary business had ended on a Thursday. As such, Blair and Brown's relationship took a while to progress. They had first met in the House of Commons bar prior to the 1983 election after an introduction by John Smith, but neither remembered much of the encounter. The dingy office that they were allocated – without windows and with erratic heating – provided an entrée of sorts but, even then, Blair would often prefer the comfort of working from home. At the very least, as Brown noted, they soon 'discovered we shared a fierce passion to see the party reform and recover'.[7] It was their shared politics – first a belief in Neil Kinnock and, then, an interest in the reforming US Democrat Party, that ignited their partnership.

Before we get to that, however, we need to further understand their internal enemy. The world of Nellist and Foot was essentially that of the New Jerusalem and the New Politics: the type of mentality that Blair had seen at Spennymoor and discussed in Chapter 1. But, as Philip Gould discovered when he started to commission his own focus groups, the issues 1980s British voters cared about were largely the same as those being told to Stan Greenberg in the US: 'those affecting their own personal and financial security: law and order, health, education, inflation, prices and taxation'. Whereas, 'defence and the role of minorities within society, two of Labour's big pre-occupations, were at the bottom of the list'. The left was thus tarred with two brushes: a nostalgic attachment to nationalisation and old-style redistribution, whilst, at the same time, the notion that, even were Labour to win power, such redistribution wouldn't ever reach the pockets of the average voter. As one focus group put it, 'Labour waste money on useless things … it's outrageous – they're spending a million pounds on parks for Gays and Lesbians in Camden'.[8] As we will see, the experience of Labour's far left in local government – Ken Livingstone and the Greater London Council on the one hand, Militant in Liverpool on the other – did not help matters.

There were undeniably legitimate concerns to be had on a range of topics in the 1980s. Whether it be apartheid in South Africa, the treatment of minorities at the hands of law and order agencies at home, the pace of economic change which threatened to engulf working-class communities from Michigan, USA to Mansfield, UK, or the use of military force overseas, there was much to be angry about. With unemployment rocketing to double digits in both countries, inequality increasing by a third in the UK and the share of national income held by the top 1 per cent of Americans increasing by a half during the 1980s, the consequences of the Thatcher–Reagan era (though not wholly negative) were clear. What was the best channel for such fury and how to talk in shades of grey rather than black and white? Too often, the left looked narcissistic and unelectable, rather than caring and serious. It talked to itself instead of the 'masses' it so often theorised about and paid the electoral consequences at every major test it faced in the long 1980s. Every mistake the left had made in the previous two decades was about to be compounded.

Reagan and Thatcher

For many progressive thinkers, though not the formerly Democratic voters of Macomb, the new Republican President Ronald Reagan was the devil incarnate. A former New Deal Democrat, Reagan had achieved notoriety as an actor and Hollywood union leader in the 1930s and 1940s. As the journalist EJ Dionne would write, 'Reagan's repeated invocations of his own past as an FDR supporter reassured many Democrats-turned-Republicans that they were not breaking with their basic political commitments but with an aberration from those commitments represented by the sixties counterculture and the New Left.'[9] Indeed, Reagan only joined the Republican Party as late as 1962 and four years later won the California Gubernatorial election on a platform to 'send the welfare bums back to work'. His Governorship, which lasted until 1975, was divided between hard stances on law and order (including putting down the 1969 People's Park protests at Berkeley)and socially liberal legislation on issues such as 'no fault divorce'.

Economically, Reagan was a free market zealot, no question. Much of this could be seen, for example, in his views on Chile – a country that would obsess the New Right and the hard left alike. In late 1973, Chile's left-wing President Salvador Allende had been overthrown by a military coup (leaving the president, his palace surrounded, to shoot himself with an assault rifle). One escapee from this coup, Oscar Soto, held the odd combination of being Allende's personal doctor and the uncle of Claudia Bracchitta, Jeremy Corbyn's second wife; left-wing north London would soon become awash with Chilean exiles. Corbyn himself had praised the 'spirit' of the deposed Allende and remarked that 'it was exciting what was achieved – the land reform, the bank nationalisations . . . all that stuff'. But the new Pinochet order had its fans too. Soon after the coup, 'stagflation' theorist Milton Friedman visited Chile to give a series of lectures on the principles of economic freedom, a decision which led to his Nobel prize award of 1976 being met by a chorus of protest from liberals across the west. In a late 1970s radio address, however, Reagan not only stuck up for Friedman but also, more or less, the Chilean military coup. He told his listeners that, 'in true Friedman tradition, twenty months ago the Generals of the junta took the drastic action politicians find so impractical. They set out to balance the budget, slashing spending ruthlessly'. Through these and other measures, 'the deep recession bottomed out a year ago and slowly, but surely, the economy is improving'. The lessons here were obvious: 'it seems that when Milton Friedman talked, someone in Chile listened. Wouldn't it be nice if just once someone in Washington would ask, 'what did he say'?' This was grandiose, almost Donald Trump level trolling.[10]

Throughout the Reagan years, Friedman would continue to influence the White House. In December 1984 he told the president that a new four-point economic programme should include 'truly extensive cuts in spending' and that his existing tax plans did 'not cut personal tax rates nearly enough'. By that point the Reagan administration had already cut the top rate from 70 to 50 per cent, but Friedman urged a 25 per cent top rate. Though Reagan would not quite get there, the 38.5 per cent (1987) and then 28 per cent (1988) top rates passed by Congress took the US close to Friedman's dream. Likewise, in the UK, the 83 per cent top rate Thatcher inherited from Labour would fall to 60 per cent and, by 1988, 40 per cent. Commenting on the latter reduction, Gordon Brown would warn the government that 'one reason for the substantial budget deficit in the United States is that predictions made in the early years of the Reagan revolution that top-rate tax reductions would yield massively increased revenues have not proved correct'. Whenever he or Blair touched on Reagan in the 1980s – and it was a comparatively rare event – it was always in a practical manner.[11]

In any event, the neoconservative agenda was never just about cuts for the rich. As George Nash noted, 'neoconservatism is a reaction of moderate liberals to the polarizing upheavals of the Sixties and particularly to the New Left, with its opposition to economic growth at home and its neo-isolationist hostility to a strong America abroad'. The point about growth was a stretch and Carter's record on that measure at least was not awful, but the other two points – a vacillating, even weak foreign policy and an addiction to 1960s New Politics cut through significantly. Indeed, for much of the 1970s the left had misdiagnosed its opponent – thinking that the high-profile tax cut message was the only game in town. In reality, the plain speaking, moralistic nature of Reagan's New Right was of equal importance. For Nash, 'the New Right ... is an anti-elitist attempt to influence our politics from below ... a revolt *by* the masses'. Whilst foreign policy was important, its 'primary interest lies elsewhere: in issues like abortion, prayer in public schools, the equal rights amendment, pornography, homosexual rights, school bussing and crime prevention'. Thatcher's moralism against crime and gay rights were a further such example and served as a wedge issue to attract new conservative voters. As Gould's focus group research suggested, 'the ridiculing of left-wing councils for intimidation and political correctness … worked partly because the brilliance of the Conservative attack; partly because of the relentless pounding of the tabloid press, but mostly because it was true'.[12]

Adjoining social conservatism to economic populism proved a heady mix. In the UK, the privatisation of state assets such as British Telecom and British Gas led not only to billions of pounds reaching the UK Exchequer (funding, in large part, increased welfare payments that rising unemployment brought), but a fast buck for millions of citizens. The general strategy was to privatise such entities through selling shares to ordinary people (usually the relevant company workforce), most of whom promptly sold them on to investors (often international) for a speedy profit. In the case of Rolls Royce, over half its shares were resold on the first day of trading, mostly to Japanese buyers. For British Airways, privatised in February 1987, over two-thirds of its shares had been sold within two years. Such foreign ownership of these big domestic employers was not without concern. Still, for the 4 million applicants who successfully applied for shares in British Gas, the 2 million for BT or the 2 million for British Aerospace, this was popular and profitable capitalism. As Tony Blair had remarked in 1982, Thatcher's strategy had a 'simple, gut appeal'.[13]

In another seemingly successful privatisation, as Labour pollster Deborah Mattinson recalls, 'the Tories could boast what I believe to this day remains the most effective example of a symbolic policy: giving [social] tenants the right to buy their own council house'. This 'meant voters had a clear and accurate view of what they believed in because their vision was translated into a simple tangible idea and one that delivered a clear benefit to the voter'. Even into the 2000s, Mattinson's focus groups would still reference the policy and the success of Thatcher's popular capitalism can scarcely be overestimated. Together with her taking on the trade unions, council house sales regularly poll as Thatcher's most positive legacy – not only to the over 1 million tenants who bought such a property at an average discount of 44 per cent of the true market value. Under Thatcher the electorate had moved away from collective concerns – what were the consequences of reducing the social housing stock for the remaining tenants – and into those of the individual – why shouldn't the decent, law-abiding tenant be able to join the property ladder? As one focus group told Philip Gould, 'if by voting Tory I'll get a flat or a job then I'll do it ... I'm not going to vote Labour to get a job for someone in Newcastle'.[14]

Progressives were unable to adjust to this reality. Despite the fact that one in four social tenants had backed Thatcher in 1983 and almost half of trade union households had voted for Reagan in 1980, the European left continued to unsuccessfully press the idea that there was a global neoconservative conspiracy against the working man and woman.[15] As Tony Benn put it in a February 1982 speech in Dublin, 'President Reagan is slashing welfare payments and boosting arms expenditure at a time when unemployment is rising in America'. Meanwhile, 'Mrs Thatcher is following the same course and attacking the historic rights of the Trade Union and Labour Movement in Britain'.[16] Though there was much to question about the pace of change, there were two flaws in Benn's argument.

First, Republicans were usually more adroit than Benn – and very often presented their arms spending in the Keynesian language of the left. As Casper Weinberger, Reagan's Defense Secretary remarked a few months after Benn's speech, 'these are new jobs that we are talking about ... Generally, unemployment declines and the economy grows a little faster as a result of the additional spending that we propose on defense'. The actual effects were more ambiguous and, depending on where one lived, could even be negative, but the public presentation of Reaganomics was never as unwaveringly monetarist as the left claimed, nor as its architect himself asserted. One politician who 'got' this was the British Liberal leader David Steel. In a July 1984 speech in San Francisco, Steel claimed that 'while our Prime Minister has opted for sky-high unemployment, your president has blundered into a warped Keynesianism'. Although Steel argued that such investment was not the most efficient way to create jobs, he still conceded, unlike Benn, that 'American unemployment has fallen simply as a result of a classic programme of counter-cyclical spending'. Much was funded by staggering increases to the US deficit but, to fix the problem, after all, one at least had to correctly diagnose it.[17]

Secondly, what Benn could not acknowledge was that Margaret Thatcher had an electoral mandate for her attack on the unions. Indeed, the 1979 Conservative manifesto had given her broad scope to deal with the trade union question and, after the turmoil of the 1970s, the electorate had voted her into office to act on it. Seven months into her Premiership the Prime Minister was being briefed of Gallup polling which said that although a majority (59%) of union members thought her new administration 'hostile' towards trade unions, the government's proposals that no strike should be called before a postal ballot of members was issued (83%), its belief that 'closed shop' practices should be limited to occasions only when a majority of workers voted for it (78%) and the idea that secondary picketing should be banned (72%), were all strongly supported. This formed the basis for her Employment Acts of 1980 and 1982. Even Jimmy Carter would tell the outgoing British Ambassador to Washington, Peter Jay, that there was a need for 'some government, fiscal and trade union reform along the lines H[er] M[ajesty's] G[overnment] is proposing'.[18]

As Thatcher took action to solve 'the British disease', American politicians from moderate Democrats to Reaganite Republicans were increasingly acknowledging that they would have to deal with the union question, too. As such, in August 1981 the newspaper of choice for British liberals, the *Guardian*, soon lent its front page to the story of 'Reagan's deadline to air [traffic] controllers'. This was the standoff between the administration and the 15,000 members of the PATCO union who had gone on strike to achieve higher wages. Since federal employees were forbidden to strike, this action was illegal and Reagan came down hard. Within days, fines of $6 million had been imposed on the union, five of its officials had been imprisoned and 13,000 air traffic controllers had been fired. Days later, the *Guardian* acknowledged that Reagan had taken a 'calculated decision to throw the book at PATCO because it is a small, impoverished union whose well-heeled members have precious little support' and that he wanted to 'damp down a potentially inflationary wage round before it gets under way'.[19] The right had seen the unpopularity of the unions in the 1970s and had moved against them early in the 1980s. Interestingly, for all the talk that the Third Way was anti-union, Reagan's lifetime ban on the federal government re-hiring the fired PATCO workers would only be repealed after the election of Bill Clinton.

Sensing the anger on the left, Thatcher soon baited her opponents by inviting Reagan for a state visit. The very idea that Reagan should be accorded such an honour provoked a two-fold reaction from Michael Foot. First, on 8 March 1982, he paid a visit to see Margaret Thatcher and her Foreign Secretary Peter Carrington. As Thatcher told Foot in a letter the following day, 'it is very natural to think of offering President Reagan, as the leader of one of this country's closest allies and friends, the opportunity of making a major speech before members of both our Houses of Parliament'. As the invitation was to be made on behalf of the

FIGURE 3 Despite their differences, Bill Clinton acknowledged Ronald Reagan's skill in portraying the Democrats as 'the party of government'. Here, Bill and Hillary meet the then President, February 1983 (Courtesy: Ronald Reagan Library).

Houses of Parliament rather than the government itself, there was a matter of protocol as to whether Foot should have been consulted first. But Foot used this procedural matter to make a political point against the American administration. Writing back to Thatcher, he claimed that 'an address in Westminster Hall ... is a special parliamentary occasion and should be offered to foreign statesmen only with the agreement of the major parties ... Had we been consulted in advance ... we would have been able to give the reasons why we believe such an arrangements [sic] would not be appropriate'. Perhaps the issue was indeed that Reagan was 'so newly in office' as Foot claimed in another draft of the letter, but Labour's public posturing suggested this was hardly the primary consideration.[20]

On 9 March 1982, the International Committee of the Labour Party passed a motion decrying the idea that 'the proposed honour of addressing both Houses of Parliament would go to a man who has worsened East–West relations and therefore the prospects for preventing a nuclear war and nuclear arms reductions and who has also backed brutal right-wing dictatorships in Central America'. They urged 'cancellation of the visit'. This did not occur, so the Labour Party decided to take matters further.

On 8 June 1982, Labour's General Secretary Ron Hayward issued an open letter to Reagan which was hardly evident of the 'long established ties of friendship and admiration for the American people' he claimed. According to Hayward, 'Labour's approach to East–West relations means that we utterly reject an ideological crusade against the Soviet Union and its identification as the sole or even primary source of conflicts in the world'. Militarily, Hayward 'emphasise[d] our view that NATO's activities should be confined to the European continent and the Atlantic only north of the tropic of Cancer' and noted that 'Britain currently makes a disproportionate contribution to the defence effort of NATO, which a Labour Government would seek to reduce'.[21] Welcome to Britain, Mr President. In the end, however, Thatcher would accord Reagan three state visits – one for each of her election victories. The left protested, she governed.

Anti-semitism, anti-Americanism

Dislike for America on the left was often bound up with its unwavering support for the state of Israel. For the British hard left, through the 1980s and beyond, the line between sympathy for the plight of the Palestinians and justifiable criticism of the Israeli state could blur into a thinly veiled and conspiratorial anti-Semitism. The actor turned Labour MP Andrew Faulds, who would vote against the moderate Neil Kinnock in the leadership election of 1983, was emblematic of this all-too-regular tendency. Having been sacked by Harold Wilson in 1973 as front-bench spokesman for the arts after accusing 'Zionists in the Labour Party' of having double loyalties, Faulds continued such rhetoric into the 1980s. Within his papers are letters from like-minded individuals detailing the so-called 'Extremists "Waiting in the Wings"' – Israeli policy advisors Ronald Reagan had taken on after becoming the Republican nominee in 1980 and who would presumably be pulling strings to ensure there was no 'balanced approach' to Middle Eastern affairs. By way of comparison, Margaret Thatcher was being briefed about then-candidate Reagan's 'pro-Israeli statements', but also the fact that 'his three closest friends are in businesses solidly locked into the Arab world'. But speaking to the Arab–American University Graduates Convention in 1980, Faulds made his own views clear. Denouncing the 'Zionist sympathisers [who] have resorted to the old chestnut about the strategic military importance of Israel to the United States', he criticised Jimmy Carter as a turncoat on the issue. 'It looked for a time as though President Carter was the one who would change this general pattern of hypocrisy . . . but it is all too obvious now when he declared in his inaugural address that "we can never be indifferent to the fate of freedom elsewhere", he would make an exception when "elsewhere" was Palestine and when we're after the Jewish vote.'[22]

Faulds was not the only left-wing figure to espouse such views, however. Ken Livingstone was a major figure in London politics from taking over as leader of the Greater London Council (GLC) in 1981 to serving as the Mayor of London between 2000 and 2008. But part of his political appeal rested on combining identity politics with some controversial public comments. In August 1983, Peter Shore was running for the Labour leadership after the resignation of Foot and glad of the rest the Bank Holiday weekend seemed to offer. He noted in his diary that 'the only event that moved me, during that period, was an outrageous speech by Ken Livingstone, or rather a radio interview, in which he compared British rule in Ireland with that of the Nazi genocide of the Jews'. Shore issued a 'strong, rebuking statement', but even having to comment on such matters dragged the collective party reputation into the ground. Just over a year later, Livingstone would rant about the British Board of Deputies of British Jews having 'been taken over by Jews who hold extreme right-wing views . . . After [Israel Prime Minister] Begin's emergence on to the political stage, suddenly the Jews became reactionaries, turned right to be nearly fascists'. For Livingstone this trend was 'happening in many countries, not just Britain'.[23]

Later, after the GLC was abolished by Thatcher in 1986, its former leader was interviewed by William F. Buckley. The Jews only came up obliquely in this discussion, but there were other hobby-horses to be outlined. At the beginning of *Firing Line*, Buckley introduced Livingstone as 'one of the most influential and also one of the most colourful members of the British left ... a lively spokesman for far-out British socialism'. Buckley began by probing Livingstone on whether his brand of socialism would stick to the democratic path and not attempt a communistic seizure of power. Livingstone, to his credit, started by noting that his 'concept of socialism is inseparable from democracy'. But his answers soon grew more dramatic. First, he claimed that 'I also have not the slightest doubt that if you had some sort of attempted left-wing coup in Britain, America would just immediately step in and slaughter us all'. For Livingstone, 'I don't think we could necessarily expect any better out of America than, say, Salvador Allende received in Chile'. As with the leftist view of 1931 and 1976, 'we could be just pushed aside either by economic destabilization by America, or by assassination'.[24]

After briefly holding court on his regular topic of Nazi Germany ('most of the British establishment was actually sympathetic towards Hitler'), Ken turned to events in Central America. When Buckley asked whether 'it is possible to have a fair election [in Nicaragua] where you don't have a robust press', Livingstone reeled off the greatest hits of leftist grievance. The British press had been 'bought up by people who basically follow American interests. We get millionaire pornographers coming out here from Australia, like [Rupert] Murdoch, they buy out papers, pump out anti-left-wing propaganda, squash anything that might suggest that there might be something wrong with our relationship with America'. When Tony Blair later flew to Australia to meet the same figure Livingstone had previously criticised, three years after Murdoch's newspaper *The Sun* had bombastically claimed to have swung the 1992 election to the Tories, he would take a slightly different tack.

Livingstone saw himself as a new 'Harvey Milk who put together that coalition of minorities and so on and took very much the same sort of positions that my GLC did'. As such, he believed that 'my socialism is a very much more democratic participatory one. It's one that I should imagine those people who fought for lesbian and gay rights and black rights in America would have quite an understanding of'. Here, at least, unlike his tinpot historical analysis, he had an actual record. It was politically brave for Livingstone's GLC to promote gay rights in the face of a hostile press and sceptical public. Indeed, there is an emerging academic consensus – forwarded most recently by Jonathan Davis and Rohan McWilliam – that whilst Labour most certainly lost the economic argument in 1980s, it managed to win the social argument for better treatment of women, ethnic minorities and homosexuals.[25] Livingstone was part of that. But to actually legislate on such matters it had to win power. As Blair and other moderates warned, the route towards this did not lie in obsessing about Chile or the Jews.

Against defending our own country

Views on Reagan and Israel were, if anything, just the tip of the iceberg. On matters of defence, it was not entirely clear what the left was for and this led to the perception that they were soft on foreign policy. In August

1981, Jack Straw, foreign and home secretary under Blair but at the time friendly with the Foot leadership, wrote an internal document detailing Labour's recent poor performance at a by-election in Warrington (where Roy Jenkins had almost captured the seat for the newly formed Social Democratic Party – a moderate force we consider more fully in the next chapter). In the provocatively titled paper 'The SDP – The Wolves at the Door', Straw dutifully recorded that 'opinion polls would suggest that a substantial proportion of the public are deeply apprehensive about the warmongering position of Reagan and Thatcher and have sympathy for Labour's strong desire (shared by all wings of the party) for disarmament'. But there was a catch. He also noted that 'we are also vulnerable to political attack, not least because of the confusion about our policy (both unilateralist and a pro-NATO multilateralist motion was passed at the last conference) and the fact that it is made up of negatives'. As Straw noted, carping from the wilderness was one thing, but 'we have not spelt out what kind of defence policy we are *for*'.[26]

Straw was right. In 1981, a party conference resolution to withdraw Britain from NATO was moved by local Manchester activist Eddie Newman. In his speech supporting the motion, Newman stated that 'it is really the interests of the United States Government and of international capitalism which determine NATO policies' and asked 'how can we obtain a Labour Government, moving forward with socialist policies, whilst in a pro-capitalist international alliance like NATO?' This motion was roundly defeated, but a year later conference would declare a clear majority (4,927,000 to 1,975,000) in favour of closing down all 'nuclear bases, British or American on British soil or in British waters'.[27] Further, in 1983, the Labour manifesto would state that 'the ultimate objective of a satisfactory relationship in Europe is the mutual and concurrent phasing out of both NATO and the Warsaw Pact' and the Bennites would continue to push the agenda through the decade.

The sense of equivalence between the Soviet Union and America was striking and a Labour-led Britain apparently wanted a piece of neither. During the 1983 election campaign Shadow Chancellor Peter Shore switched on *Question Time* where Tony Benn was making an appearance alongside Thatcher's Chancellor Geoffrey Howe and the Liberal MP David Penhaligan. Shore was a relatively balanced figure within the party and had even spoken up for Benn in the cabinet debate over the 1976 IMF loan. But, watching the BBC panel discussion, he noted that 'Benn cleared up all doubts about what the Party's policy [on nuclear weapons] was by stating the unconditional unilateralist case: every weapon, every American base, would be removed from Britain within the lifetime of the next parliament. Conference had decided. And the old policies had been swept away'. Two weeks away from polling day, Howe and Penhaligan 'didn't really enter into debate with him, they were content for him to make his point'. Shore mournfully recorded that 'this is an election loser, if ever there was one' and promptly went to bed.[28]

After the defeat and the subsequent election of Neil Kinnock as Labour leader, Shadow Foreign Secretary Denis Healey gave a speech at Labour Party conference in which he spelt out the problems all this had created. Outlining his desire for a nuclear freeze, a halfway house between disarmament and increasing the numbers of weapons, Healey noted that 'I cannot help feeling that one reason [Labour did not win the election] is that we added to these policies ... longer-term commitments on which the party was divided, some of which were profoundly unpopular with our own working class supporters'. Healey continued, 'worse still, some of these proposals were too easily represented as indicating that the Labour Party is against NATO ... and that we were against defending our own country'. Healey sat down to polite applause, evidence perhaps of nudging the debate along a little. However, with almost comic timing, the chair of the meeting then called Bill Edgar of Dundee East CLP to speak. Edgar thundered that 'this conference *condemns* the Tories compliance with the NATO plan to site in Britain 160 American-owned and controlled Cruise missiles and their enthusiasm to squander Britain's scarce financial resources on the first-strike Trident nuclear missile system'. And, 'further, it rejects Britain's membership of *any Pentagon dominated military pact* based on the first use of nuclear weapons'. Edgar's motion was carried by conference. Labour remained complaining, but not governing.[29]

In the wake of their own catastrophic defeat in 1984, the Democrats would soon wrestle with the same dilemmas. In April 1985, Wisconsin's Les Aspin delivered a speech to fellow Congressional Democrats entitled 'A Democratic Defence Policy: Defence without nonsense'. His verdict on the recent history of the left was damning. 'Throughout those 15 years, Democrats have been cast consistently in the role of chief "anti." Anti-ABM. Anti-B-1. Anti-neutron bomb. Anti-MX. Anti-SDI. And, thus, in the public mind: anti-defence'. On spending at least there was scarcely a huge divide: the Republican-dominated Senate had voted for 95 per cent of Reagan's defence requests and the Democratic-controlled House for 91 per cent. In short, 'this is a problem of perceptions', noted Aspin, 'but ... perceptions this stark can be devastating'. Aspin's point was not that 'we should start mindlessly supporting whatever gold-plated gizmo the inventive brain of defence industry can come up with'. Yet, equally, 'if Democrats ... want to make defense policy in the White House and the Pentagon, then we had better stand *for* something'.[30]

Aspin proposed three solutions: first to 'not simply oppose a weapon [but also to] stand for an alternative'. This would shift the debate to one of effectiveness rather than a black and white battle they had generally been losing. The second was to 'support additions to the defense budget'. In other words, to act in a deliberately counter intuitive manner even if it still meant undershooting – perhaps literally – the proposals of the Reagan White House. And, lastly, 'to accentuate the positive: speaking loudly and often of things we stand for'. This included doing 'more to identify with our people in uniform'. Aspin argued that 'many brilliant young men and women are donning the uniforms of our services. We ought to be encouraging the best to join – including the best of young Democrats'. To align, in other words, with the forces of patriotism. A few months after Aspin's speech, a new House Democratic Defence Task Force was forged which sought the participation of New Democrats Dave McCurdy, Barbara Kennelly and Dick Gephardt. The latter's run for the Presidency is addressed in the next chapter.

During the 1980s the right was talking tough on defence whilst continuing to follow the terms of the Strategic Arms Limitation Treaty (SALT II) negotiated under Ford and Carter. Meanwhile, Reagan's Strategic Defence Initiative (SDI), popularly known as 'Star Wars', captured the imagination but was years away from even potential implementation by the time the President left office. Indeed, in his second term, the Reykjavik talks of October 1986 would pave the way for the Intermediate Range Nuclear Forces Treaty, which eliminated all nuclear missiles up to a distance of 5,500km (save sea-launched missiles like Trident). This could all have presented an historic opportunity for the left. But, as moderate Labour MP Giles Radice put it, 'you might suppose that the thaw in international relations as a consequence of Gorbachev's arrival in power and the new hope for disarmament following the Reykjavik summit ... might make Labour's unilateralist policies seem more attractive'. Instead, 'the change in the world scene has the effect of making Labour's unilateralism seem self-indulgent and irrelevant'.[31]

This was given wider symbolism when, in March 1987, Neil Kinnock visited Washington to meet with Reagan. Although Kinnock had been allotted half an hour, Reagan would cut the meeting short and his press secretary Marlin Fitzwater briefed journalists that the President had told his visitor that Labour's defence policy would threaten NATO. As Philip Gould later noted, 'this contrasted badly with a successful trip made by Thatcher to Moscow at the end of March, when she was mobbed by crowds'.[32] Thatcher was talking tough and making friends. Kinnock, despite his best efforts, looked incapable of leading a divided Labour Party to do either. For much of the 1980s, the left remained obsessed with the politics of the gesture. Conference motions, marches and letters to newspapers which made the left feel virtuous, stood in lieu of serious engagement with the world as it was.

Siege economy and ideological purity

Isolation on foreign policy was to be allied to a generally pessimistic vision for Britain's economic future. As we will note, there was a real desire for change from workers on both sides of the Atlantic. But the case for economic isolationism rested on the view that British industry could no longer compete and that only the gifted man or woman in Whitehall could arrest the decline through erecting tariffs to foreign goods. Whilst a case for a siege economy at least could have been theoretically made in the early 1930s, when Britain still possessed an empire (the combined GDP of the UK, Australia, Canada, India and New Zealand then making up about three-quarters the contemporary American level), by the 1970s or 1980s it was a ludicrous position. To take the year of Britain's loan from the IMF as indicative, by 1976 the UK's GDP constituted just 18 per cent of the level of its American equivalent. The fall in Britain's global influence over the twentieth century was obvious.

In the face of industrial decline, Thatcherism offered two solutions: tax cuts across the board and an openness to international free trade (including signing the Single European Act – creating a truly Common Market across the European Economic Community). From the opposite perspective, the Bennites within Labour continued to press the case for the so-called Alternative Economic Strategy (AES) first floated in 1976. As *Marxism Today* proudly noted in January 1981, 'this strategy is not simply a creation of the Labour left and both the trade unions and the Communist Party have played a major role in its development and dissemination'. Unlike previous calls to global solidarity, however, 'its primary frame of reference is the nation and many of its measures involve a unilateral attempt to weaken our links with the rest of the capitalist world, with the aim of strengthening Britain's power to make independent decisions'.

The AES sought to reflate the economy by massively increasing government spending, introducing import controls to protect industries on the verge of collapse and, simultaneously, initiate price controls to stop firms exploiting the lack of foreign goods entering the market. The nationalisation of key industries was only a precursor 'to provid[ing] the public sector with the skill and knowledge required to control the private sector' and '*public ownership* of the major financial institutions [should] give the state control over the investment policies of pension funds and other sources of industrial finance'. Withdrawing from the European Common Market would make all the above possible for, as Benn had put it, 'protectionism is a perfectly respectable course of action. It is compatible with our strategy. You withdraw behind walls and reconstruct and re-emerge'. On a tactical level, *Marxism Today* argued, 'using the AES as a programme, the Left can present itself as a realistic alternative to both Thatcherism and the ineffectual moralising of the "moderates"'.[33]

In 1983, to all intents and purposes, this *was* Labour's offer to the British electorate. A year earlier, after he had been soundly defeated in a longshot by-election in Beaconsfield, Tony Blair had told Labour's National Executive Committee that the AES had not engaged with 'people's everyday lives' and made the party seem irrelevant 'to the problems they faced'. Such warnings were, of course, to no avail. Egged on by the trade unions, AES advocates in the press and Benn and his supporters, the public were given the real choice under Foot they had supposedly been denied in 1979. After the catastrophic 1983 election, Neil Kinnock noted, 'Tony Benn took comfort from the fact that "over 8 million people voted for the most Socialist Manifesto ever put by the Labour Party" and subsequently argued that Labour lost because we were not "sufficiently radical"'. Losing by 4.5 million votes to a government presiding over 3 million unemployed, the worst level seen since the 1930s, was hardly something to crow about, however. Indeed, just prior to the defeat, only 5 per cent of voters (36% to 31%) thought Labour were better placed to deal with the unemployment question than the Tories. This was an issue they should have been nailing. Given they were miles behind on defence (63% to 19%), law and order (54% to 20%)and inflation (50% to 25%), Labour's core voter strategy was hardly likely to yield much electoral gain. Even Foot's Shadow Chancellor, Peter Shore, sadly recorded in his diary during the campaign that 'Michael on the economy, I really regret to say, is so unconvincing, so uninformed and he looked so vulnerable and tired'. The voters agreed.[34]

The movement or the voters

Nuclear policy and left-wing economics were symptomatic of a British left that, through the 1980s, became inwardly more democratic but outwardly more irrelevant. With the notable exception of Thatcher's victory in 1979, turnout at British elections had been in consistent decline since the 1950s. The view amongst the moderates was, generally, it was best to try and win with the electorate that bothered to vote, but this was not a universal position. For many on the hard left, the way to counter 'disillusion in democratic politics' was to 'take away the drafting of the manifesto from the small group of politicians at the top of the party and make sure the whole of that party has it: the trade unions, the constituents, the activists'. One embodiment of this principle was the Campaign for Labour Party Democracy (CLPD), founded in 1973. With ten founding MPs and based out of the Golders Green house of its leading organiser Vladimir Derer, the CLPD campaigned for the re-selection of MPs (achieved by 1980), the election of Labour leader by an electoral college system rather than just parliamentarians (delivered in 1981) and greater power for the party conference to determine policy (after Harold Wilson had refused to nationalise 25 large manufacturing companies after a 1973 conference vote). Moreover, the CLPD was broadly aligned with the Bennite Campaign Group, formed in December 1982 and shared many of the same members. Through such tight associations long-term links would be formed. As Blairite MP Tom Harris later scoffed, 'it is not quite true to suggest that, because [Jeremy] Corbyn is reported to have voted against the Blair and Brown governments on more than 500 occasions, he was unable to respect a party whip; in fact he was an enthusiastic supporter of collective action, provided the collective in action was the Campaign Group'.[35]

Just as the moderates would come to look to their American partners, so too could the more radical leftists in the CLPD and Campaign Group spin their own version of the recent history of the United States. One area such groups were convinced by was the need for forms of positive discrimination. As the CLPD AGM of 1979 noted, the 'experience in

America … shows that it can be done on a far greater scale than we are advocating'. In this light, the rainbow alliance of Robert Kennedy in 1968 and the anti-Vietnam rhetoric of George McGovern in 1972, were the way to go. Together with quotas at home, the hard left's agenda promised anti-Reaganism abroad. As Jeremy Corbyn told his Campaign colleagues when agreeing to chair an event in the House of Commons in July 1986, 'the discussion will begin with an introduction from Tony Benn around the points of removing all U.S. bases from Britain, British withdrawal from NATO and the EEC and the role of a non-aligned policy in the context of liberation struggles around the world'.[36]

Like the moderates, the hard left recognised that if it could not control the levers of power, its ideology would come to nothing. As such, a key issue was naturally the election of the Labour Party leader. Prior to the reforms introduced in 1981, Labour's leader had been chosen by a secret ballot of its MPs (as would be the case with the Conservative Party until the election of David Cameron in 2005). This had some justification. After all, one of the major jobs such a figure would have would be to lead the parliamentary party. Yet groups not limited to the hard left began to argue that the wider Labour membership should have a say in the man or woman they were, de facto, selecting as their candidate for prime minister.

Given Labour's broad church of individual subscribers, trade union members, MPs and other supporters, deciding who should be represented in any new franchise was not easy, however. The eventual reforms involved a heavy degree of indirect democracy and created the electoral college system that would last until the election of Jeremy Corbyn in 2015. Under this new system MPs retained 30 per cent of the vote over their new leader, but 30 per cent was now handed to around 600 Constituency Labour Parties and the remaining 40 per cent was given to the so-called 'Affiliated Societies' dominated by the trade unions. Until the 1990s, the latter two such groups were 'block voting' categories – i.e. the General Secretaries of each trade union and each Constituency Labour Party cast their vote on behalf of *all* their individual members.[37] This meant that, by way of example, the 2 million or so members of the Transport and General Workers Union had their voice represented by just one man. Kinnock had tried to move to 'one member, one vote' in 1984, but the party would only get there under John Smith almost a decade later.

The reformed leadership selection process produced two problems which placed Labour in general in something of a death cycle and the moderates on the edge of influence. First, the reforms broadly empowered the left. There was little to be gained, for their own internal purposes, for trade union leaders to be moderate and, since they now held huge sway over who became Labour leader, this naturally shifted the debate away from the centre. Even if, like Kinnock, leaders tried to tack to the middle once in office, the legacy of these campaigns could be brutal and emboldened extremist forces within the party who could claim some nominal 'treachery' at any form of later accommodation with either the government or the wider electorate. Labour's failure to empower the actual trade union *members*, rather than just the bosses, was a dream for a Conservative Party trying to play up precisely that dividing line.

This, of course, spoke to wider questions about the role of trade unions and their effect on the political process. As Tony Blair later wrote, 'when she took on the trade unions [in the 1980s], Margaret Thatcher didn't come out of a sealed chamber with a new idea. It already existed'. Pointing to the Barbara Castle's famous pamphlet *In Place of Strife* – which failed to make it past a reticent Cabinet in 1968, but which included new proposals for mandatory union balloting before industrial action and a 'cooling-off' period before any strike action could begin – Blair praised the left-wing former Secretary of State for Employment and Productivity. He also backed Ted Heath's 1971 Industrial Relations Act, which established a National Industrial Relations Court with the power to issue injunctions to stop strike action in cases of national interest, but which was repealed under the 1974 Labour government. For Blair, Castle and Heath were 'attempt[ing] to bring union power within the purview of the law'. After such efforts had failed, 'it was clear that an evolutionary attack on trade union privileges had failed and only a revolutionary one would succeed'. As such, only Thatcher 'had the character, leadership and intelligence to make it happen'.[38] The fact that trade union leaders now held significant influence over Labour's leadership elections was a mixed blessing, to put it mildly.

It was in this wider atmosphere that supporters of Militant, the Trotskyist entry group, gained control of Liverpool City Council and began to set illegal, deficit-producing budgets which Kinnock rightly condemned. Even with such official disapproval, however, Liverpool became indicative for what many voters thought progressives were all about – and even moderates could be tarred with the same brush. After all, if Labour could not see its aggressive leftists off on Merseyside (members who even Michael Foot regarded as a 'pestilential nuisance'), how on earth was it supposed to rule in Whitehall? Even when a loan was eventually brokered for the council under considerable pressure from Neil Kinnock, this only led to accusations from the hard left that Labour's leader was doing the 'dirty work' of the Tories. Squaring internal party democracy with the wider, largely apolitical, British public was not easy.[39]

The second problem, again, was the unpopularity and increasing irrelevance of the trade unions. Arthur Scargill, the pugnacious union leader *The Sun* newspaper dubbed 'Mine Fuhrer', was an ideal foe for Britain's right wing. Calling a national strike having failed to secure the say-so of his members for such action on three separate occasions, the eventual defeat in the 1984–1985 miners' strike – under an atmosphere where Thatcher claimed her opponents were 'holding the nation to ransom' – was a further nail in the coffin. Thanks to such intransigence, residual sympathy towards the miners and the trade union movement per se, evaporated. During the strike, two-thirds of voters told pollsters that 'most trade unions are controlled by extremists and militants' and a similar number proclaimed that Labour 'should not be so closely linked to the trade unions'. The latter view has more or less held, with 77 per cent of voters saying similar in January 2017.[40] Moderate Labour figures like Kinnock had sought to condemn Scargill's 'suicidal vanity', but to no avail.

In this regard there were factors at play beyond the high-profile individuals, however. As Robert Reich wrote of the largest US trade union in the early 1990s, 'the AFL-CIO has been dying a quiet death and has been doing so for years. In the 1950s, about 35 per cent of American workers belonged to a union. Now membership is down to 11 per cent and every year the percentage drops a bit further'. As Reich argued, 'workers in big industries dominated by three or four major companies were easier to organize than workers in the small and medium size service businesses (retail, restaurant, hotel, hospital, office) which have been creating most of the jobs for twenty years'.[41] The trick for the left was to build a case for the jobs of tomorrow whilst being bankrolled by those representing the industries of yesteryear. This was not easy. The radicalism of the AES and the trade unions was, after all, often fundamentally conservative and about preserving their own powerbase.

On both sides of the Atlantic, therefore, seriously engaging with an increasingly globalised and mobile economy just wasn't on the agenda for the left. In the interim, as Stan Greenberg heard in Macomb, voters continued to complain that the left 'was turning its back to Joe Average in the street'. It was the political wing of a trade union movement that was 'limiting job opportunities, blocking entry by young people and making unreasonable wage demands that encourage companies to flee or close down'. And such views had, for now, moved blue collar voters in Britain and America into the arms of Thatcher and Reagan. As one Michigan resident told Greenberg: 'I believe in strength and that is what he is doing and I respect him for that. Some of his other politics I don't respect, some of his social policies. But we had to make a choice'. And so they did. The question remained: could the left alter its fundamental offer?

Notes

1   See Greenberg's report via ARC/HOV/TED/6.

2   Draper/172.

3   As was Warren, Macomb's biggest city, in the 1980 census.

4   Rund to Benson, 8 July 1984, ARC/HOV/WIRT/336/8.

5   Blair 1/44; Benn/4 November 1980.

6   PLP meetings, 22 and 29 June 1983.

7   Blair 2/147; Brown 1/65–68.

8   Gould/51.

9   Dionne/192.

10 *The Times*, 23 October 2018; Reagan address on 'Milton Friedman and Chile', undated, ARC/HOV/MFR/174/1.

11 Friedman to Reagan, 4 December 1984, in ARC/HOV/MFR/174/1; LR/HOC/26 April 1988, vol 132, col 229.

12 Nash essay, as above, via ARC/HOV/ABE/99; Gould/71.

13 Brown 2/99; Blair 1982 speech in Perth, Australia/20.

14 Mattinson/12; Gould/50.

15 IPSOS-Mori, 'Voting by Tenure'. Available at: www.ipsos.com/ipsos-mori/en-uk/voting-tenure-1983-2010 and https://ropercenter.cornell.edu/polls/us-elections/how-groups-voted/how-groups-voted-1980/.

16 'Cooperation between the Irish and British Labour Movements', 10 February 1982, ARC/PHM/MF/M13/1.

17 *New York Times*, 16 October 1983; 'New Trends in Anglo-American Relations', 18 July 1984, ARC/LSE/STEEL/B/1/7/12.

18 'Public Opinion After the First Seven Months of the New Government', 21 November 1979, ARC/CAC/THCR 2/6/2/38; Farewell Call on President Carter, 23 June 1979, ARC/CAC/PJAY/2/31.

19 *Guardian*, 12 August 1981.

20 Thatcher to Foot, 9 March 1982 and the reply, 11 March 1982, ARC/PHM/MF/L29/10.

21 Walworth Road News Release, 9 March 1982, ARC/PHM/MF/L29/10; Hayward to Reagan, 8 June 1982, ARC/PHM/MF/L23/38.

22 Reagan's Middle East Advisors: Extremists "Waiting in the Wings," ARC/LSE/FAULDS/3/6/1; Gordon Reece note, ARC/CAC/THCR 2/6/2/181, 8 July 1980; Speech to AAUG, ARC/LSE/FAULDS/3/6/1.

23 Diary, 29 August 1983, ARC/LSE/SHORE/1/23; LR/HOC/7 January 1985, vol 71, col 515.

24 16 September 1986, ARC/HOV/FLBR.

25 Davis and McWilliam/Introduction.

26 Blackburn Constituency Labour Party, August 1981, ARC/PHM/MF/M13/6.

27 Labour 1981/149 and 1982/279.

28 Britto report 30 May 1983, ARC/CAC/THCR/2/7/3/32; Diary, 26 May 1983, ARC/LSE/SHORE/1/22.

29 Labour 1983/148.

30 Aspin speech, 17 April 1985, ARC/LOC/HDC/65/10.

31 Radice 1/152, 11 January 1987.

32 Gould/71.

33 Benn/621; *Marxism Today*, January 1981.

34 Golding/254, Kinnock to Binns, 4 September 2001, ARC/CAC/KNNK 1/9/21; Britto report, 30 May 1983, ARC/CAC/THCR/2/7/3/32; Diary, 26 May 1983, ARC/LSE/SHORE/1/22.

35 16 September 1986, ARC/HOV/FLBR; Harris/142–43.

36 'One Case for Positive Discrimination', 1979 AGM, ARC/BGI/CLPD/42; Corbyn to the Campaign Group, 11 July 1986, ARC/BGI/CLPD/93.

37 CLPs would only rarely ballot their members and their leadership vote decision was, at best, only discussed at General Committee.

38 Blair 1/42.

39 Pye/157, 165.

40 IPSOS-Mori data. Available at: https://ems.ipsos-mori.com/researchpublications/researcharchive/94/Attitudes-to-Trade-Unions-19752011.aspx?view=wide.

41 *Guardian*, 12 March 2009; Reich 2/66.

3 HARBINGERS OF THE REVOLUTION

Let us step forward a moment – away from the turmoil and electoral irrelevance of the early 1980s and into an election that progressives were approaching a good deal more optimistically. By the summer of 1987, the 44-year-old Joe Biden seemed to have the world at his feet. The charismatic third-term Senator from Delaware had taken a significant lead in early fundraising ahead of the 1988 Democratic Primaries – with his $2 million campaign war-chest doubling the amount of the previous frontrunner, the former Colorado Senator Gary Hart. Much of this was gained through the upwardly mobile grassroots, with Biden's campaign manager claiming that 'so far our donors have been mostly very idealistic people in their thirties and forties who are now successful entrepreneurs'. For a brief moment, it seemed as if the moderate left might already have their candidate and his name wasn't Bill Clinton. As *The New York Times* gushed, 'when [Biden] connects with his audience . . . he can moisten eyes and set heads to nodding'. With the patronage of Ted Kennedy behind him, it seemed that he could do no wrong.[1]

Although a moderate, Biden was careful to play the usual progressive tunes as he geared up for the Iowa and New Hampshire caucuses. 'Why is it', he asked audiences, 'that Joe Biden is the first in his family ever to go to a university?' Jabbing his thumb in a fashion later perfected by Clinton, he continued: 'why is it that my wife . . . is the first in her family ever to go to college? Is it because our fathers and mothers were not bright?' Sensing the rising agreement in the room, he provided the answer: 'it's because they didn't have a platform on which to stand'. This went down very well on the stump. But, although delivered in Biden's Scranton drawl, there was a problem. It was *exactly* the speech Neil Kinnock had given to the Welsh Labour Party conference a few months earlier, just prior to the

1987 British General Election. Biden had copied Labour's leader verbatim and, although he had acknowledged this debt in other speeches, he had failed to acknowledge Kinnock's handiwork enough times that the press became suspicious. Previous allegations about plagiarism during college essays written 20 years earlier were soon tacked onto the Kinnock affair and Biden withdrew from the race in September 1987 admitting he had been 'cocky', 'immature' and 'naïve' about the rigours of running for the highest office on earth.[2]

Clearly, the Kinnock affair did not harm Biden in the long run. In fact, perhaps it even saved his life. Within months of leaving the race, Biden discovered he had two brain aneurisms which required immediate surgery. He would later tell Kinnock that 'if he had stayed on the campaign trail he would have kept on taking tablets to deal with his headaches, missed his symptoms and probably have died'. Fully recovered, he ruled out a presidential run in 1992 and returned to being a respected Senator on issues from foreign affairs to violence against women. When the *Washington Post* correspondent David Broder wrote in 1988 that 'as gifted as he is at 45, I think the Democrats will find him far better presidential material at 49 or 53 or 57 or 61', the journalist was only really one cycle out.[3] Biden would go on to serve as Vice President under Barack Obama, helping the Democratic ticket carry the crucial rust belt states of Michigan, Ohio and Pennsylvania in both the 2008 and 2012 elections. As such, the brief furore in 1987 has generally been understood as an embarrassing episode before an eventual political resurrection. But it also launched a further, arguably more important long-term trend – the friendship between Neil Kinnock and Joe Biden.

This association would always transcend politics, but it was emblematic of evolving politics on the centre-left. A few months after withdrawing from the presidential race, Biden visited the United Kingdom in January 1988. Although he also had a cordial meeting with Prime Minister Thatcher, he went out of his way to request time with Kinnock – and asked that no press be present. Kinnock later recalled that 'in good fun, Joe took the occasion on visiting me in the House of Commons to give me a small collection of his own speeches on foreign policy'. Biden had obviously meant this as a joke, but 'in fact [Kinnock] took the occasion to read several of them – on arms control, [the] Star Wars [missile system] and U.S. Soviet relations'. The Labour leader 'found them instructive and beautifully stated'. Kinnock would be looking to follow the kind of 'tough-minded internationalist foreign policy' Biden had long called for.[4]

During the trip to Europe Joe had taken along his son, Beau. The then Labour leader recalls that 'his son was in his late teens and very dismayed with his old man for standing down from the race'. Kinnock had a few words with Beau and said '*exactly* what had happened. Joe shouldn't be ashamed in any way and he shouldn't be ashamed of his father who as far as I'm concerned was a distinguished and admirable member of the US Senate who had overcome all kinds of appalling personal difficulties'. Beau Biden's own story would be deeply poignant – serving as a soldier in Iraq and then as Attorney General of Delaware, before tragically dying from the effects of brain cancer at just 46.

Back on that cold January morning in 1988, Kinnock and Biden senior discussed the anti-Americanism of Ken Livingstone, the Israeli-Palestinian question and the future unified German state. Perhaps with a mind to the first two of these, Kinnock told his visitor not to 'take notice of marginal zany propositions' he might see in the British papers. The issue here, as we have seen, was that throughout the 1980s it was difficult to tell what stood as 'marginal' on the Anglo-American left. All too often in terms of electability, the more extreme the idea, the more likely it had been to make it onto Labour's platform. The tide was gradually beginning to turn from the mid-1980s, however – and Kinnock and Biden's meeting now looks less like the gathering of two recent electoral losers and more like the celebration of a long road eventually to be conquered. If nothing else, it illustrates the convergence of centre-left moderates in London and Washington DC who were working up a set of proposals and a language to once again appeal to sceptical voters.[5] Such structures, associations and friendships were vital in understanding how the centre left in America and Britain re-orientated itself in the 1980s.

An alliance for change?

The first major break with the unelectable politics of Tony Benn and Michael Foot came not from within, but outside the Labour Party. As noted, two months after the 1980 annual Labour conference had pledged the party in favour of unilateral nuclear disarmament and to leave the European Economic Community without a referendum, Michael Foot had been elected as party leader. As Giles Radice later stated, 'at a time when the voters were shifting to the right, the Labour party seemed to be lurching irretrievably to the left'. Given the climate of the time, young moderates like Blair and Brown who were looking for a seat in parliament were impacted by this drift – forced, on occasion, to mouth the words of the left to 'get on' in 1980s Labour. Blair therefore dutifully included in his political CV of this period a commitment 'to support party policy as determined by party conference', a quote from Michael Foot declaring that 'Tony Glair [sic] will make a major contribution to British politics', and the work he had done as a trade union lawyer. His public utterances, whilst still calling for something 'more modern than Marxism' and for Labour supporters to meet more often with 'those whom they disagree', also poured scorn on those figures on the right of the party who were obsessed by gaining 'the praise of the leader writers of the *Financial Times*'. For moderate figures looking to make a name for themselves, what else could be done?[6]

But there were those in a greater position to act. Foot's isolationist policy shifts had not chimed well with several key figures and, at an indiscreet lunch, the Labour MP Neville Sandelson told a Tory counterpart that 'the prize for [Roy] Jenkins would be to detach Shirley Williams, David Owen and Bill Rodgers from the Labour Party and then to start a new party, which would have an electoral pact with the Liberals'.[7] The idea that four former Cabinet Ministers would leave Britain's foremost non-Conservative political party to form their own movement may have seemed like tea room gossip to some. Yet, on 25 January 1981, the day after a Special Conference of the Labour Party had handed over 40 per cent of the votes for the election of its future leaders to the trade unions, Sandelson's prediction was proved accurate. Named after the house owned by David Owen from which it was issued, the so-called 'Limehouse Declaration' launched what became known as the Social Democratic Party. Eventually, 28 Labour MPs and 1 Conservative defected to the new party and in July that year Roy Jenkins very nearly won the seat of Warrington in the North West (a Labour stronghold since 1945) in a by-election. In June 1981, as per Sandelson's discussion, the SDP formed an electoral pact with David Steel's Liberals – marking the beginning of what became known as the 'Alliance'. By the end of 1981 the Alliance was consistently leading national opinion polls – including an astonishing 50.5 per cent for Gallup on 14 December.

In many ways, the Alliance was a key ideological gateway for New Labour. For one, it allowed middle-class traditionally small 'l' liberal voters to grow comfortable with outwardly praising aspects of Thatcherism. Although the 1983 Alliance manifesto decried the 'record

FIGURE 4 Without the SDP there would have been no New Labour. One of their leading lights, Shirley Williams, is pictured here with Blair and Clinton, in December 2000. They are joined by her American academic husband, Richard Neustadt – former tutor to Ed Balls, Al Gore, and a host of Third Way figures (Courtesy: Clinton Presidential Library).

bankruptcies and liquidations' seen since 1979 and criticised the increase of unemployment 'twice the scale of the world recession', it also contended that some of the Prime Minister's 'objectives were good. Britain needed a shake-up: lower inflation, more competitive industry and a prospect of industrial growth to catch back the ground we had lost over the years'. In 1983, these were not words many within Labour were comfortable with saying aloud, but many middle- and some working-class voters had already moved on. As Tony Blair put it in 1982, the Alliance was gaining support because at least they 'offer some compromise between the over callousness of Mrs Thatcher and the old-fashioned collectivism of Labour'.[8] If anything they reduced, rather than increased, Thatcher's 1983 majority.

The Alliance provided a concrete home for several names who would come to shape the New Labour agenda. Andrew Adonis (head of Blair's Policy Unit, 2001–2005) was one such example and even future Conservative Ministers like Anna Soubry and Greg Clark dabbled with

SDP membership in the 1980s. The testimony of Roger Liddle, later Blair's Special Adviser on Europe, perhaps provides the best summary, however. Liddle had been one of the founding members of the SDP in 1981 and in retrospect praises the grouping as providing 'a very intellectually liberating experience and doing some interesting policy work'. In many ways the SDP formed a kind of re-heated Gaitskellism, a programme for a 'better yesterday' more than 'thinking about tomorrow'. As Liddle notes, 'the SDP's aim was to turn Britain into a kind of Sweden. Moderate trade unions negotiating reasonably with employers and each agreeing to share the proceeds of growth'. As such, 'barring latter day David Owenism, the SDP was not a neoliberal project at all. It didn't get to grips with that'. Though they accepted Thatcher's Right to Buy, in many ways its frames of reference and the way it conceptualised British politics, was entirely determined by traditional Labour norms. It would take, as Liddle argues, 'non-Labour types like Anthony Giddens' to really 'get globalization on the agenda'.[9]

In a period where Labour tended to view America suspiciously, the Alliance did at least inaugurate new channels for Transatlantic dialogue. One of the key figures in all of this was the Liberal leader David Steel. Travelling to the US in the summer of 1984 to observe the Democratic National Convention at the Moscone Center in San Francisco (an event also attended by Gordon Brown), Steel not only made but keenly observed several speeches. In later years, he recalled an excellent 'speech by Mario Cuomo and getting to know Walter Mondale and Geraldine Ferraro'. He also managed to see the speeches of Gary Hart (who had narrowly failed to win the nomination that year) and Jesse Jackson. Part of this was likely just to see the spectacle of US politics and its grandiose conventions which were and remain, above and beyond anything on offer in the more humdrum British affairs. Steel also dutifully asked for printed copies of speeches he had enjoyed and underlined key phrases, doubtless to be used at home. Jackson's 'the youth of this generation must exercise the right to dream' and Hart's contention that 'Mr Reagan, the American flag does not belong to you and the right-wing Republicans' seem to have impressed him. Next to a quote from Franklin Roosevelt – 'we will try something and if it works, we will keep it, [and] if it doesn't, let's try something else' – Steel pointedly noted it would be useful to 'confront Thatcher' with this. But the Liberal leader's interest went beyond mere linguistic pilfering.[10]

Steel and the Alliance were attempting, to some degree, to out pitch Thatcher from the *right*. Given that Anglo-American voters were often equating progressives with, as Stan Greenberg saw in Macomb, 'too many free programs' and 'too much "spend, spend, spend,"' there was much in such a strategy. Speaking to the Metropolitan Club on Sutter Street, Steel argued that 'American deficits have pushed up interest rates, making industrial investment even less attractive and raising the likelihood of third world debt'. The centre needed a conservative fiscal base if it was to earn the voters' trust. Equally, although his view on foreign policy was that a strong defensive alliance amongst western powers was a necessary precursor to a nuclear freeze, the point was the tough talk had to come first. Steel noted that 'those of us in Europe should take seriously the signs of [the] United States' restiveness about the state of the NATO Alliance'. There were 'some' in the UK who had 'taken for granted the protection that U.S. forces have brought to Europe, while jibbing at their own contribution or suggesting that neutrality is possible in the defence of democratic values'.[11] Essentially, here had stood Labour under Foot.

The danger was therefore clear and understood by many. In August 1981, Jack Straw penned his internal report which declared that, after the recent Warrington by-election, 'the SDP are now a very serious threat to the Labour Party'. Speaking to the local candidate, Doug Hoyle, Straw recorded that there were four issues plaguing the Labour vote: 'divisions within the Party, allegations of extremism, allegations that he [Hoyle] was an extremist and Tony Benn'. The latter was hardly news, with Neil Kinnock having been quoted in the *Guardian* saying Benn was a 'major electoral liability'. But Straw recalled that the doorstep critiques of Benn were not just parroting hostile elements in the press but could be 'surprisingly well informed'. On Europe, 'arguments about the Common Market were countered by the fact that [Benn] had once been in favour of entry'. On nationalisation, 'arguments about the need to control the economy were countered by claims that [Benn] had engineered many major mergers in the 60s'. Far from being a voice of authenticity and 'ordinary people', Benn was proving a deeply divisive figure.[12]

As Roger Liddle argues, 'post Bennism, after the turn of the Mitterrand government in France towards austerity and particularly after the miners' strike, people on the left gradually began to realise that their project wasn't going to work'. The SDP became increasingly 'conscious of the Reagan Democrats and the attraction of the skilled working class towards Reagan. To some degree we saw that amongst Thatcherism and the general scepticism towards the trade unions too'. And until Labour possessed a leader people could see as a potential prime minister, they would always bleed votes to the moderate centre. For one, when it came to Anglo-Soviet relations, in the words of Denis Healey, 'can you really see [Foot] negotiating with Andropov?' Too many voters agreed with that sentiment to ever see it come to pass.[13]

Eventually, the SDP would help frame future American politics in unexpected ways. Sixteen years after the Limehouse Declaration, the historian and urban policy wonk Fred Siegel was offered the chance to present his views ahead of Clinton's 1997 State of the Union. Surveying the global picture, he then pointed to an 'unprecedented period of centrist formations'. Though these movements took different forms – Siegel highlighted Ross Perot, the Concord Coalition around Paul Tsongas and 'the DLC/PPI Third Way' – generally 'most of the intellectual ferment is in the center'. More important in all this – even, after 1992, than Perot – 'is the British example'. There, Siegel argued, 'the Labour resurgence can, in large measure, be attributed to the way that Tony Blair has reintegrated the ideas and (even some of the individuals) involved in creating the now defunct British centrist breakaway, the Social Democrats'. The creation of a new intellectual hub both helped reshape the progressive agenda and provided a temporary home to those with residually progressive views who just couldn't vote for Michael Foot.[14]

As to why, despite its general sensibleness, the SDP–Liberal alliance didn't end up leading the *March of the Moderates*, we should leave the last word to Neil Kinnock. The history of Kinnock visiting the United States has essentially been condensed into the 'snub' delivered by Reagan in March 1987. But, in 1985, he had experienced a rather more enjoyable and certainly more intellectual affair. On that occasion he was hosted by John Brademas, the former Democrat whip in the House, who had been a friend since the Labour leader had visited the States in a parliamentary delegation in 1976. Brademas – a confirmed Anglophile since undertaking his doctoral thesis at Oxford in the 1950s – had taken over the Presidency of New York University and wanted to give his visiting friend something of a treat. As such, he arranged a dinner for Kinnock in the penthouse of NYU with the surviving members of the Kennedy cabinet and JK Galbraith, the noted economist. 'It was galactic!' Kinnock recalls. After supper, Kinnock and his Shadow Foreign Secretary, Denis Healey, made themselves available for questions from the assembled luminaries.

The first came from McGeorge Bundy, Kennedy's old National Security Advisor. 'We've known Shirley Williams, David Owen, Roy Jenkins and Bill Rodgers for many years through our Transatlantic contacts. We've always valued them as fellow progressives and democrats. Why did they do what they did and divide the Labour Party?' 'Well', Kinnock began, but he was stopped by Healey. 'Actually, could I take this one, Neil? Certainly, so far as Dr David Owen is concerned – when the young David was a small baby, lying in his cot, he was visited by the "good" fairy. This good fairy fluttered around the young David and told him, "you will be blessed, you will be tall, you will be handsome, you be successful and you will become rich – a leader of men." The good fairy then fluttered off. However, no sooner had the good fairy left, then the bad fairy came in. The "bad" fairy then fluttered around the baby and said, '. . . and you will also be a shit!'[15] The roof came off the place. If for no other reason than personality, the *March of the Moderates* in Britain would need another leader. And Labour, for all its faults in the 1980s, still possessed the structures and financial backing, more likely to get the electoral job done.

Transatlanticism

Just as Labour was splitting at the seams in early 1981, Dick Gephardt landed at London's Heathrow Airport. As part of a bipartisan Congressional delegation of eleven, Gephardt had spent the flight from DC chatting with Les Aspin, Clinton's later Defence Secretary, Jim Jones, future Ambassador to Mexico and Bill Hefner, the long-term North Carolina congressman. For just a five-day trip, the February 1981 schedule was gruelling. On the Monday, their dozens of meetings included Alan Walters, Thatcher's Chief Economic Advisor and John Biffen, Minister for Trade. For Tuesday, there were non-political types like the head of the TUC and Peter Jay, the former Ambassador to Washington. In light of the recent splits on the left, however, it was the group's meeting with Peter Shore, the Shadow Chancellor, that saw the most stimulating recent gossip, as all Congressmen – or certainly the seven Democrats on the trip – mulled over the future for the British left.

After further stops in Brussels and Rome, on the plane journey home Dick Gephardt began scribbling down his thoughts. All in all, he judged, 'a study of the recent economic experience in the United Kingdom is both relevant and useful for US policymakers'. As Gephardt noted, 'both have recently experienced high inflation and deep recession at the same time', whilst they formed 'highly industrialized western democracies with an established skilled workforce'. There were differences – 'the UK is more dependent upon foreign trade' and 'more highly unionized' – but also much to learn. For Gephardt, Thatcher had made a mistake in raising VAT [in her first budget], 'she did not make a perceptible reduction in government spending even considering that the economy is in a severe recession' and had 'tried to move on too many conflicting goals at one time, thereby complicating her ability to reach any goal'. The big mistake was to do 'her tax cuts before her spending cuts'. Whilst Thatcher could 'unquestionably . . . take credit for a remarkable reduction in inflation' the verdict in early 1981 'cannot be yet stated'. It would all ride, Gephardt thought, 'on how successfully she has changed public expectations and attitudes about wage and price increases'.

For Gephardt, the three key lessons were that any US government should first seek to 'cut spending quickly and before you cut taxes'. Secondly, 'in cutting government spending, cut capital spending last as it is the most important part . . . for economic recovery'. Thirdly, the big question for any future administration of the centre would be how to cut the economic 'deadwood' whilst not losing 'a lot of your industrial base': 'if the scattershot of a shotgun is undesirable what rifle can you use to eliminate practices or industries that are becoming outdated without harming those that are not'. These would be precisely the questions Bill Clinton's *Putting People First* agenda of 1992 would seek to grapple with.[16]

In a sense, Gephardt had visited too early. As the Joe Biden episode would later illustrate, the election of Neil Kinnock as Labour leader gave such transatlantic connections a real shot in the arm. Kinnock's role in this story can scarcely be overstated and he would eventually meet Gephardt when, it seemed, the British left was on the verge of power. He modernised the Labour Party, served as mentor to Tony Blair and Gordon Brown (promoting them to the Shadow Cabinet in his second term as leader) and encouraged both to visit Australia and the US to see how a new centre-left was being crafted overseas. But Kinnock had his own direct interests too.

Within six months of his elevation to Labour's top job in late 1983 (his old left-wing credentials helping him with the unions), Kinnock had undertaken a high-profile visit to New York and Washington DC. As his policy aide Charles Clarke recorded soon after, 'it is important to have a clear agreement on the "hidden agenda" of [US] visit[s] – in other words, the need to increase the Leader's standing as a world statesman'. The next year saw exactly that, even if there were one or two bumps with American opinion on the way. In early 1985 Kinnock had met with Fidel Castro whilst on a tour of Central America, leading to Bob Hopper at the US Embassy in London writing to Kinnock's press officer Patricia Hewitt, letting her know that he was 'sure your boss rightly found his meeting with Fidelissmo interesting and useful'. However, Hopper thought, 'he should be aware that Dr Castro's presence at the inaugural [for the Venezuelan President Daniel Ortega] had its downside implications for many in the US – including for moderates'. Hopper did, however, recommend that Hewitt get in touch with Bill Gray, affiliated with the DLC – 'when you consider contacts with additional US Democrats'. By this stage he had long been in touch with such sources, including Gary Hart, who 'eagerly await[ed] news of a Kinnock visit'. He had also had a positive lunch with Walter Mondale in April 1985, where the former vice president was 'impressed by the clarity and strength of

FIGURE 5 New Labour would have been impossible without the earlier leadership of Neil Kinnock. A regular visitor to the US, Kinnock is pictured here in the Bronx, 1984 (Express/Getty Images).

your leadership' and signed off his letter with his wishes for a 'Good Election!'[17]

Such dialogue continued throughout late 1985. Jack Loiello, who had taken his doctorate in London and would later serve as a junior staffer under Clinton, wrote after Kinnock's famous 1985 anti-Militant conference speech that 'your friends and admirers in the United States applauded your major address at your Party Congress'. It seemed, to Loiello, 'a fitting tone for a constructive tone against Mrs Thatcher' and he joked that 'you were now ready to join the Democrats'. Lastly, there was Jesse Jackson, with whom Kinnock was in semi-regular contact and saw as a means to 'ensure that black people are properly represented in every sphere of activity'. As Kinnock noted, 'there is a real problem of under registration amongst the black communities in this country and I would truly welcome your help in this campaign'.[18]

Like most aspects of his leadership, Kinnock's interactions with the American left must be read within the prism of the then state of the Labour party. There were certainly serious points of disagreement with the Republican administration. Kinnock had condemned the US bombing of Libya in 1986 and referred to Thatcher as Reagan's 'poodle' during his visit to the States a year later. But much of his dialogue was about trying to position his party to a point where, by the time of its 1987–89 policy review, some of the more outlandish elements of foreign policy could be dropped. In February 1989, after extensive negotiations with the soft left, a triumphant Kinnock was able to tell his party that he would no longer 'make that tactical argument for the unilateral independent abandonment of nuclear weapons without getting anything in return'.[19]

As part of the process of renewing his party, in October 1988 Kinnock had met with Ron Brown, chair of the DNC and followed up with a letter setting out where the Democrats and Labour could work together. In general, Kinnock felt that 'it would be useful to compare the policy approaches and campaign styles'. On the policy side, leading Labour figures and their counterparts in Washington should discuss 'the evolution of relations between the United States and Europe, particularly in light of the changes in Eastern Europe [and] the development of the European Community Single Market'. Further, global environmental issues, developments in international trade and financial relations and various forms of domestic policy – from the 'promotion of equality between women and men' to 'accountability and efficiency of public services' – should all be on the agenda.[20]

Elsewhere, Kinnock and the New York small 'c' conservative Democrat Pat Moynihan got on 'instantaneously'. Kinnock recalls Moynihan and Ted Kennedy 'were knowledgeable about British politics and doubtless would have been members of the Labour Party had they been in Britain'. Moynihan was a 'colourful, rambunctious, progressive character and a very impressive man in every possible way'. On one occasion in 1990, Pat was to meet Neil in the Senate, but had to return to New York on emergency business. This was represented by the British media as a terrible snub, akin to Reagan's treatment of Kinnock a few years earlier. As Kinnock remembers, 'when Pat found out about the stories he was absolutely bloody enraged and so the morning after I should have met him, he was back in Washington and had restored the meeting'. They gathered in Moynihan's Senate office, where the host again expressed his anger at Kinnock's experience and deliberately elongated the meeting from half an hour to an hour, just so there could be no ambiguity about his visitor's treatment. The pair then left to talk to the assembled British media. Moynihan boomed, 'is there a guy here called Kavanagh?'. The Sun's Trevor Kavanagh then sheepishly stepped forward, to be met by 'Pat ripping him from top to bottom, from the lies he had printed to the deformation of character in his stories'.[21]

Whilst British progressive powerbrokers took in 1980s DC, there were equally interesting lessons being learned in Massachusetts. There, at Harvard University, was the young Ed Balls – future advisor to Gordon Brown and later a cabinet minister in his own right. His time in the US was clearly significant for Balls and broadened his horizons in many ways. Arriving at Boston Logan in September 1988 on the first flight he had ever taken, Balls had gone to Harvard in part 'to figure out what a decent government of the centre-left might do, should it ever get the chance to lead'. There was time for some frivolity – Balls particularly enjoyed Ryles' Jazz Bar during the evening and the food at both Nicks Beef and Beer and Charlie's Kitchen – but this was certainly a time of crucial intellectual development. Balls would place much emphasis in later life on his then economics tutor, Larry Summers (then also advising Michael Dukakis and later to serve as Clinton's last Treasury Secretary). Together with Larry Katz, Summers co-authored a 1991 article with Balls on the regional dimensions of British unemployment and how they could be addressed.[22]

This was truly a grounding in the future Clinton Cabinet, for Balls also took a class with Robert Reich (Katz's future boss at the Department of

Labor). During those sessions, Reich asked his students which outcome they would prefer for the next 20 years: America growing by 3 per cent per year and Japan by 4 per cent or both economies by 2 per cent. As Balls recalled, 'the vast majority of the class voted for the latter, judging that falling behind Japan was a worse outcome than having lower growth'. Balls remained 'in a minority and was rather shocked that the largely American group of students would rather be worse off than see Japan pull ahead'. This somewhat spoke for the different perceptions of the world that could mark the individual American and British interpretations of the Third Way and their relative global standings. Yet the broader point for Balls was that 'no-one was thinking or talking of China at all'.[23]

The future Gordon Brown ally was far from the only New Labour figure to attend an American institution, however. Douglas Alexander, Britain's International Development Secretary under Brown, would spend his 1988/89 academic year at the University of Pennsylvania volunteering for Michael Dukakis. Alexander held the grandiose campaign title of Press Steward, though the day-to-day reality of his job was managing telephone canvassers in a freezing Teamsters Hall in North Philadelphia. Later, Ed Miliband, leader of the Party from 2010, would take an 18-month sabbatical from the UK Treasury in 2002 to teach at Harvard. For Miliband, who had developed a lifelong love of baseball whilst living in Boston as a child, proximity to the Red Sox was particularly appealing. More seriously, the experience of lecturing to an informed, largely American audience would prove pivotal in giving him the confidence to seek elected office himself. Between teaching, Miliband would gorge episodes of *The West Wing* and hosted a steady of stream of UK visitors – including Douglas Alexander, Stewart Wood and Spencer Livermore: all confirmed Brown acolytes. The then Chancellor himself would often ring to catch up, not taking into account the time difference, when Miliband was teaching classes. Such American links made sense. As former Kennedy Scholar at Harvard and later New Labour's first Culture Secretary, Chris Smith, acknowledges: 'whilst the Neil Kinnock [born 1942] and John Smith [born 1938] generation of Labour leaders were not as fascinated with America as their fifties or sixties born counterparts, Blair, Brown and the Milibands were absolutely riveted'. The British Third Way would indeed be led by such baby boomers seeking to ape the American success of Bill Clinton.[24]

The Democratic Leadership Council and the 'New Democrats'

A Clinton-led Democratic party was still a long way off in the 1980s. The man himself had endured a difficult start to the decade and became, as he joked, the 'youngest ex-Governor in history' when he had lost to his Republican challenger in November 1980. Part of this was the 'Reagan coat-tails' effect – the phenomenon whereby the president's popularity was said to have been lent to other candidates running for the GOP. But Clinton had contributed to his own downfall, as he later acknowledged. The decision to place thousands of Cuban refugees in Fort Chafee in the west of the state angered many, particularly when 1,000 escaped from the facility. Clinton was even advised to pull his support from Jimmy Carter, who had ordered the relocation of the refugees to Arkansas, though he remained loyal.

Even more serious, certainly on a day-to-day practical basis, was the need to fund improvements to Arkansas' dilapidated roads. To do so, the Governor had sought a progressive bill which broadly financed the initiative by taxing new, expensive vehicles more and older, lower-value vehicles less. After some horse trading in the state legislature, however, the bill Clinton had before him essentially offered 'a good road program paid for in an unfair way' – shunting much of the increased taxation onto the older cars used by the state's poor. Clinton then made the 'single dumbest mistake I ever made' and, lacking an alternative means to finance the road improvements, signed the bill. What particularly rubbed salt in the wounds was the fact that, in Arkansas, people's car license fees are due to be paid on their birthday. This provided to the voters 'a birthday present from me: the price of their car tags had doubled'. After his loss, Hillary told her husband that 'if you really want to run again, you've got to go out and talk to people and figure out why you lost, tell people you got the message and show them you've still got good ideas'. He did just that and in 1982 comfortably re-took the Governor's mansion on a 6 per cent swing. After some landmark education reforms, discussed at greater length in Chapter 7, Clinton then increased his majority in 1984 by a further 7 per cent and never looked back.[25]

Others were learning lessons too. On 25 October 1984, Al From, then staff director of the Democratic Caucus in the House of Representatives, typed a series of letters which set out where he and many on the right of the Democratic Party, thought the wind was already headed. Recipients included the New York public affairs executive Steve Stamas, Bob Rubin (then of Goldman Sachs) and the future Florida Congressman Douglas 'Pete' Peterson. Tacitly conceding that Democratic candidate Walter Mondale had likely lost the forthcoming presidential election, From noted that 'regardless of the outcome … I am confident that we can rebuild the Democratic Party [and] re-establish it as the party of growth and opportunity in America'. To do that, From argued, 'we need three things: attractive young leadership, a good legislative program and a good public relations program to sell that good legislative program'. For From, 'deficit reduction is the central issue around which to build our legislative program'. He believed that 'those, who for the lack of a better name, I'll call the New Democrats and business leaders, have a mutual interest in being on the ground floor of such a package'. Indeed, 'by pushing for a serious deficit reduction program, the New Democrats can pass the test of "toughness" which too many Americans feel the old Democrats have failed'.[26]

After Mondale's defeat, From would expand on his thesis. On 29 November 1984, Virginia Governor Chuck Robb (then head of the Democratic Governors' Association) invited several of his fellow governors to dinner. These included Bruce Babbitt (Texas), Steny Hoyer (Maryland), Tim Wirth (Colorado) and Mark White (Texas). Also invited was Al From's boss, Gillis Long. The briefing note From provided for his congressman set out six ways in which he felt the Democrats needed to change. Many of these overlapped, but the key contention was that 'putting together a coalition of liberals and minorities is not the way to win national elections and achieve majority party status'. This meant not writing 'off large areas of the country – such as the South and the West', avoiding becoming just 'a liberal party' and instead 'attract[ing] moderates and conservatives' and doing well amongst 'men, whites, independents and young voters'. It also meant revisiting the Presidential nomination process and for key figures to hold back on endorsing a nominee until they had proved themselves ready for the job.[27]

After the Robb dinner in late November 1984, From had various meetings in the south trying to rally support for a moderate candidate to become the next chair of the Democratic National Committee (DNC) – the body which determined the presidential nomination process, organised the national convention and serviced local state parties. After the most prominent candidates backed out, on 16 December From, Fred

Duval (aide to Babbitt), Chuck Dolan (representing Robb and the DGA), John Rendon (veteran party activist)and Bill Romjue (who had worked for Gary Hart in 1984) met in the backroom of a Kansas City steakhouse to work out what to do next. Unable to win control of the DNC and with forming an SDP-style third party a perennial electoral impossibility in American politics, the quintet 'agreed that we needed to start our own group – independent of the DNC – if we were to change the direction of the party'.[28]

The result was the Democratic Leadership Council (DLC). The DLC was 'independent of the DNC, free to have its own staff, raise its own money and operate under its own rules'. After initially intending to have the council sanctioned by the DGA and House and Senate Democratic Caucuses, this idea was swiftly dropped after its proponents realised this could lead to DNC control by the backdoor. Throughout January 1985, From therefore met regularly with the Georgia Senator Sam Nunn, Missouri Congressman Dick Gephardt and other leading congressional representatives to hammer out the precise architecture for the new DLC. Former academic turned Clinton advisor Bill Galston noted that 'there is something to the proposition that the DLC began as a regional movement rather than an ideological movement. The basic political argument was very simple: Democrats can't win unless they do a whole lot better in the south than Walter Mondale did. But they're not going to do a whole lot better in the south unless some things about the nominating process change'. Part of the latter point saw the eventual creation of 'Super Tuesday' – the cluster of southern states that form a key part in the nomination process for the Democratic candidature. But the problem for the DLCers was not just procedural. As Galton suggests, when it came to the mid to late 1980s, even 'the southern Democratic Party at that point had lost its center of moderate Democrats and had become – to a first approximation – a coalition of African-Americans and white liberals'.[29]

Tragically, at half time on Superbowl Sunday in January 1985 – six weeks before the DLC was to be launched – Gillis Long died of a heart attack. This placed much pressure on From – whom Nunn, Robb, Gephardt and others had asked to run the DLC – with the prospect of losing his federal paycheck by leaving his current state funded position and thereby living hand to mouth, all the while with a wife, two young kids and a mortgage. What the DLC did have, however, was a fairly fleshed out policy agenda and set of principles. This was important, for without significant intellectual underpinning, their aspirations would go nowhere.

Fundamentally, what the left needed was a way out of the bind where, in the eyes of the electorate, the right's offer of tax cuts to offset the effects of a globalising world were frequently outdoing the left's big statism. The New Right had done some hard thinking in the 1970s, now it was time for the centre-left to do similar.

The initial flourishing of this had been seen through the so-called ATARI Democrats, many of whose members later gravitated towards the DLC. As the veteran columnist John Chamberlain put it back in 1982, the ATARI Democrats 'include many of the Southern "boll weevil" contingent that has supported Reagan on taxes, [and] is for using government to channel investment money to the newer "high tech" industries. This may make more sense than an attempt to bail out a heavy industry that can no longer compete in world markets with the Japanese, the West Germans and the Swedes'.[30] As Chamberlain noted, conservative southern Democrats had already begun to vote with the Reagan administration on key financial measures. Up to 40 so-called 'boll weevils' could be relied on to vote in favour of Republican bills which trimmed spending (giving the GOP a de facto majority that a House of 242 Democrats to 193 Republicans did not suggest). But the point of the ATARI Democrat movement was not just the short-term tactics of having to deal with Reagan's popularity, but to forge a new set of positive policies to renew the centre left.

The difficulty here was, again, the vested interests. When he heard of the ATARI Democrats, California's Senator Alan Cranston argued that 'America's future will not be found in building an Atari for every home. It will be found in producing efficient, high quality, competitively priced automobiles. It will be found in reassigning the priorities of our best scientific and technological minds to funding new ways to make steel machine tools, tires and trains that will match – indeed, surpass – those built in Japan and Europe'. Even the Senate representative for Silicon Valley was therefore contending that he didn't 'think we can let those basic smokestack industries go by the boards, I don't believe we can become just a high-tech service economy'. Around the same time, nationally syndicated journalist Robert Walters was reporting that 'many members of Congress refuse to even acknowledge the fact that uncounted thousands of jobs in the auto, steel and other traditional "smokestack" industries have been irretrievably lost while employment opportunities in high technology fields are becoming available at an accelerating rate – but can be filled only by those with the required training and skills'. Here, again, was the bind: the jobs of today were well-represented within progressive structures but were also fundamentally dying, whilst the jobs of tomorrow were hypothetical, full of boundless opportunity, but lacked meaningful lobbyists backing their cause.[31]

It took guts to forge a new path. With southern congressmen feeling that association with the national Democratic Party was harmful to their political survival, a number of the younger members – including Gephardt, Les Aspin, Tim Wirth and Al Gore – organised a DC retreat to debate how to resurrect the party. Soon after this January 1981 gathering, Gillis Long would become head of a new Committee on Party Effectiveness (known as the 'Caucus Committee') and would go on to mentor these leading younger (and often southern or mid-western) lights in a number of ways. Indeed, as Chair of the House Democratic Caucus from 1981 Long would serve as a key sympathetic early powerbroker for the New Democrats to flesh out a new agenda and used his patronage to appoint several task forces to create the policies that might do just that.

In 1982, as From recalls, 'the most important task force was on long-term economic policy and we kept that one close to the family: Long, me working on his behalf, Wirth and Gephardt'. The result from this task force's research was a new report entitled *Rebuilding the Road to Opportunity: A Democratic Direction for the 1980s*. Known as the 'yellow book' (since the government printing office gave it a bright yellow cover), its 'centerpiece was private sector economic growth'. As Senator Paul Tsongas (later Clinton's chief rival for the presidential nomination in 1992) had previously told From, 'the problem with the Democratic Party is that we spend so much time passing out the golden eggs that we forget to worry about the health of the goose'. Growing the economy and thereby rewarding and promoting business small and large, would henceforth be part of the New Democratic agenda. In an open letter to sympathetic friends in May 1983, the chairs of Long's various task forces – including Aspin (National Security), Gore (Environment), Gephardt (the Economy) and Barney Frank (Housing) – laid out the yellow book's significance. As they noted, 'it proposed a fundamental shift in Democratic thinking – to a strategy of investment, growth and opportunity for the 1980s' and 'a tough, unequivocal, law enforcement effort to reduce crime'. On these two pillars the New Democratic agenda would be constructed.[32]

By 1984 this agenda had been extended through another blueprint, *Renewing America's Promise*. Here again, Long praised the 'emerging new force within our Democratic Party – made up of members of Congress, young in mindset if not in age, who will become the next generation of leaders in our country and in our party'. Although 'grounded in the fundamental principles of the Democratic Party, our program seeks not to dwell on the past, but to seize and secure the future'. This document was also used as a catalyst for Gillis Long to invite several private-sector figures, including Steve Stamas, to a Washington DC dinner which would allow 'some private, off the record, brainstorming about some new initiatives we are developing to redirect our national and the Democratic Party'. Around this time private polling was carried out hypothesising a 'Mr Smith', a Democratic nominee putting forward this type of agenda. 'Mr Smith' significantly out-performed the 1984 Democratic frontrunners, Mondale and Senator John Glenn of Ohio, again giving succour to the cause.[33]

By early 1985, the DLC was therefore ready to go ideologically and in terms of its key figures. Will Marshall, who had worked for Long as a speechwriter and would later head up the Clintonian think tank the Progressive Policy Institute (PPI), was recruited by From to help draw up its early materials. From himself had his salary guaranteed by Chuck Robb and initial seed money for the project. But there were clear obstacles to what they were trying to do. Paul Kirk, the new chairman of the DNC, was one powerful opponent and soon formed his own policy council to try and head off the breakaway faction. But this was to no avail. On 1 March 1985 newspapers across the country reported that 'Democratic governors and members of Congress from the South and West, seeking a stronger conservative voice in their party, defied Democratic chairman Paul Kirk yesterday and formed an independent leadership council'.[34]

Still hoping to strangle the new force at birth, Kirk claimed that his new DNC policy machinery would contain only one personal appointee (albeit its head, Scott Matheson) and that it would be 'broad based'. But, as Phil Gailey reported in the *New York Times*, one Kirk confidante had believed it was unclear how much of Kirk's opposition was 'presidential politics and how much is parochial politics'. As this source set out, 'the fear of a lot of people is that [the DLC] wants to take the cream of the party's leadership and leave Kirk with Jesse Jackson and the single-issue groups. Kirk needs these moderate elected officials for leverage in dealing with the interest groups'. Either way, with seed money in place, incorporation papers filed, a three-room office on the fourth floor of the Fairchild Building at 499 South Capitol Street ('no palace' and clad with 'an ink stained carpet'), the DLC was formed.[35]

Though it was a fledging upstart faced by an official DNC council led by a politician with not drastically dissimilar policy ideas, the DLC had two major trump cards. The first was that DNC rules meant that Matheson had to make sure every party constituency held appropriate balance within his policy apparatus. The process of achieving this took time and it therefore gave the under-resourced DLC a head start in trying to reinvent party policy. Secondly, Al From knew several of the policy staffers working for Matheson's body and thus 'when it finally produced its first report 18 months later, it reflected a point of view already identified with the DLC'. The appointment of Gephardt as first DLC chair helped smooth over some ruffled feathers since, as From notes, 'it was difficult not to like Dick Gephardt'.[36]

Throughout 1986, the DLC continued to 'break new ground in the ideas war'. In September 1985, the report *Winning the World Economy* had already established the DLC as the pro-trade wing of the Democrats. As From judged, 'the competition from imports [to America] keeps costs down and opening foreign markets to American goods and services creates jobs at home'. It was also a wider signal that the DLC was prepared to resist the protectionism of the trade unions and embrace capitalism in all its forms. But the key question was for how long should the DLC remain separate from the DNC and what was its eventual aim? At a gathering in Phoenix in January 1986 the matter was settled: 'we would remain in business until there was a Democrat safely ensconced in the White House, ... we would remain independent from the DNC'. Since Ted Kennedy was not running for the Presidency in 1988, Tip O'Neill was retiring as House speaker and Walter Mondale's defeat in 1984 had been so catastrophic, there was a real opportunity to 'lead the redefinition of the Democratic Party'.[37]

With Gephardt looking to hand over the reins to work on his own presidential bid for 1988, From sought to have Chuck Robb take over as DLC chairman. Prohibited from seeking a second term as Virginia Governor by the state's constitution, Robb was looking for a means to keep up his national profile whilst From wanted 'someone with the courage to take on party orthodoxy'. Robb demanded assurances that the DLC would broaden its base to involve more minorities and more liberal voices. Bill Gray, Barbara Kennelly and Bill Richardson fit this bill and Robb soon signed on. Robb's tenure would oversee the creation of the first DLC state chapter, a means whereby state and local officials could express affiliation with the organisation, in Florida. He would also lead the organisation into its first presidential cycle. But, if the experience of the British centre-left was anything to go by, this would not be easy.[38]

Labour policy review

In 1987 Labour lost its third successive election. Though gaining 20 seats and 3 per cent of the vote on 1983, the party still only held 229 seats to the Conservative's 376. England looked like a sea of blue only punctured by shades of red in London, Yorkshire, the Manchester–Liverpool conurbation and the North East. Neil Kinnock had helped draw up the party manifesto and thus bore some of the responsibility. But he had generally performed well in the campaign and earned the right for a second shot at any election in 1991 or 1992. As Kinnock's biographer Martin Westlake notes, his '1987 decision to concentrate his election campaign in the north and Midlands and to focus on social welfare rather than economic issues, may have evoked a powerful response and stabilised Labour's position, but it was clear that the leadership now needed to reach beyond the heartlands, to the all-important centre ground'.[39]

Such moves were about personnel and policy. Gordon Brown and Tony Blair, elected to parliament in the meltdown of 1983, would both reach Kinnock's Shadow Cabinet by 1988. This provided them a platform of their own, but also a reason to spend more time together. They were no longer just backbench colleagues who happened to believe in the broad direction Labour should take. The economic nature of their new portfolios meant they ended up at a lot of the same meetings, talking to the same people and just being in the same place. As the *Liverpool Echo* put it, these 'bright sparks' would 'be a strong source of support for their leader in his attempts to modernise the party and shake off the shackles of the left'. This was clearly true behind the scenes, but collective Shadow Cabinet responsibility placed certain limits on what they could say publicly – particularly given the hard policy yards Kinnock was having to grind out.

As such, Blair and Brown mostly got on with their Shadow briefs at Energy and then Employment and John Smith's Deputy at Labour's Treasury team, respectively. Media coverage for the two therefore tended to resemble fairly generic opposition on issues such as the excesses of the government's privatisation agenda or its tax cuts for the wealthy. Both were spoken of as future leaders, though the more 'human' media coverage for Blair perhaps indicated his wider public cut through. In December 1988, Blair was nominated by the publishers of romance novels *Mills and Boon* as one of the Commons' 'most romantic MPs'. Little was said to justify this claim, though the Conservative winner, MP Hugo Summerson, was apparently 'just that touch more romantic'. Blair and Brown would do what they could, then, but the modernisation process, as with the DLC in the States, needed an organisational impetus to harness such contributions and show the party was capable of change. What followed was the Labour Policy Review of 1987–89: a moment significant not least in that it drew the eye of Al From, then sitting at his desk in DC and significant chunks of the US media.[40]

After being confirmed at the party conference in September 1987, the review came in two stages. First, in the period up to the Spring of 1988, various policy groups went away and set out the conditions they felt would likely face any Labour government in the 1990s. Then, in stage two (lasting until autumn 1989), the groups would draw up more detailed policy prescriptions to solve them. The challenge for Kinnock was how to parlay his relatively credible performance in 1987 into dumping the party's more electorally dicey policies. This was not easy and, in many cases, involved halfway houses that, for the modernisers, were all too timid. Unilateral nuclear disarmament was dropped, but in its place emerged a complex pledge to use Britain's existing nuclear stock to negotiate with other nations to disarm *multilaterally*. Labour would still nationalise the water industry, but little else. And the top rate of tax should still rise, but perhaps not as much as they had pledged in 1983 or 1987. These were moves towards the electorate, but of an insufficiently radical nature. As Giles Radice recorded in his diary, 'what is required is nothing less than a "new" Labour Party, capable of putting forward an alternative political agenda for the 1990s'.[41]

During this period Radice was drafting and editing his own book, *The Path to Power: The New Revisionism*. In this 1989 work, he again called for 'Labour to go beyond policy reviews (in which we abandon the policies that made us unelectable in the 1980s) and create what amounts to a "new" Labour Party, based not on class or trade union domination but on reaching out to all citizens'. The book would be covered across the political spectrum, from the *Independent* to the *Daily Mail* and, at a party at Roy Jenkins' house that evening, Peter Mandelson, 'with a characteristic hint of menace', told Radice that 'Kinnock is outraged with me on the grounds that I have diverted attention from the policy reviews'. Radice's counter-argument was that he was 'building on the policy reviews to show the voters that we are really changing' and the party would 'never win by being cautious. We need to project ourselves as a "new" party'. Mandelson was working for Kinnock in the 1980s and thus doing his leader's bidding but would come to more fully back the Radice position as the years passed.[42]

Alongside the official work of the policy review and Radice's own freewheeling, was *Labour Listens* – a serious of events around the country where the party heard the gripes of ordinary voters and what they could do to better reflect them. Whilst Kinnock sold the idea as the 'biggest consultative exercise with the British public any political party has ever undertaken', the chair of his home policy committee, Tom Sawyer, argued that 'for too many people Labour simply lacked "X" appeal. Was it policy or image, credibility or leadership? It was all of these, in different measures for different people'. Whilst modernisers like Blair and Brown were nodding sagely, not everyone welcomed these initiatives, nor the recent change of the Labour Party symbol. As such, for Arthur Scargill, he of the miner's strike fame, the left did 'not need Saatchi and Saatchi and red roses. [Instead] Marx and Engels and the red blood flag of socialism should be put on the agenda of British politics'. At the 1988 Labour conference, Tony Benn likewise decried any moves away from wholesale nationalisation – 'you cannot control what you do not own' – and declared that 'as more and more people experience market forces in practice ... socialism reappears'. Given it was now the third term of a Thatcher government and George HW Bush was about to succeed Reagan as president, this was quite a claim.[43]

Still, at least the Americans were impressed with the heroic efforts of Kinnock. In 1989 Will Marshall's Progressive Policy Institute (PPI) stated that 'this past Spring the British Labour Party decided that it was tired of losing, dumped its extreme left stance and moved towards the centre'. The *Boston Globe* agreed and told its readers that 'Kinnock has demonstrated his capacity to recapture disaffected voters by dropping unpopular policies like ... the almost religiously held tenet of the nationalization of British industry'. Meanwhile, David Broder, in his influential syndicated US column, remarked that Kinnock had 'turned a corner in making Labor a more credible alternative' and 'now, for the first time, it looks as if the opposition Laborites may have something to teach the Democrats'. Labour seemed to be at the forefront of a modernising, centrist turn then being mirrored on the centre-left of Norwegian, German and Italian politics. Perhaps, then, the American left could be persuaded to do something similar after all.[44]

1988

Somewhat unfairly, even when praising the British Labour leader, David Broder had noted that Kinnock 'suffers a bit from the reputation of being too much of an intellectual lightweight to fill No. 10 Downing Street'. This was harsh. But it was certainly true that any modernising force would require a strong leader. Thus, when it came to American politics, the guiding mission of the DLC was to find a suitable Presidential candidate. In both 1984 and 1988 the person perhaps most suited to this position would have been Joe Biden – but after not running the first time and running into Neil Kinnock the second, this was not an option. If not Biden, the charismatic New York Governor Mario Cuomo would have been a sound choice – but again he elected not to run. For his part, Bill Clinton had announced he would not run back in July 1987 and, at 41 years old, was still rather young. Even so, DLC candidates remained on the Democratic ballot in 1988: Al Gore, Bruce Babbitt and Dick Gephardt. In the event, however, their combined 10 primary victories (compared to 13 for the left-wing Jesse Jackson and the soft left Michael Dukakis's 30) did not speak to an agenda that had yet broken through.[45]

Though he only garnered three mid-western states before withdrawing from the primaries on 29 March, Gephardt's campaign is worth attention since it forms a useful staging post in shifting attitudes on the left. Though his campaign ranged across the gamut of themes inherent in running for the presidency, throughout his career Gephardt had staked out important positions on several areas including defence, the perils of inflation and global free trade. As to the first, Gephardt gave an early nod to his views in a speech to the American University on 25 September 1987. There he told his audience that 'I am an American – and a Democrat – who believes in a strong defense . . . I am a member of the party of Harry Truman, who led the struggle to save Europe from Soviet imperialism; the party of John Kennedy, who told us that "the price of freedom is always high" and that we have to be willing to pay it'. However, he also stood before the voters 'as a member of the party that has won the White House only once in the last five elections – a party that has been equated, fairly or unfairly, with soft-headedness and faint-heartedness'. As such, 'the person Democrats

FIGURE 6 Dick Gephardt (left) was an important early DLC voice during the *March of the Moderates*. Here, in February 1993, he comments on the new Clinton administration's proposed healthcare reforms, with the First Lady and Tom Foley, then Speaker of the House (Courtesy: The Library of Congress).

nominate to carry our standard next year must be someone who has the record of resolve – the intellect and the spirit – to reclaim our rightful position as the party of a strong America'. Democratic voters would, of course, eventually select Dukakis – whose appearance in a photo-op in a tank would be widely mocked as simply unbelievable during the General Election. But Gephardt had begun to reassert a powerful and more muscular Democratic tradition in foreign policy that was 'realistic and reasonable' but also stated that, 'if the Soviets [were proven to be] pursuing only a "public relations peace", they will find a powerfully resolute America'.[46] With the Vietnam protests of the 1960s and 1970s still in voters' minds, this was a crucial bridge to cross.

During his 1988 run, attention was also turned back to some of Gephardt's previous articles which had highlighted the need for responsible management of the public purse. In the late 1970s Gephardt had written that 'inflation is more dangerous to all of us and to our way of life than anything I can think of – more dangerous than Fascism or Communism or any natural disaster'. Crucially, 'the most important step for the Federal government to take is to restrain Federal spending'. As Gephardt noted, 'it will be unpleasant to build fewer roads and airports and sewers. It will be unpleasant to build fewer tanks or buy fewer school lunches, or reduce pension payment increases ... But whatever spending cuts Congress can agree on, they will be more pleasant – in the long run – than an economy with 15% or 20% annual inflation'.[47] His trip to the UK in 1981 had further cemented this lesson and, like Tony Blair and Gordon Brown, he was not afraid to learn the lessons of Margaret Thatcher.

It was, however, the third arm – trade – which would be the most distinctive part of Gephardt's agenda. Here he made much of a congressional amendment he had put down which demanded more open markets abroad. The Gephardt amendment required, as his campaign briefings set out, 'only one thing: negotiation'. It compelled the president to negotiate with any major trading party that exports 75 per cent more to the US than it imports 'as a result of unfair barriers'. Once a pattern of unfair trade was found, the president would begin six months of talks with said country, to negotiate away the tariff or regulatory concerns. In one 1988 TV ad, Gephardt declared that 'some people say my trade policies are too tough on the Japanese, Germans and Koreans. They say a president can't demand that nations trading with us open their markets to our products, too . . . We have to stand up for our jobs, our farmers our seniors. If we don't, who will?' In a longer version of the ad, he went even harder: American factory men and women 'work their hearts out every day trying to turn out a good product at a decent price. Then the Korean government slaps on nine separate taxes and tariffs . . . It's not their fault we can't see our cars in a market like that'. Should Gephardt have become president, 'they'll know we'll still honor our treaties to defend them – because that's the kind of country we are. But they'll also be left asking themselves: How many Americans are going to pay forty-eight thousand dollars for one of their Hyundais?' This policy could be read two ways: on the one hand it was demanding more open markets, on the other it was threatening economic protectionism if it did not get them. It was not the default siege economy of the hard left (after all, it was trying to make capitalism work *better*), but it was far from liberal free trade either.[48]

This was an interesting juncture. Henceforth, after Gephardt failed to secure the nomination, the Third Way would be resolutely open to globalisation. For those like From, Gephardt 'had taken a number of positions, particularly his protectionist stand on trade, that were different from the DLC's and made me uneasy'. During his time at Harvard, Ed Balls too noted 'a level of economic nationalism around trade – certainly at a level coming from a British perspective – that was surprising'. Gephardt was the progenitor here, but, for Balls, 'Dukakis hinted at it quite a lot, too'. As Balls notes, the challenge for Third Wayers henceforth would be 'to really accept globalisation, not uncritically, but with a mindset that broadly said it was a good thing that we needed to mitigate the risks of, rather than seek to avoid'.[49]

Like Babitt and Gore, Gephardt was always a long shot in 1988. As From acknowledged, the latter two were 'essentially going after the same voters and the tension between them and their campaigns became palpable'. Gephardt had his problems over trade and Gore too 'was never willing to step out with cutting edge ideas on the economy', something From and Will Marshall had prompted him on. For the DLC itself, the 1988 process was more important to 'put us in a position to pick up the pieces if Democrats suffered another debacle'. To do so they concentrated on hosting debates in the south on key DLC issues: national security, social policy and private-sector-led economic growth. They sought to get the national service idea onto the agenda and to position From, Robb and Nunn on to the media as active opinion formers. They could at least frame the debate – and thereby have a ready-made narrative when alternative policy prescriptions very likely lost to Bush.[50]

As it was, the eventual Democratic nominee would prove problematic. Emerging from an uncharitably named contest dubbed 'Snow White and the Seven Dwarves', Michael Dukakis was a smart and able Governor unable to provide the charisma needed to win the presidency against an incumbent Vice President. Rather like Ed Miliband in the 2015 British General Election, Dukakis ended up being rather uncomfortable at being called a 'liberal', but also unable to convincingly reject the claim. Against Dukakis, the Republican offer in 1988 more or less bore the hallmarks of a simplistic crib sheet campaign chief Jim Baker sketched out for Bush ahead of the debates. The 3 'Fs' – freedom, family and future – would be embodied by 'peace through strength', 'traditional American values' and 'Jobs and Growth'. Added, almost as an afterthought, was a pledge that would get Bush into trouble in later years: 'no new taxes'.[51]

This was to be a bruising campaign. Former President Richard Nixon would write to Bush's running mate Dan Quayle, telling him that 'unless Dukakis is unmasked as the doveish liberal that he is, the Reagan Democrats will come back to their party and we will lose'.[52] Eventually, two Republican attack ads would embody this strategy. The first centred on Willie Horton, a convicted murderer who had been released on a weekend furlough programme in Massachusetts, only to flee and go on to rape a woman and stab her boyfriend. TV ads centred on the notion that

'Bush supports the death penalty for first degree murderers [whilst] Dukakis not only opposes the death penalty, he allowed first degree murderers to have weekend passes from prison'. It was certainly no accident that Republicans highlighted the case of an African American in Horton, but it also had clear cut through. Perhaps coincidentally, perhaps not, in 1990, an ambitious Bill Clinton resumed the use of the death penalty in Arkansas after a 23-year hiatus.

Secondly, the Bush campaign hammered Dukakis on his Gubernatorial veto of a 1977 bill which would have fined teachers who did not lead their class in the pledge of allegiance to the flag. This could have been something of nothing, but the Dukakis campaign's inability to counter it with a convincing display of patriotism (that didn't involve climbing into a tank) hurt him badly. From suggested he adopt the DLC's national service plan since it would allow the Democrats to redefine patriotism away from meaningless gestures and instead 'in terms of civic duty'. But, in this vacuum, it would be Bush who would propose a watered-down *volunteer* service plan of his own and the political commentators hammered Dukakis for this lapse. As David Broder wrote, 'Dukakis has ignored what may well be a recurrent impulse for community service. When the DLC last spring proposed a national service plan for young people, who would be rewarded with assistance for their own education or home buying, Dukakis gave it a cold shoulder. He left it to George Bush to propose last week an appealing but modest plan that would send young volunteers from affluent suburbs to help tutor and assist city-center youths, whose hopeless lives Bush has said "haunt" his conscience'. Clinton, again, was taking notes.[53]

One impartial witness here, again, was the fresh off the plane Ed Balls. Arriving at Harvard in September 1988, just after the Willie Horton adverts had begun to take hold of the airwaves, Balls would watch the Bush–Dukakis debates in the Forum of the Kennedy School. To the query of what punishment he would want for the assailant if his wife was raped and murdered, Dukakis would famously give a very procedural, politician's answer which explained the basis of his overall opposition to the death penalty, rather than engage with the emotive nature of the question. Balls remembers 'him going straight into the line to take about why capital punishment is a bad thing which was catastrophic and revealed Dukakis to be out of his depth at the presidential level: he couldn't engage with the voters in the way that he had to'. Having only seen the campaign from afar, the positive polling numbers across the summer of 1988 had left Balls 'arriving thinking Dukakis had been doing rather well, but within a week or so of being in the States it became obvious that he wasn't'. Dukakis would go on to lose to Bush by 7 million votes and by 10 states to 40. 'Freedom, family and future' had again put the Republicans comfortably over the line.[54]

Soon after Dukakis' defeat, Bill Galston had a breakfast with Al From, Will Marshall and others at La Colline (French for "The Hill," indicating its proximity to the Capitol). There he outlined what became *The Politics of Evasion* – a hugely influential September 1989 PPI pamphlet written with Elaine Kamarck. Kamarck contends that it was about showing that 'the current Democratic Party ... was a party that was out of touch on economics, out of touch on foreign policy and out of touch on values. You couldn't win the Presidency unless you fixed these problems in the minds of the voters'.[55] Whatever voters told pollsters before elections – as Labour would discover in 1992 – these fundamentals had to be addressed.

Three myths therefore had to go. 'The Myth of Liberal Fundamentalism' meant that the American left continued to tell itself it was losing because it had 'strayed from the true and pure faith of their ancestors'. In reality, as Galston and Kamarck showed, 'the real problem' was that 'most Democratic nominees have come to be seen as *unacceptably* liberal'. Alongside this, 'the Myth of Mobilisation' contended that if the Democrats could 'get non-participants to vote' then all would be well. Yet again, as Galston and Kamarck showed, even if levels of turnout amongst African Americans could be raised up to the national average, this would, even being generous with the numbers, only have swung Maryland and Illinois (36 votes in the electoral college) to a Dukakis campaign that was miles behind. Likewise, going big on the Hispanic community in California might, one day, lead to that state ending up being in the Democratic column (as it did in 1992), but unless the message changed, this would lead to trading votes in the South which would put any Republican candidate in sight of victory anyway. Without a truly 'national strategy' the Democrats were finished – there was no viable patchwork quilt of groups which could get them over the line. Lastly, 'the Myth of the Congressional Bastion' had Democrats convincing themselves that even losing the White House was fine – as long as they controlled a Congress which could hamstring any Republican incumbent. Given the presence of congressional boll weevils, this was hardly a certainty. For Galston and Kamarck, however, 'eventually, the massive political realignment at the top of the ticket will affect races at the bottom of the ticket'. Ceding Pennsylvania Avenue would, slowly but surely, see the Democrats cede America all told – both in terms of values and, at some stage, Capitol and city council buildings across the nation.[56]

As expected, Kamarck recalls, 'that paper caused quite a stir within Democratic Party circles. There were people who took it as an attack on them, as it was, but Bill Clinton loved it'. Indeed, after reading the pamphlet, Clinton had 'a very spirited conversation' with Galston. It was clear 'we were agreeing emphatically, but two things were clear to me on the basis of that one conversation: First of all, Bill Clinton *had* it. And secondly, he *got it*'. As such, Galston recalls, 'it was also clear to me that this alternative political analysis we were developing was something that resonated with every fiber of his being in all of his political experiences. It was clear by early 1990 that Clinton was going to be *the* guy'.[57]

Though he had not run himself, the 1988 cycle had managed to bring Bill Clinton far more into the DLC orbit. Chuck Robb managed to get some time with the Arkansas Governor in August 1987 where he broached the subject of Clinton assuming the DLC chair in the future. Clinton was not opposed and began to talk to From regularly from this point on. The politics here was a relatively easy sell. Clinton had moved to the right after his bruising loss on raising car taxes in 1980. He agreed with EJ Dionne that the core political problem 'was the defection of white voters of moderate incomes from Democratic ranks'. And gradually, as David Osborne observed in a 1995 open letter to Clinton, 'you changed your politics, publicly apologizing for trying to "lead without listening." You exiled the young, inexperienced, liberal staffers who brought so many blunders ... [and] you focused your message on just priorities: education reform and economic development'. If, say, this meant going 'to war with the state's most powerful liberal interest group, the teachers' union, to get genuine education reform', then so be it. Clinton and the DLC were picking fights and, as a combined force, it looked like they just might win a few.[58]

A whole new world

At its New Orleans convention in March 1990, the DLC issued its declaration entitled 'A Democratic Agenda for the 1990s'. At the top of the list of signatories was Bill Clinton as the new DLC Chairman and below him, his predecessors, Sam Nunn, Chuck Robb and Dick Gephardt. The document declared that 'the fundamental mission of the Democratic Party is to *expand opportunity*, not government'. More broadly, it declared that the past was indeed a foreign country: 'the old isms and the old politics must give way to new realities. The political realities of the 1930s and 1960s cannot guide us in the 1990s'. In short, this meant ditching old notions of economic interventionism to curb inequality: 'we believe the promise of America is equal opportunity, not equal outcomes'. And 'the free market, regulated in the public interest, is the best engine of prosperity'.

The declaration was also full of Cold War triumphalism. With the tearing down of the Berlin Wall, America was 'at a turning point and so is the Democratic Party. Around the world, democracy has triumphed, thanks in no small part to the faith, resolve and sacrifices of the American people'. As such, the DLC leaders promoted the 'creation of an Emerging Democracy Initiative that would move quickly to export democratic capitalism and democratic values to emerging democracies'. As they noted, 'every dollar spent transforming major dictatorships into well-functioning democracies strengthens our strategic position in the world and helps create new markets for US products'. The centre left would henceforth not be neutral to the promotion of freedom abroad, but actively seek to promote it. This would clearly have significant long-term consequences, as we show in our final chapter.

In terms of the domestic agenda a pledge to rebuild America's 'Economic Security' was predicated on expanding workers' skills and their stake in the economy. The aim to spread 'individual ownership of economic assets, though employee stock ownership, savings incentives and other means' could almost have come from a Margaret Thatcher speech. The idea of 'an economic strategy that plans to America's enormous but neglected strengths – an unparalleled scientific base, a top-flight system of higher education, a skilled and flexible workforce' was arguably more Neil Kinnock. Certainly, the desire to expand 'international trade, opening markets to U.S. goods and fighting protectionism both in our market and abroad' was more a stab at the Democratic left and, somewhat, at soft-left Gephardtism.

To harness the best out of America's youth, the Democrats pledged to make use of market mechanisms in a number of ways. In terms of teaching, the idea was to 'give parents more choice in the schools they attend', as Clinton had done in Arkansas. When it came to particular at-risk categories, the idea was to 'involve business and community leaders in dealing with the social problems that plague America more than her competitors, including high rates of teen pregnancy, alcohol and drug abuse and high school dropouts'. The Democrats should seek to expand youth apprenticeships with opportunities that include 'extensive on-the-job training at local businesses'. In this way, government should act as a 'catalyst [to facilitate] schools and businesses ... working together to blend strong academic and technical training'.

The declaration renewed the DLC committee to national service. 'For a decade, the Republicans have undermined America's sense of national purpose by exalting self-interest over common interests', urged the statement. It was time to 'replace the politics of entitlement with a new politics of reciprocal responsibility'. As such, the DLC envisioned a series of 'national service opportunities springing up in communities across the country: a Citizens corps that offers educational and housing assistance to those who volunteer for public service; a Teacher Corps that would remove barriers to entering teaching; an Earth Corps to enlist youth in the battle to protect the environment, here and abroad and a Police Corps to combat crime by putting more police officers on the streets'.

New Orleans was about the changing of the guard, too. In his speech handing over Chairmanship of the DLC to Clinton, Sam Nunn quipped that 'one of the great virtues of turning this gavel over to Bill is he's accustomed to working for a very low salary'. Nunn also joked that he 'is the very first person in the political history of the United States to be identified as a "bright, young, rising star," in three different decades'. More seriously, he praised Clinton's achievements in public education in Arkansas, particularly those he had delivered after regaining the Governorship in 1982. Clinton could, after all, point to increases in reading and math scores that had increased by 40 per cent.[59]

Much of the press coverage for the event went to Pat Moynihan's proposal to cut payroll taxes (FICA) for middle Americans – more-or-less backed in the DLC declaration. This was to take place alongside 'financing the operations of government through progressive taxation ... so that Americans are taxed according to their ability to pay'. As the deficit ballooned under Reagan, the Republicans had made 'cynical use of the social security apparatus, raised from a regressive tax on labor, to mask the true scope of America's fiscal crisis'. From a $74 billion deficit in 1980, Reagan and Bush-era spending had ballooned to the level where there was a $220 billion gap between government spending and its receipts by

1990. As a result, the federal debt had quadrupled from $200 billion to $800 billion over the same period. This was a challenge but, at the same time, an emerging opportunity – what if the Democrats could outflank the Republicans as the party of fiscal responsibility? To do so required distance from the left and there was thus some amusement that Jesse Jackson had turned up in New Orleans to make 'his annual token appearance' and had 'congratulated [the DLC] on joining him in the mainstream of a party that wishes to cut defense spending, permit choice on abortion and let Latin America solve its own problems'. Clinton quickly disassociated himself from Jackson, pointing that 'both he and the Rev. Jackson are Baptists, a faith that permits its practitioners wide latitude in how they interpret its dogma'.[60]

Still, whatever the shifts in dogma, as the 1990s began what was clear was just how far from power the DLC perceived the party to be. Clinton told the press that 'I really think we'd better forget about '92 and work on what we stand for – people don't know what a Democrat is'. The future nominee even told reporters, 'what's the worst that can happen to us if we do well and [Bush] wins in '92. That's not the end of the world if things are going well'. The future, arguably, was consensual: 'if everything we used to be for has already been done and everything the Republicans used to be for has already been done, it is inevitable that for the fight of the future, both parties will (address) some of the same things'.[61] It was entirely reasonable to court such support, given the then stratospheric popularity of President Bush. When allied forces successfully liberated Kuwait from Saddam Hussein's Iraqi Army in February 1991, that particular electoral mountain grew even higher. The question was, a few better policies or not, just how on earth were the Democrats going to stop four Republican presidential victories in a row?

Notes

1 *Fortune*, 8 June 1987; *New York Times*, 31 August 1987.

2 *International Herald Tribune*, 7 January 1988.

3 *International Herald Tribune*, 7 January 1988.

4 Biden briefing notes, January 1988 and June 1989, ARC/CAC/KNNK/19/2/60.

5 Handwritten note on Joe Biden, undated but January 1988, ARC/CAC/KNNK 19/2/60.

6 Paul Richards (ed), *Tony Blair in His Own Words*, (London, Politico's Publishing, 2004), 4–27.

7   Radice 2/24; Gow to Thatcher, 12 August 1980, ARC/CAC/ THCR 2/6/2/74. See Blair's 1982 speech in Perth for the views he felt it politic to express back then.

8   Alliance Manifesto, 1983 and Mandelson and Liddle/34

9   COR/Liddle.

10 COR/Steel; Jackson and Hart speeches, ARC/LSE/STEEL/B/1/7/12.

11 18 July 1984 speech, ARC/LSE/STEEL/B/1/7/2.

12 *Guardian*, 23 July 1981 and Blackburn CLP, August 1981, ARC/PHM/MF/ M13/6.

13 COR/Liddle and Radice/82.

14 Siegel to Edmonds, 21 December 1996, ARC/CPL/FOIA 2006-0462-F.

15 COR/Kinnock.

16 'Thatcher Trip', undated, ARC/MHM/GEP/1343/8.

17 'Notes from the USA visit', July 1984, ARC/CAC/KNNK 2/1/24; Hopper to Hewitt, 15 January 1985, Hart to Kinnock, 9 May 1985; Mondale to Kinnock, 3 May 1985, ARC/CAC/KNNK 19/2/40.

18 Loiello to Kinnock, 1 November 1985, Kinnock to Jackson, 12 December 1985, ARC/CAC/KNNK 19/2/40.

19 *Guardian*, 10 May 1989.

20 Kinnock to Brown, 5 January 1989, ARC/CAC/KNNK 19/2/60.

21 COR/Kinnock.

22 COR/Balls.

23 Balls/245–46.

24 Hasan and Macintyre/80–88; COR/Smith.

25 Clinton/265; CNN, 27 July 2016.

26 From to Stamas, 25 October 1984, ARC/LOC/HDC/16/3.

27 From/50, 49.

28 From/52.

29 MCI/Galston.

30 *News Leader* (VA), 23 December 1982.

31 *Los Angeles Times*, 12 February 1983; *Baytown Sun*, 3 March 1983.

32 From/39; Open letter, 16 May 1983, ARC/LOC/HDC/16/1.

33 From/42; Long to Stamas, 22 February 1984, ARC/LOC/HDC/16/2.

34 *Democrat and Chronicle* (Rochester, NY), 1 March 1985.

35 *St Louis Post-Dispatch*, 17 February 1985; From/56.

36 From/59–60.

37 From/67–68.

38 From/69.

39 Westlake/423.

40 *Liverpool Echo,* 3 November, *Newcastle Journal,* 13 December 1988; COR/From.

41 Radice 1/172–73.

42 Radice 1/196, 197.

43 *Guardian,* 29 October 1987, 6 October 1988 and *Times,* 14 September 1987, 3 May 1988.

44 Galston and Kamarck/28; *Boston Globe,* 7 August 1989; *San Francisco Examiner,* 17 May 1989.

45 *San Francisco Examiner,* 17 May 1989.

46 American University speech, 25 September 1987, ARC/MHM/GEP/73/49.

47 'The Economy' draft in ARC/MHM/GEP/34/11.

48 Advert scripts in ARC/HOV/TED/34.

49 From/94; COR/Balls.

50 From/94, 88.

51 'Experienced leadership for America's Future', ARC/PRN/BAKER/138/4.

52 Nixon to Quayle, 18 August 1988, ARC/PRN/BAKER/138/6.

53 From/99; *Washington Post,* 7 October 1988.

54 COR/Balls.

55 MCI/Kamarck.

56 Galston and Kamarck/passim.

57 MCI/Galston.

58 Dionne/68; *Washington Post* magazine, 8 January 1995.

59 *Los Angeles Times,* 26 March 1990.

60 *Palm Beach Post* (FL), 28 March 1990.

61 *Tyrone Daily Herald* (PA), 29 March 1990.

4 OFFICE AND OPPOSITION

In late 1992, Tony Blair and Gordon Brown sat in the Café Carlyle on Madison Avenue, New York City. The two rising modernisers would often travel to the US 'from time to time, essentially just to get away and think'. Blair was always somewhat sceptical of the Carlyle – 'the mood was formal, the décor elegant, the ambience a little austere' – but later admitted that he 'grew to like it'. In any event, it was here that Blair and Brown took in Woody Allen and the Eddy Davis New Orleans Jazz Band playing their regular set. Discussing the perception that the British left was soft on criminals, Blair explained to his then close ally that 'we should of course stress social conditions and be radical in dealing with them, but we also had to be tough on crime itself'. Newly appointed as Shadow Home Secretary, Blair was still figuring out how to 'make this into a Labour issue by combining a traditional and a modern stance'. It was in moments like these that 'Gordon, certainly in those early days, would show a streak of genius'. 'You mean', began the Scot, "tough on crime, tough on the causes of crime?"' 'Yes!' exclaimed Blair, 'that's exactly what I mean'. As Woody played on, the Third Way took another step towards formulation. Shortly after returning to the UK Blair used the pithy line in a speech 'and really never looked back'.[1]

This was not the first international trip they had shared. During a long visit to Australia the previous year, encouraged by Neil Kinnock, Blair and Brown had met with Prime Minister Bob Hawke and his Treasurer Paul Keating. On the long flight out, Blair and Brown had placed a blank sheet of paper on their seats' tray and begun scribbling, 'from first principles, what a modern social democracy would look like'. As Brown recalled in his memoirs, the two decided 'we had to endorse markets, competition and the essential role of the private sector in achieving economic growth and that we also had to change from a tax-and-spend party that appeared willing to borrow, no matter the circumstances'. Similarly, as with the New Democrats in the US, 'both of us favoured promoting opportunity and felt that equality of opportunity was a goal that no one was yet delivering'. Certainly, the two friends were not without emerging differences. As Brown noted, 'I gave more emphasis to prosecuting a war on poverty and addressing inequalities of income and wealth'.[2] But their similarities ran far deeper – driven by their own conviction and their reading of Labour's performance in the 1980s.

Yet, by the time Blair and Brown were knocking back the drinks in New York, the prospect of power was distant indeed. In April 1992, Labour had suffered its fourth General Election defeat in a row, with neither the replacement of Margaret Thatcher with John Major, nor the mounting economic woes then facing Britain, enough to convince the electorate that a change was needed. It was time for reform within the party if they ever hoped to be able to change the country. Blair felt he and Brown 'had held back too much after the 1987 defeat, being too timid'.[3] They would not be making the same mistake again. The modernisers were on the march and were now in a position to really shape the agenda. They moved as one, were in contact on a daily basis and were now genuine friends.

Their New York discussion did not just point to what was wrong, however, but how to ape what was now clearly right. For there was now an exemplar – a vision of the future victory they might yet win. A few weeks earlier, after all, Bill Clinton had achieved the first presidential victory for the Democrats since 1976. This chapter therefore tells the story of a fateful period in the rise of the Third Way which began with Clinton announcing his candidacy for the presidency and ends with Blair and Brown once again heading to America in early January 1993 to meet the victorious transition team. It is the story of one election lost under Neil Kinnock in the UK and of Clinton's triumph in the US seven months later.

Prime Minister Kinnock?

'Although it's afternoon here . . . good evening, Mr Prime Minister!' said a jubilant Ted Kennedy to Neil Kinnock, on 9 April 1992.

'Ted,' replied a deflated Kinnock, 'it's not going to happen . . .'
'What? No, you've just got election night blues, it will all work out.'
'It won't Teddy', replied Kinnock, 'it just won't.'

To be fair to Kennedy, many would have made the same assumption at different points during the 1992 British election cycle. After all, in the first major opinion poll of 1992 it looked like Labour supporters had much to be excited about. In their data gathering of 7–8 January, pollsters NOP reported that Kinnock's party held a five-point lead (45–40) over John Major's Conservatives. It was not yet time to start measuring the red curtains for Downing Street, but Labour could rightly be bullish. One such optimist was the actor, writer and long-time party supporter Stephen Fry. In November 1991 the future *QI* host had written to Kinnock, jovially noting that, 'looking ahead to your second premiership, I am seriously considering the possibility that you may well have me behind you on the government benches in 1995/6 and giving your Whips headaches'. 'When', he joked, 'should I start nursing [the constituency of] West Norfolk?'[4]

Fry was not alone. Far from a world of Clinton teaching Blair the ropes, in 1991 and early 1992 it looked like it would be Kinnock dealing with Bush, or, if all went well, the Welshman teaching a Cuomo or a Gore how to govern from the centre-left. Kinnock had even been invited by Dick Gephardt to address the DLC in 1990, to teach the New Democrats how to achieve the kind of 12- and 15-point leads he was then looking at. 'Well, first', joked Kinnock, 'you've got to get Margaret Thatcher as your president!' But, after such levity, they had a serious conversation led by Gephardt where Kinnock outlined how he had carved out what looked like an inevitable path to government. After alighting on the success of Labour's late 1980s policy review, Kinnock told his audience that 'what you will have to do is what you won't do: elect a leader of the Democrats to be there between elections and that's not in the nature of American politics'. In general, this was clearly true, though the very nature of the DLC chairmanship was at least a nod in this direction: a moderate Leader of the Opposition equivalent who it was intended could enjoy a boosted internal-party profile.

But in the first few weeks of 1992, Labour's expected vote share began to vanish. They were at 42 points with ICM in mid-January, 38.5 with Gallup at the end of February and 38 with Harris towards the end of March. There were more positive figures elsewhere and the polling picture was inconsistent, but no major pollster put them within two points of the January NOP figure at any stage until polling day. In April the electorate delivered their verdict at the ballot box: 42.8 to 35.2 in favour of the Conservatives and a fourth term in office for the Tories, albeit with a reduced majority. After his initial *faux pas*, Ted Kennedy would go on to console Kinnock over the phone as best he could, telling the Welsh leader that he 'was so sorry and I fear for your country'.

So, what had changed? Certainly, the polling numbers but not necessarily the underlying picture. Crucially, the day before NOP compiled the January 1992 data which looked so positive for Kinnock, the Conservatives had unveiled a famous election poster, warning voters of 'Labour's Tax Bombshell'. This involved some fairly simplistic calculations which took Labour's extra spending commitments of £35 billion a year, subtracted their existing pledges to raise £10 billion through additional taxation (including the controversial proposal to raise workers' national insurance) and suggested that, to fund the balance, Neil Kinnock was hiding further tax rises totalling £1,250 from each household. This message would take a while to become embedded but would begin to show as polling day drew nearer. The week before the election a much-publicised 'Shadow Budget' by John Smith attempted to plug the hole in Labour's finances, but it only confirmed that with national insurance (the UK equivalent of FICA) rises kicking in at £21,500 and with a new top rate of tax at 50p in the pound for those earning £40,000 a year or more, Labour was still the high-tax party. They were, in short, same old Labour.

For its part, the Labour leadership had clung, forlornly, to the hope that this election would be different and that the electorate could finally be persuaded to pay for better public services. In the 26 February 1992 Shadow Cabinet gathering Deputy Leader Roy Hattersley said 'that the nation would not be fooled again by *pre-election tax cutting*'. Shadow Health Secretary Robin Cook had likewise noted that 'people were all too well aware of the needs of the NHS' and, by implication, the need to give it extra funds. Gordon Brown had claimed 'that the deterioration in our industrial prospects was all too manifest' and that the voters, again, would take the necessary action to address years of under-investment by kicking the Tories out. To be fair to Brown, not only were the economic problems facing Labour voting heartlands then very real, the Scot also had to tow the party's general economic line since, as Shadow Secretary for Trade and Industry, he could not allow any difference between himself and John Smith to be visible. Still, as Jack Straw noted, 1992 showed that there was a growing 'nuance of difference' in the politics of Gordon Brown and Tony Blair. Whereas, for example, Brown favoured John Smith's plans for increasing state spending on pensioners and parents, his only concern was 'practical and tactical: how to pay for them and how and when to announce and implement them'. However, 'while Tony saw welfare increases as a commendable long-term goal, he felt that Labour's priority must be to demonstrate to middle-class voters and to our traditional working-class supporters who *aspired* to be middle class, that we would not raise their taxes'. As one post-election study noted, many southern English voters had found Labour's proposed new £21,500 national insurance threshold 'too close for comfort' – a figure that though they did not *yet* earn they could 'aspire' towards. With the average salary for UK thirtysomethings then around £15,000, this was not inconceivable. In any case, it seems 'no-one trusted Labour on spending'.[5]

One person who sensed this was Bob Shrum. Shrum had been brought in by Philip Gould to help with the 1992 campaign but, due to fears about potentially hostile newspaper coverage, he had to be kept hidden, so he worked from a London hotel. As Gordon Brown later wrote, 'party officials were afraid that the presence of an American would provoke a media storm about a foreign takeover. It was absurd; in 1997, 2001 and beyond, Americans including Bob were sitting in the middle of our election war room. It simply wasn't an issue'. Indeed, the limited work George Stephanopoulos would do on Labour's 1997 campaign would be on the front page of the *Guardian* – a sign of Labour's seriousness, not some negative Americanisation of British politics. Back in 1992, however, rather than give the right a chance of hitting Labour on tax rises, Brown would note that 'Bob's view, like mine, was that day after day we should be hammering on the Tories' economic record'. For Brown it was time to scrap 'all previous unfunded commitments and all tax increases'. The discrepancy with Straw's view of Brown as a fundamental 'tax and spender' remains difficult to unpack. What is certain, however, is that even with Kinnock sympathetic, John Smith could not be budged.[6]

The other issue was leadership. Much was talked in retrospect about an overly triumphalist – and certainly very American style – election rally Labour held in Sheffield in the week before the 1992 election. Whilst it was a little 'un-British' to see Neil Kinnock arrive by helicopter to a packed arena, this spectacle did not lose his party the election. Instead, it was the already ingrained notion that Neil Kinnock, for all his considerable merit, just wasn't the right man to lead the country – and this could be spotted in opinion polls for a long time. Sheffield should be taken not as a sign that Labour thought they had the election in the bag, but that they had to try anything they could to present Kinnock as Prime Ministerial (even if the note they eventually hit was more 'presidential'). Indeed, from the time John Major became Conservative leader in November 1990, his personal approval ratings were always higher than Kinnock's. On IPSOS-Mori's scale, Thatcher had left office with a −46 approval rating. Major's approval rating dipped from an initial honeymoon period, but he still went into the 1992 General Election on +4. Kinnock lost his positive approval rating the moment Major took office and went into the election on −20. As one Labour activist put it, 'people thought that there had already been a change of government – from Thatcher to Major – and so Major escaped being tarred with the recession or poll tax brush'.[7]

Though Labour won 3 million more votes in 1992 than they did in 1987, Kinnock had failed to convert sufficient voters in the south of England where the party remained second best to the Tories. The moderate Labour MP Giles Radice set out to find out why, leading to his writing a famous *Fabian Society* pamphlet on Labour's *Southern Discomfort*. Travelling around five marginal seats in the broad London periphery – Gravesham, Harlow, Luton South, Slough and Stevenage – Radice interviewed Labour activists, losing candidates and local journalists. In these areas, Radice noted, 'four out of five had Labour councils. There were obvious signs of recession . . . [and] if the constituencies had been in the North, one would have expected most of them to be certain Labour gains'. Yet Labour still suffered from 'a crippling weakness in Southern England' which meant, even including its urban London heartland, the party only held 45 seats out of a possible 261. Stripping out the capital, Labour had 10 seats out of a possible 177. As Radice bluntly put it, 'Labour cannot win without doing better in the South'.[8]

This meant shaking a series of assumptions that were deeply imbedded within the British left. Whilst some voters liked Labour's views on health and education, almost half those Radice talked to 'could not think of anything positive to say' about the party. When it came to the negatives the answers flowed much easier: 'taxation, strikes and unions, the past' and the fact it remained 'old fashioned' and 'weak'. The key point about wavering southern voters who had not voted Labour was 'that they consider themselves to be upwardly mobile . . . They are Britain's "aspirants."' For a party traditionally predicated on lifting people out of their malaise this was a difficult shift: the voters perceived themselves to have already done so or be in the process of doing it *on their own*. On a policy level, this shift also meant acknowledging that elements of Thatcherism had proven wildly popular. As Radice argued, 'the majority of [the waverers] own their homes, many through "Right to Buy" schemes. Home ownership is a potent symbol of their aspirations and achievements'. And, 'crucially, many no longer consider themselves to be "working class"' since 'they believe that "class" no longer has much relevance to their own lives. They believe that they have "got on" by their own efforts and not with the aid of a group or class'. Indeed, the concept of the 'working class' represented a dim and distant past from which they had escaped, not some glorious vanguard or future Valhalla. Until Labour could show that they accepted 'the market economy has been remarkably successful in bringing prosperity and that state ownership is ineffective', they were in trouble. If they could not show that they stood 'for the freedom of the individual' rather than being 'too identified with groups' then it was finished. And the ready-made proof of this, by the time Radice set to work, was President William Jefferson Clinton.[9]

Clinton takes the nomination

It was only at 5am on a Monday morning in March 1991 that Al From became aware that Clinton was seriously considering a tilt at the Presidency. Up to late 1990, Clinton's public position was that he hoped that 'one or more people' would espouse the general DLC line in the 1992 primaries. He had then retreated to Arkansas until March 1991 to see out the current state legislative session, whilst From travelled the country setting up new DLC chapters in states such as Oregon, Montana, Wyoming and Colorado. The *Washington Post's* David Broder was certainly noting that the DLC would likely be represented by Lloyd Bentsen, Al Gore and Dick Gephardt in the primaries next year, but there was no mention of Clinton. The field was clearly wide open – with some early polling, albeit implausibly, indicating that Jesse Jackson (22%), Mario Cuomo (17%) and a returning Jimmy Carter (13%) led the way in June 1990. The DLC's Gore (7%) and Gephardt (10%) trailed significantly behind. For British observers, the field was similarly unpredictable. In a late 1990 briefing note, Neil Kinnock was told by his staffers that 'we have no idea at the moment what stand on which issues will be taken by the next Democratic candidate. Sam Nunn will take a very conservative position on just about everything. Gephardt, now majority leader of the House, would push a protectionist stance again. Biden would be more progressive (but is very unlikely to run). Cuomo will not run'. Clinton, again, was not even mentioned.[10]

On 10 March 1991, the man himself turned to Al From whilst both were sat in the lobby of the Radisson Hotel in Southfield, Detroit. They had been in town to spread the DLC gospel to the northern industrial areas that had left the Democrats for Reagan. As both men waited for a car to take Clinton to the airport for an early flight back to Little Rock, the Governor said, 'I've been thinking that maybe I ought to make a run in 1992'. He continued, 'that way we could get our ideas out there and even if I lost but I ran a respectable race, people would be more receptive to our ideas the next time'.[11] Nominally, there was the problem of Clinton promising to serve a full term as Arkansas Governor (the next election was not due to take place until 1994) but such difficulties could be got around. Though Clinton maintained public denials of a run into the early summer, his mind had more or less been made up by the Spring of 1991. It was worth a shot.

A bigger issue was the ongoing DLC versus DNC row and Clinton's public differences with DNC chair Ron Brown. In April 1991 Clinton gave a lengthy interview to USA Today, where he was quoted as saying 'I'd like [the DLC] to be what people think of when they think of the Democratic National Committee'. In fact, it was a misquote – Clinton had said 'Democratic national party' rather than directly refer to the DNC – but the matter had clearly annoyed Brown. When asked by reporters what he made of Clinton's supposed comments, Brown told them that the Democrats would 'win the White House by being a unified party'. 'Maybe the DLC wants to come up with a candidate', he added with a barely concealed smirk. 'Too bad it can't be Bill Clinton since he's already announced to the people of Arkansas that he can't be a candidate.'[12]

To Al From, however, the Democrats needed new voters who had been put off by perceptions the party couldn't be trusted on defence or the economy. And, 'if changing this perception meant an intraparty fight, so be it'. Thus, for the upcoming DLC conference to be held in May in Cleveland, left-wing figures contemplating running next time round like Jesse Jackson and George McGovern were refused the opportunity of making major speeches. Clinton himself abhorred the breach with Jackson, slamming down the phone on From soon after picking it up: 'I'm so damn mad at you that I can't talk to you today'. But Clinton needed

From, respected him deeply and the row was only temporary. In Cleveland, Clinton would go on to give his own speech which broadened his platform in a series of detailed ways. Yet his address would come to be defined by the words that adorned the cover of the printed version the DLC later put out. The three words Clinton had handpicked for the design – opportunity, responsibility and community – would soon reshape global politics from DC to Berlin.

Over the next few weeks the gap between the DLCers and DNCers would only grow. Mario Cuomo denounced the 'implicit position that we have something to apologize for and, now, we have to move to the middle'. In response Clinton 'didn't say we have to apologize for anything, but did say that it is a fact that we've been getting beat … People aren't buying what we're selling'.[13] As Clinton traversed the country giving such media interviews and meeting power brokers like Chicago Mayor Richard Daley, it was becoming ever more apparent that he was running. On 15 August, Clinton announced both his resignation as chairman of the DLC and the formation of his exploratory committee to consider a presidential bid in 1992. On 3 October 1991, in front of the Old State House in Little Rock, Bill Clinton formally announced his candidacy and declared he would deliver a 'New Covenant' to America.

That at least was Clinton's path to deciding to run. He was a skilled public figure, youthful but with an extensive record as a Governor, who could appeal to the American heartland in a way many of his fellow challengers would have found more difficult. Yet Clinton was also a calculating politician. He did not want to run and lose, even if he was young enough to run again in 1996. And, for all his considerable talent, his campaign in 1992 was undeniably helped by events far beyond the reach of a small state Governor. Just as the 2003 invasion of Iraq would come to tarnish the Third Way in the minds of many, conversely it would be the 1991 war against Saddam that would indirectly launch it to power. Put simply, the Gulf War had one very important consequence: it cleared the way for Bill Clinton to be the DLC candidate for the Democratic nomination in 1992.

This thinning of the field occurred on several fronts. For one, during late 1990, Georgia Senator Sam Nunn had constantly been in the headlines through his high-profile role in holding President Bush to account for the diplomatic strategy that proceeded the Gulf War. It was widely expected he would run and could appeal to the same southern, conservative democratic circles which favoured Clinton. On 4 December

1990, Bruce Reed sent Al From a memo claiming that 'there are many different routes to the nomination, but one of the most compelling strategies for 1992 is one that has never been tried: two like-minded candidates running from the start as a ticket'.[14] In this formation the Vice President was to be Bill Clinton, operating as second in command in the administration of President Sam Nunn.

Reed's arguments were strong. As he put it, 'nobody can deliver a message of peace through strength as well as Sam Nunn, nobody delivers a message of getting America moving again better than Bill Clinton'. Combining the most experienced Democratic Governor with the most trusted Democrat in Washington seemed a slam dunk. From was therefore tasked with running the idea by Bill Clinton over a breakfast in DC. Handing a copy of Reed's memo over to the Governor, Clinton gave a semi-smile before saying he broadly liked it. As From noted, 'I'm sure he was thinking that a Clinton-Nunn ticket would be better'.[15]

But events were soon to turn. In early January 1991, Nunn would lead the opposition to putting American boots on the ground against Saddam Hussein in Kuwait. On 12 January, however, the resolution authorising US military action passed the Senate (Al Gore notably voting in favour) and on 17 January, Operation Desert Storm began. Nunn was soon pilloried by Republicans claiming his opposition to the conflict was soft liberal pre-election posturing at best and downright unpatriotic at worst. In his home state, a sign went up on a Georgia highway calling the Senator 'Saddam's Best Friend'. By 21 January, Nunn was calling Al From saying that he was willing to do any DLC events already scheduled, but that he was not to schedule any more. As From noted, 'I could tell from his voice that he had lost his stomach for politicking'. By the end of January 1991, it was 'clear that if there was a DLC candidate in 1992 – and it was far from a sure thing – it would be Clinton'.[16]

The Republican Congressman Jim Leach remembers similar. As he recalls, 'Clinton got the nomination because of a single vote taken by other Democrats in the U.S. Senate'. This event not only eliminated Nunn but also the former NBA star and New Jersey Senator Bill Bradley. It remains Leach's view 'that Bill [Bradley], who is one of my several closest political friends, chose not to run for president in 1992 because like all the other potential nominees from the U.S. Senate he had voted against authorizing force in support of President Bush's decisive actions in the Gulf War'. Once the conflict appeared to be progressing smoothly for Bush, the calculation amongst Democratic opponents of US action 'was that this vote would have been a severe liability against an incumbent who successfully managed a significant military action'. For Leach, 'Clinton got the nomination based on charm, being southern and not having a liberal voting record. Clinton's statements during and before the campaign were on both sides of the Iraq War vote' and this creative ambiguity, against his more committed Democratic opponents, was sufficient.[17]

Bob Kerrey, the former Governor of Nebraska, was another such example. Kerrey, who had won the Medal of Honor during the Vietnam conflict, had one potentially attractive contrast with Clinton, who had sought to avoid his own service, off the bat. Kerrey was a passionate advocate of health care reform and, having lost part of a leg during combat, had a story that could go along with it. Elected to the Senate in 1988, Kerrey retained ambivalent feelings about running for office and becoming president was never the 'be-all and end-all' for the likeable Nebraskan. There was nothing dishonourable about such a view, but it was perhaps a positive feature of the primary system that it weeded out such figures. In the event, like so many of his Senate colleagues, voting against the Gulf War would harm even this former war veteran when it came to the primaries.

If Iraq took out many current occupants of the Senate, it still left one former Senator, Massachusetts' Paul Tsongas, as a key rival. Tsongas had been forced to leave the Senate in 1985 due to the effects of non-Hodgkins lymphoma (his seat being taken by John Kerry) but had received a clean bill of health by 1991. His campaign stood economically to the right of Clinton's and Tsongas made much of Clinton's middle-class tax cuts supposedly exploding the federal deficit. Whilst Tsongas declared 'I'm not Santa Claus', he accused Clinton of saying 'whatever people wanted to hear'. In the end it would take the Governor of Georgia, Zell Miller, an idiosyncratic Democrat later to endorse George W Bush in 2004, to turn these arguments on their head. 'Bill Clinton is too gracious to say this', Miller told the press, 'but it's time to tell the truth'. Tsongas' programme 'sounded a lot like the trickle-down economics of the 1980s'. In this light, the idea that Clinton was performing some form of small-state hijack of the Democratic Party always had its limitations.[18]

The field, then, was not a vintage crop, but problems soon emerged. As Reuters reported, Clinton was forced to 'deny allegations that he carried on a torrid 12-year old long extramarital affair with a nightclub singer, Gennifer Flowers'. In truth, such denials were always caveated. Clinton initially rejected claims about the Flowers affair, but when asked if he had ever had an affair, his response became 'I wouldn't tell you if I did'. Clinton's womanising was well known and his closest aides were not afraid to raise the issue with him. Susan Thomases, long-time friend of both Hillary and Bill, put the thing particularly dramatically. Cornering the Governor on the campaign trail, she told him that 'you're stupid enough to blow this whole presidential thing over your dick. And if that turns out to be true, buddy, I'm going home and I'm taking people with me'. Elaine Kamarck remembers that 'the minute Gennifer Flowers appeared, we said, "Oh, shit." We had no doubt that it was true, but what dawned on us then, too late, was that she had no stake in his Presidency. Gennifer Flowers . . . had no desire to be the Assistant Secretary of State for Oceans and Treaties, right? The other women he had been linked with over the years had every incentive to be part of the team'.[19]

Still, the issue had to be managed. James Carville, Political Strategist during the Clinton campaign, recalls that 'December [1991] went fine. If you remember, [Mario] Cuomo was thinking about running. He decided that he wasn't going to run and we . . . were picking up pretty good in the polls. Then, in January, as we say in the trade, we got a little *incoming*. This was the Flowers' story'. George Stephanopoulos, Deputy Campaign Manager, remembers 'clearly watching Clinton read the *Star* story up in the top-floor suite of the Holiday Inn. He was basically reading through the whole story, almost giving a running narration as he was going through it, pointing out all the things that he could prove were not true, you know? And in fact, he got more excited as he found the things that he could hit'. During a confessional *60 Minutes* interview, 34 million Americans would tune in to hear his and Hillary's public response. As Bill told the nation: 'You know, I have acknowledged wrongdoing. I have acknowledged causing pain in my marriage. I have said things to you tonight and to the American people from the beginning that no American politician ever has. I think most Americans who are watching this tonight, they'll know what we're saying. They'll get it'. After the interview and Hillary's strong performance alongside her husband, Dee Dee Myers (later Clinton's Press Secretary) remarked that 'there was a sense that he was in debt to her and he was obliged to take seriously her advice'. Focus groups indicated that the campaign could ride out the Gennifer Flowers story and they resolved to continue into New Hampshire.

But further issues were not far off. In early February 1992, the *Wall Street Journal* reported an affidavit made public by Colonel Eugene

Holmes who, in the late 1960s and early 1970s, had run the University of Arkansas' Reserve Officers Training Corps programme. According to Holmes, Clinton had applied to the University's officer training course in the summer of 1969 whilst having no intention of either attending the institution or its ROTC – he simply wanted to use his nominal enlistment in the programme to avoid active service overseas. In a letter to Holmes in December 1969 retrospectively explaining his actions, Clinton had been starkly critical of the conflict and his political enemies began to circle. There was no criminal charge here (Jimmy Carter having pardoned all 'draft dodgers' on his second day in office) but it did raise questions of character. Against a war veteran in George HW Bush this would be less than ideal and Clinton's polling numbers dropped a dramatic 12 points.

Clinton retreated to Arkansas with a cold as the draft story took off. Less than a week before the New Hampshire primary – the first major test of the campaign, this was potential disaster territory. What saved him was his own youthful eloquence, his campaign staff's ambition and the attitudes of ordinary voters. As the story broke, senior aides in New Hampshire pored over the letter Clinton had sent to Holmes. Stan Greenberg remarked that 'this is one impressive letter. This is not as problematic – there's something revealed here that is very interesting'. James Carville agreed. Although the young Clinton had referred to Holmes 'saving me from the draft', this was not a unique sentiment. Whilst Clinton felt that 'the draft was justified in World War II because the life of the people collectively was at stake . . . Vietnam is no such case'. On a more philosophical level, he had argued that 'no government really rooted in limited, parliamentary democracy should have the power to make its citizens fight and kill and die in a war they may oppose'. This was impressive stuff from a 23-year-old. The campaign therefore elected to go on the attack – they went on *Nightline* and had the letter read out in full. They then booked out blocks of time on local television and had Clinton sit down with undecided voters and have them throw any questions they wished at him. As media consultant Frank Greer remembers, 'in the first thirty minutes not one person asked about Gennifer Flowers. Not one person asked about the draft'. 'All of a sudden', Greer recalls, 'I think even the national press corps said, "We may be a little carried away on this"'.[20]

Even so, Clinton was now clearly going to lose in New Hampshire. Given he had been ahead in the polls a month earlier (*The Boston Globe* had it at 29%–17%, Clinton over Tsongas in January) the question was how to deal with it and this took some brash showmanship. Clinton had campaigned hard in the final days and no one could accuse him of ducking the state. But Greenberg remembers that still 'none of us thought we could win' and '[we] all thought we were dead'. A good second was possible, however, so the team elected to get ahead of the story. Devising a scenario known as the 'Comeback Kid', the Clinton campaign elected to have their candidate give a speech as soon as the first results came in. 'As soon as we had anything, we'd go out, because we wanted to be out there before anybody else so we could characterize the results'. This effective media management, together with the growing perception that, whatever his personal flaws, Clinton was clearly a tough political cookie, kept the show on the road. Clinton ate a 33–25 per cent loss to Tsongas in New Hampshire but was still in the hunt. At this stage, British bookmakers had him at an 8/1 shot to win the presidency, but the odds would soon narrow.[21]

He had also gained the support, by hook or by crook, of Yvette Cooper – later Labour MP and Cabinet Minister under Gordon Brown. Cooper was in her early twenties and, like her future husband Ed Balls, very interested in the American political process. As she recalls, 'it was the New Hampshire primary. The shameful thing to admit is that my first contact with the Clinton campaign, as opposed to any of the other campaigns, was down to this: I didn't know a huge amount about any of the candidates, but the other campaign buses were going at eight in the morning and the Clinton bus went at nine!' She would, however, become a firm supporter, relocating to Little Rock and wearing a badge, which she still keeps, saying 'I'm backing Hillary's husband'. Cooper would live off baked potatoes, sweetcorn and bananas from a local farm and served as a researcher on the campaign's crime and health policies.[22]

Over the next month Clinton duked it out with Tsongas, Kerrey and Jerry Brown, the then former Governor of California. After some shadow boxing (Clinton taking Georgia but falling well behind in states like Maine and Utah), when the primaries began to take in big southern states on 7 and 10 March Clinton pulled significantly ahead, winning South Carolina on the former and Louisiana, Missouri, Mississippi, Oklahoma and Texas on the latter. With Clinton on 10 states to Tsongas' six and Brown's three (Bob Kerrey having dropped out in early March), the campaign then swung back north to Illinois and Michigan to take in the very type of 'Reagan Democrats' that Clinton claimed the party had lost and that only he could win back.

In the end, he won the two rust belt states handsomely, polling at over 50 per cent in both and winning the symbolically important Macomb County which Stan Greenberg had visited in the 1980s. Clinton had acknowledged that the Democratic Party 'didn't do right by middle America for a while' but that he now 'had a program that will restore the middle class'. This chimed with a Michigan electorate which polling showed was 'dominated by a feeling that the middle class is being squeezed to pay for the rich'. As such, Clinton's bargain, to borrow Greenberg's verdict, 'offered those white disaffected voters [a] people-centered investment approach' but only if they were willing 'to talk to your brothers and sisters of different races'. Likewise, in a speech to the predominantly black Pleasant Grove Baptist Church in Detroit, Clinton implored his audience to look north to Macomb because it was 'basically full of people who did right and were done wrong, just like the rest of us'. For the last three presidential elections, Clinton told both black and white voters, Americans had 'rewarded Ronald Reagan and George Bush and [in response] they have punished you'. Instead, he would empower millions with the skills and training to arm them in the economy of tomorrow, not give away tax cuts to the wealthiest elements of society. When Republican strategists tried to tell Michigan voters that Clinton believed 'massive taxes are the key to economic growth', this bumped up against his general message of self-reliance that voters had been buying for months. Local Democratic figures had been talking up 'the ugly mood' voters had been in for months and the need for a viable 'recovery package'. It was time for a change and Clinton was the man to deliver it.[23]

But, prior to these northern primaries and faced with the prospect of imminent elimination from the contest, Jerry Brown went hard on Clinton in a Chicago debate. Claiming Clinton had funneled business to Hillary's law firm and granted preferential treatment to a poultry company her firm had represented, Brown asserted that the Arkansas Governor had 'a big electability problem'. Clinton was able to bat away the charges and later admitted he had done so with such gusto because he 'felt guilty that Hillary had been forced to defend me so much' over Gennifer Flowers. This was certainly fair enough, but Hillary was not without her problems for the campaign. When questioned months earlier about her having continued her legal practice after marriage, she remarked that 'I could have stayed home and baked cookies and had teas, but what I decided to do was to fulfill my profession, which I entered before my husband was in public life'. Some took this as an upper mid-west liberal being disparaging to stay-at-home mothers. Hillary's more left-leaning views than her husband were generally tricky to manage and Republicans would make much play out of claims that 'Hillary believes that twelve-year-olds should have the right to sue their parents'. In the end, however, attacking the future First Lady did little for either Jerry Brown in Illinois and Michigan or, later, Bush nationwide.[24]

More seriously, Clinton's record in Arkansas was inevitably scrutinised as the campaign heated up. As governor, as we discuss later, his education record involved a three-part plan: new standards in all school districts, a competency test for teachers and a 1 per cent increase in the state sales tax to pay for them. Having faced down the teaching union and Arkansas legislators alike to achieve these reforms, 'the resulting victory established a national reputation for Clinton as a policy leader and its outcomes were clear'. For the first time, Arkansas reached the national average in its percentage of high school students going on to college – though levels of teenage pregnancy indicated more remained to do across the board. For the *Los Angeles Times*, Clinton's Governorship also indicated that he was 'addicted to corporate tax breaks to attract new jobs and hobbled by a state constitution that requires a three-fourth vote to raise any tax other than the sales tax'. As such, Clinton had repeatedly turned to that source to raise funds for new programmes, 'leaving Arkansas with one of the most regressive state tax systems'. Yet, generally, the system had worked. The number of people on welfare had come down fairly dramatically under Clinton – from considerably above the national average in 1980 to slightly below it by 1992. This was aided by Arkansas having experienced faster economic growth than any state in the region. Clinton himself saw his record as one of empowerment. As he remarked in late 1991, 'that's what we've tried to do in Arkansas – balance our budget every year, improving services and treating taxpayers like our customers and our bosses, giving them more choices in public schools, child care centers and services for the elderly'.[25] This was a platform that was eminently defendable and the Governor was a confident salesman.

The stress of winning the nomination did, however, take a temporary toll. Clinton was traversing America, seeing a lot of late nights, constantly worried that some new scandal would break and, consequently, not eating well. From the first caucus in Iowa to winning Pennsylvania on 28 April the rigors of the campaign and Clinton's poor diet, saw him put on about 30 pounds (over two stone) in weight. Making a solemn vow to

Hillary to eat right, the future First Lady told him he could eat a varied enough diet 'if you'd just be careful about the *amount*'. The issue was that, although not a big drinker, Clinton liked everything when it came to food – as the restaurant community of Little Rock already knew. For one, Juanita's proprietor Mark Abernathy told the *New York Times* that 'Bill's partial to chicken enchiladas'. Elsewhere, when going to Sims Bar-B-Que 'every chance he gets', Clinton's regular order was 'sliced pork barbecue, baked beans and slaw, sliced beef, potato salad and sweet potato pie'. At Does Eat Place it was usually a 'greasy cheeseburger or a two-pound steak'.[26] It took a lot of effort to shift twenty of the excess pounds by the General Election in November. At least, however, it looked likely he would get that shot.

The British view of Clinton through all this was interesting. Jonathan Powell would later be recruited to work for Tony Blair, but in 1992 he was still at the British Embassy in Washington DC where he 'travelled the campaign trail, following Clinton and [was] filing dispatches predicting his success that were dismissed as romantic nonsense at Whitehall'.[27] Since the Second World War, the British Embassy had maintained a position whereby one of their number would follow the candidate of the opposition party for president – a policy pursued by surprisingly few other nations, Japan being the major exception. Various high-profile figures had performed this function from Isaiah Berlin in the 1940s to Sherard Cowper Coles trailing Michael Dukakis in 1988. Powell had joined the Embassy in 1991 and immediately latched on to the Democratic candidates. 'At that stage', he recalls, 'no-one thought the Democrats were going to win'.

Powell took an interest in Clinton's campaign 'because he had been at my college at Oxford and I thereby acquired a completely undeserved reputation for being a political genius for predicting he would win in the early days'. The Englishman met with the other candidates and did occasionally visit Harkin, Tsongas and Kerrey on the stump, but he was always keen on the university connection with the Arkansas Governor. In July 1991, Powell had accompanied Clinton during his first public visit to New Hampshire, which involved stopping at a lot of fast-food restaurants – 'at that stage Clinton was very much into McDonalds'. Back then, it was all very informal and Clinton made time for some chats with Powell, but as the operation became more professional, the British diplomat sat at the back of the campaign plane with the assorted journalists. It was certainly a useful connection to have made.

However, the bigger diplomatic headache, far away from Powell, was triggered by the Republicans. With a month to go in the presidential race, Bush's staff asked John Major's Conservative administration to look into Clinton's student activities in England and whether there was any evidence he had applied for British citizenship to avoid the draft in Vietnam. British connections of Clinton were interviewed; immigration records checked. Nothing came up. As Clinton later wrote, 'it just showed how desperate the Bush people were to hang on to power and how little they had to offer to offer for America's future'. Powell recalls one long-term legacy – when Tony Blair looked like he was set to become Britain's new Prime Minister, 'Clinton went out of his way to help, which was not great for John Major. Clinton always claimed he wasn't seeking revenge for the Tory investigations of 1992, but there's a strong argument that he was'.[28]

There was a broader British political relevance to Clinton, however. Neil Kinnock had, after all, long been seeking to orientate Labour in a generally more transnational direction. Borrowing ideas and exchanging views with kindred spirits abroad was both a useful way of looking statesmanlike and provided some ammunition for his battles within the party. This meant cooperation with US Democrats, but it also meant, as noted, changing the party symbol from the Red Flag to the more European social democratic red rose and looking to Bob Hawke and Paul Keating's Australian Labor Party. Indeed, for Geoff Mulgan, who would work for both Blair and Brown, 'in some ways Australian Labor had had more influence and was a more similar party, than the US Democrats. Under Hawke and Keating it had had a complete overhaul in policy and outlook and had won successive elections [from 1983 to 1993]'. But the major difference was that 'the Clintonites and DLCers basically thought they were in a conservative country – and this was different from the Australian context. In this regard, Labour modernisers felt the same as their US equivalents – that the conservatives were the natural party of government and politics was to some degree played on their terms'.[29] Clinton understood this too and it lent his and Blair's future relationship a key building block.

Beating Bush

Although an all-round better candidate and certainly one who challenged rather than confirmed what voters thought progressives were about,

Clinton had a distinct advantage over Kinnock in 1992. As Jim Leach remembers, Clinton 'won the election because despite the country respecting Bush for his international leadership, a key voting block was angered at his never raise taxes pledge ("read my lips", his oft quoted statement from the 1988 election) – a pledge that he broke'.[30] Combined with the shift the DLC had already made, this neutralised the charge that a Democratic candidate would just be about big government and, therefore, big tax. That said, had Bush had the ability to call a snap election earlier, as in the British system, he may well have won re-election convincingly.

In March 1991, as American forces began arriving home after driving Saddam Hussein out of Kuwait, their beaming Commander-in-Chief saw his approval rating hit an incredible 89 per cent. But Bush, who always enjoyed being president more than running for office (arguably the reverse of Clinton), soon made a strategic mistake. As he delayed and delayed formally beginning his campaign for re-election, the Republican right soon sought to fill this vacuum. On 10 December 1991, Pat Buchanan, Ronald Reagan's former Chief of Staff, announced his candidacy for the presidency. Rather than having a free run, Bush would have to enter his own set of primaries. Buchanan was no shrinking violet and his campaign adverts went big on Bush's broken tax promise. Even if Buchanan was unsuccessful, his anti-Bush rhetoric in the primaries helped insulate Clinton from charges that he would be another same old tax-and-spend Democrat when it came to the General Election.

Buchanan's social conservatism, even when eventually endorsing Bush at the RNC in August 1992, would also help paint the Republicans as simultaneously divided and to the right of respectable America. Some of his lines at the RNC were quite witty: 'Bill Clinton's foreign policy experience is pretty much confined to having breakfast at the international house of pancakes', but others were deeply controversial. He railed against the 'radical feminism' of the Democrats: 'Abortion on demand. A litmus test for the Supreme Court. Homosexual rights. Women in combat units. That's "change" alright, but it's not the kind of change America needs.' To such rhetoric, the auditorium applauded. Buchanan then pointed to those claiming that 'Bill Clinton and Al Gore represent the most pro-lesbian and pro-gay ticket in history' and concluded, 'so they do!' The crowd then responded with the expected boos. But here the Republicans were falling into the same trap as the Democrats had in the 1980s: retreating to merely pleasing their own supporters and failing to see the nation for what it was.

Republican strategists like Robert Teeter confidently noted that 'two million *more* Republicans voted in the 1992 primaries than in 1988 [whilst] two million *less* Democrats voted'. But it depended who was being energised and, crucially for a system with an electoral college, in which states. For Clinton, Buchanan was always playing 'to the dark side of middle-class insecurities' – the politics of division.[31]

Bush would eventually see off his Republican opponent, but in February 1992 a much graver threat would enter the presidential race in the shape of the Texan businessman, Ross Perot. It is difficult to recapture what a phenomenon Perot seemed at the time, but Newt Gingrich for one was telling fellow Republicans that Perot's 'personal life and personal credibility makes him more acceptable than Clinton for most Americans'. At the beginning of June 1992, Gingrich contended that 'the odds are at least even money that Clinton will fade as the third-party candidate' behind the independent Perot.[32] This, of course, was nonsense – and would have been the first such outcome since 1912. But in many ways Perot would come to define the Clinton presidency – helping him in some ways over the electoral line in November 1992 by shifting the debate, but then leading to his team obsessing about winning over the 'Perot voter' thereafter.

That said, rather like the myth that the SDP supposedly ensured Labour's defeat in the 1983 British election, the case for Perot 'costing' Bush in 1992 is not without problem. A Perot-less race would possibly have seen Bush carry Ohio, but his near 20 million votes are generally seen as coming more or less equally from both major parties. Some studies even conclude that he 'stole more votes from Clinton than from Bush'. In the end, we cannot know the outcome of a straight contest between Bush and Clinton. Perot altered the electoral terrain which make any post-facto assumptions about his impact necessarily speculative. What we can say is that, like Buchanan, he formed another non-Democrat voice hammering the president on 'no new taxes' and the national debt and that this may have harmed the attractiveness of Bush's incumbency somewhat. As British Ambassador Robin Renwick messaged home to London, 'the attempt to portray Clinton as another tax-and-spend Democrat is not really working because of Bush's own quote' on that subject.[33] Equally, in a private dinner with British Conservative MPs soon after the election, Richard Nixon claimed that 'the energy has been drained from Bush ... the voters have sensed it and moved on. You can smell a winner and Clinton is a formidable campaigner'.[34]

That, of course, was after the fact. Bush's heroism in the Second World War and his role in the Cold War victory under Reagan appeared a far greater problem for the Democrats in the run up to November. Clinton would continually tell his advisors: 'I've never served in the military, we've just had a war [and] George Bush is a war hero. How are they going to elect someone who has never served?'[35] In part, this required the persuasion of figures like Frank Greer, who told the president that post-Vietnam any appeals to patriotism were more mixed. Certainly, Bush was a hero, but in a world where millions had joined Clinton in seeking creative ways out of military service (or being grateful they were never drafted) the lack of such a record was not a guaranteed pathway to electoral failure. If the campaign was concise on its message and kept the narrative on terrain in which it held the advantage, then all was possible.

Crucially, during the Fall of 1991, Clinton had given three speeches at Georgetown University designed to do just that. From 'opportunity, responsibility, community' to Blair's 'education, education, education', the Third Way would come to find various forms of holy trinity in both its British and American incarnations. True to form, the Georgetown speeches addressed, in turn, rebuilding the American community, economic change and national security – all of which sought to place meat on the bones of the 'New Covenant'. On 23 October, Clinton denounced both the Reagan–Bush era and the Democrats' response to it. Whilst 'the American Dream reigns supreme abroad', he argued, 'the very fiber of *our* nation is breaking down: families are coming apart, kids are dropping out of school, [and] drugs and crime dominate our streets'. Such resentment had 'produce[d] votes for David Duke – not just from racists, but from voters so desperate for change, they'll support the most anti-establishment message, even from an ex-Klansman'. The 1980s had 'exalted private gain over public obligations' and thereby 'usher in a gilded age of greed, selfishness, irresponsibility, excess and neglect'. But just as Republicans had denigrated the power of government, so Democrats had relied too heavily on it. Turning to his largely liberal audience, Clinton remarked that 'it's been 30 years since a Democrat ran for president and asked something of all the American people. I intend to challenge you *to do more and to do better*'. This helped blunt later accusations that electing Clinton would mean a return to 'the disastrous policies of the Carter years' in particular.[36]

The New Covenant would therefore 'break the cycle of welfare'. 'In a Clinton administration', he pledged, 'we're going to put an end to welfare as we know it'. Americans could 'no longer stay on welfare forever'. But there was carrot as well as stick. To the young, the New Covenant meant 'new challenges' to be delivered through 'a system of voluntary national service for all Americans'. A new domestic GI Bill would 'say to the middle class as well as low-income people: We want you to go to college, we'll pay for it, it will be the best money we ever spent, but you've got to give something back to your country in return'. As such, Clinton promised 'a trust fund out of which any American can borrow money for a college education, so long as they pay it back either as a small percentage of their income over time or with a couple of years of national service as teachers, police officers, child care workers – doing work our country desperately needs'. For those accessing public services, Clinton promised to 'make government more efficient and more effective by eliminating unnecessary layers of bureaucracy and cutting administrative costs'. Taxpayers would be given 'more choices in the services they get' and be empower[ed] to make those choices'.

In late November 1991, he fleshed out his economic agenda in the second Georgetown address. He would deliver a 'middle class tax cut' which would cut income taxes for the average family by 10 per cent (equating to a $350 average benefit). This would be paid for by raising the taxes of those earning over $200,000 a year – 'not to soak the rich but to return to basic fairness'. He would insist on 3 per cent annual cuts in federal administrative costs and limiting federal spending to actual revenue growth, not growth estimates – which he claimed had encouraged a 'bipartisan conspiracy' of overestimating future revenues, thereby inflating the deficit. Again, while the left had to move away from the 'old Democratic theory that says we can just tax and spend our way out of any problem', the right was left telling voters facing economic hardship that 'tough luck, it's your fault'. It was economic mismanagement by the administration, not its affirmative action programmes, Clinton argued, which was producing widespread resentment amongst white America. He would become more nuanced on such questions when in office.[37]

On 12 December, he then gave his final Georgetown address on foreign policy. The president had, he asserted, 'devoted his time to foreign concerns and ignored dire problems here at home. As a result, we're drifting in the longest economic slump since World War II'. Bush had also erroneously sided with the Chinese in putting down the democratic rise of students at Tiananmen Square. On the plus side and there was little point in hiding from it, Bush had performed 'a masterful job in pulling together the victorious multilateral coalition' which had removed Saddam from Kuwait. Clinton also backed giving the administration 'authority to negotiate a sound and fair free trade agreement with Mexico'. But, though he had been a good Cold War leader, if America wasn't careful, Bush would fail to address some of the major challenges of tomorrow.

Clinton's New Covenant foreign policy would therefore be based on three core themes. First, as the Cold War ended, it was time to restructure America's military. This meant a one-third cut in the military budget by 1997, with other allies stepping up to fill the gap. Expensive projects such as the B-2 bomber would go, as would Reagan's Star Wars programme. Likewise, nuclear weapons would be scaled down. Unlike the hard left, however, he did acknowledge that, 'as an irreducible minimum, we must retain a survivable nuclear force to deter any conceivable threat'. Nor were the spending reductions a retreat to isolationism. Clinton argued America 'must do more to stop the threat of weapons of mass destruction. We need to clamp down on countries and companies that sell these technologies ... and work urgently with all countries for tough, enforceable, international non-proliferation agreements'.

Secondly, it was time to work with allies to encourage 'the spread and consolidation of democracy abroad'. In the short term, this meant increasing investment into Russia to aid nuclear decommissioning programmes and to provide food for impoverished parts of the former Soviet Union. But, in a broader sense, the global community mattered. As Clinton argued, 'it should matter to us how others govern themselves'. This was a matter of self-interest as much as it was idealism. For candidate Clinton, 'we cannot disregard how other governments treat their own people ... whether they help, encourage or check illegal conduct beyond their borders'. In practical terms, this meant 'regard[ing] increased funding for democratic assistance as a legitimate part of our national security budget'.

Thirdly, in place of the mistrust and economic isolationism of the Cold War era, there was a genuine opportunity to remake the global order. 'If individual liberty, political pluralism and free enterprise take root in Latin America, Eastern and Central Europe, Africa, Asia and the former Soviet Union, we can look forward to a grand new era'. In this world, America must regain its place as global economic leader to the advantage of all. On the one hand, 'we need a commitment from American business and labor to work together to make world-class products ... We must organize to compete and win in the global economy'. But others should grow too. As Clinton argued, 'free trade abroad means more jobs at home. Every $1bn in US exports generates 20–30,000 more jobs'. Indeed, 'without global growth, healthy international competition turns all too readily to economic warfare'. Debt cancellation measures to the poorest countries should henceforth be part of the US agenda. The Third Way would truly embrace the global. It might be America First, but there was no hiding from the world, either.

In an election cycle, some partisan points were to be expected, but there was a wider canvas here. Just as the hard left had sought to break the bipartisan New Deal–New Jerusalem consensus on foreign policy in the UK and US in the early 1980s, Bill Clinton sought to restore it in the 1990s. An intriguing glimpse into this mindset can be found in the papers of Charles Hill, former advisor to both Kissinger and Reagan. In early 1992, the Clinton team reached out to Hill asking him for his verdict on the third Georgetown address. Hill found it 'comprehensive', 'filled with good sense' and agreed 'with almost any point in it'. But he felt Clinton was battling Bush's diplomatic record in the wrong way. Clinton had structured his speech around the idea that the end of the Cold War necessitated the promotion of democracy around the world – which then, in turn, would allow America 'to be able to rebuild our economic health'.[38] For Hill, though the points were entirely sensible, they were the wrong way round. Instead, Clinton should devote over half his future foreign policy speeches to 'economic strength at home' and 'strengthening our own democracy'. He should begin on such themes since 'others around the world now look to us as a model'.

That, then, was the collective policy agenda outlined at Georgetown. But it needed a frame. This was partly for defensive reasons – if the campaign, or the candidate on the stump, needed a rebuttal, they couldn't relentlessly quote policies back at the media or the electorate, but needed an overall narrative which could smooth over differences and reach the median voter. To do so, Clinton and his aides, principally James Carville, maintained that the campaign should focus on three main messages. The first was the idea of 'change versus more of the same'. The 1980s had been a decade where 'the rich got richer' whilst 'the forgotten middle class ... took it on the chin'. Washington was dominated by 'special powerful interests and an entrenched bureaucracy' and the result was a government that had 'betrayed the values that made America great: providing opportunity, taking responsibility, rewarding work'.[39] Bush couldn't take on an establishment he was so much a part of, but maybe a fresh-faced southern Governor could.

The second frame, as Carville famously put it, was 'the economy, stupid'. This was about both perception *and* reality. As political scientist Marc Hetherington has observed, 'relentlessly negative reporting on economic performance during the [1992] election year negatively affected voters' perceptions of the economy, [and this] influenced voting behavior'. The broad economic conditions of 1992 were not disastrous: growth was better than 2 per cent and inflation lower than when Bush had won in 1988. Certainly, unemployment had been on the rise since mid-1990, but at 7.4 per cent on election day was still more or less the same as the level seen at Reagan's re-election in 1984. Still, as Seymour Lipset noted just after Bush's defeat, 'what economists will have to put into their equations next time, in addition to the economic numbers, is what people *believe* the numbers are'. Bush's haughty form of leadership had played very well during Desert Storm – the composed global statesman dealing with the weight of big decisions. But he was ill at ease with domestic issues and, after 12 years in the White House, understandably somewhat 'out of touch'. The Bush recession was voter catnip for Clinton.[40]

Lastly, Carville told his charges, 'don't forget health care'. With a Washington establishment beholden to the drug and insurance lobbyists, 'working Americans are paying the price'. Health policy was truly the brake on the lives of many Americans. Healthcare costs were the leading cause of labour disputes, bankruptcies and – defence aside – the federal deficit. They made it tough to change job should any new insurance company cite some pre-existing condition and they placed stringent costs on small businesses to protect their workers. Meanwhile, drug prices were rising three times above the rate of inflation. This was an area where an opposition candidate could make much hay. For Clinton, the key was to avoid the excesses of the single-payer British and Canadian systems – 'no incentives to manage cost and taxpayer financed, with no incentives for citizen-contribution restraint – and achieve a 'mixed system, with sweeping insurance reforms'. Whether he could deliver on this in office, of course, remained to be seen.[41]

All told, this amounted to a mantra of *Putting People First* – a campaign slogan which became the title of a book, ostensibly 'written' by Clinton and Gore. This set out a path to cutting the deficit in half by 1996. It involved investing $50 billion each year, including a $20 billion annual Rebuild America Fund to deliver large-scale infrastructure, the 'information super highway' Al Gore had been an early adopter of in the 1980s and particular frontline public sector jobs, such as 100,000 new police officers on the streets. Lifetime learning, long an interest of Clinton's, was to hit $20 billion of new investment by the end of his presidential term. This was the pro-tech, future facing and exciting carrot of pre-election Clintonism.

The stick was spending cuts that dwarfed the new investments in each year. Defence would account for the largest chunk ($19bn) of savings intended to reach an annual high of $89 billion, whilst administrative savings (largely what would become Gore's Reinventing Government Agenda), would contribute $8.5 billion by the end of the term. What the manifesto called 'Tax Fairness' raising rates on the top 2 per cent of Americans, with a surtax on millionaires, would produce another $23 billion a year, with various forms of clamp down on tax avoidance raising a further $17.3 billion by 1996. Some of these revenue numbers were optimistic. But the real story and the place where Clinton arguably boxed himself in was in having to accept the Congressional Budget Office's sluggish expectations on growth. As it turned out, the CBO growth assumptions, on which the Democrats costed their future spending pledges were, with the exception of 1993, fairly conservative underestimates. In 1993, the US economy would undershoot a 3.5 per cent projected growth, coming in at 2.7 per cent. But in 1994 (4% compared to a 2.9% projection) and 1996 (3.8% compared to 2.6%) the economy dramatically overperformed. 1995 also saw a modest over-performance (2.7%, 0.2% above expectations).[42] Cumulatively, this created greater economic headroom than seemed likely in 1992 or indeed the chaotic early weeks of the eventual Clinton administration. There was more money around than they realised.

On 10 July 1992, Clinton had announced Senator Al Gore of Tennessee as his running mate. Gore was selected for his foreign policy knowledge, his small 'c' conservative social leanings and his ATARI Democrat background. He was a confirmatory rather than balancing candidate and showed that Clinton was serious about reform. Elaine Kamarck remembers a personal dimension too: 'Clinton essentially picked in Gore his wife. He picked Hillary. In fact, Hillary and Al never liked each other. The rest of us thought, Of course they don't like each other, because they *are* each other. They're exactly the same person: wooden on the stump; come off as cold and phony and preachy; nobody likes them because they're the smartest kid in the class. But in fact they were also both very organized, linear, conscientious thinkers.'[43]

After Clinton gave his convention speech a week after announcing Gore, he received the biggest polling bounce in US history. That speech united both old and new Democrats and the hopeful with the downtrodden. The New York audience heard transactional promises to 'cut 100,000 bureaucrats and put 100,000 new police officers on the streets'. They were told that 'if you are sick and tired of a government that doesn't work to create jobs, if you're sick and tired of a tax system that's stacked against you, if you're sick and tired of exploding debt and reduced investments in our future, or if, like the great civil rights pioneer Fannie Lou Hamer, you're just plain old sick and tired of being sick and tired, then join us'. Clinton stated that 'we didn't get into this mess overnight and we won't get out of it overnight. But we can do it – with commitment, creativity, diversity and drive'. And, as for the final lines, famously, 'my fellow Americans, I end tonight where it all began for me – I still believe in a place called Hope'.

Democrats were understandably cautious. Following Clinton's New York address Robert Reich noted that 'after Michael [Dukakis]'s experience four years ago and the [Boston] Red Sox experience in most years, I am not drawing any conclusions'. Still, the numbers were there.

FIGURE 7 In 1992 Bill Clinton secured the Democratic nomination. At the New York convention which confirmed his candidacy, Gordon Brown stood cheering in the audience (Steve Liss/The LIFE Images Collection/Getty Images).

The combination of a biting recession and Clinton's own charisma saw the Democratic nominee leap from just 25 per cent in the spring to 55 per cent after his convention speech. Standing in the crowd, Gordon Brown was swept away too. His aide Sue Nye had contacted the British Embassy for help with gaining accreditation for the convention and Jonathan Powell had managed to secure him a full pass. Powell squired Gordon around for a day or two, including taking him to Brooks Brothers to buy some shirts, which Brown always liked to do when he came to the States. Having hoovered up all the DLC publications he could get his hands on and indeed briefly meeting Clinton in 1991, Brown finally got to see the man in action. Clinton had restored his party to the brink of power. And if it could happen in the US, why not Britain?[44]

An Englishman in Little Rock

For a start, many British moderates were punch drunk after Labour's shocking defeat of April 1992 – and scrabbling around for work. After Neil Kinnock resigned in the wake of the loss, his old communications guard was soon cut loose. Peter Mandelson had been elected as MP for Hartlepool but was so out of the loop that, on one occasion, he recalled saving a visit to the supermarket on Sunday so that he would have something to do with his weekend. Gould conducted the odd focus group for the new leadership, but he was 'clearly and rightly, at the very fringes ... out in the cold'. The Strategic Communications Agency, at the heart of the modernisation agenda since late 1985, was quietly wound up in October 1992. 'A chapter was closed' recalls Gould, 'it was time to move on'.[45]

If John Smith was lukewarm, Stan Greenberg was raining sunshine. Greenberg and Gould had reached similar polling conclusions regarding the future direction of the Anglo-American left and, in September 1992, a fax arrived in Gould's office which was 'like water in the desert' for the 'depleted, dejected, depressed' pollster. Greenberg was 'anxious to meet ... here in Little Rock, at the Clinton campaign headquarters'. He wanted Gould to 'observe the campaign and to hear about your efforts'.[46] Gould got on the first flight he could to St Louis where, at Lambert Airport, he was told by Democratic volunteers to hurry up on his connection to Little Rock. The Bush campaign was stealing the tactics of John Major's Conservatives and going hard on Clinton's supposed Soviet sympathies – cooked up from his student visit to the country in the late 1960s. Gould was needed again.

Arriving in Little Rock was like 'leaving the shadows and coming into the sunlight'. Gould was 'greeted with more warmth than I imagined possible'. He was told repeatedly that 'everyone here has been defeated two or three times in presidential elections. Defeat is how you learn [and] we want to learn from you'. With Bush drawing heavily on Tory tactics, he had much to offer. Shaun Woodward (who later defected to New Labour, but in 1992 was the Conservative Communications Director) recalls that senior Bush officials had visited him in London and 'left his office bare' after taking away so much material.[47] Gould was to provide the antidote to these right-wing weapons.

The Bush campaign had released a statement claiming that 'six weeks after he organised a massive anti-war protest in London, then student Bill Clinton turned up at the Soviet Union for a visit during the dead of winter'. This was the episode with the border guard and Clinton's disappointing lack of 'dirty books'. The immediate response was to brief the media that Bush was 'borrowing almost all his campaign strategy from British Prime Minister John Major' and that 'this was a smear modelled after a similar attack on Neil Kinnock'. More broadly, working with Bennett Freeman, Gould wrote a long memo about the similarities between the British and American campaigns and the dangers for Clinton. For Gould, 'tax and trust are the only issues that matter'. This, as he noted, would become 'the genesis of the defensive strategy used by the Blair campaign five years later'.[48]

By 11 o'clock on polling day it was clear that Clinton had won. He'd gained 3 million more votes than Dukakis in 1988 and flipped the rust belt (Michigan, Ohio and Pennsylvania), mountain (such as Colorado and Montana) and west coast (the huge prize of California) states alike. This was a truly national victory, albeit seen by millions across the globe. Watching the coverage through the night were many Labour politicians including, perhaps most poignantly, Neil Kinnock. Ed Balls saw the news come in on his television at home and 'remembers the results so well because by that time there had not been a left of centre American president or British prime minister all my adult life – and I hadn't really believed it could happen'. 'My God', he mused, 'it is actually possible to win in modern politics from the centre left rather than the centre right'. The next day Balls walked into the *Financial Times*, where he had gone to work as an economics writer after leaving Harvard, with a slight element of 'I told you so'. As he recalls, 'having been an optimist and an enthusiast for Clinton and for what he embodied, which was that the centre left could have an economic agenda that was fair and efficient, I remember having being verbally dumped on for a few months by numerous pessimists in the room who were very sceptical of his candidacy'.

The bleary-eyed London commentariat was one thing, but for those who were in the US the experience was virtually euphoric. Having returned to where it all began, Gould stood in the freezing cold outside the Old State House in Little Rock as it became evident that Clinton had the electoral college votes he needed to become president. Next to him was the BBC's Martha Kearney. Turning to Gould, she asked, 'when is this going to happen for Labour?' He answered, 'when Labour has got rid of high taxes and trade-union dominance'. Kearney smiled politely at Gould, 'as though I had gone temporarily insane'.[49]

So, who would be Labour's Clinton? After the 1992 election, Kinnock clearly had to go. But the obvious options to follow the Welshman all seemed fraught with problems. As Peter Mandelson observed, Robin Cook was a 'thinking man's Tony Benn', whose chief innovation seemed to be an obsession with the introduction of a proportional electoral system. The eventual winner, John Smith, was 'Kinnock with a different face'. The third, more radical option of Gordon Brown could not be persuaded to stand – largely because he assumed (probably correctly) he could not win. At this stage, Mandelson recalls, 'neither I nor anyone else seriously saw [Tony Blair] as the next Labour leader'. Indeed, in so far as he discussed the leadership, in 1992 Blair viewed himself as a potential deputy to Gordon Brown on a joint modernising platform – nothing more.[50] As with the Nunn–Clinton abortive ticket in the States, Blair was initially underestimated by many – even those sympathetic to his eventual ambitions.

The election of John Smith as Labour leader in July 1992 (in a 91% landslide victory over the left-wing Bryan Gould) was symptomatic that the Labour Party was intending 'one last heave' on the same Kinnockite policies: not going back to the ultra-nationalising agenda of Foot, but not jettisoning their image of statist tinkerers either. Smith had served in various junior ministerial positions in the Wilson–Callaghan administration from 1974, finally reaching the Cabinet in 1978 as Secretary of State for Trade. He had had health problems, including suffering a heart attack in 1988, but it was thought that these had been permanently alleviated by a gruelling 1,000 calorie a day dietary regime (he lost over 30 pounds) and by regular mountain walking in Scotland.

Smith was a serious figure and, the pressures of political life aside, a mostly jovial man. He was, as Mandelson acknowledged, someone who projected 'authority and knowledge' and would 'be a stable and unifying figure for Labour'.[51] In 1993, Smith achieved what Kinnock had failed to deliver in 1984, with 'One Member One Vote' introduced for trade union affiliates of the Labour Party – handing power to the individual worker rather than the old 'block vote' of trade union leaders. But he was not a modernising zealot like the younger generation. Since Gordon Brown and Tony Blair had topped the July 1992 Shadow Cabinet election this was bound to come to a head, particularly since they were given the key portfolios of Shadow Chancellor and Shadow Home Secretary respectively. As Ed Balls remembers, 'in their respective areas' Blair and Brown 'were constantly pushing the envelope in terms of demonstrating their commitment to modernisation – whether it was Tony's "tough" language on crime or Gordon's ditching of John's 1992 pre-election budget'. This, as Balls recalls, 'clearly irritated John and his office'. Labour's future remained uncertain.

Clinton transition and New Labour comes to town

In Washington, people were also making decisions about their futures and that of progressive politics per se. Al From decided early that he did not want to join the administration: 'even if he had appointed me to a top job, chances were good that I'd have a limited portfolio.' The smart choice from personal, political and financial points of view was to remain a critical friend from the outside. But he did join the transition team as its head of domestic policy. This was a very busy and, occasionally, for From, a troubling time. On 15 November, while From was back in Washington, Clinton held a dinner of the Democratic congressional leadership at the Governor's Mansion in Little Rock. With George Mitchell, Tom Foley and Dick Gephardt, Clinton agreed to back off on a campaign promise to cut congressional staffing by a quarter. Whilst these proposals were not 'particularly significant', 'they had been symbolic of Clinton's intention to depart from business as usual'.[52] Their jettisoning did not bode well.

On 7 December, Will Marshall's Progressive Policy Institute published its work, *Mandate for Change*. This became a best seller and laid out the Clinton agenda: 100,000 new police officers, time-limited welfare, expanding the income tax credit, national service, an assault weapons ban, apprenticeships, business tax credits and using the market to stimulate a greener economy. With From's domestic policy hat on, he and Bruce Reed subsequently urged the president to concentrate on five areas: national service, reinventing government, welfare reform, youth apprenticeships and community policing. But beneath even these, they argued, his presidency would be judged on two criteria: 'to get the economy moving again' and to 'be a different kind of Democrat'. A major target, they argued, should be the 19 per cent of Americans who had just voted for Ross Perot – the 'most change oriented and most hostile to the status quo' voters.[53] After all, Stan Greenberg's Macomb County still hadn't voted Democrat in 1992 and, thanks to Perot, Clinton had actually fallen back on Dukakis' performance there. There was still something holding these, and other, voters back.

Such challenges paled into insignificance compared to the major issue: the economy. As Clinton would go on to put it in his first weekly radio address, during the transition he had learned that 'the economic situation has some greater problems than we thought. Shortly after the election, the Federal Government announced that the proposed deficit for next year and the year after that and the year after that was about $50 billion more than we'd been told last August'. As Robert Reich recalls, this 'meant – and [Clinton] knew that it meant – that we couldn't do everything that he wanted to do, everything that he had promised the public. The administration's language therefore changed. As Clinton told Americans on 6 February 1993, 'today the government is spending about $1.20 for every $1.00 it takes in taxes. We've got to act and act now. There is simply no alternative'.[54] The latter phrase was famously one borrowed from Britain's Margaret Thatcher.

Still, Labour would have killed to be in a position to have to make such tough calls. Though there remained left-wing British sceptics of the New Democrats, the election of Bill Clinton had certainly whetted Tony Blair and Gordon Brown's appetite for change. In the first week of January 1993 both travelled to Washington DC where they met Democratic congressmen and members of the transition team. Larry Summers, Alan Greenspan and Sidney Blumenthal would be amongst those to press the flesh with the two British politicians that week. This came at a time where, as the American press reported, 'some Labour traditionalists are suspicious, labelling Clinton's program [as] "Keynesian economics with an electric chair"'. Yet, as the papers also noted, 'many echo Gordon Brown's feeling of "common roots" with the Clintonites and his call for a "new settlement" sounds very like Bill Clinton's "new covenant"'. The divisions this was opening up were by then obvious. The day before Blair and Brown flew to Washington, an irate John Smith picked up the phone to Peter Mandelson. 'I know what their game is!' he shouted. 'Well, I can tell you that we don't need any of this fucking Clinton stuff over here. They're just drawing attention to themselves and rocking the boat'.[55]

Whether it was attention or policy lessons they were after, the Washington trip certainly provided plenty of both. Shown around by Jonathan Powell, the modernising MPs secured three hours with Al From and probed him 'about the New Democrat themes we had developed and the role they played as we reshaped our party and broke our losing streak in national elections'. From highlighted 'moving from redistribution to a dependence on private sector growth', 'moving from welfare to work' and 'the whole crime and social justice agenda which Blair picked up'. For Elaine Kamarck, present at the gathering, Blair 'looked like a kid', though he was also 'very courteous, very humble, very focused'. From went away believing 'Blair had taken it all more to heart than Gordon'.[56]

Either way, from then on America would form a powerful reference point for both New Labour's key figures. If you wanted to get on in Labour after 1994, it helped to have some transatlantic experience. Jonathan Powell for one had had little contact with Labour figures during the Clinton campaign itself. He had been at Oxford with Blair 'but didn't know him'. But, apart from his strong civil service background, 'the fact that I had experience of Clinton and the whole New Democrat thing' would prove crucial in landing his later job as Blair's Chief of Staff. Ed Balls too notes that 'part of the reason I spent a lot of time talking to Tony Blair and Gordon Brown when back at the *Financial Times* in 1992/93 was that they looked to what the Americans were doing in terms of enhancing and sustaining modernisation and embracing the challenge of globalisation, that were both central to Clinton. And this was something I had done at Harvard, thought about and knew lots of the people'.[57] If Blair and Brown could get their hands on the reins of power, then, to paraphrase John Smith, there would be *plenty* of that Clinton stuff over in the UK.

Notes

1 Blair 1/56.

2 Brown 1/81–82.

3 Blair 1/51.

4 COR/Kinnock; Fry to Kinnock, November 1991, ARC/CAC/NEWB/1.

5 ARC/PHM/SHADCAB, 26 February 1992; Straw/131; Radice 3/20.

6 Brown/83.

7 Radice 3/5.

8 Radice 3/4, 1.

9 Radice 3/10, 7, 19, 15.

10 Polling data, 10 June 1990, in ARC/PHM/GEP/118/16 and Ron Brown briefing note, ARC/CAC/KNNK 19/2/81.

11 From/140.

12 From/141.

13 From/152.

14 From/136.

15 From/137.

16 From/137–38.

17 COR/Leach.

18 Greenberg 2/45, 49.

19 Cited in *Philadelphia Daily News*, 24 January 1992; Riley/22; MCI/Kamarck.

20 Riley/42.

21 Riley/42, 43; French to Powell, 17 February 1992, ARC/KEW/PREM/19/4496.

22 *Huffington Post*, 9 May 2015; *Guardian*, 24 July 2015.

23 Greenberg 2/220–21; 'Bush Versus Clinton' ARC/BHL/JENG/289, Michigan House Democrat Report, January 1992 in ARC/BHL/DPM/46.

24 Clinton/396; Pat Buchanan keynote at RNC.

25 *Los Angeles Times*, 14 January 1992; Georgetown speech, 23 October 1991.

26 *New York Times*, 23 December 1992.

27 Blumenthal/301.

28 Clinton/433; COR/Powell.

29 COR/Mulgan.

30 COR/Leach.

31 Clinton/397; 7 July 1992 memo in ARC/FORD/RT/138.

32 '1992 as a unique year' ARC/PRN/BAKER/100/14.

33 Renwick memo, October 1992 ARC/KEW/PREM/19/4496.

34 *Washington* Post, 8 November 1992, Dean Lacy and Barry C Burden, 'The Vote-Stealing and Turnout Effects of Ross Perot in the 1992 US Presidential Election', *American Journal of Political Science,* Vol 43, No 1 (Jan 1999), 233–55; Brandreth/138.

35 Riley/19.

36 Teeter to Axe, 7 August 1992 ARC/FORD/RT/141.

37 *News-journal* (Mansfield, OH), 21 November 1991; *The Tribune* (Coshocton, OH), 21 November 1991.

38 Hill to Johnson, 20 March 1992, ARC/HOV/HILL/69.

39 Clinton and Gore/3.

40 Marc J Hetherington, 'The Media's Role in Forming Voters' National Economic Evaluations in 1992' *American Journal of Political Science*, Vol 40, No 2 (May, 1996), 372–95; Seymour Martin Lipset, 'The Significance of the 1992 Election' *Political Science and Politics*, Vol 26, No 1 (March, 1993), 7–16.

41 *Rolling Stone*, September 1992.

42 CBO Budget Economic Outlook 1991–92 versus World Bank data.

43 MCI/Kamarck.

44 Reich to Galbraith, 19 August 1992, ARC/JFK/JKG/78; *New York Times*, 18 July 1992.

45 Gould/162.

46 Gould/163.

47 Gould/166.

48 Gould/164, 167; *Washington Post,* 8 October 1992.

49 COR/Balls; Gould/170.

50 Mandelson/134–35.

51 Mandelson/141.

52 From/185.

53 From/188–89.

54 President's Radio Address, 6 February 1993.

55 *Democrat and Chronicle* (Rochester, NY), 20 January 1993; Mandelson/151.

56 From/186; COR/From; Greenberg 2/180.

57 COR/Balls.

5 NEW DEMOCRATS, NEW AMERICA

On the morning of 21 January 1993, Labour's Giles Radice pored over his morning newspapers. Later that day there was business in the House, including PMQs, but all MPs knew what the big story that Thursday was. The modernising centre-left was now in power. Against what seemed like insurmountable odds a decade ago, even a year ago, a moderate Democratic president had finally stood up to deliver an inaugural address. Radice was delighted: 'the papers are full of Clinton's inaugural. A beautiful winter's day in Washington and a feeling that a new generation is taking over the helm'. It was, Radice thought, 'shades of Kennedy'.[1]

In clear overtones of JFK, Clinton's address pledged to 'do what America does best: offer opportunity to all and demand responsibility from all'. This would involve several challenges. Clinton demanded that America 'invest more in our own people, in their jobs and in their future and at the same time cut our massive debt'. He challenged 'a new generation of young Americans to a season of service: to act on your idealism by helping troubled children, keeping company with those in need, reconnecting our torn communities'. And he pointed to the new, 'almost magical' technological revolutions which meant 'ambition for a better life is now universal'. At least in spirit, Camelot was back.

Whilst inauguration was perhaps not the time to level with the American public, there was, however, a major problem: Clinton was taking office in a time of severe economic constraint. Although the new president alluded to an 'economy that is still the world's strongest but is weakened by business failures, stagnant wages and increasing inequality', the reality was much starker. As British Foreign Office officials were briefing to their ministers, 'unless Clinton takes the difficult steps in the first year of his Presidency, he could find himself running into the same

FIGURE 8 John F Kennedy was a president Bill Clinton both wanted to emulate and eclipse. Here he watches an old JFK speech, alongside Senator Edward Kennedy, at the JFK Presidential Library, February 1993 (Courtesy: Clinton Presidential Library).

sort of gridlock as President Bush'.[2] Before they could dream of loftier goals, the new administration had to clear up its predecessor's mess.

Delivering a new economic agenda

On 7 January 1993 the first meeting of Clinton's economic team took place in the Dining Room of the Governor's Mansion at Little Rock. Al Gore, Hillary Clinton, George Stephanopoulos and others gathered at the table, where the nation's future path would be set out. The inauguration was two weeks away, but Clinton, *de facto*, already held the reins of office. He had spent much of the transition hearing from voices such as Alan Greenspan and the news was fairly catastrophic. Now, the latest numbers were laid before the president elect. The deficit was climbing towards $360 billion and, all things being equal, would probably hit $500 billion by the end of the century – equivalent to a third of then federal spending. Unemployment was nearly 8 per cent and only modest growth could be expected over the next few months. The administration could certainly seek to bring the mounting deficit down by slashing spending, but this would have trade-offs in terms of an already fragile economic picture. As it was, any economic gains, such as they were, would be over the medium to long term and this would require buy-in from both Greenspan at the Fed in keeping short-term interest rates low and cooperation from investors on Wall Street – who would largely determine the cost of long-term borrowing. As Clinton chewed all of this over he muttered, 'you mean the success of the program and my re-election hinges on the Federal Reserve and a bunch of fucking bond traders?'[3]

A few days later Greenspan would tell Leon Panetta and Lloyd Bentsen that Clinton had two basic choices: 'a package of spending programs that would fulfil some of his campaign promises, or . . . a deficit-cutting plan. There was no in-between'. These were well chosen targets – Panetta was a former Republican and Bentsen, the incoming Treasury Secretary, was such a 'deficit hawk' that his very appointment left Robert Reich asking himself, 'how committed can [Bill and Hillary] be to raising the prospects of the working class and the poor?' The elevation of such figures led British diplomatic sources to brief that 'Clinton is perhaps one of the least ideological American presidents since Eisenhower'. In some sense confirming this verdict, Clinton would essentially opt for the latter option mapped out by Greenspan, a major casualty of which became the middle-class tax cut he had made so much of during the campaign. When they heard of this, members of his economic team quickly voiced concerns. David Wilhelm, new chair of the DNC, asked 'when did the deficit become the main goal?' Al From, too, demanded to know, 'where is the economic growth?' And Greenberg would write to the president claiming that 'you would think from watching the news that cutting the deficit in half was our only goal'. Reich believed that 'going into debt in order to help our people become better educated and more productive is entirely reasonable' and was concerned that '*the deficit* is already framing our discussions about what we want to accomplish in the future'. An important point here was that the focus on bringing down the deficit was not voter led. As Greenberg lamented, it was a 'goal the president had locked himself into without consulting any polls'. Still, 'none of that mattered, of course, since the decisions had been made'.[4]

Still, six days after Clinton took the oath of office, Greenberg made one last pass at changing his mind. Running reams of polling numbers before the president, Greenberg told him that Americans had never really expected a huge middle-class tax cut, but if he went and did the opposite, a middle class tax hike to try and lower the deficit, it 'could easily be seen as a betrayal'. Instead, the pollster urged the new president to 'go long. The country will support a bold program – a major stimulus, serious investment, serious deficit reduction, broad tax increase'. Little of this cut through. After all, it was smack bang in the realm of the same old Democrat solutions that Clinton had been so keen to avoid and delivering Keynesianism on the economy and 'big government' healthcare reform at the same time was a legislative impossibility. Indeed, Greenberg's was a relatively solitary voice. As Rubin and Bentsen reassured the president that significant action on the deficit would be met by Greenspan with an interest rate reduction to stave off a depression, Clinton was finally convinced. As he told Greenberg, 'we can't do anything for people unless we reduce the deficit'. Some key Clintonian priorities such as the extension to the Earned Income Tax Credit would stay, but to provide the 'serious' and 'plausible' plan the Fed demanded, several of the future-orientated investments would be scaled back significantly.[5]

After all, Clinton was not the only leader with a mandate. Any budget would need approval from the Senate and the House – both then controlled by the Democrats, but close enough that 40 lost votes in the House would leave the budget's fate in jeopardy. Since many of the Democrats first elected in November were deficit hawks this was not a moot point and, as the Minnesotan Congressman Marty Sabo put it, even the more established representatives had 'given up on the little guys' in the mid-1980s and were owned by 'business'. After pre-existing legislative caps from the Bush years wiped $100 billion off Clinton's proposed spending even before the budget entered serious horse-trading, his $50 billion of new strategic investments were gutted to barely half that amount as it went before the new Congress. By early April 1993, Clinton was ranting that they had 'gone too far' and were 'losing our soul'. 'We're doing everything Wall Street wants!' 'Everything Wall Street doesn't want gets slashed!' The proposed $30 billion of short-term stimulus money had been reduced to just $16 billion, the equivalent, for Robert Reich, of 'a pinch in the ass' – a more colourful version of the 'much too weak' verdict JK Galbraith had offered to Reich. Meanwhile, Al Gore's desire for some form of climate-friendly levy (eventually accommodated in 4.3 cents a gallon increase in the gas tax) was also creating problems vis-à-vis the cost of living for average Americans. Clinton had won on a ticket of middle-class tax cuts and had envisaged a modest stimulus during the transition as a means of tiding the economy over. Now he couldn't do either.[6]

The president wanted answers. 'I know what's wrong', he told Greenberg, 'give me a strategy'. Greenberg's answer was for Clinton to appeal to the country above and beyond Washington and to frame the debate more positively. Deficit reduction on its own sounded gloomy and tough. The pollster himself remained privately doubtful of its efficacy, but he did his job and tested various ways it could be sold to the American people. In his surveys of voters, Greenberg sought to present 'the deficit reduction option as a genuinely bold move with economic consequences – "lower interest rates" and "more job-creating investment"'. He found, 'amazingly, that it tested as strong as our economic growth message with investments'.[7]

The trick was to spread the pain. Greenberg's numbers showed Americans could be convinced on a change of agenda if it was presented as 'bold steps to put our house in order'. But it needed to be a simple message which spread the burden evenly. After some thought Greenberg wrote a memo to Clinton in June 1993 which stated:

[For] Every $10 devoted to deficit reduction
    $5 comes from spending cuts
  $4 comes from taxes on the wealthy (over $100,000)
    $1 comes from everybody else.

Clinton loved it. The economic team and communications staff were told within a day that this formulation should govern everything they put out and when it came to giving an Oval Office address two days before the crucial congressional votes on the budget, Clinton reeled off this exact formula. 'This plan is fair', Clinton argued, 'it is balanced and it will work'.[8]

That said, it still only crawled across the line in Congress. Although the Senate had at long last approved Gore's gas tax hike, the overall budget vote was still on a knife edge. The House passed the bill 218 to 216, but even as this was going through, Bob Kerrey, Clinton's old presidential foe from 1992, was making noises that he would vote against the full plan when it came to the Senate. Kerrey felt that the bill did not address entitlements and its tax increases would send the economy into a tailspin. He was summoned to the White House where he met a furious president. 'If you want to bring this Presidency down, then go ahead' thundered Clinton. Kerrey was angry that Clinton was trying to blame him for not being able to get to 50 votes in the Senate, to which the president bellowed 'fuck you'.[9] In the end Kerrey was talked down and though he claimed on the Senate floor that the bill 'challenged America too little', voted for its passage. It was vital that he did. The Senate was deadlocked at 50 votes a piece and it took Al Gore's casting vote to deliver victory to the White House.

The budget was not tax and spend, but largely tax and cut on the formula Greenberg had framed. As the *Boston Globe* noted, 'if this year's budget does nothing else, it once again demonstrates that the American middle class is politically sacrosanct'. Five million or so social security recipients stood to pay a little more in tax. But, with the exception of this and Gore's gas tax, this was a budget largely targeted to hit the very wealthy. A new 36 per cent bracket of income tax was created for incomes above $51,900 with 39.6 per cent for those earning over $250,000. Corporate incomes too received new surtax rates – 35 per cent for income between $10 and $15 million and 38 per cent for income between $15 and 18.33 million. On the revenue side, as the *Globe* sympathetically pointed out, 'Clinton's budget bypasses middle-income Americans in favour of taxing the rich'. The British Embassy in DC was similarly impressed and conceded that, whatever problems the budget may have had in passing, 'Clinton has succeeded in persuading the American people and Congress of the need to raise taxes, which was simply ducked by his predecessors'. As such, the revenue-raising measures totalled some $241 billion over five years.[10]

The slightly larger measure of deficit reduction ($255 billion) would come from spending cuts. The biggest casualty here would be defence spending ($77 billion), though devolving some of the federal government's Medicaid administrative costs to state level and reducing the federal government by 100,000 employees also helped. These sums did not quite hit Greenberg's dictum of five dollars in ten from spending cuts and four from taxing the rich, but they were not far off. In the end, thanks to the economic expansion that America witnessed in the mid-to-late 1990s, the 1993 package would lead to well over double its planned levels of deficit reduction ($1,200 billion instead of a projected $496 billion). For South Dakota Senator Tom Daschle, the 1993 budget was a sound, clear piece of legislation. As he noted, 'rather than the vague predictions with rosy scenarios of [Reagan's first budget in] 1981 – the 1993 proposal put details into black and white – details involving cuts, details involving revenue, details requiring major changes in the way we do business'. And, in the long run, it delivered.[11]

Even in the dire straits of 1993, however, Clinton was emphatically not a right-wing president. His was a presidency steadfastly aiming to assist low income Americans' pockets and to ensure the taxes they did pay were efficiently spent. The most high-profile example of the first was the Earned Income Tax Credit – a helping hand for both the American worker and, indirectly, a British Labour Party seeking to re-orientate itself. By way of brief explanation, the EITC constitutes a refundable federal payment to low-paid workers – or, in non-jargon, a top-up in their wages from the state. The credit is equal to a percentage of their earnings up to a maximum level and is at its most generous in the lowest portion of earnings before tapering off entirely. It is largely, though not exclusively, targeted at those with children.

With around 11 million Americans working full time but not earning above the poverty line improving the lives of the working poor had always been a big Clintonian priority. Although the EITC had been introduced in 1975, Clinton's 1993 increase of an average of annual $2,000 for low-paid families with one child (and $3,700 for those with two) was the largest such rise in the policy's history. Initially pushed by proto-Clintonian congressional New Democrats in the 1970s, it had been vigorously opposed by advisors of President Ford as an 'undesirable welfare type program' whose only redeeming feature was making 'other, worse approaches somewhat less likely'. Sitting in Cabinet, Caspar Weinberger for one advised his president that it was a 'disaster'. Still, Reagan had warmed to the idea and expanded its remit in the 1986 Tax Reform Act. Its benefits were numerous – it tapered away to a degree that ensured work always paid, it was delivered without stigma since all claimants had to do was fill their tax return as normal and, most obviously, it put money into the hands of lower income Americans. This was a redistributive, interventionist side of the New Democrats platform that made meaningful changes to millions of Americans. Between 1993 and 2001 the number of Americans receiving EITC increased from 15.1 million to 19.6 million and the average pay out by 65 per cent.[12]

One witness to the policy was Simon Crine, then General Secretary of the Fabian Society, but also serving as a Harkness Fellow at the Center for Policy Alternatives in Washington DC. For Crine, there were several lessons New Labour could draw from Clinton's welfare agenda. As he wrote in a September 1994 pamphlet, 'Clinton's increase in the EITC suggests that the best way to help the low paid is through the tax system'. Whilst raising the personal allowance threshold (i.e. the level below which no worker paid income tax) to offset the changes in early 1990s Conservative budgets would be a good first step, the larger 'advantages of the Earned Income Tax Credit, which goes to 90% of eligible working families in the US', were obvious. With a future Blair government not beholden to state level politics (only six states had introduced any form of local EITC, meaning the federal EITC had to do all the work), it could truly 'make work pay' across the UK, should it wish. For Crine, the EITC stood as Clinton's 'greatest success on the poverty front so far'. Back in the UK, Cambridge MP Anne Campbell recalls 'lots of conversations with Harriet [Harman] on tax credits and what Clinton was doing in that area'.[13]

Clinton did not just put money into the bank accounts of working Americans whilst simultaneously cutting the deficit, he oversaw a more efficient form of government per se. A month after the budget had been signed into law, Al Gore's National Performance Review called for $108 billion of federal efficiency savings. As Gore noted, 'we suffer not only a budget deficit, but a performance deficit'. Part of the solution was thus to create an entrepreneurial public sector, where performance targets were not just used by federal government to self-aggrandize, but to unleash competition between and within agencies for the benefit of service user and taxpayer alike. Air Combat Command, the IRS and the Forest Service had led the way in this regard and others would follow. Chapter 1 of Gore's review concentrated on 'cutting red tape' to stop the climate of 'fewer people doing real work [and] more people getting in their way'. The overall effect of this would streamline procurement processes, speed up the process of government and get the private sector to do the heavy lifting.[14]

A further admirer of all this was the then Labour policy advisor Liam Byrne. Byrne would be elected as MP for Birmingham Hodge Hill in 2004, but in late 1997 was arguing that 'the fabulous success of Clinton and Gore's reinventing programme' should be at the heart of Labour's agenda. As he wrote in an influential *Fabian Society* pamphlet, 'the administration of the British state ... resembles a state-of-the-art industrial age bureaucracy circa 1950'. UK Government departments were mandated to deal with piecemeal issues 'with an unrelated collection of needs, each one of which is to be satisfied separately'. The co-ordination of activities was thus thrust upon the individual service user, relegated to 'running round collecting them all – rather than *internally* by the bureaucracy'. With British single mothers, for example, needing to visit up to seven different sorts of government or private agency to service their needs or shopkeepers encountering up to ten inspection agencies each and every year, this needed to change. Byrne had read Osborne and Gaebler's *Reinventing Government* and was firmly behind the concept of public entities 'steering not rowing': giving service users and taxpayers the information and ability to make their own decisions, safe in the knowledge they would see a swift and tangible return.

Byrne had his own figure too: billions of pounds could be saved, he argued, by a more efficient government. For one, new technology had not fostered the leaner public sector workforce it should have done: compared to 17 per cent reductions in banking headcounts since 1989, central government had only shrunk by 5.8 per cent. Government agencies which replicated much of the same functions could be merged, such as the Inland Revenue and Customs and Excise (the future combined HMRC). And American-inspired solutions at a local government level, such as Michigan's Employment Security Commission's use of interactive voice response software to service users out of office hours or the Californian Human Service Agency's automation of eligibility for access to federal benefits, indicated more could be done to devolve functions to the lowest appropriate level – thereby freeing staff for other tasks. As liberal writer Robert Kuttner argued, 'a dollar liberated by efficiency gains buys just as much as a dollar borrowed or taxed'. New Labour would build on this legacy.[15]

Internal debates

Such early measures were symptomatic of the difficulties and general trade-offs of government, but also the internal conversation that was still going on as to what Clinton's administration should prioritise. Whilst Stan Greenberg was soon in and out of Clinton's office with his new polling numbers, Al From had pledged to stay out of the White House melee for three months. He intended to use 'the DLC to support the administration's New Democrat initiatives and nudge it back to them when necessary' and 'this meant going straight to the president when I thought things were veering off course'. On 16 April 1993, a few days before his self-imposed deadline ended, From began to do exactly this. He had taken the early flight from Clarksburg, West Virginia to Washington DC – a journey which proved eventful when his plane suddenly dropped several hundred feet in the sky after hitting an air pocket. One woman sat in the front seat of the aircraft continually yelled 'we're all gonna die! We're all gonna die!'. To From, 'it didn't feel like a good omen'.[16]

Arriving at his desk at 8am, From sat down and typed a memorandum directly addressed to the president entitled 'the Next Hundred Days'. After reassuring Clinton that he 'didn't want into the administration' personally, this document went on to pull very few punches. For From, 'there is a pervasive and growing perception that something about the Administration is not quite right'. Clinton had got off to a 'very mixed start' with the budget and his charismatic authority was on the wane. From the perspective of the 'forgotten middle class [Clinton] courted so assiduously during the campaign', the combination of dropping 'that middle class tax cut' and being seen to 'fight for a stimulus package', even in the limited form eventually reached, was just old statist leftism and not the 'change' he had promised. Raising taxes on gasoline to pacify environmentally minded supporters was another red flag. For From, 'the failure of both the liberal (pre-Reagan) agenda as championed by Congress and Democratic interest groups and the Conservative Republican agenda running out of intellectual steam' meant there was a chance for 'a new synthesis, a third way'. Yet, as From noted, 'with the emphasis on diversity (a lot of people read quotas) on appointments, gays in the military and abortion being the dominant social issues in your first 100 days, many average Americans are going to begin questioning whether you really stand for their values'. Clinton remained 'right' on these questions, but his ticket needed more 'clear balancing messages before you get tabbed as a Hollywood cultural liberal'. These included two-year welfare limits, national service, reminding voters 'you're for the death penalty', re-inventing government and charter schools. Welfare would be the 'single issue that demonstrates your willingness to break with old Democratic orthodoxy'.

This was all about balancing Democratic goals with political realities. On abortion, Clinton had signed executive orders in his first week in office that undid much of the more draconian policies of the Reagan–Bush era. He would go on to twice veto Congress' attempts to ban partial birth abortion later in his first term. But, as From reminded him in the spring of 1993, this should be balanced with 'a government wide campaign to discourage teenage pregnancy and out of wedlock births' and Clinton should 'talk about that every time you talk about abortion'. Signing the 1996 welfare bill would eventually deliver this, but it would still take the chastening experience of the 1994 elections to tip Clinton in this direction.

Likewise, on the vexed question of allowing openly gay men and women to serve in the military, the president should 'do whatever you're going to do' according to From, but he should 'do it quickly'. With some Democratic DLCers, including Sam Nunn, in favour of maintaining the absolute ban, but maverick Republicans like Barry Goldwater ('you don't have to be straight to shoot straight') backing the president's line, the issue wasn't necessarily a party political one. 'Don't Ask, Don't Tell' was the eventual compromise – precisely the type of arrangement ('call in the gay groups and tell them that's the best you can do right now') that From had argued for. Again, on getting more women and ethnic minority candidates into high office, Clinton should continue to do just that, but he should also 'talk about the quality of your appointments and slightly cool the talk about diversity'. The symbolism mattered and this was From's advice on a whole range of matters. Going to high-tech businesses and emphasising private sector growth as 'the key to opportunity'. Visiting 'welfare reform projects or charter schools'. Getting the president to 'walk the beat with a community policeman'. As From noted, 'you know the drill'.[17]

A few weeks later, From fired another memo to Clinton and enclosed a Tom Edsall article from the *Washington Post*. Edsall's piece had claimed that whilst Clinton had issued a pointed 'rejection of the Democratic Party as a "tax and spend" institution' in his 1992 campaign, he had stumbled in this regard in his first 100 days. More acutely, he had also 'acceded to the culturally liberal pressures within his own party' and failed 'to affirm the middle-class values of family, work and responsibility' that had got him into office. From knew Clinton had not 'dropped the new Democrat ideas from your agenda', but 'they are no longer center stage'. Issues which should have been smuggled through were being thrust into the limelight. Some of this was a hangover from the transition period. What communications officials like George Stephanopoulos had failed to see 'was Rush Limbaugh and Newt Gingrich bearing down on us from the right' and 'hammer[ing] us as self-indulgent, overprivileged yuppies who thought it was permissible to break the law if you were wealthy and went to Yale'.[18]

The embodiment of this was Zoe Baird. Baird was a talented lawyer who had risen to be chief counsel at Aetna Insurance, a multi-billion-dollar healthcare plan provider. At barely 40 she was an impressive figure and Clinton wanted her to be his first Attorney General. However, her nomination was withdrawn after it was discovered she had failed to pay social security taxes for a nanny and a chauffeur – both of whom were also illegal aliens. After 'Nannygate', Baird was promptly canned as the nominee and the slot was filled by Janet Reno who served throughout the Clinton years. But there was a wider question above and beyond poor vetting. As Stephanopoulos recalled, 'although I can't point to a discrete moment of decision, we worked from the assumption that keeping Clinton's pledge to have an administration that "looked like America" meant appointing a woman to one of the big four cabinet posts'. Whilst this 'was a worthy goal ... by turning in a quota, we put ourselves in a box'. For Stephanopoulos, 'after twelve years out of power, the pool of Democrats with high-level government experience was limited [and] the pool of women Democrats was even smaller'. The transition team had therefore scrambled 'to find the best female attorney general rather than the best attorney general – period'.[19] After Baird had withdrawn, Clinton could just about see the funny side. Turning to a newly appointed aide, David Dreyer, he asked when the fresh face before him had started work. To Dreyer's answer of 'yesterday', Clinton chuckled, 'well, it sure didn't take you long to screw everything up'.

Legislative successes

Internal wrangling aside, from an international perspective all looked well. Indeed, from London Giles Radice recorded in his diary on 8 January 1994 that 'Clinton, despite the continuing Republican attacks on his vivid private life, has turned out to be a "good thing". He has succeeded in getting reforms through Congress – the budget, NAFTA – and has come up with a viable health reform package'.[20] Health was clearly easier proposed than enacted. As for the North American Free Trade Agreement, agreed under Bush and then passed in a bi-partisan manner in the House, it might have superficially looked like an easy sell for Clinton. Though he had pressed for tougher Mexican environmental standards, protections for labour and a commission to be set up to monitor its implementation, Clinton had broadly supported NAFTA during his 1992 campaign – certainly more so than another DLC Democrat, Dick Gephardt. The globalist within Clinton believed that whilst there might be political costs in heavy manufacturing states, the wider signal that he was pro-business would be worth the pain – certainly in the electoral college.

It was no free ride, however. The trade union movement rigidly opposed the bill since hundreds of American factories, they argued, would soon relocate to Mexico where they could sell goods back to the States for far cheaper. As AFL–CIO president Lane Kirkland later told Robert Reich, 'we worked our asses off to elect Bill Clinton. I'll be goddamned if my members are going to lose their fucking jobs on some vague promise by Mexico to improve their labor standards'.[21] The unions lobbied congressmen and hoped to derail the president away from NAFTA and into spending his political capital on healthcare reform instead. But when Al Gore successfully defended the bill against its most prominent opponent, Ross Perot, in a debate on *Larry King*, its passage in Congress looked likely. Ironically, given later events, it would be Newt Gingrich who would deliver one of the president's key 1993 achievements – 132 Republicans would join the 102 Democrats in voting for NAFTA in the House on 17 November 1993, thereby getting it over the line. A year after NAFTA, in December 1994, Congress would go further in approving the terms of the new Global Agreement on Tariffs and Trade, which reduced global tariffs by $740 billion and created a new World Trade Organization (WTO).

Around this time, EJ Dionne contended that 'having embraced global competition, Clinton had to live with the sometimes-chaotic change it could impose'. Whilst he bought the ideas of Robert Reich that globalisation must be met with significant investment in worker re-training in theory, deficit reduction placed limits on how far the president could arm the American workforce in practice. So, Reich, whilst continuing to press his case, looked elsewhere. The Labor Secretary's dream became to broker a deal whereby the business community got NAFTA whilst Clinton acted to introduce a law banning strike replacements – the controversial practice whereby factories would fire striking employees and replace them with new staff, thus undermining the efficacy and point of industrial action. By early 1994 this was still rumbling on – NAFTA had been passed, but as one union audience told Reich in a Florida meeting, 'you and Clinton sold us down the drain'. In his quieter moments, Reich reflected that 'Clinton has already delivered to corporate America what even George Bush was unable to deliver – a shrinking deficit and NAFTA'. He underestimated his president, however. Clinton couldn't get a bill on nationwide action through Congress, but he could do something about one of the US economy's biggest spenders – the government. On 8 March 1995 Clinton therefore signed executive order 12954 which declared that Federal Government agencies would not procure from any employer which permanently replaced lawful striking workers. The next day a bill was introduced by Congressional Republicans which sought to effectively overturn the order and even Democrats like Sam Nunn declared that 'the President has no authority whatsoever to do this'. Pat Moynihan, too, recommended to the administration that it was better to 'save your energies'. Still, the Democrats got their 40 votes in the Senate and the order was safe.[22]

The other big three reforms in his first year were vintage Clinton – and akin to his mantra of responsibility, opportunity and community. As for responsibility, the Clinton administration 'believed in preventing crime and punishing criminals'. To deliver on this, the Violent Crime Control and Law Enforcement Act put 100,000 new police officers on the beat, provided for an assault weapons ban and put $1.6 billion into initiatives aimed at violence against women. Meanwhile, the Brady Bill, signed into law in late 1993, provided for mandatory background checks prior to the purchase of a firearm –thereby preventing more than half a million felons and fugitives getting their hands on weapons. For those who claimed Clinton was all about triangulation and political calculation, there was a clear cost to this – readily acknowledged at the time. It is estimated that 1 in 3 of the seats the Democrats would lose in the House in 1994 were down to representatives having voted for gun control. This was politically brave on behalf of both the president and the deposed Congressmen.

Clinton, however, did not just want to protect Americans, he wanted to unleash their opportunity – and much emerged here from personal experience. When Chelsea had been born in 1980, Hillary Clinton had been given four months of parental leave by her law firm. Meanwhile, Bill, as Governor, could afford to take a lot of his work home with him. But not all Americans were so lucky. Hillary told Bill of the comparatively generous offerings abroad and the president entered office determined to act. A bill lay on the president's desk, having been vetoed by Bush. And so, in February 1993 Clinton signed the Family and Medical Leave Act (FMLA) which gave Americans three months of unpaid leave after the birth of a baby or when a relative was unwell. As press secretary Joe Lockhart put it, Clinton wanted to 'dominate the center' and part of this was to show that government should 'start doing things that people would get'. Whilst 'government does hugely complicated things that the public is just never going to get', Clinton's view was that if it did 'a simple thing every day' the public would go to bed every night saying 'that's a pretty good idea. He's working for me, Clinton's all right'. FMLA fitted into the 'bitesize initiatives' the White House had thereby laid out, but it had profound consequences – by the time Clinton had left office over 35 million Americans had made use of its provisions. Business groups from the US Chamber of Commerce to the National Federation of Small Businesses had lobbied against it and, as the influential Michigan Congressman Bill Ford told Robert Reich, 'it took us seven years to get this fucking bill enacted. Goddamn Republicans'.[23] Now, on 5 February 1993, Clinton could make Americans' lives a little easier.

But what of community? Kennedy's call to 'ask not what your country can do for you, ask what you can do for your country', had long resonated. By the late 1980s, academics and columnists from across the political spectrum, from David Broder to William F. Buckley, had become 'worried that the baby boomer's rights-based liberalism and me-first conservatism had severed rights from obligations'. Taking a more communitarian approach – against the values free and rights-based notions of many on the contemporary left – DLC figures began to muse that some form of national service should be a key part of their agenda. In 1989, Oklahoman Congressman Dave McCurdy convinced Sam Nunn to co-sponsor a bill, the Citizenship and National Service Act, which Milton Friedman compared to 'the Hitler *jugend* [youth]'. In reality, the legislation proposed to replace $9 billion of Pell Grants of loans and grants for higher education with a system of federal tax credits earned for national service – military or civil – which one could redeem against the cost of college. Though unwilling to pass the DLC-inspired bill, Bush was savvy enough to pass a watered-down bill, which, by 1992, was awarding $64 million worth of grants to various forms of community service.[24]

Clinton wanted to go much further, however. Through the National and Community Service Trust Act, the new administration created AmeriCorps. In its first 20 years, this body would facilitate 900,000 volunteers delivering 1.2 billion hours of service in thousands of communities. Such volunteerism involved tutoring at-risk high-school students, cleaning up after hurricanes and tornados and helping build homes for low-income families. In doing so, the volunteers earned more than $2.7 billion from the government to go to college or pay back student loans. Later, New Labour would struggle to match this record. In 2002, Gordon Brown announced that, 'based on the success of the United States *AmeriCorps*, we will pilot a financial scheme to help British young volunteers from lower-income backgrounds take a year out after school to undertake community service'.[25] They would leave office pledging to roll out a National Service along the AmeriCorps model – though David Cameron's 'Big Society' agenda was able to steal much of the press attention, at least in opposition. Though it undershot the dreams of the 1980s, Clinton's achievement should certainly be set against New Labour's limited achievements on volunteerism.

Healthcare

As Clinton took the oath of office, it looked like there was a strong and binding consensus for healthcare reform. The president's proposals broadly matched those of moderate Republicans in the house and the prospect of consumer choice within a framework of universal coverage seemed set. In January 1993, the president therefore created a Task Force on Health Care Reform to be headed by the First Lady. Elaine Kamarck, working for Gore, remembers that 'the first thing that happened was that he set up this health care mess and gave it to Hillary. This came on top of the transition period, when Hillary's people were saying things to the *New York Times* like, "Al Gore is going to have to get used to the fact that there are two Vice Presidents".[26] Still, with 37 million Americans uninsured and tens of millions with inadequate coverage, there was much to do. Even viewed from a purely budgetary standpoint, the cost of healthcare, $900 billion a year, was the highest in the world and rising at twice the rate of inflation. Reform was needed and quickly.

The problem was certainly not the First Lady's lack of diligence. Hillary had been researching the subject heavily since the beginning of 1992, including studying the systems in France and Canada and the myriad of regimes within the various US states. This would prove useful in her testimony before the house committees which would scrutinise the proposed reforms and she received ovations for her appearances. Indeed, it looked like momentum was with a major policy shift. The Clinton victory aside, in November 1991 Harris Wofford had managed to win an upset victory (from 40 points behind) in a Pennsylvania Senate special election after making universal health coverage a central issue of his campaign. With costs rising at double-digit rates and the recession increasing unemployment (thereby affecting levels of health coverage), the issue had cross-class cut through. Twenty-three Republican senators even signed on to a bill which would have provided a universal individual mandate – that is to say, place into law the responsibility for each American (save some set aside categories) to purchase health insurance.

Nevertheless, through the middle of 1993, healthcare began to sputter. On a procedural matter, Senator Byrd declared that healthcare could not be moved into the budget reconciliation process (where it would only need 51 votes to pass, rather than require a filibuster-breaking 60). With 43 Republicans in the Senate this was an issue – if they sensed the administration was faltering elsewhere and it was, the temptation to block the bill to harm a president fast losing popularity would grow. As it was, the budget was proving problematic, thus any new spending measures, which major healthcare reform certainly involve, were placed on the back burner. But it was Clinton's own authority, upon which passage of the bill would depend, which was the biggest problem. As Paul

Starr, who worked on Clinton's healthcare team recalls, 'there is no logical connection between views on health care reform and, say, gays in the military or the role of women in society. But the identification of the Clintons with the reform of health care became so strong that sentiments crossed over'.[27] When the *Wall Street Journal* asked focus groups about particular health care packages with and without the Clinton name attached, the principle of change won more than 70 per cent support. With the Clinton label this dropped dramatically, by at least 30 points.

On 22 September 1993, Clinton gave a major speech to Congress outlining his plan in detail. All employers would be required to obtain health insurance and pay 80 per cent of premium costs (the employee providing the balance, with set asides for low-income workers) for their workers. All in-work citizens would be guaranteed health insurance coverage at a level similar to current employer packages, with primary care and preventative services prioritised and pre-existing conditions could not be used to deny coverage. As for the administrative questions, each state would set up regional health alliances from which individuals would purchase their insurance and which would negotiate with health plans made up of doctors and hospitals. Meanwhile, a National Health Board would determine the cost of the basic benefit package, set spending limits for each state-wide alliance and cap future premium increases. Revenue for the plan would come through cutting costs to Medicare and Medicaid (the latter would be rolled into the new system), a $1 per pack cigarette tax and increases to income tax, financed, in part, from employer health cost savings.[28] There were economies of scale here, but these were achieved by 'big government' and therein lay the problem.

Criticism came from both left and right. For the Democratic left – Congressmen like Jim McDermott – a government-financed, Canadian-style health care system was a more efficient model than that proposed by Clinton and this general view commanded 89 supporters in the House. However, even should it muster enough support to pass, such a proposal would have had close to zero prospect of getting through the Senate. From the opposite perspective, the official Republican responder to Clinton's Congressional address, South Carolina Governor Carroll Campbell, called it 'a giant social experiment, devised by theorists who have never met a payroll'. Meanwhile, Senate GOP leader Bob Dole, with an eye on the Republican nomination in 1996, argued that 'the big winners were big government, big labor and big business'. Still, the White House remained confident. Greenberg pointed to polling showing two-thirds approval for the president's plan, whilst *The New York Times* thought the case had been made so convincingly that Clinton could already nail it to the wall.[29]

This was optimistic for several reasons. First, as the clock ticked on, the November 1994 mid-terms grew ever nearer. The Republicans did not know that they would make the stunning gains they would achieve, but significant pickups in both houses were likely, which would affect the congressional numbers. Strategist Bill Kristol's advice for Republicans therefore remained, 'sight unseen, oppose it'. This was utterly craven, but nevertheless carried a degree of sly logic. Secondly, there was no realistic back-up option if, as proved to be the case, private-sector special interests successfully bounced Congress away from business carrying the tab for any potential changes. With Whitewater dominating the headlines in early 1994, the Chamber of Commerce and American Medical Association withdrew their support for the main thrust of the Clinton plan. As Paul Starr notes, 'if there is a simple answer to the question, "Why did universal coverage fail?" it is simply this: Congress would not enact the employer mandate in any form and when the mandate failed, so did universal coverage, because there was no willingness to consider a broad-based tax [to fund the reforms instead]'.[30] Even some Democratic senators, including Pat Moynihan, found the estimates behind the plan – which relied on speedy take-up rates and savings elsewhere in the congressional budget – 'fantasy, pure fantasy'.

But popular presidents usually find a way round such impasses. Neither Congressional opponents nor private-sector lobbyists would have attempted this strategy if it did not stand a significant chance of success. Certainly, the collapse of healthcare reform in 1993 and 1994 was 'a story of compromises that never happened, of deals that were never closed, of Republicans, moderate Democrats and key interest groups that backpedaled from proposals they themselves had earlier co-sponsored or endorsed'.[31] It was also a failure of the Clinton brand. The fact was that the votes could not even be found for a compromise bill that would have delayed most of the responsibilities for business until 2002. In many ways the failure of health was the failure of an administration overconfident and flush in the wake of an historic victory. A plan cooked up in the White House and then taken out to stakeholders only late in 1993 was judged to be an inside job, rather than something Americans had crafted together on an issue that affected millions. Of course, this was all a matter of perception, but perception would come to matter. The administration would return to health in its second term, but in a chastened, more moderate form. The debate continues to rumble on.

Before leaving the vexed issue of healthcare, a final word should also be added on Whitewater, since it would become a watchword for the Clintons' wider trustworthiness and hamper their ability to deliver in that area. Compared to more recent political scandals, Whitewater was of limited seriousness. In 1979, Bill and Hillary had formed a property company, Whitewater Development Corporation, with old Arkansas political contacts Jim and Susan McDougal, as a means of supplementing their respective incomes. The new company borrowed $203,000 to purchase 230 acres of land in the Ozark Mountains, with the intention to hold the land for a few years and sell sub-divided plots of land at a profit. Yet, when interest rates rose, the Whitewater Development Corporation saw the demand for its land plummet, losing all its contributors' money. The Clintons argued they had done nothing wrong save invest in a losing scheme and the fact that they had lost less money than the McDougals on the deal was proof of precisely nothing – despite what opponents speculated.

But Whitewater did two things. First, it tied the Clintons to Jim McDougal, who later funneled money to secure a 1985 property deal – Castle Grande – upon which he relied on the legal services of Hillary Clinton. The same year, the bank McDougal had previously purchased, Madison Guaranty Savings & Loan, had hosted a fundraiser to clear Bill's gubernatorial campaign debt from his 1984 campaign and McDougal had helped secure many of the donations. Through such dealings the Clintons became connected, in short, to a man eventually found guilty of 18 counts of fraud and conspiracy and whose financial malpractice would require the taxpayer to underwrite $68 million of bad loans. This wasn't ideal. Secondly, however, such conduct also attracted the attention of an ambitious prosecutor, Kenneth Starr, appointed to look into the affair by a panel of judges. As he came to develop a hatred for the president and widened the scope of his inquiry, Starr would come to dog the administration – leading the prosecutor to Monica Lewinsky.

That was a problem for the second term, however. Watching Clinton's first year from the British Embassy, Jonathan Powell recalls that many of his colleagues felt that 'from the outside it was obvious they were making mistakes'. Certainly, 'Whitewater was an issue, [with Clinton] having to appoint a special counsel and so forth, but the real problem was healthcare – normally in the British system you would have a royal commission, whereas you can't do that in America. By handing it to Hillary and having her take it forward in quite a liberal way without taking account of Congress was a pretty big mistake'. When New Labour would go on to hand over major questions – electoral reform, university fees, care for the elderly among countless other examples – in government to independent policy commissions, it owed something of its legacy to the Clintons steaming ahead on healthcare in 1993. The centre-left would aim for radicalism in government, but this had to be properly sequenced and not everything could be achieved at once. Elaine Kamarck contends that 'in retrospect, what we should have done is done nothing but reinventing government for the first two years, cut deficits, cut employees, tried to reverse those distrust numbers and then try to do health care [and] welfare reform'.[32]

1994

On 8 November 1994, the American public had their first major chance to deliver a verdict on the Clinton administration. It had passed a budget whose long-term economic effects remained uncertain, bungled health and was bogged down in largely irrelevant presentational scandals. When the verdict came in it was, as the British strategist Alastair Campbell recorded in his diary, 'a disaster'.[33] The Republicans gained eight Senate seats to take their total to 52, making them the majority party. Gains included Maine (where retiring Majority Leader George Mitchell had served), Michigan and Pennsylvania (which elected future presidential candidate Rick Santorum). Even Dianne Feinstein only held on by 2 per cent in California. In a further blow, a day after the 'Republican Revolution' was cast at the ballot box, Alabama Senator Dick Shelby announced his defection to the Republicans. Even this paled into insignificance compared to what had happened in the House. There, the leadership of Newt Gingrich delivered 54 new seats to the Republicans, taking them to 230 and providing them with majority party status for the first time since 1952. The Republicans also gained 10 Governorships, including George Pataki defeating Mario Cuomo in New York and George W. Bush taking Texas. From January 1995, Clinton would be a Democratic president surrounded by Republican influence at almost every level of American democracy.

For Stan Greenberg, 'this surge was a reaction against governmental activism and obtrusiveness, made visible and real by unified Democratic control of Congress and the presidency'. Gun control had accounted for

FIGURE 9 Having achieved an historic 1994 mid-term result for the GOP, Newt Gingrich would prove a thorn in Bill Clinton's side. Here he and Al Gore take in the 1998 State of the Union (Courtesy: Clinton Presidential Library).

much, but it was more than that. Newt Gingrich's 'Contract with America', written with the Texan Congressman Dick Armey and based on rehashing Reaganomics with some new ideas pickled at the Heritage Foundation think tank, had proven wildly popular. Based on so-called '60 per cent issues' – policies which polled higher than that number – this de facto manifesto pledged Republican candidates to support a number of state-shrinking measures, including cutting the staff of house committees, requiring tax increases to gain a three-fifths majority and zero base-line budgeting (i.e. assuming no element of public spending was ever sacrosanct). It avoided more controversial issues such as abortion and school prayer and was nakedly populist.[34] After 'the big tax hikes and government run health care' initiatives of Clinton's first two years, this strategy worked. This was a 'values' election and one which further exposed where the Democrats were out of touch.

Still, as Al From and Will Marshall wrote soon after the election, 'Democrats should view the 1994 election as liberating. The election ended any illusion that any New Deal coalition, which cracked three decades ago in presidential elections, could somehow be put back together'. For independent voters, Clinton was still a New Democrat at heart, but he wasn't governing as one. Health care had proven harmful and he was identified with 'an agenda for cultural liberalism, typified by his support for gays in the military'. Rather than big government, independents were 'looking for a new kind of government that helps them solve their problems without overtaxing or overregulating them'. A 'third choice' between left and right would have to now involve 'ruthlessly cutting unproductive federal spending that benefits special interests', 'reforming welfare' to 'repair the nation's tattered social fabric' and injecting 'choice, competition and market incentives into the public sector'.[35]

Aside from DLCers looking to reassert their own relevance, one interested observer was Labour's Peter Mandelson. He collected his thoughts in a *Guardian* article three days after the 1994 election. There, Mandelson noted that Clinton's own personal problems – 'Whitewater and alleged female skeletons in his cupboard' – made any comparisons between the president and the new opposition leader Tony Blair rather tough.[36] We cover Blair's rise in the next chapter, but there were clear lessons for the broad British centre left. First, 'the failure to secure healthcare reform was a colossal setback. Spearheaded by Hillary Clinton, drawn up in total secrecy, the reforms were easily portrayed by hostile political and commercial interests as too "big government liberal" for American tastes'. It was 'not that the Clintons were wrong to take the issue on'. But, to deal with the fights the issue was bound to trigger, 'the president needed much greater administrative and political capacity than he created . . . Too many of the Clinton officials did not have either the skill or the bottle to cope'. Organisationally, there were lessons here.

Yet there were also specific policy questions for the high-polling Blair to consider, particularly in terms of tax. As Mandelson noted, Clinton had run on the idea that 'the burden on ordinary taxpayers had become too great and needed to be lightened'. Yet, 'as the Tories have discovered here, hell hath no fury like taxpayers betrayed. Promises on tax needed to be fully baked and Labour is right not to make casual commitments prematurely'. Much internal New Labour debate would be given to the issue of tax, particularly for high earners. Clinton's legacy in part paved the way here. 'If, as Labour is doing, more active government is being promised, this must be accompanied by a pledge of better government – more accountable, less wasteful and decentralised . . . Clinton had failed to put enough stress on political reform'. Both New Labour and the New Democrats needed to forge anew, rather than merely return to the 'tax and spend solutions' of old.

For Jonathan Powell, 'the spectre of Clinton's first term' would account for much of New Labour's decision to 'hoard our political capital rather than spending it' in its first term. As Clinton 'frittered away his support on a series of missteps over gays in the military and health-care reform' he had threatened the long-term success of his overall project.[37] In private, Tony Blair would probe Stan Greenberg on all this. As Greenberg recalls, 'Blair was a committed reformer and he wanted to know if Clinton was a real reformer. Given the problems in Congress, the healthcare plan, big government, all that stuff, he was looking for more inside reading on his instincts as a reformer. He was interested in both his effectiveness and his reformer's credentials . . . Every meeting began there. He wanted to know about Clinton'.[38] All that we cover in the next chapter.

Back to the centre

1994 was a disaster electorally, but it also served as a litmus test for where one assumed the New Democrats should go. For some, Stan Greenberg included, the party would go on from this point to kowtow too much to a Republican-controlled Congress. Clinton was clearly rattled in the weeks that followed. When Al From told him that 'remember, we're your friends', the president would snap back, 'then act like it'.[39] But the left-leaning Greenbergs were losing the battle. On 8 January 1995, David Osborne – of *Reinventing Government* fame – wrote a 7,000-word op-ed in the *Washington Post Magazine* which suggested the tide was already turning. Provocatively entitled 'Can This President Be Saved?' Osborne savaged the Clinton administration's record to date. Clinton's 'fear of offending liberal interest' had stymied the necessary attacks on statist 'sacred cows'. Since 'most' of Clinton's 'advisors believed in the spending side of your vision, but not the cutting and reinventing side', the result was a president served by 'bad advice' that was antithetical to the New Democrat vision. Gore had got a few parts of his Performance Review through the naysayers, but Stephanopoulos had nixed the more radical cuts to federal bureaucracy as 'too radical [and] too dangerous'. The healthcare debacle smacked of 'big government' and had obscured the few interesting measures on the *Reinventing Government* agenda that had managed to sneak through.

The article was more or less kicking against an open door. Privately, Clinton would rant against 'those kids who got me elected' and claimed he 'never should have brought anyone under forty into the White House'. This, of course, included Stephanopoulos. A few weeks after the election Clinton flat out told the 33-year-old that 'we hired too many people in this White House who are smart but not wise'. As Stephanopoulos conceded, a 'pretty fair description of me'. The DLCers then took aim at what they saw as 'the liberal tilt' in the administration and Dave McCurdy, who had failed to take the Senate seat for Oklahoma that November, called for Stephanopoulos' sacking whilst the communications chief was standing only yards away. The loyal Pat Griffin, listening in, mouthed 'cocksucker' in the direction of McCurdy, whilst the president tactfully ignored both.[40]

Change was needed. Like McCurdy, Osborne proposed that Clinton clean house and sack or move the blockers of reform. Those moderates who stayed, like Leon Panetta, should be given New Democrat deputies. Clinton should himself 'be presidential' and 'quit jogging in public and answering questions about your underwear'. On the policy side, he should be bold. He should pass meaningful civil service reform, giving managers freedom to hire and fire, promote or demote. Rather than devolving funds to level of the state, as the Republicans demanded, he should instead go to the individual. As Osborne argued, 'state welfare bureaucracies are the *problem*, not the solution. To 'end welfare as we know it', Clinton should fund the *individual* through measures like Individual Skills Account – tax-free accounts that could be used for education, training and job placement assistance. Because he was now seen as part of 'the system', Americans now put Clinton in the category of the 'cultural elite – people who graduated from Yale and Harvard and Oxford [and] . . . who hang out with movie stars and vacation in places like Martha's Vineyard'. But this was not America. Whereas the Democrats could still just about command polling leads when voters were asked who understood family financial pressures, the Republicans cleaned up when it came to 'strengthening families, honouring middle-class values, insisting on moral standards, [and] having people take greater responsibility'. The New Covenant was dead and it needed to be brought back sharpish. As Panetta told Reich a week after the election, 'the radical center – that's where we're headed'. The more cynical Reich felt this was a 'fictitious place'.[41]

Clinton listened and, in his 1995 State of the Union, he returned to the tunes of 1992. Over ten weeks Al From, Bruce Reed, Don Baer and others had carefully used the Republican resurgence to finally and decisively, jettison the 'Old' Democratic norms from the president's lexicon. In the words of From, Clinton was a 'cat in its ninth life' who had 'one more chance to seize control of our party and of the national agenda'.[42] For too many Americans, Clinton in 1994 had been defined by gays in the military and a failed attempt at a big government health system. Within weeks of the election, indeed, a new Blue Dog Coalition of Democratic Congressmen would be formed designed to stop the party going further down that road. Not that Clinton had much intention of that. The 1995 State of the Union provided a chance to reset the clock.

With Newt Gingrich sat behind him, a looming reminder of the recent defeat, Clinton gave what Bill Kristol called the 'most conservative State of the Union by a Democratic president in history'. As the *Post* reported, Clinton 'offered no new massive government efforts, like the health care plan that was the foundation of his address from the podium only a year ago'. Instead, he 'bowed to the political imperative of redefining a more centrist, visionary presidency'.[43] Clinton recalled when, as a Governor, 'I had the honor of working with the Reagan administration to write the last welfare reform bill back in 1988'. He again played to the Republicans when recalling that 'our administration gave two dozen States the right ... to reform their own welfare systems and to try to promote work and responsibility over welfare and dependency'. On families in need, he argued that 'we can promote, together, education and work and good parenting. I have no problem with punishing bad behavior or the refusal to be a worker or a student or a responsible parent. I just don't want to punish poverty and past mistakes'. On law and order the administration had 'passed a very tough crime bill: longer sentences, "three strikes and you're out," almost 60 new capital punishment offences, more prisons, more prevention, 100,000 more police. And we paid for it all by reducing the size of the Federal bureaucracy and giving the money back to local communities to lower the crime rate'. In short, he could be a good centrist leader who the Republicans could work with.

But this was a speech which was still triangulating more than conceding all the way. As *The Post* noted, Republicans 'glowered or sat on their hands when he invoked his own [agenda] – gun control; government programs that he believes work; his version of the crime bill, not theirs; his version of welfare reform, not theirs'. On tax cuts, Clinton would consider all proposals from left or right, but his test 'will be: Will it create jobs and raise incomes; will it strengthen our families and support our children; is it paid for; will it build the middle class and shrink the under class? If it does, I'll support it. But if it doesn't, I won't'. He proposed to work with Congress to create a higher minimum wage which 'rewards work'. In doing so, he continued to argue that 'the weight of the evidence is that a modest increase does not cost jobs and may even lure people back into the job market. But the most important thing is, you can't make a living on $4.25 an hour, especially if you have children'. This was a masterclass of a speech which combined social conservatism with meaningful economic reform. It formed a fork in the road. Down one path lay a probable defeat in 1996 and down another, as it turned out, a 'new' New Democrats. Watching on, Tony Blair believed it showed that Clinton 'was determined then to make sure he got that center ground back and kept it. So, the lesson we took out of that was get there as soon as possible, because that's where it's smart to be'.[44]

The State of the Union was a success, but on its own it was not a strategy. That would come from 'the dark Buddha whose belly Clinton rubbed in desperate times', Dick Morris. Though Clinton was averse to sacking people, he could essentially replace them in all but name. After the '1994 debacle', as Stephanopoulos noted, 'Clinton would occasionally take my suggestions on minor tactical matters', but no longer 'fully trust[ed] me or my judgement'. Morris was the new flavor of the month, initially meeting with the president in secret (a codename 'Charlie' was designed to keep anxious liberal staffers off the scent) and then, through early 1995, being integrated more formally into the White House team. Clinton and Morris had first met in 1978 when the former was an ambitious Arkansas Attorney General and the latter a fledgling consultant looking for his vehicle to prominence. Morris 'had literally no shame' and, as Stephanopoulos recalled, 'when Dick looked at Bill, he saw a future president; when Bill looked at Dick, he saw the devil he knew – the part of himself that confused power and popularity with public service and principle'. In 1978 they won the Arkansas Governorship together and, when Clinton needed some hard-headed pragmatism again, he called up Morris to get him re-elected in 1982. Dick knew his client well. As he told Stephanopoulos in a 'getting to know you' dinner in May 1995, 'Bill only wants me around when his dark political side is coming out'.[45]

It was Hillary who had suggested Morris be brought back on board, but Clinton had not taken much convincing. Morris had been on the phone with the president in the weeks after the 1994 defeat, framing the very story Clinton himself would use to staffers. Rants about knowing 'going after the Contract with America was a loser' and never 'letting myself get sucked into campaigning so much' were lines fed by Morris that Clinton, subconsciously or not, had taken as his own. The strategy under Morris would be to 'neutralise the Republicans' and 'triangulate' the Democrats. Neutralisation required the passage of key Republican policies: 'a balanced budget, tax cuts, welfare reform [and] and end to affirmative action'. Venting these concerns among certain voters would allow Clinton breathing room on issues like abortion and gun control where there would be no going back. Equally, 'triangulating' the Democrats demanded Clinton abandon 'tradition class-warfare dogma' and inhabit a 'center above and between the two parties'. This meant 'deliberately pick[ing] fights' with Democrats and adopting a 'strong foreign policy'.[46]

Stephanopoulos' initial reaction was that this meant abandoning 'our promises and piss[ing] on our friends'. But, after listening to Morris expound his vision, he began to realise that his position was more precarious than he let on. Clinton trusted Morris, but he was still only one man in a sea of relatively liberal Democrats. Even the former Republican Leon Panetta 'could barely stand to be in the same room as him', whilst Harold Ickes was his 'mortal enemy'. Morris' mania to win at all costs also saw him take odd political positions. Certainly, his advice to enact a big 'national crusade' against domestic terrorism after the Oklahoma bombing or to give police officers the power to use stringent background checks on those suspected of being illegal immigrants, was of a piece with Republican thinking. However, when it came to the budget showdown across late 1995 and early 1996, Morris 'didn't really care' about the policies – 'as long as it was ready by Tuesday and we could claim it reached balance'. Clinton had brought Morris on board because he had won with him previously and felt the administration needed greater creative tension, not because he was going to make Dick Morris *de facto* Vice President. Personally, Morris was also abrasive and unreliable. His association with Clinton would be cut when newspapers got wind that he had been involved with a prostitute who, in turn, had been allowed to listen on his conversations with the president. The fact that his resignation occurred the same day as Clinton's accepting the Democratic nomination was a further blow.[47]

But Morris' essential arguments were incontrovertible. America had elected a New Democrat in 1992 and rejected an Old Democrat in 1994. In any case, the Republicans now controlled Congress, severely limiting Clinton's freedom of movement. His own spin on the necessary shift was therefore, inevitably, far more positive than Stephanpolous'. Morris told Clinton that he should 'triangulate, create a third position, not just in between the old positions of the two parties but above them as well. Identify a new course that accommodates the needs the Republicans address but does it in a way that is uniquely yours'. This was a way 'to change, not abandon, the Democratic party'. A key issue here was tax cuts – which Clinton had promised in 1992, but economic realities and a Democratic Congress with other priorities had meant lay undelivered. Clinton told Morris he wanted to go back to the idea of a 'middle class tax cut', though Morris 'disagreed with triangulation based on class. I said it must be based on substance'. Talking it through with Clinton, Morris said that 'the key here is not which income level gets the tax cut but what they have to do to get it'. Instead of the Democrats saying 'no tax cuts' and the Republicans 'tax cuts for everyone', the administration should say 'tax cuts if you are going to college or raising children or buying a first home or saving for retirement ... Triangulate by functional differences'. Clinton didn't buy this all the way – he still wanted an upper income limit to the cuts built in – but the language he fundamentally agreed with. And this 'push-pull between the traditional class-warfare language and the new language of opportunity-responsibility' was to dominate the period up to 1996.[48]

Certainly, Clinton was helped by his opponents' mistakes. Republican nominee Bob Dole's 1996 pledge for an across-the-board 15 per cent tax cut was superficially attractive but did not chime with the spirit of the 1990s. If, as Morris argued, the '1980s were the "me" decade, we realized that the 1990s were the "we" decade'. Again, his polling showed that 'people wanted a tax cut to go to those who merit it and needed it to do good things like raise children or go to college'. Where Clinton was different was 'using the Republican means of cutting taxes to accomplish the Democratic end of helping families meet the cost of a college education'. 'In the old days of big government, he would have done it through a national scholarship program, with grants and a bureaucracy'. But now, in the age of smaller government, it makes sense to cut taxes to accomplish the same goal – sending people to college'. When Clinton formally declared that 'the era of big government is over' in his 1996 State of the Union (a phrase suggested by Morris), Sidney Blumenthal saw this as 'just the beginning of the battle. Once he had outmaneuvered the Republicans during the government shutdowns and won reelection in 1996, he wanted to move the country beyond Reagan's debilitating simplifications'.[49]

But first he had to win. In November 1996, flushed by the heat of victory, Stephanopoulos would breezily tell reporters that 'this election was over nine months ago' – referring to the end of the budget shutdown.[50] A year earlier, however, Clinton's victory was far from certain. By the end of the fiscal year, on 30 September 1995, the president and his new

Republican Congress had failed to agree a budget for the coming year. An interim resolution was passed to kick the can down the road in the hope of reaching a deal but, on 14 November, with no agreement reached, all non-essential federal services shut down. From November 1995 to January 1996 a total of 27 days saw suspended operations, thereby making American democracy a laughing stock to the rest of the world. The questions for the administration were twofold: who would get the blame and what would Clinton do to accommodate a rabid Republican congress armed with its small government Contract with America?

The answer to the first question, eventually, would prove to be Newt Gingrich. At first, Clinton rather liked Gingrich and certainly respected his 1994 electoral achievement. He saw the new Speaker as a fellow intellectual 'with whom it was fun to match wits'. Panetta and Stephanopoulos even began to believe that Clinton might be bamboozled by Gingrich's charm into signing a budget deal that would harm the administration. But this was to underrate the president. By 1995, Clinton had cut the deficit by 60 per cent, reduced the federal workforce by a quarter of a million jobs and expanded the Earned Income Tax Credit. These were significant achievements, some of which tilted towards the traditional right, but Clinton had his lines in the sand. Even Dick Morris argued that the strategy must be to 'reject emphatically and inflexibly the efforts to cut Medicare benefits, eliminate Medicaid guarantees, weaken environmental-protection laws and reduce federal aid to schools'. As his polling had shown, 'Medicare cuts are ... hated by the public, old and young'. The trick was to transition the Republicans away from the vague language of small government – which generally voters liked – to the more concrete consequences of cutting particular line items.[51]

There were tactics here but, as Stephanopoulos noted, 'it also revolved around fundamental questions of philosophy, economics and politics'. Namely, 'what is the proper size, scope and role of the federal government?' Up to November 1994, the Republicans had successfully parried the charge that their proposed massive tax cuts and increased defence spending would require up to 30 per cent cuts in Medicare and Medicaid. The strategy from the administration was initially to extend the same deficit reduction policies as seen in 1993, but Clinton gradually became convinced he should go more on the offensive. A Republican Congress putting forward unreasonable proposals being met with a worthy but equally intransigent president was not appealing to him. He was growing gradually uneasy with being questioned by journalists about what his own plan was and being forced to act like 'Who am I? I'm *just* the president of the United States'. In reality, the economy would grow far faster than the Office of Management and Budget and Congressional Budget Office analysts realised – thus rendering the projections on which the 1995 debacle was based essentially hollow. By summer 1995, the choice before the administration was what the numbers were then telling them: either no budget at all or 'big cuts in programs that affected broad slices of the population'.[52]

Clinton's first play was to publicly rule out a balanced budget in seven years' time, as proposed by the House and Senate, though he hedged on whether nine or ten years would be doable. Behind closed doors it was increasingly clear that Clinton had settled on a balance in ten years and all presentations were to be geared to that agenda. Still, discussing the issue in Cabinet and listening to Secretaries Brown, Reich, Riley and Shalala in particular, it was clear that if each had their various hobbyhorses protected then the budget would be $100–150 billion short of balance over the cycle. On 13 June 1995, Clinton thus took to the airwaves to outline his plans for a ten-year balance, the consequences of which took on Democratic interests, but were worlds apart from 'Gingrichism'. Whereas the Gingrich-controlled House wanted $288 billion saved from Medicare, Clinton wanted $127 billion. From Medicaid, the difference was between a $187 billion set of House reductions, or $55 billion in the Clinton plan. Whilst $350 billion should be wiped off personal and corporate taxes, Clinton wanted a $176 billion middle-class tax cut. Clinton's plan also proposed to raise new money from closing corporate loopholes, though he placed the burden on Congress to figure out what they might be.[53]

The debate over the budget not only split America, it also spilt old and new Democrats. To liberals in the administration, 1995 looked set to be the year 'that swept away the Great Society'. Medicare would be privatised, Medicaid sent to the states, immigration would be frozen and the civil rights won in the 1960s rolled back by a Republican-dominated Supreme Court. The budget aside, the Republicans in the 1995 Congress were also making huge attacks on affirmative action. This type of wedge issue, as Bill Kristol argued, could indeed drive the Democratic base apart as it had in the 1980s. What was more, many within the administration agreed with the substance of Republican criticisms: New Democrats like Bill Galston and Joel Klein believed that 'affirmative action was a good idea that had gone bad over time' and was now 'just another form of discrimination, with severe moral and political costs'.[54]

Conducting a review, the administration discovered that, in terms of education and employment programmes, the system was more or less working as it should. A bland statement from the president about not rewarding 'unqualified people' and avoiding quotas would just about do. But when it came to various set-aside projects, which reserved a percentage of government procurement for minority businesses, there were far deeper issues. These programmes were often abused by 'scam artists who won the contracts fronting for minority firms' and the practical effect could be akin to hanging a sign out of the front of the White House saying 'Whites Need Not Apply'.[55] For all the reasons Stan Greenberg had identified in *Middle Class Dreams*, this needed addressing.

But it was part of a wider agenda. Through the 1996 campaign, as Dick Morris acknowledged, 'we made it harder for Dole by taking away his key issues: balancing the budget, crime, welfare reform, toughness in foreign affairs and cutting taxes'. Social conservatives were certainly given much succour. In May 1996, Clinton signed an amendment to the Wetterling Act. Popularly known as 'Megan's Law', the change meant that not only were states required to track sex offenders by confirming their place of residence, they now had to give public disclosure of their location. A few months later, Clinton signed the Defence of Marriage Act in September 1996, explicitly defining marriage as between a man and a woman. This was eventually ruled as unconstitutional. Clinton himself was 'personally embarrassed and remorseful' in later years and Mike McCurry, as press secretary, noted that 'his posture was quite frankly driven by the political realities of an election year in 1996'.[56]

But it was welfare where the biggest call needed to be made. What became the Personal Responsibility and Work Opportunity Reconciliation Act (PRWORA) of 1996 had two aims: to tackle what it saw as the 1960s inspired scourge of illegitimacy and to promote incentives to work for single parents, particularly mothers. The almost threefold growth in the number of American children receiving Aid for Families with Dependent Children (AFDC) between 1965 and 1992 was indicative, the legislation set out, of a 'crisis in our nation'. This lifecycle of welfare dependency – 'children born into families receiving welfare assistance are 3 times more likely to be on welfare when they reach adulthood than [their peers]' – was one Clinton was determined to tackle having pledged to 'end welfare as we know it' in 1992. The Democratic left hated the Clintons for this. In the 2016 primaries, Bernie Sanders would somewhat unfairly hammer Hillary Clinton for 'scapegoating people who were helpless' during the reforms and even the president himself seemed on the fence on the issue in the summer of 1996.

Unlike Ronald Reagan, Bill Clinton did not buy that there were hundreds of thousands of 'welfare queens' defrauding the American taxpayer. The image of Clinton as 'Republican-lite' was also palpably wrong. Indeed, Morris remembers Clinton screaming down the phone to him during the 1996 campaign that his Republican challenger Bob Dole was 'an evil, evil man. He *likes* cutting food stamps. He *likes* it. He enjoys cutting Medicare. He *relishes* slashing education. He *loves* cutting immigrants. It's how he gets his kicks'.[57] But Clinton was sympathetic to the various workfare measures enacted by Republican governors in the 1980s, including Wisconsin's Tommy Thompson, later to serve in George W. Bush's cabinet. The new Temporary Assistance to Needy Families (TANF), enacted to replace AFDC, would largely square this circle. It was temporary. It provided dollars for the majority of needy cases whilst cutting some of the waste in the system. It allowed flexibility at the state level – allowing for greater innovation, but still protecting the match funding element of the old AFDC (i.e. to secure federal dollars, the states had to deliver their own spending too).

In December 1995 and January 1996 Congress had sent two bills to the president, which would have ended both welfare and health care benefits to low income children (through slashing the relevant parts of Medicaid). Clinton had vetoed both and asked Congress to come back to him. On 31 July and 1 August, a new bill passed both Houses of Congress and the White House team gathered to discuss the new legislation. The entitlement to health care had been restored, but welfare was explicitly removed from entitlement status. The bill proposed a requirement to work after two years of benefits, enacted a five-year lifetime limit on the receipt of such benefits and handed power down to the states in the form of a relatively open-ended block grant for the administration of the new system. As to the latter, federal incentives were provided whereby states were to be awarded a bonus of up to $25 million a year for demonstrating a decrease in the number of illegitimate births. Meanwhile, the majority of legal immigrants were barred from claiming federal TANF benefits for at least five years – more or less the arrangement, coincidence or not, that David Cameron would later attempt to secure from the EU prior to the Brexit referendum of 2016.

Back in 1996, demands to veto came from both the left (Reich) and right (Rubin) of Clinton's inner circle. Hillary Clinton, too, was doubtful, fearing the abolition of the safety net for needy mothers would jeopardise millions, though took care not to break with the president in front of others. But the arguments in favour were simple. The core proposals of a time limit and work requirements were close to Clinton's own proposals and what DLC voices had told him to do. The Republicans had come some of the way on child care, child support enforcement and school lunches to a degree that meant the administration could plausibly argue that it was a genuinely new bill. And, crucially, as Dick Morris and Bruce Reed both argued, a third veto would break faith with the promises of 1992 and might lose the election. This was a 'good welfare bill wrapped in a bad budget bill' and the president should sign.[58]

On 22 August, he did and, electorally, was proven right. To be sure, TANF was not without its critics. Some claim it has been insufficiently targeted towards the needy families in question (states using the bill's flexibility to invest in tangential schemes such as those which sought to reduce levels of unmarried pregnancy) and that by not raising its block grant of $16.5 billion since 1997 it had been undermined by inflation. Others have argued that it has been unable to respond to economic depression – though separate provisions within Obama's American Recovery and Reinvestment Act (the 2009 'stimulus package' containing $5 billion of extra TANF monies) and PRWORA's own $2 billion contingency fund, have somewhat addressed these. But such arguments are to view TANF in a vacuum and to ignore, for one, the 70 per cent increase ($4 bn) in the amount set aside for child-care provision that the White House secured from the original congressional legislation. Crucially, however, welfare reform was only one part of four intersecting policy agendas. The Earned Income Tax Credit incentivised work to a far greater degree than hitherto. Training programmes gave workers a greater ability to gain the jobs that a growing economy provided. Raising the minimum wage provided an immediate boost to pay packets. If action on welfare was the price for a second term in office, then the administration judged it worth paying.

Ultimately, for the survival of the Third Way, it was. Seventy-six days after he signed PRWORA, America took to the polls and confidently re-elected Bill Clinton. Defeating Bob Dole by 8 million votes and a landslide 220 seats in the electoral college, Clinton also saw off a returning third-party challenge from Ross Perot. This was an utter vindication for his electoral strategy and flew in the face of outcomes political pundits had previously hypothesised. Hispanics deemed to be alienated by the anti-immigration rhetoric of the welfare bill were 12 per cent more likely to vote Clinton in 1996 than they had been in 1992. The union households (5% increase) or self-defined liberals (13% rise) allegedly put off by his tack to the centre were more likely to back him against Dole than they had against Bush. Only the LGBT community showed slight disproval of Clinton, with 3 per cent of gays and lesbians turning against him from 1992.[59] If 1994 was a disaster for the incumbent, then 1996 was a ringing endorsement.

As in 1992, the architects of New Labour would be watching all this intently. Seeing the results come in from Winfield House, the residence of the US Ambassador in London, Alastair Campbell found Clinton 'on great form'. As such, many Labour politicians would cast a wry eye over the *Guardian*'s view that Clinton's was a 'modest agenda to reward the beleaguered wage-earners, elderly and poor'.[60] Whether helping these groups was indeed 'modest' – and not decent centre-left policy – was one question. Either way, the *Guardian* still felt compelled to compare the first re-elected Democratic president since Roosevelt unfavourably with both the New Deal and the Great Society. Labour would have killed to be in that boat. To be sure, there were lessons to be learned from Clinton's first term – both about what to push on and when. But if Blair could win, then, in a parliamentary system, he would not face the same difficulties of a hostile Congress. Health care was not the loaded pistol in British politics that it remains in the US. And the economic picture, for all the necessary campaign criticism against the Tories, was also far better than that the New Democrats had inherited in 1993. If New Labour could win power, perhaps they could even eclipse Clinton.

Notes

1   Radice 1/293.

2   'A Clinton Administration', circulated 2 November 1992, ARC/KEW/ PREM/19/4496.

3   Greenberg 2/68.

4   Reich 2/17–18, 29; Pellew memo, 29 January 1993, ARC/KEW/ PREM/19/4496; Greenberg 2/69–72; Greenspan/146.

5   Greenberg 2/73, 77.

6   Reich 2/92, 80; Galbraith to Reich, 18 March 1993, ARC/JFK/JKG/78.

7   Greenberg 2/91.

8   Greenberg 2/94.

9   Greenberg 2/96.

10 As syndicated in *Rochester Chronicle*, 4 August 1993; Renwick memo,
    29 April 1993, KEW/ PREM/19/4496.

11 Flavio Romano, *Clinton and Blair: The Political Economy of the Third Way*
    (Abingdon, Routledge, 2006), 55; ARC/SDS/DAS/DA3/4/9/33.

12 'Tax Cut Bill', March 1975, ARC/FORD/JM/32 and Weinberger memo,
    27 March 1975, ARC/FORD/PHF/C17; Falk/8.

13 Crine, passim; COR/Campbell.

14 Gore/2, 5, 12.

15 Dionne/99; Byrne, passim.

16 From/193, 196.

17 From to Clinton, 16 April 1993, ARC/CPL/REF/OA/ID 3520.

18 From to Clinton, 4 May 1993, ARC/CPL/REF/OA/ID 3520;
    Stephanopoulos/119.

19 Stephanopoulos/118.

20 Radice 1/311.

21 Reich 2/68.

22 Dionne/94; Reich 2/151, 168, 255.

23 Reich 2/57.

24 Bloodworth/233–34.

25 LR/HOC, 27 November 2002, vol 395, col 324.

26 MCI/Kamarck.

27 *Prospect*, Winter 1995.

28 *Cincinnati Enquirer*, 23 September 1993.

29 *Journal News* (White Plains, NY) and *Ithaca Journal* (Ithaca, NY),
    23 September 1993.

30 *Prospect*, Winter 1995.

31 Ibid.

32 COR/Powell; MCI/Kamarck.

33 Campbell 1/84.

34 Greenberg 1/261, 262.

35 'New Democrats and the 1994 Elections', in *Third Force*, November 1994,
    ARC/LOC/HDC/76/4.

36 *Guardian*, 11 November 1994.

37 Powell 2/28.

38 MCI/Greenberg.

39 From/217.

40 Stephanopoulos/322, 324, 326.

41 Reich 2/207.

42 From/215.

43 *Washington Post*, 25 January 1995.

44 MCI/Blair.

45 Stephanopoulos/332–33.

46 Stephanopoulos/334–35.

47 Stephanopoulos/338–39, 351.

48 Morris/80–83.

49 Morris/86; Blumenthal/310.

50 *Guardian*, 6 November 1996.

51 Morris/268, 93.

52 Stephanopoulos/344, 346.

53 *Los Angeles Times*, 14 June 1995.

54 Stephanopoulos/363.

55 Stephanopoulos/366.

56 Morris/269; *New York Times*, 25 March 2013.

57 Morris/268.

58 Stephanopoulos/420.

59 Exit poll data. Available at: www.ropercenter.cornell.edu.

60 *Guardian*, 6 November 1996.

6 LEARNING FROM THE BEST

Tony Blair was nervous. More nervous than his confidants had seen him in a long time. Leading his press adviser Alastair Campbell to one side, he furtively asked, 'Do I call him Bill or Mr President?' On the morning of 12 April 1996 Blair sat in a waiting room in the White House – thousands of miles from Spennymoor Town Hall in 1983, but not yet in actual power himself. The memory of Ronald Reagan's 'snub' to Neil Kinnock in 1987 laid heavy on Blair who 'felt very awed, hoping as you do that the meeting isn't too short ("Blair snubbed"), praying it overruns ("Blair welcomed"), but in either event begging to avoid disaster'. After a slight delay Blair, Campbell, Anji Hunter (Blair's Private Secretary), Jonathan Powell and Sir John Kerr (British Ambassador to the US) were all then ushered into the Oval Office. Greeting everyone individually at the entrance stood Bill Clinton, 'suit and tie immaculate, as was his hair'.[1]

The occasion was clearly a bigger deal for the British leader of the opposition than it was for the sitting American president. Yet Alastair Campbell remembers being 'surprised at the level of turnout from their side'. In the room alongside Clinton were Secretary of State Warren Christopher, Bob Rubin, Leon Panetta, Nancy Soderberg (then leading policy on Ireland), Tony Lake and two other officials. Lake had drawn up Clinton's briefing note for the occasion and this document helps explain the strong US presence. As Lake put it, the purpose for Clinton was 'to deepen your acquaintance with Blair, who appears likely to be the next prime minister in the UK'. Much of Clinton's immediate interest, certainly, was to ascertain whether Blair would continue incumbent Conservative Prime Minister John Major's open and flexible policy on peace in Northern Ireland. The Labour leader most certainly would, but the sympathies clearly ran deeper, as Lake acknowledged. 'Blair is personally responsible for moving his party to the center in order to appeal to the middle class. He speaks of broadening the Thatcher revolution rather than dismantling it.' As such, Blair's 1995 conference speech – where he stated that 'Labour had already made a deal with British Telecom to link every school, library and hospital to the information superhighway for free in return for greater market access' – particularly impressed Lake.[2]

There were clear policy crossovers between Blair and Clinton, in fact to a degree that was almost embarrassing. Before their private conversation began, Blair and Clinton had allowed a few questions from the Anglo-American press. Peter Riddell of *The Times* soon piped up, 'Mr President, do you think you're sitting next to the next Prime Minister?' Since John Major already had that job and, after some early wobbles, had gone on to form a productive relationship with Clinton, this was not an easy question to answer. Alastair Campbell could 'feel Clinton's mind whirring, thinking carefully about what to say'. Tony Blair even butted in, semi-joking but with underlying ice to his voice, 'now, that is not a diplomatic question!' Clinton chuckled, 'if I were in that position that's the question I'd ask'. Then he concluded, referring to his own forthcoming campaign against the Republican Bob Dole: 'it's all I can do to keep up with American politics. I only hope he's talking to the next American president!' For Blair this proved that Clinton 'was quick witted, he would have shone at PMQs'.[3] Whatever the mutual admiration, until May 1997 it was Clinton who had the power and Blair who wanted it. Though things would evolve, their relationship would undeniably begin as tutor and apprentice.

Over there

Clinton remained a moveable feast in British political discourse in the early 1990s – useable by both sides of the political divide and by anyone looking to promote their particular policy hobby horse. Certainly, progressives saw much hope in his having finally ended the Thatcher–Reagan era. In September 1992 the Liberal Democrat peer Lord Russell declared that 'when I read last week that US business is now busy giving its money not to [President] Bush but to [candidate] Clinton, I think that we are entering a world of new economic thinking'. Clinton's subsequent election then saw several Labour figures begin to read up on the theories of Robert Reich, who, according to Mike O'Brien, the new Labour MP for

North Warwickshire, was right to argue that 'in the age of new technology a nation's economic progress depends not so much on individual entrepreneurs as on collective entrepreneurial talent'. And for Robin Cook, then shadowing Trade and Industry, the key lesson from Clinton was in industrial policy. As Cook told the Commons in March 1994, 'in north America, home of capitalism, the Clinton administration have brought the automobile industry together in a national project to design the car of the future: a car low on gas and pollution and high on safety and export orders. What a contrast that is with the British Government, who look the other way while Rover is taken over'. It should be said that this was not all one way. The Conservative MP Phillip Oppenheim was keen, for example, to point out that, despite his campaign pledges on the matter, Clinton 'has done absolutely nothing' about raising the minimum wage 'because his own Labour Secretary, Robert Reich, said that it would threaten the recovery'. For Oppenheim, 'even the left-leaning Democratic Leadership Council recently said that the minimum wage is "anachronistic, it's a loser, it's got no life"'. 'No wonder it is Labour party policy', he mocked. This line would not hold long – Clinton would twice go on to raise the federal minimum wage.[4]

The point, however, is that the election of Clinton kickstarted a free flow of ideas across the Atlantic and this began early in his tenure. In January 1993, not only did Blair and Brown visit Washington, but Democratic advisors travelled to London to try and gee-up their Labour counterparts still depressed after their recent defeat. A couple of months earlier Denis MacShane had been standing in the queue for a cup of tea at Labour's European conference in Brighton and found himself behind Bill Morris, the head of the TGWU. MacShane was on the lookout for a parliamentary seat (he would eventually alight on Rotherham in 1994), but he was also intellectually curious about Clintonism. Taking the opportunity to chat to the influential trade unionists, MacShane told them that 'there's more to this Clinton guy than all the "Slick Willy" stuff we've seen in the press you know, he's not just about "spin"'. After consulting with Margaret Prosser, Morris agreed that the TGWU would put forward £50,000 to sponsor a landmark event to debate 'Clintonomics' at London's QE2 conference centre. Prosser recalls that Morris was certainly excited by Clinton's victory, but recalled a wider 'frisson within the trade union movement and certainly within the TGWU. This wasn't necessarily about the Americans, it was more the negative attitude within Tony Blair's group at the time towards the trade unions'.[5] Still, Clinton's appeal to 'youth' and 'freshness' contrasted well with the 'disarray at the Tory government at home' and TGWU put up the money.

As it gathered steam, numerous high-profile Labour types were roped into the event's organisation including Prosser, Margaret Hodge and, inevitably, Philip Gould who asked a group of Clinton advisors including Elaine Kamarck, Paul Begala and Stan Greenberg to come to the event. Greenberg viewed it as a holiday before the hard work of office began, but the opportunity to present on Clinton's economic strategy to the British left intrigued him. As Greenberg recalls, 'the audience was a mix of the curious and the hostile'. John Prescott sat in the front row, his expression dour and his arms crossed. The future Deputy Prime Minister would routinely mock the so-called 'beautiful people' enthralled by Clinton and as MacShane recalls, he 'of course attacked [the event] – "bloody hell, importing *American* ideas, we can't have any of that" – which was wonderful and made it the lead story in the *Sunday Times*'. Equally, Anne Campbell notes that there was a general 'suspicion' of Clinton at this stage and it was felt that 'the Democrats were not, nor had ever been, a truly socialist party'. Labour, as yet, 'hadn't come to terms with the need for reform'. For his part, Neil Kinnock could be seen in the back row and spoke up in a more supportive form when claiming that 'winning is better than losing, unfortunately I wasn't able to convince everyone else in the Labour Party'. Macshane, meanwhile, 'saw Gordon and Tony walking from breakout session to breakout session absolutely gawping at the wave of Americans, of their own generation, exuding success, achievement and confidence'.[6]

On the day, Greenberg tried to ingratiate himself by claiming that it was only after the Tories had used their tax-scare campaign against Kinnock in April 1992 that the Democrats realised that similar heat was coming their direction in November. This went down well. What did not go down so well with Labour thinkers in early 1993 was Clinton's actual policy. When Greenberg declared that 'Clinton centered his campaign on the broadly defined "middle class," promoting its economic interests and respecting its values, including toughness on crime, a work ethic and welfare reform, ideas that won support with the poor and working class as well', he was met with tumbleweed. Under John Smith, Labour was not yet ready to jettison some of its old shibboleths. As such, when Greenberg was led to the leader's office to meet in private, the occasion was 'polite enough and [Smith] thanked us for sharing our experience, but there was no sense of a shared political project'.[7]

This was the general impression most moderates got from Smith. After his time in Little Rock, Philip Gould had also tried to nudge the debate along. He wrote a long document summarising the Clinton campaign and sent it to Smith's advisors. In arguing that Labour was perceived to be looking 'downwards not upwards', was 'not trusted to run the economy properly' and was 'for minorities and not the mainstream', he recalled that such views 'went down like a lead balloon'. With Patricia Hewitt, Gould then took the argument public through an article in the newly formed journal *Renewal* in early 1993. According to the pair, 'the lessons which the British left can learn [from Clinton] are not so much about *content* – although there is valuable intellectual exchange already underway – as about *process*'. This involved better voter identification and a 'databank' of facts about their opponents which could be used as instant rebuttal. But even for the communications' strategists Gould and Hewitt, policy remained important, as was the need to hear what voters were saying. As they noted, 'political strategists like Stanley Greenberg – people outside the leadership circle but who were to play a vital part in the Clinton campaign – *listened* to disillusioned Democrats. They found that the majority of Americans – the self-defined middle class – felt themselves squeezed between the 'undeserving rich' and the 'undeserving poor'. Their central values were those of the New Deal Democrats: work, reward for work and responsibility. Throughout 1993, Gould continued to fire off a series of internal memoranda, in turn met by stony silence, all of which suggested Clinton had not yet found a viable British equivalent.[8]

Still, none of this deterred the modernisers. In November 1993, Blair visited the new Republican Mayor of New York Rudy Giuliani and took notes on his 'zero tolerance' methods to reducing crime. As per his usual American schedule, the then Shadow Home Secretary travelled to Washington DC where he had dinner at the house of Sidney Blumenthal – then a correspondent for the *New Yorker*, but later to join the Clinton team. Toasts were raised to the 'next leader of the Labour Party and prime minister' though this seemed a long shot with John Smith currently leading Britain's opposition to a strong position in the polls. Sitting to Blair's left on that occasion was Greenberg, who found his British visitor 'like a Bill Clinton without all the complexity' and a man who 'exhibited no sign of Clinton's explosive anger'. Blair was genial, interested in the machinations of Congress and, politically, generally Clintonian. Yet he was already showing a steel beneath the smile. Greenberg noted that 'he seemed to relish the prospect of confrontation with the unions, which suggested to me that Blair's politeness had another side'.

Interestingly, two months later Greenberg saw the second great figure of New Labour and the contrast was telling. Whereas Blair was about grand visions projected amiably, Gordon Brown marched into his office with a stance that was both more detailed and more combative. Having read a recent essay by his host, Brown told Greenberg that 'I've read your article and I can't agree with you on one point: voters will not trust the left if they are making the case for more government'. Brown had 'read everything America's new Democrats had been producing and was loaded down with a pile of policy reports from the DLC as well as his impressions from his meetings with Bob Reich, Larry Summers and Alan Greenspan'. With a messianic zeal to make Labour electable by proving it could manage Britain's economy, the Shadow Chancellor seemed to Greenberg like the American fullback Alan Ameche, 'who would grind out five yards each time toward the goal, each time carrying a bunch of defenders with him'.[9] Whether Brown or Blair would be best placed to take *the country* with them was about to become a pressing concern.

New Labour, new leader

A few months later, on 11 May 1994, Brown's advisor Ed Balls attended a Labour fundraising dinner at the Park Lane hotel in London. John Smith was doing the speaking honours and gave a barnstorming defence in favour of the NHS. The purpose of the gathering, according to another audience member, Tony Blair, was to 'consolidate what was then fairly limited support' from business for Labour. Such a difference of understanding regarding the same event was already suggestive of diverging views between the then leader and his Shadow Home Secretary. In any event, such machinations were above Ed Balls' pay grade. Balls clearly had a good time and in the early hours he, Smith and others were tucking into the celebratory drinks. The leader was in good spirits and, when it was time to leave, he gave Balls a great bear hug. Whilst in a clench with the young advisor, Smith said, 'Ed, listen: we must get all the thinkers together, plan the future'. Balls 'felt really chuffed … that's what I'd come into politics for'. Feeling upbeat, everyone dutifully went on their separate ways.[10]

Driving into work the next day in his small Renault 5, Ed Balls flicked on the radio. John Smith had suffered a heart attack. This had happened six years earlier, but the latest episode was far graver. By the time Balls arrived at parliament it had been confirmed that Smith had died. Gordon Brown was distraught at the death of his long-time mentor and retreated to his flat near parliament to write Smith's obituary. Brown then called Blair shortly after nine that morning, the two men still both shocked. Blair received the news at Aberdeen Airport where he had flown to be briefed on the party's forthcoming local election prospects in Scotland. None of that mattered now.

As Blair recalls, 'I knew what was coming now [Smith] was gone: even as people tried to assimilate the news, even as they mourned, even as they reflected about John Smith the man, as a political leader, as a friend, attention would shift and they would ask the question that is asked every time a leader falls and immediately a leader falls: who will be the successor?' It was clear that it would have to be Tony or Gordon and that two into one would not go. The two had conversations at a couple of houses owned by Blair's friends in Edinburgh at which, it was decided that Tony would be the one to stand for the leadership. Later, Gordon Brown would tell Blair's ally, Giles Radice, that he could not have won the contest regardless. In a subsequent dinner at the Granita Restaurant in Islington the Edinburgh deal was firmed up.[11]

Granita was certainly an awkward occasion. Ed Balls had been cajoled into joining Blair and Brown at the table before sloping off at some opportune moment. Polenta was on the menu that evening, a fact notable only for the fact that Brown did not know what it was – perhaps, for Blair, evidence of his inability to appeal to the English middle class. Balls left before the 'pact' – loose as it was – was ironed out. Indeed, had Balls been there, as he later recalled, 'I'd be able to tell the media and biographers what was right and wrong'. As it was, the meeting confirmed at least one and possibly two, elements ahead of any future Labour government. What is certain is that Brown was to have 'control of the broad range of economic policy' – in effect making him the most powerful Chancellor of the Exchequer in history.[12] Both Blair and Brown were agreed on this and it was more or less the line briefed to the press the next day. More contentious was the fact that the then Shadow Chancellor also appears to have left Granita with the understanding, accurate or not, that whilst Blair would serve two terms as Prime Minister, he would not serve a third and would, in turn, support Brown's candidacy as his successor.

From the wilderness of a fourth successive Conservative government, a third New Labour term looked utterly fanciful, even with the Major administration's then difficulties. Perhaps Blair hinted at standing down at some stage, perhaps not. Arguably the most impactful element of Granita, however, was to ensure that Blair would not dictate the government's economic strategy. He would go on to make several important interventions – including bouncing his Chancellor into raising national insurance in 2002 by simply going on the BBC and declaring that health spending would reach the European average. New Labour's public service reforms would also involve the say-so of Brown's Treasury in several key ways. But the economy was Gordon's terrain, a fact helped by the relative similarity in their world views.

There were two consequences here. First, Brown's elevation to a form of 'Super Chancellor' perhaps encouraged his sense of anger at having missed out on the top job. This led to a strained working relationship to say the very least, with Brown occasionally refusing to show up for meetings to illustrate who was boss. On one occasion, Jonathan Powell notes, Brown refused to attend a meeting on the grounds he was doing TV interviews, but when Blair rang him it was clear through his puffing and heavy breathing that he was on an exercise bike. Still, Powell knew this going in. When Powell flew over to London to be interviewed by Blair for the job of Chief of Staff in September 1994, he had been under strict instructions not to let Gordon know he was in line for the position. But then, on the journey home, Powell was horrified to spot Gordon Brown and Ed Balls in Terminal 4 at Heathrow. Sheepishly, Powell ducked into the newsagent WH Smith's to hide from the pair only, farcically, to have to meet them both the very next day in DC and pretend that nothing had happened.[13]

In terms of working method, Blair was something of a Third Way between Gordon Brown and Bill Clinton. For Clinton staffer James Steinberg, 'Blair is a little more methodical in his style [whereas] Clinton kind of grabs [a] whole thing'. Compared to the president, Blair would 'focus a lot on the details, whereas Clinton would get people in the room and get it done'. Indeed, 'Blair tried to use his ideas, his mind and his arguments more. Clinton thought he could do it with force of personality'.[14] Such an assessment was doubtless forged in Steinberg's experience of the unique Northern Ireland peace process, where Blair had to handle the day-to-day matters and Clinton could lend the strategic vision. But it always contained a grain of truth. With Brown grinding the hard policy yards, Blair the visionary quarterback who could also run with the football and Clinton directing traffic from the sidelines, the Third Way was a serious political force on a number of levels.

Still, the working patterns of the leaders could produce the odd gripe. By July 1994 – the month, coincidentally, Blair became Labour leader – Clinton's Cabinet Secretary Robert Reich was becoming increasingly concerned that his memos were simply not reaching the president or, not much better, were being deliberately leaked to the media. When Federico Pena, Secretary of Transportation, rang to ask him how he found out what was going on at the White House, Reich snippily remarked that 'the place was so disorganized that information is hard to come by'. Indeed, 'the decision-making loop depends on physical proximity' to Clinton, 'who's whispering in his ear most regularly, whose office is closest to the Oval, who's standing or sitting next to him when a key issue arises'. Reich had at least known the Clintons for over two decades, for newer 'friends of Bill' there wasn't even a long-standing personal connection to draw on. Hillary was at least helpful, counselling Reich to send her memos (on blank sheets of paper 'without any letterhead or other identifying characteristics') and she would see what she could do. By 1996, however, with Dick Morris in the ascendance and the administration tacking towards the centre, Reich would be reduced to roaming the corridors of the West Wing, 'like an itinerant peddler', trying to button-hole anyone he could to get his agenda across.[15]

Tony Blair's much debated 'sofa' style of government would come to rely on similar physical proximity to the Prime Minister – above and beyond the traditional Cabinet approach. Having introduced the UK's first Freedom of Information Act in 2000, Blair would later write that he was a 'naïve, foolish, irresponsible nincompoop' and quaked at the imbecility of it. This wasn't out of some Machiavellian aim to thwart the public, but because 'governments, like any organisations, needed to be able to debate, discuss and decide issues with a reasonable level of confidentiality'. As Blair correctly noted, 'in every system that goes down [the FOI] path, what happens is that people watch what they put in writing and talk without committing to paper'. For Jonathan Powell, 'Tony was not a natural chairman. He didn't as a rule feel bound to follow an agenda or sum up the discussion. There were never any votes in Cabinet and usually any dramatic differences had been resolved before they got there'.[16]

Yet, like any leader in power for a long time, Blair could also be oddly vacillating. Powell was on several occasions told to sack particular members of staff on the Prime Minister's behalf, only to see them reinstated once they appealed for clemency to the man himself. Much emerged through the various leaders somewhat different personalities. For one, Clinton was a political junkie, whereas Blair was always more rounded. Blair insisted on taking his full holiday allocation as Prime Minister – leading to much criticism in the press – but Clinton could barely get enough of political intrigue. Like Steve Richards' description of Gordon Brown, Clinton 'followed the media the way a music critic listens to a concert'. John Podesta, Clinton's Chief of Staff, once told Jonathan Powell that his problem was never having to wake the president at 3am due to some urgent international crisis, but Clinton ringing Podesta in the middle of the night wanting to chat about something he had seen on C-SPAN. This led, as Joe Biden told him, to Clinton suffering from 'Rhodes scholar disease'. When Clinton asked him what he meant, Biden remarked that 'you are so accustomed to having facts at your disposal, you don't trust your instincts'. Peter Hyman meanwhile notes that Blair tended to favour the opposite: 'his criterion for a good minister was the boldness in which he or she carried out reform'.[17]

Clause IV

Winning the party leadership would prove easy enough for Blair. With the semi-grudging backing of Brown he was able to comprehensively win the June 1994 contest in all three affiliate, constituency and parliamentary sections over Margaret Beckett and John Prescott, the latter of whom became Deputy Leader. With the former trade unionist Prescott by Blair's side, the new ticket balanced the party's left and right well enough. But winning the soul of the party beyond this gesture required a whole new set of challenges, particularly as the press – who dubbed him 'Bambi' – were keen to portray the young leader as lightweight.

The Major government was on the ropes, no question. Whilst the Conservative USP under Margaret Thatcher had been a ruthless competence, Major, largely due to external circumstance, could rarely project either characteristic. Sandwiched between Eurosceptic Rebels on his party's right and a broadly pro-European Labour and Liberal Democrat opposition, Major had achieved a considerable success in agreeing the Maastricht Treaty on further European integration in February 1992. By September that year, however, the UK was forced to exit the Exchange Rate Mechanism – the precursor to the Euro currency – which was largely regarded as a national humiliation. In February 1993, the murder of a young boy, James Bulger, by two boys from single-parent families then intensified a media storm over the issue of single mothers. Conservative ministers held court on the subject for much of that year and Major tried to respond in his annual conference speech with a plea for the country to go 'back to basics' with notions of 'sound money, free trade, traditional teaching, respect for the family and respect for the law'. What he did not know was what his parliamentary party had been up to. In just one month, January 1994, one MP resigned from the government following stories he had fathered a child in an extra-marital affair, another was found dead in his home with an electrical cable around his neck having performed autoerotic asphyxiation and a third confirmed rumours that he had fathered a child with the secretary of another parliamentarian. These were far from the end of the list. An image of sleaze and chaos had replaced responsibility and order.

These issues mattered because the government also looked incompetent and uncaring. For many, for example, the experience of public services in early 1990s Britain was clearly sub-par. As Gordon Brown later wrote, 'few people were in any doubt that the NHS we had inherited in 1997 was not fit for purpose' and the UK certainly had the fewest number of doctors per capita in any developed nation.[18] Likewise, from the late 1980s onwards, the proportion of children being educated in classes of 30 or more rocketed to the point that, by 1997, over one-third of primary school pupils were in this boat. This led to Blair's famous emphasis on 'education, education, education' at the 1996 party conference.

But unless Labour looked like a government in waiting it might all come to nought. Major was not the incompetent many, particularly Labour at the time, would come to allege. The economy began to boom from 1994 onwards. He had brought hospital waiting lists dramatically down since 1990. He had been pragmatic on Ireland and steely enough to see off a Eurosceptic challenge to his leadership in 1995. His public service reforms were largely ones New Labour would ape. In any event, even if he was electorally toast, perhaps a Michael Heseltine figure could usurp him and persuade the electorate that, just as Major had seemed to offer a change of direction from Thatcher in 1990, the Conservatives could also pivot ahead of any 1996 or 1997 election. According to Sidney Blumenthal, even Bill Clinton was 'sceptical about Tony Blair's political prospects' at this stage.[19] Sitting in opposition, the incumbency factor was always a fear even for the most upbeat Blairite. And, in 1994, Blair could not yet change the country. But he could change his party.

What followed was an act of pure symbolism, but one, crucially, that showed the party had not only moved on from the 1980s, but also the short-term leadership of John Smith. In July 1992, Gordon Brown had given the annual *Tribune* lecture which argued that it was time for the 'party to break with a one-dimensional view of state power'. Governments, he argued, 'could be sponsor, catalyst and coordinator of services or industries: they did not always need to be owners'. In reviewing the recent election defeat, Jack Straw had likewise concluded that whilst 'there were plenty of obvious reasons why we'd lost the election, of which our tax-and-spend policies were the most significant', the problems were deeper. 'Beyond those specific policies, people didn't really understand what we stood for, because we weren't certain ourselves.' Labour could apply a new coat of gloss to the cracks the public didn't like, but until it fundamentally questioned why there were cracks in the first place, the party was going nowhere near office.[20]

The major element here was that the party 'was tied by its constitution to one of the most explicit statements of Marxist-Leninist values of any left-wing party in western Europe'. This was the old Clause IV. Plunging himself into the Labour Party archives, Straw began to research a pamphlet calling for its fundamental re-wording (to text very similar to that eventually passed under Tony Blair in April 1995). Thinking his leader would be sympathetic personally, even if he might have to box clever in public, he faxed over a copy of his first draft to John Smith. However, the actual response was negative, with Smith arguing Clause IV should 'be allowed to wither on the vine' and that it was a 'sentimental souvenir, best ignored'. Undeterred, Straw ploughed on. It all came to a head in January 1993, first with a phone call and then a meeting in Smith's office. Whilst Straw argued that 'the party – and he – had to have the confidence to acknowledge that what was right in October 1917 wasn't necessarily right seventy-five years later', Smith was furious. He predicted that if Straw went ahead, he would lose his place in the Shadow Cabinet and demanded the idea be dropped. Straw began to take his leave, to be met by a shouting Smith: 'you can take this with you, too!' as the pamphlet was hurled towards him. He published it, regardless, in March 1993.[21]

Blair therefore became leader in a situation where the case for reform was clear and he took his chance. In his first conference speech as leader, Blair declared that the party should adopt 'a modern constitution that says what we are in terms the public cannot misunderstand and the Tories cannot misrepresent'. He continued: 'let this party's determination to change be the symbol of the trust that they can place in us to change the country'. Or, in simpler terms, 'our party – new Labour; our mission – new Britain. New Labour, new Britain'. Instead of the nationalisation dreams of the First World War era, the new text, when it was agreed in April 1995, described Labour as 'a democratic socialist party' which backed a 'community in which power, wealth and opportunity' should be in the hands of the many, not the few' and where 'the rights we enjoy reflect the duties we owe'. This was virtually 'responsibility, opportunity and community'. Indeed, when Blair achieved this aim, Bill Glauber, reporting for the *Baltimore Sun*, described the new text as 'a jargon filled statement that is as controversial as a Chamber of Commerce manifesto'. When interviewing David Winnick, the left-wing Labour MP, he found him in agreement: 'the new Clause 4 is meant to be quite meaningless'. Still, Winnick conceded that 'Tony Blair will get the credit. He will be seen as taking on the left and winning'.[22]

Clause IV would form Blair's 'Sister Souljah' moment – akin to the time, during the 1992 campaign, when Clinton had proven he could stand up to Jesse Jackson and the special interests within his own party by condemning the hip-hop activist's comment that it might be time to start 'kill[ing] white people'. One person who had first-hand experience of this very moment was Stan Greenberg. Having left Clinton's team, Greenberg flew to London in May 1995 to observe how the policy and New Labour, was panning out. For the pollster, Labour was now emerging with a 'classless quality', being simultaneously 'for everyone' whilst not 'being for the special interests and the unions'. Whilst the right-wing *Daily Mail* would declare that it was Greenberg who had 'persuaded the modernisers to dump Labour's traditional, crime and welfare policies and its socialist ideology to lure back working-class voters', the reality was that Blair had already begun to achieve this.[23]

Ultimately, Greenberg believed Clause IV was evidence of Blair's utter ruthlessness. Whereas Clinton 'wanted to embrace—you know, after Sister Souljah he wanted to call Jesse Jackson. He wants to embrace him. Tony Blair is like, "Just kick him again." He did it when . . . chang[ing] the rules on bloc voting for unions within the party. Instead of saying, "All right, this was hard, let's pause", he would immediately, before they had a chance to get up, move to the next thing. Let's repeal the provision on nationalization from the party rules'. Fundamentally, 'Blair enjoyed conflict and Clinton didn't enjoy conflict'.[24] When it came to the power of the trade unions and other advocates of nationalisation, this was certainly true. Still, for a true comparison, the two would have to come face to face.

Bill and Tony 1: November 1995

Clinton had met the 'brilliant Scottish Labour Party member' Gordon Brown at the Bilderberg Conference in Baden Baden back in 1991. Today, Brown remembers travelling to the event with John Smith, where he met both Clinton and his advisor, the civil rights activist, Vernon Jordan. There, Clinton told Brown he was thinking of 'standing for president [even] at a time when Bush was 15 per cent ahead in the polls'. But Clinton would only encounter 'the impressive young opposition leader' Tony Blair in the flesh in late 1995. This was a rather awkward occasion, certainly more awkward than even their later 1996 White House meeting. As Campbell wrote in his diary, 'Clinton was in town and unfortunately going into overdrive in his praise of [John] Major'. Campbell turned to ask Clinton's press secretary Mike McCurry, 'only half in jest ... if he couldn't rein him in a bit'. Blair and Clinton would go on to have a brief chat in the hall of Winfield House. The Labour leader was clearly as nervous as he would be in their later Washington meeting. He even introduced Campbell to the president as 'a legend in his own lifetime' which, as the diarist noted, 'must have baffled him a bit'. Still, Blair was hardly unique in being starstruck. Attending the address Clinton gave to the Houses of Parliament, the Tory MP Giles Brandreth thought he looked 'tall, slim, handsome, his eye meets your eye'. And 'the way he talks ...' For Brandreth, 'his language was simple and the manner almost conversational. He brought us towards him. It did what oratory should'. Even for sceptical Tories who were attending out of mere politeness, 'if we walked in wondering how he ever got to the White House, by the time we shuffled out we knew'.[25]

In their meeting away from the usual formalities, Jonathan Powell felt Blair and Clinton had a 'very special chemistry', which Campbell felt 'overdid it'. On the broad Third Way agenda, at least, the two were as one. Clinton had been briefed by Wendy Gray that 'pragmatism is the hallmark of Blair's approach'. Indeed, 'since he became leader in 1994, Blair has accelerated Labour's move to the political center, notably ending the doctrinal commitment to nationalization and further curbing trade union influence within the party'. Rather aping the language (if not the sentiment) of Blair's critics on the Labour left, Lake further noted that 'on a number of issues, including law and order, there is now very little daylight between Labour and the Conservatives'. Whilst Robin Cook was judged to be a little reticent on NATO's eastwards expansion into the former Soviet bloc, the 'party leadership has generally moved to adopt centrist, mainstream positions' on foreign policy too. Blair was judged to be an 'admirer' of Clinton's who, on Northern Ireland, 'generally avoided specifics'.[26]

For Alastair Campbell the first impression of the president was a man who 'was much bigger than I imagined him to be, both taller and fatter. He had enormous strong hands and size 13 feet'. Clinton chuckled in recalling that he and Boris Yeltsin had swapped shoes to see who had the bigger feet – a contest won by the American. But other than meeting McCurry, 'one of those people [Campbell] liked immediately', the occasion was more awkward than anything else. This was compounded by a Downing Street dinner held for Clinton that evening – to which Blair, as opposition leader, was invited. The future Prime Minister 'hated being photographed arriving at the door [of No. 10] because it looked so presumptuous'. At the dinner itself John Major had been 'all over' Cherie Blair with 'false bonhomie, making jokes about tape measures and whether she would want to change the curtains' when and if Labour won the election. By the evening Blair and Campbell had 'been getting pretty sick of Bill shoving the boat out for Major'.[27]

Perhaps this led Blair to overplaying his hand. During this November 1995 visit, the British leader of the opposition handed Clinton a single-page note which set out three problems 'left of centre' parties would have which would leave them out of control, even if they managed to win elections: definition, differentiation and dissemination. In age where 'the era of grand ideologies is over', the left needed to show that 'the right was sectarian [and] selfish' whilst the left was able to 'find radically different means of meeting traditional ends'. To do this, however, would require an 'academic and intellectual backbone to sustain a modern left-of-centre project'.[28] Maybe Clinton bristled at the implication his own administration had not yet achieved these goals, but he respected Blair's chutzpah in raising them.

Stakeholding

Many were turning over how to achieve traditional ends with different means. In the early to mid-1990s, Democratic politicians such as Ted

Kennedy, Jeff Bingaman and, most impressively, Dick Gephardt began to speak of the 'stakeholder society'. This had many technocratic implications. As the economist Sanford M Jacoby notes, partly it involved Democrats 'encouraging companies to treat employees more like "stakeholders"'. The carrot here was that any 'employers who train their workers, give them decent health, family and pension benefits and have measures to cushion them from layoffs, would receive preferential tax and regulatory treatment'. 'In effect, such legislation would require government to subsidize the cost of private welfare capitalism.'[29]

In Britain the concept was similar, though its precise legislative agenda would await the election of a Labour government. In the interim, Roger Liddle and Peter Mandelson would write approvingly of embracing 'the modern concept of a partnership between business and the wider community and between employers and employees'. This could, they argued, obviate the old arguments of labour versus capital – or Labour versus capitalism – and bring forward 'competitiveness and partnership in a stakeholding economy'. Will Hutton and David Marquand were likewise major voices in favour of an 'economy in which all have an interest' and where 'we think creatively about how companies are owned and governed'. Though he would not be uncritical of the concept, Anthony Giddens would see *stake*holder capitalism as fundamentally different to *share*holder capitalism – the latter a top-down, management driven affair only concerned with 'maximising returns to its owners', whilst the former recognised that 'trust networks' brokered between different arms – or stakes – of the economy could have mutually beneficial ends.[30]

This was the kind of intellectualising that could be done when twenty points ahead in the polls. *The Observer* even dedicated a double-page spread in August 1996 to Labour's search for its 'big idea' and the various powerbrokers advancing each subset of new thinking. Whilst Hutton's 'stakeholders' would give people 'access to training and education' they would expect 'people to engage in productive work'. Meanwhile, the 'Communitarians' – including Michael Sandel – pointed to the role of associational blocks such as churches and neighbourhoods as providing the 'moral and social glue for a market society', even if this held 'overtones of authoritarianism' and was 'bad for women'. Neil Kinnock argued such a view 'had elements of fascism in it – to be in the community is great, but what if you're excluded' – but overall didn't think Blair 'had put a lot of thought into it'. Lastly, the 'New Progressives', including EJ Dionne, were 'basically pro-market but worried that declining living standards will mean the middle class will not survive [the] transition into [the] new information age economy'. All would compete for influence in New Labour thinking through the world of the think tank seminar, newspaper op-ed and behind the scenes lobbying.[31]

All in all, this was a transatlantic and intellectually stimulating moment for the centre left. On 7 February 1996, Blair would write to Gephardt, thanking him for a recent letter enclosing a pro-stakeholding speech. In a piece of Third Way one-upmanship, Blair provided not one but three of his own speeches in reply to the Congressman. Perhaps the most important, 'Faith in the City: Ten Years On', had taken place in Southwark Cathedral in January 1996. The title referenced a 1985 pamphlet, produced by the Church of England, which had included scathing and very direct criticisms of the then Thatcher government. It had noted that 'social welfare and taxation policies have tended to benefit the rich at the expense of the poor' and declared that by the mid-1980s 'social disintegration has reached a point in some areas that shop windows are boarded up, cars cannot be left on the street, residents are afraid either to go out themselves or to ask others in and there is a pervading sense of powerlessness and despair'.[32]

For mid-1990s Blair, 'ten years on, our society is [even] more divided, it squanders more of our talent in unemployment and low paid insecure work, our NHS is creaking at the joints, our children's education is at risk; there is fear on our streets and our economy is falling behind'. This was a series of symptoms that added up to a national crisis. In place of this 'feel-bad factor', Blair argued 'people want an alternative moral and political compass'. And this was 'a society in which everyone has a stake'. In early 1996, the stakeholder economy was Blair's guiding vision and, Alastair Campbell felt, 'was really taking off'. Though John Prescott groused about the lack of working-class voters in his focus groups, Philip Gould's canvassing of marginal seats seemed to indicate likewise.[33]

By the time he wrote to Gephardt, Blair had taken his stakeholder vision to Singapore, where he sought to 'present the economic justification for social cohesion'. As he argued in a keynote speech, 'the recognition of a mutual purpose' between business, labour and government would lead to 'the inventing and producing of goods and services of high quality' which would arm Britain in the 'new global economy of today'. This was Robert Reich's point about moving from high volume to high value production and was a positive, hopeful vision cloaked in just enough meat to appeal to both left and right. Meeting with Lee Kuan Yew after his speech, Blair and Campbell were told that Yew was convinced 'we would win and would need at least two terms to do the job', remarks the Singaporean would go on to helpfully repeat in public. Mark Lawson's write-up in the *Guardian* was a little less effusive – Blair still came across like 'a sane, male, Princess of Wales: shyly smiley, above the dirt, compassionate'. But with a polling lead then somewhere between 14 and 30 points something was obviously going right.[34]

Two weeks after the triumphant set piece of Singapore, however, Tony Blair would be sitting in a dingy hotel room, in his underpants and dressing gown, muttering to Campbell that the party lacked 'a real message' and was 'underestimating the strength of the Tory fightback'. Some of this was an unjustified pessimism, but much also lay in the argumentative relationship between Blair and Brown. In the days after Singapore Brown was 'already moving against the stakeholder economy, suggesting we should broaden it to the stakeholder society'. To Campbell, this was evidence that 'he didn't like the idea of TB giving the key economy speech that had made an impact'. Ironically, having just given a speech defining stakeholder economics as one with 'sense of team and [the] main players working in harmony', Blair presided over a Shadow Cabinet that, on the brink of power, showed a 'lack of any real team spirit'. Cook, Prescott and Brown could erupt over comparatively minor issues on a regular basis. On 11 January 1996 Campbell simply ended his diary entry of the Shadow Cabinet meeting that day with the exasperation, 'aaargh!'[35]

As for the stakeholder economy, Brown half-heartedly defended the concept on the *Today Programme* but sought to place much emphasis on the *opportunity* economy too. Later that day Blair and Brown had a meeting where the latter complained he had never been consulted over Singapore and argued that 'we had not yet thought through the consequences of the speech'. Blair was spooked, not least when, on the train to Derby for a campaign visit, Brown rang twice to try and re-hammer home his points. Blair wistfully remarked that it was 'tragic. The guy devoted his whole life to becoming leader of the Labour Party and he feels he had it taken away at the last minute by friends who betrayed him'. Brown's mission was to get Labour on to a vision of the economy which explained voter's pain and, as Stan Greenberg recalled, showed 'them how to vote for change'. Greenberg was sympathetic, not least when his own focus groups on the stakeholder speeches soon returned verdicts entirely different to Gould's: 'heard it all before', 'hopeful but wishful thinking' and 'brilliant, [but] nothing new'. Brown, therefore, came to see Greenberg with Ed Balls and tried to get across 'on your side, hardworking families' economic message to 'which I was more than sympathetic'.[36]

For now, however, the most important attacks would come from the Conservatives. Cabinet Minister William Waldegrave told the Commons that 'we all know why the "stakeholder" soundbite was deployed. It is because it can mean two completely different things to two different audiences'. Indeed, 'to the floating voter, it can be made to sound like the good old Conservative idea of the property-owning democracy ... [and] wider ownership of homes, shares and pension funds. There is nothing threatening in that, which is why the phrase was used'. Whilst, at the same time, 'to the soft left the phrase can be dressed up to sound like Will Hutton or Andrew Gamble or any of the old leftist think-tankers – a miasma of failed corporatist wheezes and schemes all involving more legislation and costs imposed by politicians and civil servants on business'.[37]

This was as true for 'stakeholding' as it was for 'one nation', the other idea Labour floated around this time – a political ideology associated with the nineteenth-century Tory, Benjamin Disraeli. Stan Greenberg, carrying out broad polling for Blair during a de facto sabbatical from the White House, was pointedly not told to poll on the concept of 'One Nation'. 'Maybe', he concludes, 'they thought "One Nation" was too remote to get buy-in from Brown, let alone the rest of the shadow Cabinet?'[38] Certainly, in their 1997 manifesto, the party moved away from anything that smacked of the statist spreading of ownership. It declared that 'our long-term objective is high and stable levels of employment. This is the true meaning of a stakeholder economy – where everyone has a stake in society and owes responsibilities to it'. It also declared that 'an independent and creative voluntary sector ... is central our vision of a stakeholder society'. In both regards, this was not a million miles away from the Clinton's 'responsibility, opportunity, community' agenda in 1992.

Bill and Tony 2: April 1996

For all Blair's nerves, his American trip on April 1996 was clearly better than his meeting with Clinton in London six months earlier. For Alastair Campbell, preparation for the half-hour White House chat and press call scheduled for 12 April had begun in earnest nine days earlier. Briefing the British media on 3 April, 'it was clear from the questioning the tabloids were trying to build up to present it as a snub situation'. Peter Westacott, number two at the British Embassy in DC, had warned his former colleague Jonathan Powell that 'there was concern that the hype was being overdone'. Still, Campbell 'went ahead and continued to hype'. By 4 April, the American news magazines were starting to trail the future Blair government – 'both the *New York Times* and the *Wall Street Journal* went on the line that he would not undo Thatcherism'. By 6 April, the *Sunday Express* had run a story about Blair's supposed 'un-Americanism', which Campbell felt to be 'unbelievably useless' since 'none of the Yanks saw him as anti-American and all it would do would heighten interest in the visit'. In fact, it was a domestic story – the allegation that Blair felt voters 'couldn't be a Tory and a Christian' – that exercised Campbell's mind that Sunday. This type of comment led to Campbell's later stance that 'we don't do God'.[39]

On 10 April, Labour's team flew out to New York – 'thankfully we had been upgraded to first class', thereby avoiding the 13 journalists on the same plane. Blair sat working on a speech he would give to the Anglo-American Chamber of Commerce the next day, 'big writing, hair awry, head down and clearly totally focused'. But a problem soon emerged. As Campbell passed the time on the long flight, he got chatting to the BBC's Jeremy Vine. Vine told him that the *Financial Times'* Robert Peston was 'getting terribly excited and telling the others that [Blair] had ruled out tax rises for people on £40,000'. In fact, as Campbell told him, 'the figure had been used as a figure of speech for a band that people on average earnings might think was a lot, but it's not really' and Blair had 'not go[ne] beyond the line – no plans'. Campbell and Peston ended up in a 'very public argument' with Campbell saying that 'if he wrote it, based upon what TB just said, it was akin to making it up'. With New Labour still fudging their policy on taxing the comparatively wealthy (Brown was then saying they could 'not rule out' a 60p top rate and would go on to press the case for an additional levy on those earning £100,000 well into late 1996), Peston had 'single-handedly inspired headless chicken syndrome in the media'.[40]

Finally arriving at the presidential suite at the Hyatt in New York, Blair's team continued to work on their speech, which would be written up as 'Blair: we're the centre party now', marking the success of Campbell's attempt to 'drive home the radical centre theme'. As Blair, suit on and standing at a lectern, would declare the next day: 'I am a radical. I believe the centre can be fertile ground for radical politics. The extremes of left or right simply will not meet the real challenge'. Late into the early hours, as they worked on the speech, things were scarcely so grandiose, however. Instructing Campbell to work up the final passage, Blair 'went to the corner of the room, ostentatiously sat down at the piano, flicking back the bottom of his dressing gown like it was a pianist's coat and started to play *Frère Jacques*'. Campbell continued to type away: if at times policy 'cross[es] left–right boundaries, so be it'. But, as Blair 'continued to play badly on the piano', his dressing gradually began to bow more and more open, eventually 'exposing his private parts to the world'. Campbell joked, 'what would a fly-on-the-wall documentary make of this particular scene' and the pair fell about laughing.[41]

The 11 April would be another long day. Speaking to John Prescott early in the morning, Campbell had learnt that Gordon Brown was furious about the top rate of tax story that Peston had pushed on the plane. As he was on the way to appear on *Good Morning America*, Blair told Campbell that it was all very sad, 'he and GB had been so close, had a great laugh together and now it was just very hard work'. There was another eleven years of such discord to go. Still the speech went well, as did the questions from the American press. At one point Blair clearly did not know the answer to a question on Taiwan and simply replied that 'obviously our position is close to that of the government', to which Campbell muttered to Jonathan Powell, 'whatever that may be'.[42] The group then flew down to Washington DC where they met Alan Greenspan and Campbell peeled off to meet Mike McCurry in a bar to further discuss the Blair-Clinton meeting scheduled for the next day. McCurry would prove particularly useful throughout the opposition years and had previously met Powell to lay the groundwork for the 1996 visit.

So came the big day itself. Campbell could not have been more relaxed and even organised a bet with staffers that he could get Bill Clinton to say the words 'Brian Jenkins' – the name of Labour's candidate for a forthcoming by-election in South East Staffordshire which they would win with a swing of 22 per cent. Agreeing beforehand on the rule that he couldn't just ask Clinton to 'say Brian Jenkins', Campbell put a few 'Vote Brian Jenkins' stickers on his notebook and whenever he spoke held it close to his chest. After a while Clinton took the bait, said 'Who's Brian Jenkins?' and the British delegation fell about laughing. But Blair remained nervous and pulled Campbell aside once more. Campbell thought he 'was going to bollock me for the Jenkins scam' but 'in fact he just wanted my reassurance: "Am I doing OK?" "Yes", replied Campbell, "but you are letting your nerves show, just be yourself".[43]

For all the nerves, the policy content of their chat remains interesting. Clinton was mostly feeling Blair out on NATO, Northern Ireland, the EU and areas of diplomatic interest. Blair was clearly trying to press home his centrist credentials. After Clinton enquired what he had been up to in the US, Blair told him that 'I visited Wall Street yesterday and saw the hard-faced men of banking'. Sensing the former Goldman Sachs presence on his shoulder, British Ambassador Kerr jokingly remarked, 'watch out, Secretary Rubin is here'. But Blair pressed on, 'it is important to reassure the business community' and, with a mind to the recent Peston debacle, asked Clinton how he 'put the message of equity and justice across without people seeing increased taxes behind it'. Clinton's answer showed all the 'amount of detail he carried in his head' which so impressed Campbell. Clinton argued that 'we need to find ways to add to the value of labor by re-educating the existing workforce ... One way is to use the tax code to get the private sector to do more, for instance in the inner cities'. He pointed to Detroit, where 'we are trying "empowerment zones" in which some cash and tax credits leverage business development'. Elsewhere, as with Mayor Henry Cisneros in San Antonio, 'we had a competition ... it forced citizens to come up with a plan. You simply cannot raise enough tax dollars to succeed; you have to have the private sector'. Seven hundred communities had bid for the empowerment zones, which were built on the idea that the 'tax code will give companies a credit if a worker has to be trained for a new job'.[44]

Blair was in awe of the president at this stage, no question. Chatting to Neil Kinnock soon after their 1996 meeting, he told him, 'Neil, Clinton's quite extraordinary – you should see him work a room'. Kinnock had offered no advice to Blair prior to the meeting, thinking the two would get on well. But Kinnock wasn't yet totally sold on the president. 'That's great, Tony. But have you ever seen Nelson Mandela work a room? Have you ever seen Lenny Henry work a room?' Blair's brow furrowed, 'What do you mean?' 'Well, I'm certain Bill Clinton has got great gifts, I've heard him speak on television and he's bloody impressive. Like most American politicians, he's not saying a hell of a lot, but what he says sounds really impressive. Not everyone can be Abe Lincoln or Roosevelt and I'm not denigrating him. But I am saying that the leader of the free world has to be better than a game show host'. Blair was somewhat crestfallen: 'Oh ...'.[45]

For Blair, however, the domestic context perhaps mattered as much as the impressive pomp and ceremony of visiting the president. For, in a way,

Clinton served as a means for Blair to face down Gordon Brown on the issue raised by Peston on the plane. Whilst Blair and Brown shared the view that 'we needed to be wise spenders rather than big spenders', there was a fundamental difference on taxes for the wealthy. Though both thought it prudent to rule out raising taxes on the low paid (they would eventually settle on a lower, 10 per cent rate) Brown wanted to leave greater room to raise income taxes at the upper end to pay for improvements to public services. On this point Blair was adamant: 'no party he led would ever raise the top rate of tax', a position with which many 'Third Wayers' agreed. Having spoken to Australian Prime Minister Paul Keating, a centre-left reformer *par excellence*, Blair was told that 'I've got some good advice for you about income tax – don't put it up. Ever. Tony, promise me you won't raise income tax. It's death. Labour parties around the world have enough to contend with without hanging that round their necks. It's not worth it'. Having dealt with the Murdoch press for far longer than Blair, Keating knew of which he spoke. American pollsters like Stan Greenberg would back this strategy, telling Blair that 'voters need relentless reassurance [on the tax issue], over forty per cent thought Labour would raise taxes on the rich, but would eventually wind up raising them on everyone'. Since Major's 1993 budget had raised taxes on national insurance and rolled out VAT to fuel and electricity bills, the Tories had dumped their own tax bombshell on the country. It was time to draw a dividing line.[46]

This would lead Brown as Chancellor into the type of wheezes for which the right-wing press would later criticise him. Raising national insurance, a windfall tax on the privatised utilities, 'stealth taxes' on alcohol or cigarettes – any revenue raiser that avoided breaking a rule Blair considered sacrosanct. Clinton had, of course, raised the top rate of income tax in his 1993 budget to just under 40 per cent, where the British rate had stood since 1988. But this line of 40 per cent was not to be breached until Brown himself was in 10 Downing Street, with the rise to 50 per cent in the wake of the 2007–2008 financial crisis. Forty cents or pence would become the Third Way's guiding light when it came to soaking the rich even if, in 1998, Blair tried to bounce Brown into *reducing* the rate, to 35 per cent. When left-wing thinkers prodded New Labour to *raise* taxes on income they were told, in the understated words of David Miliband, 'that this would not be helpful'. In a way 40 per cent was its own compromise policy between the leader and his future Chancellor.[47]

Polling, presentation and, finally, power

Effective policy still needed good presentation. With this in mind, just prior to Christmas 1996, Peter Mandelson flew to the States. This was far from his first trip. In 1989, Mandelson and Philip Gould had visited the Democratic National Committee – a visit that did not go terribly well. After a long and rambling meeting with DNC strategists, Mandelson had turned to Gould and whispered: 'Do you know what the best thing about this meeting is, Philip? The best thing is the doughnuts.' Still, though he used the opportunity to take in a little skiing in Aspen, the primary purpose of the 1996 trip was to meet the Clinton campaign team. Speaking to Alastair Campbell, Mandelson said that 'the big difference between the Clinton operation and ours was (a) cohesion and (b) attention to detail'. The American president would rehearse on video four or five times before a major interview and the campaign team ironed out any perceived mistakes. Coincidentally, Campbell had just met George Stephanopoulos at Philip Gould's house. Stephanopoulos was 'less than flattering about' Mandelson, who he had met previously. Still, he raised the same point about 'cohesion'. The only problem, as Campbell saw it, was that 'we all had big egos and [had] sometimes competing interests'. This was not just figures like Brown and Mandelson, but certainly Campbell had both in mind.[48]

The gift and curse of Blair, like Clinton, was that he was quite difficult to pin down. In late 1995, Stan Greenberg had pitched up to Tony Blair's house to present him with the details of the latest polling data. During their conversation, Greenberg realised that 'I didn't really know Tony Blair at all'. 'The likenesses to Clinton were too simple. The common language of "opportunity," "responsibility" and "community" had allowed me to presume I knew much more than I did about his political mission'. As Greenberg began to wonder, 'why was he so uncomfortable bringing inequality and fairness into his indictment of the Tories dissolution of society?' The stakeholding debate had been one facet of that, but it was broader. Roy Jenkins' verdict was that 'Tony is like a man who is carrying a precious vase across a crowded and slippery ballroom. He is desperate above all that the vase should not fall and be smashed'. Listening to Blair's 1996 Conference speech – the last, after all, before the election – Giles Radice was struck by the vacuousness of some of the rhetoric: '"What on earth does Labour's coming home" mean?' He knew about the 1996 European Championship anthem by comedians David Baddiel and Frank Skinner which used this line, but it was still slightly thin for a political speech. That said, Radice noted, 'he looks and sounds like a leader'.[49]

As such, various figures within the Labour backroom including Peter Hyman and Margaret McDonagh were keen to nail that leader down to some key policy pledges. McDonagh, head of the campaign, urged that a small set of policies should be printed on a wallet-sized card – like one she had seen in California listing the yes votes for a ballot initiative. The idea was taken up and the pledges became:

- to cut class sizes to 30 for all primary age children by using money from a scheme whereby the state subsidised some high-performing children to attend private schools;

- to fast track punishment for young offenders by halving the time from arrest to sentencing;

- to cut NHS waiting lists by 100,000 by releasing £100 million saved from cutting red tape;

- in what became the New Deal, to get a quarter of a million under 25-year-olds into jobs by using money taken from a windfall levy on the privatised utilities – including firms such as British Gas, BT, Scottish Power and Railtrack; and

- that New Labour would broker no income tax rises, would reduce VAT on heating to 5 per cent and would keep interest rates as low as possible.

These pledges, fiscally, were rather limited. But this was because, in large part, New Labour had boxed itself in. After the whole Peston debate, in January 1997 Gordon Brown pledged that there would be no rise in either the basic or top rates of tax and that he would keep to Conservative spending estimates overall for the first two years of the next parliament. Unlike Clinton, who had promised big amidst a constrained early 1990s economy, Blair and Brown were offering a limited programme for a first term at a point when the domestic and international picture looked a lot rosier. As such, for the American journalist Joe Klein, Blair was 'blithely gadding out and repeating the [Clintonian] mantra – Opportunity, Responsibility and Community – as if he had invented it and vowing to devote himself to those who "work hard and play by the rules"'.[50]

Many in Washington were following such reports keenly. Dick Gephardt asked his team to clip the numerous stories in the American press on Blair's path to power and thus encountered the *New York Times'* verdict that he was offering 'no specifics, few promises'. As Gephardt read, Blair was 'a reassuring figure, but not a galvanizing one'. He was 'intelligent, articulate and in command of his facts' and offered a 'smiling promise "to do better" to anyone who asked for a specific commitment'. Later, Gephardt read *The Washington Post*'s view that whilst the 'Labor Party has always stood squarely for something ... Now, according to pollsters and pundits alike, it stands primarily for its capacity to unseat the Conservatives'. As such, 'the Clintonesque Blair' was the 'inspiration for the party's thin platform'.[51]

For those in the know, however, Blair was always about more than that. Joy Drucker, Gephardt's foreign policy advisor, compiled a note for her boss the day the election results came in. As Drucker accurately noted, 'Blair is expected to develop a good relationship with Clinton, having used Clinton's 1992 campaign strategy and policy agenda as a model for his own campaign'. Noting the 'minimal policy differences', Drucker did, however, point to Blair's new 'radical centre' agenda including eliminating 'Labour's emphasis on using taxes to redistribute income, nationalization of British industries and a reduction in the party's economic and political dependence on British labor unions'. Decisions to 'enhance economic growth through low inflation and "pro-business" policies, rebuild Britain's health care system and crack down on crime' were also evidence of Blair having remade Labour 'into a mainstream alternative'.[52]

The campaign itself was both short by American standards and slightly tiresome for the British public. As Stan Greenberg later wrote, 'with presidential campaigns lasting more than a year, forty-five days seemed pretty civilized to me, but nobody else thought so, certainly not the voters'. John Major had called the election on 17 March which, thanks to the parliamentary calendar, made for a longer than usual six-week campaign. Greenberg and Gould managed focus groups throughout the period, with the latter 'obsessed about the campaign going all wrong as it had in 1992'. Borrowing from the Clinton playbook, a War Room was set up in Millbank Tower, which 'had the feel of a 24 hour operation, with a full staff monitoring the media through the night, ready for [Gordon] Brown's 7am ... meeting, previewing the 8.30am daily press conference [of the party leaders]'. On most days Blair would address the London media and then be bussed into various marginal seats. Though the campaign

FIGURE 10 The Tories threw everything at New Labour in 1997, including, here, invoking a Clinton-based pun. Thanks to Blair and Brown's caution, however, the Conservative's tax-based tactics of 1992 failed to cut through (The Conservative Party Archive/Getty Images).

machine was slick, the fundamentals were already set. As Greenberg noted, 'the voters in the [focus] groups were not undecided and were not struggling with their vote'. Given Blair's lead in the polls, Labour had no incentive to agree to any TV debates – despite the valiant efforts of a man dressed as a chicken that the Tories had paid to follow the supposedly cowardly opposition leader around. The campaign was certainly a success in that it did not blow anything, but the victory had already been won.[53]

At 10pm on 1 May the exit poll came in: it was Labour by a landslide. New Labour had held its core working class base in the north and Scotland but bolted on swathes of seats in southern England. In Essex, Labour had gone from one seat in 1992 to six in 1997 and in Kent they rose from zero to eight. This was a revolution that indicated the party had told the truly national story the left had lacked for decades. The party won four in ten home owners across the country, half of Britain's renters and two-thirds of social housing tenants. In each case, this was higher than the Tories. From a position in 1983 where Labour had lost the skilled working class vote to Thatcher (40% to 32%), in 1997 they achieved virtually double the Conservative tally amongst that group (50% to 27%). It is true that, ever keen to manage the public perception, New Labour ensured staffers waiving Union Jacks were in place to mob Blair as he entered Downing Street for the first time. But the truth was that whether a voter read the tabloid *Sun* or broadsheet *Guardian* in the morning, they had been more likely to vote Labour in 1997 than not. This was an astonishing achievement.[54]

The next few days and weeks were like a blur. It included appointing a new Cabinet, awarding the Bank of England the power to set interest rates for the first time and releasing the details of the £5 billion windfall tax on the privatised utilities. Yet amidst the flurry of activity, two figures could sit back and consider the bigger picture. Sitting at his desk in Brussels, Neil Kinnock composed a personalised letter to hundreds of new and returning Labour MPs. Many wrote back. Margaret Beckett (now Secretary of State at the Department of Trade and Industry) told him that he had forced 'the Labour party to be a party that looked to the future instead of sticking in the present or harking back to the past'. Jack Straw, now Home Secretary, effused that 'what was achieved in '97 would not have been possible without your extraordinary effort between '83 and '92'. Clare Short, Secretary of State for the new Department for International Development, gave similar thanks, but also semi-jokingly asked Kinnock to 'please keep close or we would blow it!!'[55]

In his own post-election comments, Bill Clinton was careful to pay fulsome public tribute to the outgoing John Major. Not only had Major shown courage over Northern Ireland, Clinton had been 'profoundly impressed by his patriotism, by his willingness to take tough decisions'. But there can be little doubt about his joy at Blair's election. When he first heard the news, Clinton reportedly danced a jig around the Oval Office. In public, after giving his weekly radio address to the nation that Saturday, Clinton turned to the British result. 'I think it once again proves that the people do not want political parties and political leadership tied to the rhetoric of the past'. He continued: 'if you go back to … President Roosevelt, he said that if you have new times, you have to have new policies. You don't have new values, but you do have new directions'.[56] Where those new directions would take the world remained to be seen.

Notes

1   Blair 1/232; Campbell 1/418.
2   Campbell 1/417; CPL/MDR, Meeting with British Labour Party Leader, 12 April 1996.
3   Blair 1/232.

4   LR/HOL/24 September 1992, vol 539, col 464; LR/HOC/19 November 1992, vol 214, col 478, 2 March 1994 vol 238, col 957 and 7 March 1995, vol 256, col 136. See also Gould to Spearing, 9 February 1993, ARC/CAC/SPRG/1/2.

5   COR/Prosser.

6   COR/Campbell and COR/Macshane.

7   Greenberg 2/182.

8   Gould/175; Hewitt and Gould/passim.

9   Greenberg 2/187.

10 Blair 1/39, 37.

11 Blair 1/39; Radice 1/409.

12 Balls/63.

13 Powell 2/121, 107.

14 MCI/Steinberg.

15 Reich 2/181, 311.

16 Blair 1/517; Powell 2/63.

17 Richards/51; Powell/94; Biden/275; Hyman/174.

18 Brown 1/166.

19 Blumenthal/299.

20 Brown 1/87; Straw/185.

21 Straw/189–90.

22 *Baltimore Sun*, 28 April 1995.

23 Greenberg 2/191.

24 MCI/Greenberg.

25 COR/Brown; Clinton/367, 686; Campbell 1/329; Brandreth/365.

26 Gray note, 24 November 1995, ARC/CPL/MDR.

27 Campbell 1/330.

28 Blumenthal/305.

29 Sanford M Jacoby, *Modern Manors: Welfare Capitalism Since the New Deal*, (Princeton, 1997), 265.

30 Mandelson and Liddle/71; *Guardian*, 31 October 1994, 7 October 1994; Gidden/151, 78.

31 *Observer*, 4 August 1996; COR/Kinnock.

32 Blair to Gephardt, 7 February 1996, ARC/MHM/GEP/1062/10; and *Faith in the City*, contained in the same.

33 Blair's speech, 29 January 1996, in ARC/MHM/GEP/1062/10; Campbell 1, 352 and 356.

34 *Guardian*, 8 January 1996; Campbell 1/352.

35 Campbell 1/358, 355.

36 Campbell 1/358; Greenberg 2/205.

37 LR/HOC/15 January 1996, vol 269, col 419.

38 Greenberg 2/203.

39 Campbell 1/410–11.

40 Campbell 1/413–14.

41 E.g. *The Independent*, 11 April 1996; Campbell 1/415.

42 Campbell 1/415.

43 Campbell 1/418–19.

44 ARC/CPL/MDR, 12 April 1996 meeting.

45 COR/Kinnock.

46 Brown 1/101; *Sydney Morning Herald*, 5 June 2010; Greenberg 2/183.

47 COR/OTR.

48 Gould/163; Campbell 1/594–95.

49 Greenberg 2/198; Radice 1/359, 361.

50 *Guardian*, 24 May 2001.

51 *New York Times*, 2 April 1997 and *Washington Post*, 26 April 1997.

52 Drucker to Gephardt, 2 May 1997, in ARC/MHM/GEP/540/2.

53 Greenberg 1/214–16.

54 Available at: www.ipsos.com/ipsos-mori/en-uk/how-britain-voted-october-1974.

55 Beckett (3 May 1997), Straw (3 May 1997)and Short (16 June 1997) letters, ARC/CAC/KNNK/1/9/9.

56 Presidential radio address, 3 May 1997.

7 BLAIR AND BROWN'S BRITAIN

On 2 May 1997 Tony Blair picked up the telephone. It was the middle of the night and he was exhausted, but, frankly, who cared. He'd made it. Labour had made it. And the Third Way had made it. At the other end was a beaming Bill Clinton. 'Tony? congratulations! I'm really happy for you'.

'Yes, well you showed the way.'
'I'm sorry you got so much grief from the press.'
'That's right. Always the Right attack you and the Left don't defend you.'
'Well, the *people* voted for you!'[1]

They definitely had. Labour had gained 43 per cent of the vote. Thirteen-and-a-half million Britons had backed Blair, 2 million more than 1992 and the new House of Commons was almost two-thirds Labour. Blair had secured more MPs than even Clement Attlee in 1945 and, thanks to All Women Shortlists for key parliamentary seats, this included a record 101 women. Little wonder that, a couple of hours after speaking to Clinton, Blair would famously declare to an adoring public that a 'new dawn has broken, has it not?' This was an objective statement of fact. After all, it had been over three decades since the party had achieved a stable parliamentary majority. When Labour had last won a General Election, Chris Leslie, the newly elected moderate MP for Shipley, had been just two years old. His new Prime Minister had never served in even the most junior of government posts previously and would now broker Britain's future. And Labour's Chancellor, Gordon Brown, had not even been inside the Treasury building in his entire life and would now control over £300 billion of public spending. This was a dramatic shift in a country as nominally politically stable as Great Britain.

As discussed, Labour's nominal retail offer had been limited. But their pledge card had not only made various specific promises, it had broadly signalled the areas Blair's administration would go on to prioritise: educational opportunity for all, improving Britain's communal healthcare system and a responsible welfare model which would get the young back into work. All this would be accomplished within a mostly stable tax system, the initial windfall levy on the utilities notwithstanding. Though it would need to deliver in all these areas, in reality, Blair's government would be far more redistributive, if not always by the usual left-wing means, than it often projected. Whereas Bill Clinton had campaigned from the centre-left and governed, in some ways, from the centre-right, Blair had talked like a Tory only to deliver goals that had alluded to far more traditionally Labour Prime Ministers like Clement Attlee and Harold Wilson. The 1997 manifesto's unwillingness to name a figure on Britain's new 'sensibly set' National Minimum Wage and its failure to use the words 'redistribution' and 'tax credits' masked the radical intent of the new administration, particularly its Treasury. As one former Brown aide told the journalist Steve Richards, his boss had 'redistributed quite extensively without making the case overtly for redistribution ... But once the controversial policies, such as tax credits and discreet increases in public spending, had been implemented and middle England or the media was not raging, he would make the case for them'.[2]

National Minimum Wage

In office, Labour would adopt a progressive universalism – all should benefit from its governance, but the poorest should benefit the most. A big part of the new administration's agenda was naturally, therefore, the low paid. Whilst the US had operated a federal minimum wage since the Roosevelt era, the British state, generally more interventionist, had lagged behind. Various state-appointed Wage Councils had set a minimum pay level in industries from catering to clothes manufacturing since 1909, but in 1993 the Major government had abolished them, arguing that they did not assist the poorest households in the UK (who often had zero wage earners), tended to increase unemployment by raising costs for business and were not relevant in a flexible, late twentieth century economy. In large part, however, they had become *more* relevant. Prior to the 1980s, the low paid had relied on the collective bargaining power of trade unions to see their pay rise. But with Thatcher's reforms, the legal recourse and, after the miner's strike, public support for industry-wide bargaining dissipated. Unusually, therefore, the recent American example was more radical. The federal minimum wage had risen twice under Clinton. Inheriting a $4.25 minimum from Bush, Clinton had managed to raise the level first in 1996 to $4.75 and then to $5.15 a year later. To secure Republican support in a hostile Congress, this was tied to tax breaks for small business owners.

Clinton was one context. Indeed, Labour's 1997 manifesto acknowledged that 'every modern industrial country has a minimum wage, including the US and Japan'. But the internal Labour debate and its history, was another. In 1983, Michael Foot's notoriously left-wing manifesto had actually only promised to 'discuss with the TUC the *possibility* of introducing a minimum wage'. Neil Kinnock had gone a good deal further, pledging the party in 1992 to a statutory minimum wage of £3.40 an hour. But, given the propensity of New Labour to ditch the parts of the 1992 manifesto they felt unpalatable to middle England, there was seemingly no guarantee the policy would remain.

In 1991, Ed Balls, fresh from Harvard and then working at the *Financial Times*, had been to see Tony Blair to discuss the research he had carried out on the federal minimum wage in the US, a meeting where the future leader made all the usual noises about being cautiously in favour, but also noted his worries about the effects on business. In general, the image of Blair in the early 1990s is as a reluctant adopter of the policy. Prior to the 1992 election, as Shadow Employment Secretary, Blair had, in the words of his biographer John Rentoul, 'defended it as a lawyer' rather than 'promote it as a salesman'. He helped ditch the party's previous commitment to affix the rate to two-thirds the median male wage (curious, since most of its beneficiaries would be women), but still backed the policy in public. Still, John Fryer, the BBC's Industrial Correspondent, felt that 'when you looked into the whites of his eyes you detected a lack of true conviction'.[3]

There were two competing forces in Blair's mind: an aggressively hostile business community on the one hand and the 2.5 million low-paid workers no longer protected by the Wage Councils on the other. The hostility towards the policy should not be forgotten. In 1992, a few weeks before the election, the Confederation of British Industry (CBI) had made a direct political intervention in claiming that Kinnock's minimum wage would cost 150,000 jobs.[4] In the run up to 1997, the estimates given by Conservative MPs to their sympathetic media varied anywhere from 750,000 job losses to up to 2 million. The minimum wage was generally bundled by the Conservatives into claiming Blair was a bit too European and far too interventionist for the British national interest. It ran alongside arguments against New Labour's commitment to reverse Major's opt-out from joining the European Social Chapter – a slew of policies from a 48-hour maximum working week to rights over parental leave.

Contrary to later criticism of the man, the Tory argument in 1997 was that Blair did not *get* globalisation. Their manifesto stated that 'many countries in Europe have tried to cocoon themselves from global competition behind layers of red tape and regulation – such as the Social Chapter and a national minimum wage. This provides a false sense of security, playing a cruel trick on working people. It also excludes the unemployed from work'. In short, intervening in this manner was not only 'Old Labour', but bad for jobs. John Major's argument was that 'as companies in the rest of Europe have grown more uncompetitive, employers have found it too expensive to employ new workers, investment has gone elsewhere and the dole queues have lengthened'. So it would be, allegedly, under Blair.

As leader, Blair therefore pledged to introduce a National Minimum Wage, but at a level not to be determined by politicians, but by the recommendations of a new, independent Low Pay Commission. This fudge allowed the opposition not to be tied to a particular figure but this, in turn, caused its own problems. In May 1995, Alastair Campbell had worried that 'we were going to have to do a lot more to win the argument on economic grounds as well as pure fairness, particularly when [the Tories] started coming at us over job losses'. As the major trade unions held votes on calling for a £4.15 or even a £4.26 minimum wage, this helped neither the jobs' case, nor the perception that 'same old Labour' was still in the pocket of the unions. Blair was comfortable with a minimum wage near the £3 mark, but the closer it got to £4 the more New Labour became jittery. In general, Blair thought unions' leadership a hindrance. In one meeting on the minimum wage, Campbell recalls, Blair was 'determined to make the unions understand that he did not operate on the basis of them asking for something and us agreeing to something just short of it. He wanted to have the argument on the basis of it being a real argument about the rights and wrongs [of the policy]'.[5]

It was the diligent work of Harriet Harman that tipped Blair in favour. Harman was often regarded by the more tedious end of the right leaning press as an 'ultra-feminist gender warrior trapped in a student radical time-warp'.[6] But, like many Labour MPs, she had seen the practical realities of low-paid Britain and her South London constituents would often bring in pay slips of just £1.60 an hour, a rate sometimes held for years. In her first meeting with Blair after he became leader, Harman recalls that 'he made clear that this was the one policy that he was not going ahead with'.[7] But Harman doggedly stuck to the task of convincing him, producing detailed policy work which illustrated the ways European countries had introduced 'social partnership' arrangements whereby the employers and the unions had got together to propose to the government different arrangements for different sectors (not far off the old Wage Council model). Harman feared that a NMW set at too high a level might well be of political benefit to male union leaders, but would also see thousands of women thrown out of work. But the need to act was clear. Her 'Low Pay Map of Britain', published in March 1995 to much press coverage, illustrated the over 1 million people being paid less than £2.50 an hour.

FIGURE 11 If Neil Kinnock saved Labour from its radicals in the 1980s, other soft left figures like Harriet Harman sought to keep its offer truly progressive in the 1990s. Harman would prove instrumental in maintaining Labour's promise of a meaningful, and new, National Minimum Wage (Steve Eason/Hulton Archive/ Getty Images).

In one meeting at TUC headquarters, Harman's notion of what became the Low Pay Commission went down like a lead balloon – the unions sensing that the policy was a Blairite fudge to avoid committing to a precise figure. To spare embarrassment, the assembled union chiefs offered Blair and Harman the chance to cook up some form of words which appeared to show consensus. But, Harman argued, 'we needed a proper policy' and a 'form of words wouldn't survive a radio phone-in'. She held her breath as Blair decided. Union bosses continued to press that unless some placatory language was briefed from the meeting there would be a row. Mulling it over, Blair finally decided that 'if it's a choice between a row and a fudge, I'd rather have a row'.[8] He backed Harman and the Low Pay Commission was now on track. Even in Blair's mind, better a semi-statist solution than a union driven one.

The National Minimum Wage was introduced at £3.60 an hour from April 1999. Exempting the armed services from the purview of the policy briefly caused something of an internal battle, as did initial noises that the Low Pay Commission was going to call for a £3.75 rate. At a February 1998 gathering, as Alastair Campbell scribbled in his diary, Blair 'went off on one, ranting that they were all going native and not understanding the bigger picture'. 'Have they thought of the effect on business?' he spat. Campbell and Sally Morgan sat furtively passing notes throughout. After Blair had declared that 'just because we have some superhumanly mad people running the unions does not mean we are obliged to meet them halfway in their madness', Morgan jokingly communicated to Campbell, 'has he been seeing Thatcher again?'[9]

The policy was a landmark success. But it remains one taken for granted, largely because it does not fit the narrative of a 'Thatcherite' Blair. Even amongst New Labour figures, it has almost been eroded. In the memoirs of Blair, Brown and Mandelson for example, over 500,000 words all told, there are a combined eleven references to the policy – and mostly within a suite of other positive measures New Labour enacted. But by the 2001 election Labour could claim that the National Minimum Wage had helped 1.5 million people, mostly women and had taken place alongside a 700,000 *drop* in unemployment. In 2015, Conservative Chancellor George Osborne even pledged a new extension to the policy – a National Living Wage for the over 25s. The policy had reached consensus, and stuck.

Perhaps the reason the policy hasn't become embedded in Third Way folklore is the other narrative that it doesn't fit: the destructive relationship between Gordon Brown and Tony Blair. Though they could certainly diverge elsewhere on economic policy, Brown and Blair agreed two overarching principles on the minimum wage. First, it was time to right the historic wrong of previous Labour governments and introduce the policy. In short, they would *do it*. Secondly, they agreed it was 'best to start from a lower rate than we would ideally have wanted before raising faster in successive years'.[10] It was most effective, in other words, to enshrine the principle and deal with the detail later. In this approach they were in lock step. Through such cooperation, the Third Way was capable of targeted interventions to help the low paid in a manner that demolishes the comparisons with Reagan or Thatcher. In her 1986 Conservative conference speech, Margaret Thatcher had declared that 'the prospects of young people would be blighted by Labour's minimum wage policy, because people could not then afford to employ them and give them a start in life. A quarter of a million jobs could be at risk'. Reagan did not raise the federal minimum at all in his eight years in the White House. Blair and Clinton would both go far further, far faster.

Opportunity

In early June 1997, Tony Blair visited a housing estate in South London to give a landmark speech. Since the Prime Minister was very much flavour of the month, this occasion gained much coverage in the American press. The *New York Times* reported Blair as saying that 'there will be and should be no option of an inactive life on benefits. Where opportunities are given, for example, to young people, for real jobs and skills, there should be a reciprocal duty to take them up'. In doing so, Blair called for an 'ethic of mutual responsibility in Britain'. 'It is something for something', he said. 'A society where we play by the rules. You only take out if you put in. That's the bargain.'[11] This was entirely in line with the Third Way position that the society should be about contribution, not automatic entitlement. A 'hand up, not a hand out', as Clinton had laid down all the way back in 1974.

The Congressman who read the *New York Times* article into the record was Jim Leach of Iowa. Leach had been a Republican Congressman since 1977 and a relatively moderate voice within the party. In 1997, when speaking in support of legislation to deregulate the public housing program, he 'hoped Members on the other side would recognize that the party of liberalism that is doing well in the world is the party of Tony Blair, not parties of extremism that object to free markets, to change programs that fail, to restrained budgets'. A month later, Leach remarked that 'many of the concepts expressed by Prime Minister Blair in his [South London] speech are surprisingly similar to the ideals contained in the House's public housing reform bill. Much like Leach's reading of '"New Labor" philosophies,' his bill intended to create 'a mutuality of obligation between public housing residents and the Federal Government, to help end the cycle of poverty, where generation follows generation in an environment devoid of hope and opportunity and instead encourage self-sufficiency and the process of moving people from welfare to work'. Blair's adoration on the Republican benches predated Iraq.[12]

A good test of whether Blair could deliver would be seen through the New Deal – a policy that took its name from Roosevelt but was far more Clintonian. Like Clinton, Blair wanted to end the dependency culture of low expectations. The New Deal had first been floated by Gordon Brown when Shadow Chancellor under John Smith and long worked up in opposition. Its flagship promise was the power to withdraw benefits to those who refused 'reasonable employment' and formed part of a workfare continuum in British politics that extended back to Thatcher and Major. That at least was the stick. The carrot was the promise for a quarter of a million 18–24-year-olds (those unemployed for six months or more) of the services of a personal careers adviser and one of four options: a private sector job (employers were to be subsidised for six months to the tune of £60 per week), a volunteering position (very Clintonian) with benefits retained plus a full allowance, or to enter either full time education or vocational re-training. As Gordon Brown thundered, there would be 'no fifth option'. Those who refused to take part would lose their benefits. This would all be funded through the one-off windfall tax on the privatised utilities, though Blair was clear on the long-term aim. Two weeks after becoming Prime Minister he told the Commons that 'we have reached the limits of the public's willingness simply to fund an unreformed welfare system through ever higher taxes and spending'.[13]

The New Deal would be expanded in subsequent budgets beyond its original goal of trimming youth unemployment, to programmes for all those unemployed for 18 months or longer, lone parents with school-age children, disabled workers and those aged over 50. Many of these would eventually be merged into the Flexible New Deal, a programme for anyone claiming Job Seeker's Allowance for more than a year. As academics Ken Mayhew and Mark Wickham-Jones note, while Labour frequently used 'conservative rhetoric over welfare, such as in the harsh tone surrounding the New Deals, many of its interventions were redistributive in their practical orientation'.[14] Whilst critics of the government, including former minister Frank Field, would argue that levels of youth joblessness would begin to creep up from 2001, it was only in 2008/2009, as the global economy went into meltdown, that the unemployment rate amongst 18–24-year-olds exceeded what Labour had inherited in May 1997.

Helping the unemployed was classic left-wing territory. It would, however, be the so-called 'squeezed middle' identified by Gordon Brown's team (and later resurrected under the leadership of one of its cohort, Ed Miliband) that would prove critical in showing that the party really had evolved. These were much the same type of Michigan voters that Stan Greenberg had seen in Reagan's America. As Deborah Mattinson noted, this group had previously seen themselves as 'too well off to be on the receiving end of Labour handouts, while too poor to be able to survive a more laissez-faire Conservative approach'. Just as Thatcher had dipped into Labour's electorate through the right-to-buy council houses, Brown therefore was seeking to reclaim the vulnerable lower-middle and upper working-class voter. A key symbolic way to do this was tax credits, where Brown was keen to set them 'at a figure that was above the average wage and would include middle ground voters – a bold move that sent a powerful message to Middle England'. One voter in Sheffield told Mattinson that 'this is the first time that the likes of us have ever got anything from government', whilst normally 'handouts go to the lazy ones who never do a hard day's work'.[15]

It is difficult to overestimate the role of the Clinton administration in convincing Brown and particularly Blair to go for tax credits in a big way. Michael Jacobs, then at the Fabian Society but later to work for Brown, was 'very conscious of the way in which the Blairites and No 10 looked to Clinton and the New Democrats for relations and policies – and the EITC and Welfare to Work were definitely two of the most significant'. Gordon Brown, a long-term reader of DLC publications, had been bombarded with ideas that could bulk up Britain's tax credits for years. But anyone with a passing interest in American affairs could hardly have missed the impact of both tax credits and welfare to work. Clinton's 1993 increase of the EITC had effectively made a $4.25 minimum wage job a $6 an hour position and, within five years of taking office, the EITC had lifted over 4 million low-paid Americans out of poverty. Later, in his 1997 State of the Union, Clinton would go beyond the PRWORA Act which had helped secure his re-election and announce a new Welfare to Work partnership, led by Eli Segal, which engaged 20,000 companies in hiring over 1 million welfare recipients by the time he left office.[16]

Following Clinton's lead, in his 1999 budget Gordon Brown increased child benefit, replaced Family Credit with the Working Families Tax Credit and passed on greater allowances for young children in workless households. This represented approximately £2 billion in new money for the low paid and greatly incentivised mothers, in particular, back into the workplace. In 2003, the system was brought into the income tax structure, with WFTC split into Child Tax Credit and a new Working Tax Credit for the low paid (regardless of children). Taking these and many subsequent changes into account, spending in cash benefits to support children under the age of five increased by around £1,600 per head (in 2009/2010 prices), more than double what it was in 1997. On cash transfers, in short, 'Labour adopted the "progressive universalist" approach. Many households benefited but the poorest benefited most'.[17]

The second landmark policy to aid the squeezed middle was child care. With thousands of women locked out of the labour market due to the cost of early years provision, New Labour borrowed substantially from America's Head Start. Clinton's success in this area had been demonstrable and, by the end of his first term, a federal funding increase of 70 per cent had opened up services for over 1 million children. These helped convince New Labour to initially resource 250 Sure Start Local Programmes for 150,000 children living in deprived areas and then, from the 2002 spending review, rolling out the Sure Start Children Centre (SSCC) model which sought to provide a universal one-stop shop for local provision for the under fours. As with the New Deal, Gordon Brown initially helped a vulnerable group, before expanding his scheme nationwide. By the time Labour left office in 2010 there were 3,633 SSCCs open in England, offering services to 2.9 million children: an over delivery on the promise of 3,500 by that year. The previous year SSCCs had been placed into statute – giving them both an independent legal standing and the local authority in which they sat a duty to provide the services they catered for, in one form or another.[18] The combination of tax credits and childcare would help Labour over the line in its difficult 2005 post-Iraq election and remain a substantial part of its legacy. The Coalition government which succeeded Gordon Brown's administration would expand the number of free hours of childcare provision, indicating that, like the minimum wage, the policy had achieved cross-party consensus.

Invest more, demand more: health

If the minimum wage was a straight steal, there remained limits to transnational learning. The UK and US healthcare systems were so fundamentally different that any joint Third Way work, compared to areas like welfare or education, was always at the margins. Simon Stevens talked to American healthcare providers 'on how to increase capacity' – but Patrick Diamond recalls there was no serious look 'at their private healthcare model'. Indeed, with good cause, amongst New Labourites 'there was a feeling that the Americans were behind *us*'. In 1997, Clinton had managed to get his Children's Health Insurance Program on the statute book (thanks to bipartisan work from Ted Kennedy and Orrin Hatch), thereby awarding matched federal funding to states for families with children who were above the income threshold covered under Medicaid. But US enrolment levels (1 million under CHIP by 1999) lagged behind the British system of universal healthcare.

Resourcing the NHS was, however, not easy. The toughest nut to crack when it came to public services, as pollsters and policy makers alike acknowledged, was how to get money to the front line and then for people to actually perceive the results. In part, New Labour had boxed itself in. By pledging to stick to Conservative spending plans for the first two years of the new parliament, Gordon Brown had to play a little fast and loose with his early spending pledges. His first budget in the summer of 1997 was written up by the media as a triumph, with an unexpected £3.5 billion for health and education. But most of this money was to be spent over the lifetime of a five-year parliament and, by 1999, focus groups were telling Mattinson that 'they may say that they've spent more ... they would do, but we're not seeing any of it'.[19]

Because of the spending rules, at least initially, health was also an area that made significant use of the Private Finance Initiative (PFI). Set up under the Major government but drastically extended by Blair and Brown, PFI schemes involve private capital paying for the construction of new infrastructure, which is then leased to the public sector over a significant period, often up to three decades. Importantly, because there is little to no upfront cost for the Exchequer, PFI would prove a useful way of keeping substantial infrastructure investment off of the government's books and thereby, for the most part, it did not count towards its deficit. As of 2018, the UK state had underwritten over 700 PFI deals, with a capital value of £60 billion and for which it was paying £10 billion annually. It is expected that these 700 deals will produce a total bill of £190 billion by the time the last expires in the 2040s. Yet, as Gordon Brown would argue, 'while controversial, private finance initiatives allowed us to have the largest hospital-building programme the country has ever seen and this could never have been achieved using only public funds then available'. The question would thus be framed in internal circles as 'Do you want new schools and hospitals, or not?' Certainly, using conventional government borrowing (gilts) would have involved trading off Labour's hard-won reputation on economic prudence and possibly endangered the later majorities. From the 1998/1999 to 2000/2001 financial years, Labour was able to run a current budget surplus, in part on the back of PFI.[20]

Even with such creative use of new borrowing methods, it was clear that a step change was needed once the spending reins came off. Like Mattinson, through 1998, Stan Greenberg's polling started to show disquiet on the NHS. In July 1998, Gordon Brown's comprehensive spending review found an extra £30 billion for health, but it was only to start filtering through from the next year. In early 1999, Blair asked for new estimates from his policy advisors as to the likely progress made on key policy areas by December 2000 – six months prior to a likely General Election. On education, the government had cut class sizes but missed other targets. The economy was going well, with the New Deal exceeding its 250,000 new young workers in employment target. But health remained difficult. Peter Hyman recorded that 'we have convinced ourselves that we have allocated historic sums of money. We have not'. The required 'quantum leap' had not been reached.[21]

Though Labour's polling lead remained consistent, Greenberg told Blair the NHS was a potential 'bombshell'. Barely half the electorate thought the government was meeting its commitment and the time the money was taking to filter through was contributing to a growing perception that the government was 'all spin'. It was clear that a big shift was needed. How that change occurred says much about the policy-making process under the Third Way, but also its willingness to listen to the argument. In March 2001, Derek Wanless, the former CEO of the

NatWest bank, was brought in by Gordon Brown to conduct a review of long-term challenges affecting the NHS – not least increased longevity and obesity. Projecting 20 years into the future, Wanless declared that to deliver a health service where both outcomes and user confidence rose significantly, there would need to be between a 4 and 5 per cent increase in health spend each year up to 2022, with the major investment frontloaded over the next decade. The idea of using Wanless had itself been rigorously focus grouped and he was viewed as a 'money man' and 'not obviously a Labour supporter'. Wanless made no direct call in his review as to where the money for his changes should come from, as long as they were long-term and sustainable.

Running parallel to this story was the case of Michael Jacobs. In 1997, Jacobs, an environmentalist by background, had secured an interview for the position of General Secretary of the Fabian Society think tank, 'very much as an outsider'. Part of his application had included the pitch of doing a Commission on Taxation and he felt New Labour needed to move somewhat away from 'its taboo – post the Shadow Budget of 1992 – on raising taxes'. Jacobs retained a 'philosophical and deeply political, objection' to the decision to rule out raising income taxes in the first parliament and went to his interview with this proposal. Despite being warned that the Fabians were New Labourites who would reject the notion out of hand and facing a panel of Margaret Hodge, Chris Smith and Denis MacShane – 'all good Blairites'– Jacobs pressed his case and got the job. Pressing his Commission on Taxation once in situ, Brown's advisers were initially similarly reticent, though, eventually, Ed Balls got in touch and became interested. In November 2000, the Fabians would recommend a directly hypothecated NHS tax which, combined with Wanless' call for new funding, finally convinced Blair and Brown that a truly radical change was in order.[22]

In the 2001 manifesto, Labour noted that 'we will, if elected, be able to sustain significant funding increases throughout the next Parliament. So over time we will bring UK health spending up to the EU average'. In their 2002 budget New Labour went bold. As Brown told the Commons, 'from April next year, there will be an additional 1% National Insurance contribution from employers, employees and the self-employed on all earnings above £4,615 pounds'. As Brown noted, 'it is right that when everyone – employees and employers – benefits from the insurance provided by the National Health Service, everyone who can should make a fair contribution'. Billions of new money flooded into the NHS and, as

Brown later noted, 'by 2010 Labour policy had helped the NHS achieve a 22 per cent fall in cancer deaths, a 52 per cent reduction in fatalities from circulatory diseases among men under seventy-five, the lowest infant mortality rate ever and all our waiting-time targets – no more than four hours for treatment at A&E, forty-eight hours to see a GP, sixty-two days before cancer treatment and eighteen weeks prior to hospital operations – were being met'.[23]

As in the other major public service reform area of education, there were two parallel conversations here: investing more and demanding more. After the 2002 budget, the money was beginning to flow at historically strong levels. But the debate over management within the NHS raged on. For Gordon Brown, 'there were fundamental limits to the ability of markets to provide a public service such as healthcare: because nobody can be sure if or when they will need medical treatment or of what sort, the consumer is simply unable – as in a conventional market – to seek out the best product at the lowest price'. He opposed the ability of new foundation hospitals to borrow money against their own assets because 'if a hospital went bankrupt, it would fall on the Treasury to bail it out'. This all played out across 2003 when, that August, the Blairite Health Secretary Alan Milburn argued in the *Times* that 'the battle in the party is now between consolidators and transformers'. For Brown, 'the implicit depiction of Tony and himself as "transformers" and of me and supporters of my position as "consolidators" was both disingenuous and vacuous'. Ever the academic, Brown had the Treasury circulate a 50-page document to fellow cabinet ministers setting out the case against allowing foundation hospitals to run up debts. Blair was furious, but it was Brown who won the argument: the new foundation hospitals would remain substantially within the public sector and its overall borrowing requirements. Charles Clarke, a critic of the Chancellor, would note that 'the leadership issue has to be seen as at the heart of Gordon's inability to truly embrace the reform agenda on health, or indeed education. Since he knew he would be reliant upon the trade unions and local activist votes in any future leadership contest, this always limited his willingness to challenge the status quo'. Brown remained 'fundamentally committed to doing things in a twentieth century manner: from Whitehall'.[24]

Whatever the fudge it eventually involved, New Labour's record on improving Britain's healthcare system would prove astonishing. In its prosaic, analytical prose, the influential think tank the Institute for Fiscal Studies laid this out when noting that 'over the period from 1997 to

2010 – including the crisis – the UK had the largest increase ... in spending as a share of national income out of 28 industrial countries for which we have comparable data.[25] Some of this involved procuring additional capacity from the private sector, but even as Labour left office less than 5 per cent of NHS spending was going to such non-public sources. As Blair and Brown had promised, Labour looked after its traditional heartland – voters who believed in the public provision of healthcare.

Invest more, demand more: education

The Third Way education strategy had four basic tenets: more money should reach the front line, that same front line should be freer to innovate away from the whims of government bureaucrats whilst, at the same time, being held to exacting overall standards, and the net result should be a system which armed those it taught with the skills that would best serve them in an ever-changing economy. Much of this emerged from Bill Clinton's own record as Governor of Arkansas. In 1983, he had passed a series of education reforms which simultaneously raised teacher salaries but subjected them to compulsory competence tests. He also mandated that schools had to teach subjects like physics (previously less than half public schools had) and lengthened the school day and year. To finance the measure, Governor Clinton used that old left-wing tactic – raising taxes, in this case the state-wide sales tax going up by 1 per cent. In 1989, he then pushed ahead with measures on choice and accountability. Parents were given the right to choose schools (Arkansas becoming only the second state in the union to permit this), providing that a broad racial balance of pupils continued. The State Board of Education could henceforth also compel under-performing districts to merge with stronger ones. In 1991, Arkansas began to offer $1,000 annual scholarships to assist low-income students to attend college.

Clinton had also begun to look enviously at the fledgling charter school model, whereby schools received direct federal funding but operated outside the confines of the state system. This was all very new and, when president took office, only one state in the union, Minnesota, had enacted a charter school law. Minnesota's journey to this point would be of profound interest to reforming Democrats and Republicans alike, however, not least because the parental clamour for choice in the education system had emerged from poor performance. As David Osborne and Ted Gaebler noted, Americans were used to a system where 'students don't choose, parents don't choose and schools don't compete for their customers'. In 1984, after several attempts to introduce voucher-based schemes for low income students, Governor Rudy Pepich of Minnesota had passed an education bill which contained the provision for 16- and 17-year-olds to take state educational dollars to a college and finish high school while earning dual credits. This saw an initially modest take up, but some high satisfaction rates amongst those students taking advantage of it. Through 1987 and 1988 further measures allowed students to change school whilst taking all the public dollars allocated to them, even should they change district. Finally, in 1991, Minnesota passed a law giving teachers the power to create new public schools. As Osborne and Gaebler argued, 'in truly competitive markets, the [pro Charter lobby] reasoned, much of the significant competition comes from new firms that have discovered a better way to please their customers'.[26]

Clinton was a big fan. Even before he became president, Al From recalls the then Governor travelling to California to have a fund raising dinner 'with a bunch of Hollywood liberals'. 'You're not for Charter Schools are you?' they demanded because then, as From recalls, 'all the liberal establishment was against them'. Clinton's answer was 'yes I am and you should be too and here's why'. In the first four months of his presidency, he went on the record over 50 times calling for more Charter Schools. In 1994, federal legislation backed by Clinton paved the way for nearly $400 million of seed money to organise more schools in the remainder of his presidency. By 2000, 32 states had charter school laws and 1,700 such institutions had been founded across America. Clinton's ethos was to challenge the public sector to do more, to create a sense of competition which would drive up standards and New Labour was watching intently.[27]

But Clinton was not just about challenging the system, he also invested more money into it. In 1992, the federal government allocated $14.2 billion to elementary, secondary and vocational programmes, as well as $12.1 billion to higher education. By 2000, Clinton had added $6.6 billion to the schools' budget, $4.9 billion to higher education and nearly $30 billion was available for student aid. Indeed, no previous administration had devoted so much federal money to education.[28] Clinton's Community Learning Centres Programme provided evening and summer educational opportunities for 850,000 students, most of whom came from poor rural and urban districts. His Class Size Reduction Initiative saw 100,000 new teachers in America's schools and a reduction in average class sizes from 23 to 18 students where these new teachers were hired. And, to arm American children for the future, internet connectivity was drastically expanded under Clinton, with over 95 per cent of schools connected by the end of his tenure compared to barely a third in 1994.

By the late 1990s, the crossover in education policy between Blair and Clinton was almost embarrassing. In early 1998, White House aide Jordan Tamagni was tasked with producing a list of the 'similarities between [the] Clinton and Blair education agendas'. On top of efforts to reduce class sizes in the equivalents of the American grades 1 through 3, Tamagni noted the pledges to get 'every school wired to the internet', Blair's 'individual learning account' bearing a striking similarity to Clinton's Lifetime Learning Credit, the concurrent improvements to teaching training and the 'better school-business links' that both were providing. Perhaps most visible were the connections between the American Head Start – expanded by 1 million children under Clinton to that point – and New Labour's Sure Start programme: 'a nursery place (pre-school) guaranteed for all 4-year-olds'.[29]

The links were broader than even these landmark reforms, however. As Tamagni remembers today, 'a lot gets said about teacher accountability and so-called performance-based reform, but I think both Clinton and Blair were real friends to educators and big believers in teacher training and professional support – and hiring more teachers – as a linchpin of all education reform'. Speaking of Clinton, she recalls that 'educational opportunity – at every level, from pre-Kindergarten to making college affordable – was his passion, something he and Mrs. Clinton had been focused on since their days in the governor's mansion in Little Rock – a southern state with huge disparities in educational outcomes'. She notes that: 'Clinton thundered mightily about the "tyranny of low expectations" and was determined to expand educational opportunities for underserved communities. I believe Blair was equally focused on this'.

Certainly, Blair was 'invest more, demand more' to his core. As Peter Hyman recalls, 'Tony made two gambles, both of which were courageous'. The first was, 'despite the clamour of the Right to abandon the traditional tax funded public services and move to a private or social insurance model, we would keep them in place and in the second term raise the taxes to fund them'. Equally, however, 'there had to be root and branch reform of the public services'. In private, Blair would roam No 10 declaring that 'we will end up suffering not for reforming too much but for doing too little'.[30] This meant targets – a rod for the government's back in that they would either be missed, a public relations disaster, or hit, in which case they were viewed as too 'soft'. It meant reforming the accountability of, and funding streams for, education. But it also meant investment.

In their 13 years of office, New Labour presided over a 78 per cent real-term increase in education spending compared to the 5 per cent total increase seen under the six years of John Major. As a percentage of GDP, British education spending increased by six times the additional spend seen in the same period in the United States and Italy and three times that of Germany and Japan. By consequence, the UK moved from a nation where education spending significantly lagged behind that of France, America and Canada, to a country which was outspending the latter two and close to the parity with the first. This was a serious shift – new money, which led to real results at every stage of the education system. By the end of 2000, Britain had fewer than 30,000 youngsters in infant schools with class sizes of over 30, compared to 485,000 when Labour had taken office. Likewise, in 1997, half of Britain's secondary schools had been below the minimum standard. By 2010, because of the money Labour pumped in, the equivalent figure was just one in 12. The proceeds of the sustained economic growth seen before 2008 went to education in a manner above and beyond what the Tories had delivered.[31]

Like Clinton, since he had 'invested more' Blair 'demanded more' too. This was undeniably more controversial. From 2001 onwards, many would argue that Blair's education reforms owed more to Stockholm than they did to Washington DC. From the perspective of 2018, former Education Secretary Ruth Kelly recalls that 'while the [US] Charter school movement was clearly known to us, we were much more interested in the evidence from the school system in Sweden'. Patrick Diamond likewise remembers that 'when we were developing ideas on education in the early 2000s the Nordic countries and the Netherlands were the areas we were keen to make the link towards. America was seen as a more dangerous country to be seen to be talking about. That doesn't mean that there wasn't an underlying intellectual interest, but it was not quite as strong'. In the June 2002 Third Way summit (discussed in the next chapter), Denis MacShane recalled the 'good contributions from two Swedes, Par Nuder and Thomas Ostros, who is the Education Minister. He wants to see the National Curriculum abolished in Sweden and all power returned to schools to decide what and how they will teach. It sounds like a nightmare by British standards but I'm sure it's the right way forward'.[32]

By Diamond's time in No 10 from June 2001, the issue was that Bush was now in the White House and thus the potential for transatlantic cooperation was more limited. Partly this was the gap between a British government of the centre-left and a right-wing Republican administration. As such, under Bush Charter Schools were 'definitely something we looked towards in terms of the lessons of competition', but this was crucially a matter of 'more diversity driven in the public sector and the not-for-profit sector' rather than any creeping privatisation. Rather than policy difference, however, the biggest problem was that No 10 found the Republican domestic agenda a little thin. As Diamond recalls, the 'Bush administration didn't really have much of a domestic policy agenda to look towards. I remember we did see one of Bush's education advisors when they came to London – but it was a bit of a non-conversation'.

The Americanisation of the British education system was a tricky sell and driving up standards alienated New Labour from a public-sector base the party had historically courted. David Blunkett, Blair's first Secretary of State for Education and Employment, was one strong advocate of reform. When Roy Hattersley penned a critical article of New Labour education policy shortly after the 1997 election, Blunkett recorded that 'defending the [teaching] profession has taken on much greater salience with people like Roy than actually defending the children'.[33] Hattersley had previously called for the abolition of Grant Maintained Schools – institutions free from local authority control and funded by a grant from central government. Such institutions only made up around 3 per cent of all schools at the time Labour took office, but, like the various selective grammar schools that had survived the comprehensive movement of the 1960s, assumed a symbolic importance. Labour allowed Grant Maintained Schools to keep their freedoms as Foundation Schools and all schools were given the chance to take on greater financial independence, particularly through new building grants being sent directly to the institution itself, rather than the local council.

The trick for New Labour was to balance reform within the education sector with a clear signal that there would be no return to the old, selective model detested on the left. Blunkett had given a 1995 Conference speech where, parodying George H W Bush, he remarked: 'read my lips, no selection under a Labour government'. Despite giving 17 interviews that day clarifying that he had meant no *further* selection, i.e. no *new* grammar schools under a Labour administration, the party's left continued to hammer Blunkett on the policy. In the minister's favour, the 1997 manifesto had declared that 'Labour will never force the abolition of good schools whether in the private or state sector' and that 'standards, more than structures, are the key to success'. But there were also voices urging Blair to go further than the pragmatic approach he began his administration with. Will Hutton's influential *The State We're In* had argued that to stop the middle classes from sending their children to private schools, a future government might have to hardwire inequality into the public sector to a degree many would have found uncomfortable. As he wrote, 'grammar schools and grammar school streams in comprehensives need to be revived in order to attract members of the middle class back to the state system; nationalizing inequality'.[34] Whilst there was a marginal expansion of the grammar system under Labour, with 4.2 per cent of pupils educated at such institutions in 1997 compared to 4.8 per cent by 2010 – this was almost entirely achieved through the expansion of existing institutions.

The inequalities of education where also thrown into stark relief by the presence of Oxford and Cambridge universities – institutions which took around half their intake from private schools at the turn of the century, at a time when only 7 per cent of British children attended such schools. In 1999, Laura Spence, an A-level student at a state school in the north-east of England, applied for a place at Oxford to read medicine. Spence had 10 A* GCSEs and was predicted the top grade in each of her A-level exams. She was not offered one of the five places on offer at her chosen college, however, because, at her interview, 'she did not show potential'. Later, she would accept a scholarship at Harvard, but in May 2000 a row erupted over the class implications of her rejection from Oxford, triggered in large part by Gordon Brown. Coincidentally, when the Spence story broke, Al From was in London, staying at Winfield House. The two discussed the details of the Spence affair and, based on From's advice, Brown rushed out an op-ed going on the attack. Calling the Oxford decision to reject Spence 'an absolute scandal', Brown denounced 'an interview system that is more reminiscent of the old boy network and the old school tie than genuine justice in our society'.[35]

For Alastair Campbell, 'it was tricky. On the one hand, it was a classic opportunity message where there seemed to be a British elitist bias against a girl from an ordinary background. On the other it was always risky when politicians alighted upon individual stories without knowing the facts'. When the news emerged that Spence had underperformed in her interview, Brown admitted that, collectively, they should have done more to check the facts of the case, but did not concede to voices like Peter Mandelson that it was a mistake to have engineered the row altogether. Campbell agreed that it was worth the fight – even with Oxford University voices lining up against the government. There was, after all, a bigger topline message to come. By the Comprehensive Spending Review a couple of months later, Labour's claim to increase 'opportunity for all' would be backed by an annual increase of 6.6 per cent in education spending over the next four years.[36]

If opportunity was truly to be embedded, such improvements could not only be about money, however. In 2005, the government published a white paper entitled, 'Higher Standards, Better Schools for All: More Choice for Parents and Pupils'. In his foreword, Blair argued that 'the local authority must move from being a provider of education to being its local commissioner and the champion of parent choice'. All schools should be given the right to become a self-governing Trust School, 'with the benefit of external drive and new freedoms' in areas like staff pay, the curriculum pupils took and the length of the school day. To sweeten the pill for any doubters, he pointed to the money Labour had already pumped in to the system: 'teachers' pay is 20% higher in real terms and schools employ an extra 32,000 teachers and 130,000 support staff. Schools have access to twice as many computers, as well as new interactive whiteboards and broadband technology'. But, he contended, 'there is too little choice and standards are not yet high enough'. Looking abroad, Blair pointed to 'Swedish parents choos[ing] an alternative school to their local one, including a diverse range of state-funded independent schools'. Meanwhile, 'in Florida, parents can choose an alternative school if their school has "failed" in two of the last four years. Again, studies showed test scores improved fastest where schools knew children were free to go elsewhere'. Where individual parents and children could be empowered to act like consumers, so the argument went, they would act like intelligent market actors and improvements would follow for the system as whole.

Not everyone viewed the situation so rosily, however, and some argued that, by the mid-2000s, 'harping on about radical change sent the message that public services were still rubbish'. Patrick Diamond later reflected that the 2005 White Paper had been 'the high point of the competition agenda'. By then, he and others had 'got the sense that some of it had become a little bit detached from what was really going on in the education system. There was around this time a certain type of reform fetishism that was frankly getting a little bit out of control'. Gordon Brown and his allies continued to press No 10 on questions of accountability and where the buck would stop if local councils saw their role in the education system diminished. Left-wing opponents of the agenda, including Diane Abbott, Jeremy Corbyn and John McDonnell, claimed that 'there is an uncomfortable fit between what is a supportable and a very obvious Labour White Paper and those sections which import proposals from the Charter Schools experiment in the USA, which has been shown to fail the poorer and more vulnerable families'. Because of such doubting voices, what became the 2006 Education and Inspections Act would only pass on the back of votes from David Cameron's Conservatives.[37]

Cameron had begun his first Prime Minister's Questions as Leader of the Opposition by telling Blair that 'with our support ... there is no danger of losing these education reforms in a parliamentary vote. So [the PM] can afford to be as bold as he wants to be'. Blair, however, responded that there remained significant divergence between the two on the role of admissions procedures – Labour against a return to the grammar system by the back door and Cameron seeking to indicate his sympathy towards that model, not least to the right-wing press. But the investment mattered too. As Blair began his final answer of that week's questions, Gordon Brown, sitting next to him, leant forward and reminded the Prime Minister not to forget about 'the money'. As Brown jabbed his finger at his new Conservative opposite number, George Osborne, Blair told Cameron that if he indeed wanted a truly bold new consensus 'we also have to agree that the investment that is so necessary to back up that reform continues'. Brown was more of an academy sceptic than Blair, but he still believed in that old Clintonian mantra: 'Invest more, demand more.'

These reforms were risky, but in a sense that was the point. As Jonathan Powell has noted, 'sometimes in government Tony metaphorically drove the car at the wall, daring others to give in and secure the reforms he thought were vital'. Cameron's pledge meant he would always be able to pass some form of bill but, as Powell notes, 'there are real dangers for a Labour leader in depending on Conservative votes. The ghost of Ramsay MacDonald hangs heavy over the Labour Party and no leader wants to find himself as a Judas, clinging on to power by selling out'. Fundamentally, he believed in the legislation and daring the soft left and Brownite rebels in the PLP to kick him out of office was worth it. By 2006, like Clinton after Gingrich took Congress 12 years earlier, Blair had become a Prime Minister without a party. John Prescott would thunder at his boss, 'Look at the Tories, they are saying the same as you', to which Blair would reply 'and what does that tell you?' – hoping in response that Prescott would see the reform's overall popularity. Prescott's reply – it shows 'that you're a Tory!' – didn't quite suggest total buy-in. Once Cameron had swung in behind Blair on education, the Prime Minister's authority was sunk. At the Party Conference in September, Blair would announce he would stand down the next year. His performance at the event would, however, be so slick that several Labour aides murmured to one another, 'why are we getting rid of this guy?'[38]

Though damaging to Blair's personal fortunes, the results, however, were obvious to anyone familiar with the British education system. The number of academies rose from three in 2003 to 202 by 2010, meaning they still constituted less than 1 per cent of schools as Labour left office, though were dramatically extended under the Cameron government that followed. According to academics Andrew Eyles and Stephen Machin, New Labour's academies programme 'gave struggling schools more freedom and stronger leadership, leading to significant improvements in pupil performance'. The more bound into previous local government structures the new academies had been, the better they performed. Freedom, in other words, worked. But better results across the board were undeniable, at both primary and secondary level. The numbers of those achieving level 4 at Key Stage 2 Maths increased from 62 per cent in 1997 to 79 per cent by 2010. The percentage of A-Level examinees with at least a pass rose from 79 per cent when the Tories left office to 95 per cent by the time Labour lost power. About 100,000 more students each year would go on to gain university degrees across the same time period. These improvements were about money and reform.[39]

Financial crisis

In order to pay for such progressive priorities, the Third Way's brand of globalisation attempted to ride the wave of two innovations: big tech and big finance. The first was more or less the legacy of the ATARI Democrats in the 1980s and could be seen from increased internet connectivity to the billions that flowed into Treasury coffers from mobile phone licenses. In short, increased productivity above the rate of natural inflation would generate additional receipts that could be poured into public services. But the second was more controversial. The expansion of financial services in the late 1990s and early 2000s in part helped fund Sure Start, tax credits and other such reforms, but they also needed to be carefully managed, particularly given their often opaque and complex nature.

Shortly after Blair had become Labour leader in 1994, he and Brown had gone to visit Alan Greenspan at the Fed. During their conversation, it soon appeared to their host that 'Brown was the senior person' as the Shadow Chancellor 'did most of the talking about a "new" Labour'. Given that Greenspan was so antipathetic to the British left embodied by Michael Foot and Arthur Scargill, he was delighted that 'Brown espoused globalization and free markets and did not seem interested in reversing much of what Thatcher had changed in Britain'. Regardless of any words, 'the fact that he and Blair had arrived on the doorstep of a renowned defender of capitalism (namely, me) solidified my impressions'. After May 1997, Greenspan approvingly noted that 'Britain has welcomed foreign investment and takeovers of British corporate icons' and pointed to the 'increased incomes for financial expertise' and the fact that 'UK finance has prospered'. This was part of a broader notion, often espoused by Blair, of 'open' versus 'closed' societies. In 2007, just before the financial music stopped, Greenspan confidently predicted that 'if Britain continues its new openness (a highly reasonable expectation), it should do well in the world of 2030'.[40] Within a decade of Greenspan's words, of course, Britain would vote to leave the European Union.

It wasn't all pro-Greenspan deregulation under New Labour, however. One of Brown's first acts as Chancellor had been to beef up the old Securities and Investments Board, a self-regulating body within London's financial centre which oversaw stock and associated markets. Newly named the Financial Services Authority, the organisation was now underpinned by statute, had taken over responsibility for banking supervision from the Bank of England and absorbed the previous work of the Securities and Futures Authority – which regulated both such markets. After the collapse of Barings in early 1995, when derivatives trader Nick Leeson had caused the demise of Britain's oldest merchant bank by betting the wrong way on the Japanese stock market, there was much clamour for financial service reform. Indeed, in February 1995,

Brown had mocked the then Conservative Chancellor, Ken Clarke, for having 'felt that there was no need to worry about the derivatives market' and his belief that 'American legislators were wrong to become excited at the need for regulation'.[41] Labour's 1997 manifesto itself had failed to mention any specific reform. But given that Brown's landmark move to give control over interest rates to the Bank of England had been couched in the vague desire to see 'monetary policy ... free from short-term political manipulation' – this did not preclude something more radical in office.

Certainly, meaningful action on financial services would be best coordinated internationally. In the February 1998 visit to DC – best known for Blair's Lewinsky press conference heroics – the British delegation had also included Helen Liddell, then the minister with direct responsibility for financial services. Liddell remembers the trip was 'hugely valuable because we were working on financial services regulation and we were also looking at the establishment of the Debt Management Office. It was therefore hugely valuable to be able to talk to US regulators'. When Liddell had discussed the changing landscape with the financial services community at home, she found them 'very supportive' of the new government. The Edinburgh asset management community in particular was keen to go head to head with Chicago. Wall Street was also keen to have access to the London market as a route into Europe, particularly with regard to small business investment.[42]

The issue, even amongst Third Way partners, was the inevitable competition between the United Kingdom and the United States in a sector in which they they both had historic dominance. In April 1998, Brooksley Born, head of the Commodity Futures Trading Commission (CFTC), raised major concerns regarding the Over-the-Counter (OTC) Derivatives market. Sometimes used to spread risk but, increasingly, to make speculative bets or avoid taxation, OTCs – contracts traded away from the formal stock exchanges – were evidently ballooning in size and beginning to worry many. Yet, when she asked whether the government was doing enough to keep a check on this market, Born's question was instantly shot down. For Bob Rubin, subjecting derivatives to further regulation would create 'uncertainty over trillions of dollars of transactions'. With the 'financial community ... petrified' by the notion of greater federal oversight, Rubin warned that the 'Treasury will put out [a] statement that the CFTC has no jurisdiction' over the area, should Born press her case. Alan Greenspan piped in with the Fed's view: 'the OTC derivatives market could flee to London (or Europe) if this isn't handled well. That would be a failure on CFTC's part'.[43]

Faced with the two most powerful men in the American economy, Born bravely ploughed on regardless. On 7 May, the CFTC released a statement noting it was 'reexamining its approach to the OTC derivatives market' and asked for respondents to analyse 'the benefits and burdens of any potential regulatory modifications in light of current market realities'. For those who wished to keep a lid on regulation, this was a virtual declaration of war. Unusually, Rubin and Greenspan put out a joint statement publicly criticising Born's move, stating that they had 'grave concerns about this action and its possible consequences'. For Rubin and Greenspan, 'the OTC derivatives market is a large and important global market' and the CFTC had overstepped the mark.

But voices in the administration continued to express doubt. Deputy Director of the National Economic Council, Sarah Rosen, noted that simply arguing regulating derivatives was bad because it 'inhibits use of a risk management tool and has global implications' was a paper-thin position. As she noted: 'Why should an American citizen care? Who are the users of these instruments that would be harmed by limiting the market? This isn't compelling as a public policy issue. Without better justification, [it] just sounds like Treasury wants to protect the traders from regulation'. But Greenspan and Rubin won the argument. A few months after Born left the CFTC in June 1999, the President's Working Group on Financial Markets – the senior members of which were Greenspan and Rubin – argued to 'clearly exclude most OTC financial derivatives' from the purview of impending regulation. The Commodity Futures Modernization Act of December 2000, one of the last pieces of legislation Bill Clinton signed in office, would enshrine this principle and see off the CFTC's attempts to police these trades.

The consequences would soon be obvious. To take one measure, in April 1998, there had been $58 billion worth of daily OTC interest rate derivative trades on US markets. By 2004, this figure had reached $317 billion and, by 2007, just before the crash, $525 billion. A nearly tenfold increase in such activity was hardly evidence of a mounting interest in hedging, risk spreading and other claims made by proponents of keeping derivatives unregulated. Its increase dwarfed even the 72 per cent increase in the average US house price across the same period and the 59 per cent increase in the DOW Jones. The real economy – the thing, after all, derivatives were supposed to *derive* their value from – had grown, but nowhere near the level the OTC markets suggested. The building up of contracts between banks, institutional funds and high net individuals created a quicksand that meant that when key real world markets began to dip – in 2008, the US housing market – the entire global economy was threatened with being pulled under.[44]

Derivatives were just a piece in the puzzle, however. From the British point of view, Helen Liddell argues that 'what [the centre left] got right on financial services was establishing a relationship where there were no barriers to discussion and we were not perceived as pursuing some overtly ideological agenda'. That said, 'what latterly broke down is that atmosphere of openness deteriorated and the global attitudes to risk changed. Globally, it became overly relaxed with banks over extending and thinking the good times will always be there'. Derivatives traders could be speculative parasites on the system, but seemingly more trustworthy institutions were also making catastrophic decisions. For Damian McBride, 'the reality was that if even the highest paid accountants in the country – working for the most profitable banks – had no idea that those banks' balance sheets were reliant on worthless assets and debt that would be impossible to recover, how on earth was the Treasury, let alone No 10, meant to guess that at a dozen steps removed?' For years the major banks had been operating at excessive leverage and were becoming dangerously under-capitalised – in layman's terms keeping absurdly small amounts of money compared to the volume of loans they were making. In turn, many of the toxic loans, including the subprime mortgage loans that gained such later notoriety in the US, had been parcelled up and sold off. Such 'securitisation' not only increased the volume of institutions affected, it hampered the ability of the markets to distinguish good from bad assets on their own balance sheets. In the wake of institutions like RBS and HBOS collapsing, when Gordon Brown spoke over the phone to banking figureheads like Fred 'the Shred' Goodwin, he would tell them information about their own banks which they themselves did not know. Afterwards he would thunder 'How is this possible? How do these guys not know this stuff?'[45]

By then Brown was in Number 10, having finally, Granita Pact stretched to breaking point, ousted Blair a year earlier. In October 2008 he would take the unprecedented step of injecting £37 billion of government capital into RBS, Lloyds and HBOS to prevent a run on the banks. This steadied the hand of global forces and prompted the Europeans, followed by the Bush administration, to take similar action.

Even Nicolas Sarkozy, the centre-right French President, commented that 'Gordon, I should not like you. You are Scottish, we have nothing in common and you are an economist. But somehow, Gordon, I love you.' As Brown considered these words, Sarkozy hastened to add, 'but not in a sexual way'.[46] In December that year, Brown would be mocked by David Cameron for having stumbled into saying 'we not only saved the world' (he meant 'the banking system'), but even his slight gaffe was, in reality, not so far off. In early October 2008, major financial institutions were about to go bust, their customers might panic and withdraw all their savings at once (making the collapse of the banks certain) and advanced industrial economies might be reduced to using the army to restore order. Brown bulldozed the Bush administration to go further than its initial plan just to purchase troubled assets in major banks and actually inject capital. In that sense, he *did* help save the world.

Although the problems on Wall Street and the City of London were strikingly similar, they altered the centre-left in two ways. First, most obviously, the crash paved the way for the election of Barack Obama. A Democrat would be back in the White House but, as Liam Bryne notes, 'Obama represented something of a break with Third Way orthodoxy. Obama really did see himself as an anti-establishment candidate'. Having only served in the Senate since 2005, the new president could plausibly claim an ideological break from 'Clintonomics', even if he had himself sought advice from Clintonian figures like Bob Rubin. The Keynesian nature of the Obama stimulus was certainly an option Clinton had rejected – and had to reject, given the congressional numbers – in 1993. As Byrne continues, however, 'Gordon Brown was at a very different stage of his political cycle' with a record to defend rather than trash. Thus, for former No 10 advisor Kirsty McNeill, whilst the relationship Brown had built up 'with, say, Ted Kennedy was not bilateral UK–US or between the parties, but a properly personal relationship', the Prime Minister's association with 'Obama would be closer to a normal bilateral intergovernmental relationship'.[47]

Secondly, the crisis evidently challenged the model upon which the Third Way had been built. For many years, as Byrne notes, financial services 'was a sector that was making the single biggest contribution to the tax base. There was a wariness to regulate because we were generating huge revenues from the financial services industry'. The other issue was that most of the 'perverse deregulation happened under George W Bush and there wasn't much we could do about that'. As such, the crisis 'was a floodwave that came in from the US'. To this credit, Brown foresaw the problem more than most. In December 1998, in the wake of the financial crisis then gripping much of east Asia, the then Chancellor called for 'four major reforms that add up to a transformation of the international financial system – a new economic constitution for the new global economy'. These included accurate reporting of financial flows, a new permanent standing committee for global financial regulation under the IMF, greater surveillance of both public and private sectors (and responsible action from the latter in times of crisis) and an undertaking that when the 'IMF and World Bank help a country in trouble – the agreed programme of reform will preserve investment in the social, education and employment programmes which are essential for growth'. Certainly, a lack of transparency and an inability to foresee the interconnected nature of the financial system were both at the heart of what would go wrong. Brown, a committed multilateralist, attempted to nudge the IMF through his role as chair of its International Monetary and Financial Committee in all these four areas, but there were limits to what was achievable – particularly when Bush entered the White House. Brown's calls for 'an early warning system for the world economy', as he later understatedly put it, 'did not win the support it required'. In the meantime, as Greenspan acknowledged, 'the large tax revenues that have emerged [from an enlarged financial sector] have been used by the Labour government to counter the income inequality that is an inevitable by-product of increasing technologically oriented financial competition'. That was the trade-off.[48]

Community

The flows of globalisation were not just financial, but deeply human. New Labour's initial challenge in this regard was with processing the claims of asylum seekers – mostly citizens from war-torn countries in the global south, relatively small in number but over whom the administration found it difficult to balance liberal and conservative instincts. By 2002 and 2003 this had mostly fallen off the radar, after the civil service found more efficient means of assessing individual cases.

More significantly, with the expansion of the European Union in 2004 – admitting ten new countries most of whose economies remained far behind the west – old assumptions about the freedom of movement of labour within broadly convergent advanced economies significantly shifted. Though UKIP and other forces would exaggerate the threat of en masse migration to the UK, there were now tens of millions more workers with access to the British economy and, due to the difference between wages then seen in the former Soviet influenced countries in particular, these workers had much incentive to relocate. To put this into context, when Labour won re-election in 2001 there were around 100,000 Eastern European migrants in the UK. By the time it left office there were around 1.5 million. This was some change. Reflecting back, Ed Balls argues that in the mid-1990s Blair and Brown had seen globalisation as 'in terms of the globalisation of capital and trade – of finance and goods moving around the world – which offered opportunities we needed to harness and risk we needed to manage'. However, 'the one aspect of globalisation which Tony and Gordon didn't foresee was the extent to which it would result in the movement of people across borders looking for work'.[49]

Unlike France and Germany, Britain did not place any restrictions as to when workers from the new member states could begin work in the UK. Much of this decision lay in servicing a growing economy. Indeed, in January 2005 Blair confidently told internal critics that 'thirty four percent of [British] strawberries are picked by Poles and migrant workers help to prevent inflation by keeping wage rises down in UK regions'. But there were wider issues at play. Britain's failure to join the Euro – the single European currency which Blair had hoped to join, but Brown firmly resisted – also played a key role. As Balls notes, 'the Foreign Office and Number Ten definitely saw Britain turning down the opportunity to have transition controls on the movement of workers . . . as a way to signal our continued commitment to the European project'. All in all, 'the fact is that the Home Office, the Treasury and the Foreign Office never expected migration within the European Union on the scale that occurred in the second half of the last decade. It was a failure of forecasting, of foresight, of politics and understanding'. In the wake of Britain voting to leave the European Union in 2016, many would argue that at least British citizens had the reciprocal right to work in dozens of other EU states. But, for Balls, 'whilst it is true that one million British people do migrate to work in the rest of Europe, they are more likely to be working for higher wages in Brussels, Frankfurt and Milan than undercutting unskilled wages in the poorer parts of Europe'. The changes were obvious. In every year since 2010 (when it replaced Pakistan), Poland has formed the foreign country most likely to see its citizens give birth in the UK and over 80 per cent of

British population growth between 2001 and 2016 has been estimated to be due to the effects of migration (either new migrants themselves, or their children).[50]

Initial forecasts for the numbers of EU workers coming into the UK were clearly way off. In June 2003, Lord McIntosh outlined the government's position that the total flows from the new Member States would be somewhere between 3,000 and 14,000 each year. Official statistics would later have the figure at about four times even that higher estimate. Still, the broad liberal establishment accepted this line. Lib Dem Lord Wallace noted that 'all the evidence from previous enlargements has been that when states join the European Union, people go back to their own country rather than leave ... So long as their domestic economies enlarge, they are likely to stay in their own country'. This was the view forwarded by Jack Straw and others at the Home Office, too. In actual fact, falling unemployment in states like Poland and Czech Republic after 2004 went alongside increased migration to Britain. New Labour had inherited an economy with total annual net migration of about 60,000 and presided over an increase – in the boom years – to over 300,000.[51]

Some of this was due to inherited policy, some of it, again, was wider geopolitics. In 1994, the Conservatives had withdrawn exit checks from ports and the smaller and medium airports, a policy extended universally by Labour a year after coming to power – in both cases justified on cost. But the argument remained that Britain needed the workers. Just as immigrant labourers from the Commonwealth had kept Britain's new National Health Service and nationalised transport system going in the full employment economy of the 1950s, so too would eastern European migrants service a British economy where unemployment had nudged under 5 per cent by the mid-2000s. Many also noted that this was an historic moment: the true end of the Cold War. Just as the Czechs, Poles and Hungarians had joined NATO in 1999, it made sense to lock down the eastward expansion of liberal democracy by having such nations join the world's largest trading block. These nations could not be denied the full EU rights of other Member States, nor, innately did Blair want to stop them. As Kirsty McNeill argues: 'TB was a deeply European character. He loved the EU as an institution. Rather than Gordon's general preference for multilateralism, Blair liked *that* institution.' For some, latterly on the Brexit side of the debate, he bent too far in its direction.[52]

Still, New Labour did at least try to marry a globalised world with national concerns. A big part of this was the furore over the proposed introduction of Identity (ID) Cards, planned to be held by every resident in the UK. David Blunkett would record in late 2004 that 'the acceptability ... of ID Cards is going to be crucially dependent on ... people feeling that this is something that is good for them individually and critical in terms of knowing who is in the country and rooting out illegal migration and illegal working'. Gordon Brown started out as a sceptic, thinking the policy a waste of money, though pivoted in public once he saw their popularity with voters. Charles Clarke, Blunkett's successor as Home Secretary recalls 'furious rows with Gordon, partly driven by cost, partly by his awareness that the kinds of constituencies that were against the policy might prove useful in any impending leadership contest once Tony stood down'. As external opponents, particularly the Lib Dems, tried to move the debate onto issues of counter terrorism (and ID Cards' inability to deliver in that regard), Blunkett believed the issue would be better framed as 'entitlement cards' – that were 'about beneficial gains for the individuals and not just the state'. In the end the ID Cards bill would face colossal problems in both houses of parliament before it reached the statute book in March 2006 and would only be implemented for certain categories of non-EU nationals, a few hundred airport workers and others who had voluntarily signed up. Blair would bemoan that 'the Tories could not run a serious campaign on immigration while opposing ID cards' but the policy would indeed be formally scrapped by the cost-cutting Conservative-Liberal Democrat coalition in 2010.[53]

The difficulty here was dealing with the pace of change – for policymakers reared in Cold War norms and the British population having to deal with the consequences. Ed Balls had started thinking about questions of immigration back at Harvard under Reich and Summers, but in the late 1980s, 'the basic assumption about globalisation was that British people would risk losing their jobs to cheaper competition from overseas, not that that they would feel threatened by competition from immigrants in this country'. Although faced with the largest far-right British National Party membership in the country in his parliamentary constituency, Balls acknowledged that 'the vast majority of people were in what I'd call the pragmatic centre: they certainly knew we needed skilled labour to come in ... but they also felt that things had been happening too fast, that there was a lack of control on the numbers coming in'. Having pledged 'British jobs for British workers' after becoming Prime Minister, by 2010 Gordon Brown confirmed he would expand the Migration Impact Fund he had introduced the previous year, to help those areas of the country experiencing high levels of new arrivals. Again, this would be scrapped by his successor in Downing Street.[54]

For pollster Deborah Mattinson, immigration became a 'Vortex issue' for New Labour – one which sucked all others in.[55] A struggling NHS was due to overcrowding with immigrants. Under performance in schools was equated to teachers being overworked dealing with children with poor English skills. By the mid-2000s immigration had become 'the elephant in the room', an issue that as soon as it was pointed out in focus groups, would light a fire under participants. The fact that there was a strong case that immigration was *generally* good for the country – particularly in generating new tax receipts – could not offset the lived experience of some. Fluctuating demand for public services due to the influx of seasonal labour meant it was difficult to plan for decent long-term provision. The very centralised nature of the UK state also meant that, where there were particular geographic pinch points, there was not always the flexibility in the system to address local concerns.

There was also the concurrent question of domestic integration and a society in flux. The conundrum for New Labour was to square the notion of cultural diversity with a society where 'everyone is the same'. Demonstrably, this was and remains tricky – particularly when it comes to social attitudes. In 2015, IPSOS-Mori polling revealed that 'approaching half (45%) of British Muslim men and a third (33%) of Muslim women agree that "Wives should always obey their husbands"'. As the pollsters somewhat understatedly put it, 'agreement levels are much lower among the general public as a whole, indicating that a significant number of Muslims have more traditional views on gender roles'. A majority of Muslims in the same poll also backed the recriminalisation of homosexuality, a policy for which there is next to no clamour amongst the wider population. Likewise, almost a quarter of Muslims polled by ICM in 2016 'would support . . . there being areas of Britain in which Sharia law is introduced instead of British law'. There are some limited signs of a generational shift, but the idea that multiculturalism would lead to unity through diversity was simply untrue. Between 2001 and 2011 the number of British Muslims nearly doubled, from 1.5 million to nearly 2.75 million. This brought policy challenges, as Blair would later acknowledge – not least after four home-grown Muslims carried out a series of suicide attacks in central London which killed 56 people in July 2005.[56]

In the wake of Donald Trump's astonishing victory in the 2016 presidential election, Blair noted that 'there is a reaction against globalization ... [and] feelings of culture and identity are bound to happen at a period of rapid change. The sensible thing is to deal with those issues and anxieties. And to deal with them by having strong, clear policy positions on them – that then allows you to make the sensible case for immigration, but with controls'. Moving further, he argued the case went beyond the two candidates: 'Leave aside Hillary Clinton and Donald Trump. Just look at those two platforms and you'll see what the problem is. For example, when it comes to a discussion of radical Islam and the Islamist threat, the Democrats felt that, for reasons I completely understand, that if you talked about it in that language, the general prevailing sense is that you were then stigmatising all Muslims. I don't personally agree with that. I think that you're perfectly able to distinguish between Islamists and Muslims. But there is a threat that is based on the perversion of religion and you should acknowledge it as such. Whereas the Republicans had a whole section that was all about that. Again, if you're looking at America and how they feel about things, what they feel is that the liberal left is unwilling to have a discussion about these things.'[57]

For Trevor Phillips, head of Britain's Commission for Racial Equality, 'in recent years we've focused far too much on the 'multi' and not enough on the common culture. We've emphasised what divides us over what unites us. We have allowed tolerance of diversity to harden into the effective isolation of communities, in which some people think special separate values ought to apply'. The emergence of widespread sexual abuse by South Asian men of predominantly white girls as young as 11 in the town of Rotherham between 1997 and 2013 was one high-profile example. The Jay Report commissioned to evaluate these crimes – of which it suggested, conservatively, there had been at least 1,400 victims (a staggering figure for a town of 100,000) – was scathing of the public service response to the problem at almost every level. It concluded that 'agencies should acknowledge the suspected model of localised grooming of young white girls by men of Pakistani heritage, instead of being inhibited by the fear of affecting community relations. People must be able to raise concerns without fear of being labelled racist'. Of course, the vast majority of British Muslims, like any other community, had been law-abiding citizens. But Rotherham and wider social attitudes amongst Muslim communities posited a challenge to the Third Way it did not always adequately address. Denis MacShane, the MP for the town, would later note that 'I think there was a culture of not wanting to rock the multicultural community boat'. Whilst no victims ever approached him, he had been aware of the 'the oppression of women within bits of the Muslim community in Britain'. But, 'as a true Guardian reader and liberal leftie, I suppose I didn't want to raise that too hard'.[58]

Responsibility

With the free movement of capital and people and its diversifying effects on the community, the Third Way had to decide what to do to imbed notions of common citizenship and, ultimately, responsibility. In British politics, the Conservatives had long been identified as the party of law and order. During the Thatcher years, tough talking rhetoric on punishing criminals, particularly the young offenders to be treated to a 'short, sharp, shock' to scare them straight, contrasted sharply with what voters perceived Labour to be offering. For the left, crime was a product of circumstance, though also most acutely felt by those in poverty. From the time Thatcher took office until the mid-1990s, the number of offences steadily grew, particularly in areas like burglary and violent crime. By 1994, there were over 19 million criminal offences occurring each year (up from about 11 million in 1981), the product of economic deprivation, heavy handed policing and, of course, the individuals convicted. Though the scale was drastically different, Blair's manifesto offer in 1997 was textbook Clinton: 'the Conservatives have broken their 1992 general election pledge to provide an extra 1,000 police officers. We will relieve the police of unnecessary bureaucratic burdens to get more officers back on the beat'.

Under Labour, crime dramatically fell and, by 2010, there were less than 10 million offences each year. Part of this was about the economic boom, but much was due to the government effectively walking a line the left had previously struggled with. One witness to this was Home Secretary David Blunkett who faced a pincer movement between a rabid 'hang 'em and flog 'em' right-wing press and liberal *bien pensants* who prioritised civil liberties to a degree many voters did not understand. As Coalition forces entered Baghdad in May 2003, Blunkett was floating tougher sentences for high order offences at home. As he confided to his diary, 'on sentencing for murderers – life meaning life, twenty years increased to thirty years, no definable floor up to fifteen years. God! You'd think I had announced something akin to chopping people's hands off or putting them to death. The libertarians were out in force in the *Guardian* and the *Mirror*'. When it came to what became the 2003 Criminal Justice Act (which increased 'stop and search' powers and introduced mandatory life sentences for over 150 types of violent crime), however, Blunkett knew that 'the world outside [the media bubble] agrees with me, because at every meeting, whenever I mention changes in sentencing I get a round for applause. Everyone I've spoken to in the real world is up for it'. Likewise, when in early 2004 newspapers began to harangue the Home Secretary over the potential release of Maxine Carr – guilty of providing a false alibi for Ian Huntley, who had killed two young girls in Soham – Blunkett again bemoaned that 'of course the liberal media commentary was [about] how awful it was that we were going to stop her automatically being let out'.[59]

Whilst the left-wing press talked of civil liberties, the right-wing media harped on about a malaise in British youth through the early to mid-2000s. To some degree, this was a repetition of the debates of the early 1990s – sparked by the horrific murder of James Bulger, which led Blair into his 'tough on crime' stance as shadow Home Secretary. But its roots went back further. In July 2004, after many stories of feckless criminality amongst the young, the Downing Street operation began briefing that 'a great many of the troubles we were facing originated back in the 1960s and the "flower power" era'. For Blunkett, however, it was the period of economic unrest in the 1970s and 1980s that really was behind it all. As he then recorded, 'I knew precisely what Tony was getting at – a kind of *laissez-faire*, look after yourself libertarianism – but mass unemployment, disintegration of the family and downright selfish individualism are just as much to blame as the "anything goes" attitude of the 1960s and early 1970s. It is perhaps because in the 1960s anything didn't go with me and those around me that colours my view!'

As Blair remarked in early 2006, his view was that 'ultimately, the change has to come from within the community, from individuals exercising a sense of responsibility. Rights have to be paired with responsibilities'.[60] The 'respect' agenda introduced late in his premiership owed much to this. In both language and policy, the legacy of Clinton ran deep. Yet, for all their occasional faults, Blair and Brown's achievements eclipsed the benchmark their mentor had laid down. They had used their more secure parliamentary majority to achieve something substantial. Their long period in office was marked by significant achievements.

Notes

1   ARC/CPL/MDR, 1 May 1997 call.

2   Richards/43.

3   Rentoul/166–67.

4   *Guardian*, 27 March 1992.

5   Campbell/1, 196, 201.

6   *Daily Mail,* 14 January 2009.

7   Harman/175.

8   Harman/178.

9   Campbell 1/281.

10 Brown 1/133.

11 *New York Times*, 3 June 1997.

12 LR/CRH, 14 May 1997, H2646 and 27 June 1997, E1355.

13 LR/HOC/14 May 1997, vol 294, col 65.

14 K Mayhew and M Wickham-Jones, (2014). 'The United Kingdom's Social Model: From Labour's New Deal to the Economic Crisis and the Coalition' in JE Dølvik and A. Martin (eds), *European Social Models from Crisis to Crisis*, 144–76, 153.

15 Mattinson/76.

16 COR/Jacobs.

17 Via the Ruth Lupton-led research. Available at: www.casedata.org.uk.

18 House of Commons Briefing Paper 7257.

19 Mattinson/109.

20 Brown 1/170; Black (NEC, 3 October 2002).

21 Greenberg 2/223.

22 COR/Jacobs.

23 Brown 1/231.

24 COR/Clarke.

25 Institute of Fiscal Studies, 2010 Election Briefing Note 5.

26 Gaebler and Osborne/93, 102.

27 COR/From.

28 ARC/CPL/FOIA 2006-04648-F, Similarities Between Clinton and Blair Education Agendas.

29 COR/Tamagni.

30 Hyman/171.

31 Ruth Lupton and Polina Obolenskaya, 'Labour's Record on Education: Policy, Spending and Outcomes 1997–2010', LSE Working Paper 3, July 2013; Blunkett/219.

32 COR/Kelly and Diamond; DMAC/8 June 2002.

33 Blunkett/16.

34 Hutton/311.

35 *Guardian*, 26 May 2000.

36 Campbell 3/325; Treasury Cmmd Paper 4807 (July 2000).

37 Compass, Shaping the Education Bill: Reaching for Consensus, (2005); Black (NEC, 29 June 2004).

38 Powell 2/35, 67; COR/OTR.

39 *The Conversation*, 14 August 2015; House of Commons Research Briefings, SN02627 and SN04252.

40 Greenspan/283, 499.

41 LR/HOC/27 February 1995, vol 255, col 695.

42 COR/Liddell.

43 See material in the President's Working Group on Financial Markets at ARC/CPL/FOIA-2010-0673-F.

44 See relevant data at https://fred.stlouisfed.org/series/MSPUS; DOW stats at www.finance.yahoo.com and OTC numbers at the Bank of International Settlements.

45 COR/Liddell; McBride/376.

46 *Guardian*, 14 October 2009.

47 COR/Byrne and McNeill.

48 Kennedy School speech, 15 December 1998; Brown/126; Greenspan/499.

49 Balls/184.

50 Balls/185; *Guardian*, 6 June 2010; ONS births, deaths and marriages register; Migration Watch Briefing Paper 452 (August 2018), Black (NEC, 25 January 2005).

51 LR/HOL/25 June 2003 vol 650, col 293; BBC News Online, 20 October 2005; LR/HOL/27 October 2003 vol 654, col 14.

52 COR/McNeill.

53 Blunkett/713 and 293; COR/Clarke; Black (NPF, 3 February 2007).

54 Balls/247, 186.

55 Mattinson/133.

56 ipsos-MORI, 21 March 2018; Channel 4, 11 April 2016.

57 *New Statesman*, November 2016.

58 Richard Race, *Multiculturalism and Education*, (London, Continuum, 2011); 55; Jay Inquiry (2014), *Telegraph*, 27 August 2014.

59 Blunkett/492, 577.

60 Blunkett/669; BBC News Online, 10 January 2006.

8 THE THIRD WAY INTERNATIONAL

As Bill Clinton reached to place a hand on his wife's arm, Alastair Campbell saw that Hillary 'literally froze when he touched her and avoided any eye contact at all'. Her 'icy cold' demeanour was understandable. During what the British delegation called '*le sommet surrealiste*' of Third Way leaders, the whole world was glued to televisions relaying the president's newly released testimony to a grand jury investigating whether he had sought to cover up his affair with Monica Lewinsky. Meanwhile, Tony Blair, Bill Clinton, the Italian Prime Minister Romano Prodi and Bulgarian President Peter Stoyanov were sitting in the New York Stock Exchange discussing 'the progressive rebirth' of the centre-left. The First Lady remained a consummate professional throughout, even chairing a seminar on the role of civil society organisations in a modern, globalised economy. But it cannot have been easy and the British were somewhat bemused. Having been in long dialogue with Hillary Clinton about its importance, David Miliband tried to put a brave face on it. But Blair had always viewed the limited turnout from European partners, with no German and French representation, as likely to lead to 'me and the Prime Ministers of Sweden and Bulgaria sitting around gassing on comfy chairs'.[1]

Whilst the September 1998 New York summit did not garner the widespread coverage its organisers had hoped (though the write-ups were mostly positive for Blair), it was emblematic of a series of policy discussions that took place over five years between May 1997 and June 2002 which seemed to offer a radical new consensus for western progressives. As Clinton waded through what Campbell called 'the deep shit' of the Lewinsky case, sometimes the seriousness of this agenda was obscured by the media's focus elsewhere. But, in retrospect, it is important to view this moment very seriously indeed. With the Democrats in the White House, Labour in Downing Street and Gerhard Schroeder, Lionel Jospin and Romano Prodi in power in Europe, the centre-left had a chance to codify a unifying set of principles that would, it was intended, see it in office for a generation. From 1997 onwards, the Third Way went global and, for a while, seemed to have achieved the hegemony that the New Right had crowed about only a decade or so earlier.

Blair in charge

On 1 November 1997, Tony Blair strode into the living room at his Prime Ministerial country residence of Chequers wearing a pair of old blue jeans. 'Opportunity, responsibility, community', Blair told his audience as he brandished a piece of paper, 'these are the notes from our first meeting during the Clinton transition'. Standing in the room were Al From, Larry Summers, Sidney Blumenthal and, leading the US delegation, First Lady Hillary Clinton. The official press release from the White House had been remarkably cryptic: 'in England, Mrs Clinton will participate in a closed seminar hosted by Prime Minister Blair at Chequers. The seminar, which will include participants from the United States and the United Kingdom, will focus on shared policy and common challenges'. But the agenda was further reaching than that. As Blair remarked, 'unless we define the political territory with our ideas, people would grow disillusioned with our parties, just as they had with the governments they had replaced'. The trick was to avoid the 'danger of winning power but not the battle of ideas'.[2]

Sidney Blumenthal, who had helped connect Blair to the Clintons years earlier, remembers 'a full day of intensive seminars, very serious policy talk, back and forth, about what we did, our views on economic policy and globalization and worker adjustment, education, healthcare, how you deal with poverty'. This involved reconfiguring old positions anew: 'it was as if new synapses and nerve endings were being laid down'. Of course, the particular answers that might be reached remained unique to each territory: 'we understood our systems were different, not just politically, but for example, our education systems are very different. Healthcare systems are different and so on and so forth'. But Blumenthal believed that 'there are things that can be learned [and] this is how you develop the relationship, as you talk about policy'.[3] The Third Way was being codified, somewhat on the hoof. Bill Clinton had been first to achieve office, but others were now stepping up to the plate.

While the relationship between Blair and Clinton began as unequals, after 1997 it shifted dramatically. As Blumenthal recalls, 'it was not until the election of Tony Blair ... that the global imperatives of Clinton's politics began at last to come into focus'. Blair allowed Clinton's rise to appear no longer 'a matter of mere chance, skill and personality' but to re-frame him 'as the leader of an international movement'. On 27 October 1997, Al From told his DLC colleagues that Clinton had been at the vanguard of 'the forces of global, social and economic change that have brought about new progressive movements all over the world, most notably ... New Labor in Great Britain'. Due to the two-term limits on the US Presidency, Blair would even, in time, come to outdo Clinton. As David Osborne notes, 'we were envious of the success Tony Blair had as a third-way leader, given that our leader, Bill Clinton, was sidelined by scandal, which was a big factor in Al Gore's loss in 2000. Until Blair decided to back George W. Bush's invasion of Iraq, he appeared from afar to be accomplishing what we hoped Bill Clinton would: creating a modern Labour Party that could rule for some time to come and address the social and economic inequities that Conservatives generally don't address'.[4]

Unlike Clinton, after 1997 Blair could now more or less do what he wanted. When Stan Greenberg had claimed Labour would not only win the 1997 election, but would accomplish something truly astonishing, Blair had shot back, 'this is not a landslide country'. Yet now, demonstrably, it was. The oft-repeated notion that Blair was a 'presidential figure' was therefore untrue. Presidents, as Clinton would attest, often have to deal with knife-edge or even adversarial Congresses which can block their agenda. Between 1997 and 2005, for the most part, Blair had no such checks and balances. And from May 1997 onwards, both because of his parliamentary majority and Clinton's personal scandals (Labour advisor Derek Draper called him 'the first lame fuck president'), it would be the Englishman who would decisively shape what the Third Way was all about.[5]

Northern Ireland

One key achievement of the Third Way, which saw both landmark early successes and some tough long-term policy grind, was Northern Ireland.

There was a personal dimension here. Despite scant actual evidence, Bill Clinton claimed an Irish background, whereas Blair's mother Hazel had most certainly been born in Donegal. But, for Clinton at least, the politics were obvious – with over 30 million Americans having some form of Irish heritage and making up over 1 in 8 voters in potentially marginal states like Pennsylvania, West Virginia and Ohio, they were a significant electoral constituency that would not look kindly on any errors in policy. Such considerations, together with the prodding of influential Irish Catholic Senators like Ted Kennedy, undeniably influenced Clinton's decision to grant Gerry Adams a special 48-hour visa to fund raise for Sinn Fein in the US in January 1994. John Major was so angry about this decision – which ran contrary to the British government's campaign to delegitimise Adams' position in global opinion – that he refused to speak to Clinton for days afterwards.

Such anger had long marked the politics of Northern Ireland. Cleaved off from the remainder of Ireland in 1921 (after the entire island had been occupied by the British in one form or another since the twelfth century), the six counties of Ulster had been the subject of inter-religious conflict between Catholic Republicans campaigning for a united Ireland and Protestant Unionists determined to remain within the UK. After protests against predominantly Catholic internment were met with the British Army opening fire and killing 14 civilians in January 1972 (dubbed 'Bloody Sunday'), the parliament of Northern Ireland was suspended and direct rule imposed on the province from London. The 1980s brought IRA hunger strikes and an attempt on the life of Margaret Thatcher through the bombing of the Conservative Party Conference at Brighton, which killed five people. Then, in February 1991, a mortar was fired into the garden of Downing Street, intending to kill the entire British cabinet. Whilst the American media generally described the IRA in this period as 'activists' and 'guerrillas', the British media usually went with 'terrorists'.

Whatever the views of his domestic press, Major's attempts to broker a settlement in Northern Ireland were laudable. The Downing Street Declaration of 1993 – which affirmed that the north could be transferred to the Republic of Ireland if and only if a majority of its population favoured such a move – even produced a temporary IRA ceasefire in late 1994. Clinton saluted Major's 'courage and vision' for having pursued such a path and the British Government worked constructively with the former Democratic Senator George Mitchell, appointed as US Special Envoy to Northern Ireland. From 1995 onwards, Mitchell would become

Clinton's point man on the issue, serving as a chair for all-party talks in the province the next year. With Blair in power, the atmosphere then shifted even further towards a long-term deal.

When visiting Downing Street just after the 1997 election, Clinton told the new Prime Minister, that 'with regard to Northern Ireland, when it comes time that you think it would be helpful for us to say something about a cease-fire or decommissioning, let me know. We may have to wait for the Irish election. I have some pull and can call in chits; just let me know'. The issue of what came first – the IRA giving up its weapons, or the politicians consenting to a deal – would indeed be thorny. But Clinton was certainly delighted with Blair's choice for Northern Ireland Secretary, Mo Mowlam: 'she is good, great on TV. Her happy face inspires confidence. She seems solid and not full of herself; you don't need another person over there posturing like a peacock'. Clinton believed it was good to have such pragmatists in charge for, rather like the moderate's views on the hard left, there was a gap between views on the ground and what politicians were saying: 'one problem is that the people are farther along than the leaders. For people like Sinn Féin and [Democratic Unionist] Ian Paisley, the conflict is their whole life'.

By September 1997, Clinton told Blair that he saw the problem as generational and that leaders on all sides, though particularly the Unionists, were 'worried about being rendered irrelevant in 20 years: given the way the demographics are going, it's better to make a deal now rather than later'. Clinton's analysis was simple: 'if you look at it, their popular majority is eroding over time with the increasing birth rates, so now is the time [for a deal]. You'll have to come up with some sort of creative dual relationship'. This idea of creative ambiguity was crucial to getting a deal. Both the Unionists, who desired no material change to Northern Ireland's membership of the United Kingdom and the Republicans, seeking union with the Irish Republic, needed both a genuine victory (for their own conscience) and a victory they could sell (to their supporters). Two into one wouldn't go. Or at least it seemed as such.

Blair and Clinton received much criticism during their careers for being somehow duplicitous. It would be Tony B-*liar* over Iraq and, according to Christopher Hitchens, there would be *No One Left to Lie To* for the triangulating Clinton. For the most part, such accusations would be materially untrue. But the point also misses those cases where politicians must operate in shades of grey and, for Blair and Clinton, Northern Ireland was a perfect example of this. The Good Friday Agreement eventually brokered in April 1998 acknowledged there was presently a majority in Northern Ireland for continued membership of the UK but, equally, that a substantial minority wished for reunification with the Republic. On the one hand, it bound the Republic of Ireland for the first time into a formal agreement that acknowledged the six counties as part of the United Kingdom (requiring a change to the Irish constitution). On the other, the right of Northern Irish citizens to identify with and acquire the citizenship of both the United Kingdom and the Republic of Ireland was rendered into law. This was creative ambiguity at its best.

The Good Friday Agreement required both Third Way leaders to be at their best and to think on the hoof. By Friday 3 April, its key terms were set – the aforementioned position of Northern Ireland being matched by a commitment from all sides to 'exclusively democratic and peaceful means' of resolving issues and the creation of new institutions within the province, between North and Southern Ireland, and between Great Britain and Ireland. Blair, therefore, was helicoptered into Hillsborough fairly confident a deal was close. But then unionist leader David Trimble became worried about the long list of proposed North/South bodies to be created and asked that they be made accountable to Stormont rather than Westminster. This, in turn, led Sinn Fein to 'resent being taken for granted' and to begin briefing that there would be no deal. On Thursday 9 April, Gerry Adams and Nigel McGuinness produced their own 40 pages of detailed amendments, over policing, the Irish language and IRA prisoners, which seemed to present another roadblock.

Crucially, at this point, in came Clinton. As Jonathan Powell recalls, the crucial element for Sinn Fein was 'the promise [from Blair] to remain engaged' and to make Good Friday the beginning of a process and not the end. As Powell himself noted, the agreement, after all, 'was an agreement to disagree' and thus the continued role of a honest broker – or a prime minister that at least would not be viewed as actively hostile to either side – was crucial. For this, Gerry Adams had to trust Blair. Through the early hours of Friday 10 April, at the behest of Blair, Clinton called Adams three times – at 1am, 2.30am and 4.45am. Clinton stayed awake all through the night, waiting by the phone for anything he could do and would call Adams 'to shoot the breeze, rather than put pressure on him'. Such commitment not only cemented Blair as a figure all sides could trust, it showed the US would not be walking away either. Later that morning, Good Friday, the agreement was announced.

The Adams scenario was not unusual and Clinton and Blair conversed on Northern Ireland regularly. In February 1998, after the murder of pro-union Ulster Defence Association (UDA) member Robert Dougan, Clinton told Blair, 'give me one more chance to hit these people, to get them to make a tough statement because you can't be caught in the middle of *this:* you are in a hell of a pickle'. Still, he reassured his friend, 'you are the best friend they have and they are lucky there'. Throughout the process, into Good Friday and beyond, Clinton would offer to act as go between for Blair's overtures to Gerry Adams, David Trimble, Bertie Ahern and the Canadian expert in charge of weapons' decommissioning, John de Chastelain. By April 2000, with the clock running on his presidency, Clinton told Blair that: 'You know how badly I want this to work. I really think it's important. You have a good economy and good social reform. And, if you could get a breakthrough here, I think you would secure your place and your party's place for a long time to come. You could help New Labor in ways we can't even evaluate. I just want to do whatever I can for you before I have to leave here.'[6]

The achievements were considerable. Months after Good Friday and fulfilling its terms, the Northern Ireland Act created a new Assembly at

FIGURE 12 Northern Ireland would prove one of Blair and Clinton's strongest team efforts. But peace took some winning. Here both leaders, and Hillary, inspect the aftermath of the Omagh Bombing in September 1998 (Courtesy: Clinton Presidential Library).

Stormont. The Assembly would see several suspensions, most notably from October 2002 to May 2007, as rows over the decommissioning of IRA arms rumbled on. In 2006, however, the landmark St Andrew's Agreement created the means by which a power-sharing arrangement was possible (the First and Deputy First Minister in the new Assembly positions being awarded to the largest and second-largest political – and, *de facto*, religious – block respectively) and which took full effect from May 2007 – a month before Blair left Downing Street. Building on John Major's efforts, the Blair–Clinton partnership had delivered what successive administrations had thought impossible.

Blair, Clinton and Lewinsky

Northern Ireland was the culmination of centuries of history. Still, one cannot ignore the backdrop to such serious discussions. As Mike McCurry remarked to Alastair Campbell during Blair's visit to Washington in February 1998, Clinton was 'a fifty-year old man and what is he doing trying to chase a girl like this?' The 'girl', of course, was former White House intern Monica Lewinsky. After months of 'intense flirting' Clinton had begun an affair with Lewinsky during November 1995. Had it not been for an ongoing independent investigation by Ken Starr into Clinton's conduct in the Paula Jones case (Jones had claimed Clinton had exposed himself to her in a Little Rock hotel in 1991 and was suing for damages), the Lewinsky affair may have run its course. But Lewinsky had confided in her then friend Linda Tripp, who decided to tape their telephone conversations and pass them on to Starr. The issue of whether Clinton had lied in his testimony during the Jones case – he had claimed under affidavit not to have had an affair with Lewinsky – thus became an explosive news story in January 1998.

Part of this was trivial. The locations of the acts ('the hallway ... the office and then also in the bathroom'), whether Clinton's semen had come into contact with Lewinsky's blue dress (as she put it, 'it could be spinach dip or something') and, more crucially, whether he had lied about the affair, soon became the subject of forensic public discussion. But it also created intense difficulties between the Blairs and the Clintons. First, what kind of man did this make the president and how should they handle Hillary? Cherie Blair believed that there were three possibilities as to why Hillary had elected to stay with Bill. Cherie thought either Hillary

FIGURE 13 The Lewinsky affair caused understandable strain in the Clinton's marriage, and led to much debate amongst Blair's team as to how to handle a president taking much domestic flack. During this February 1998 visit from the Blairs, everyone just about managed to grin and bear it (Courtesy: Clinton Presidential Library).

'was religious and her marriage was a religious union', 'she was besotted [and] could not believe she was married to Bill Clinton' – which Cherie considered unlikely – or 'it was a power partnership'. For Cherie, 'Hillary knew what [Bill] was like but lived with it for the access to power and the feeling of power and occasionally the reality of power'. If so, the Prime Minister's line of general sympathy towards the predicament should just about hold. But, more immediately, what if Clinton would be exposed as a liar and was therefore politically finished?[7]

The obvious friendship between the Blairs and the Clintons undeniably added an extra layer of awkwardness. As Cherie Blair notes, 'Bill is an incredibly sociable person who loves ideas and loves talking, but only really gets going after ten'. This meant late nights for the Blairs whenever the couples got together, but some clearly fun times. The relationship between the two marriages was so close that, in the lead up to the birth of Leo Blair in 2000, Clinton joked that 'after January I'm available for babysitting duties . . . You said you wanted to continue my work with the Third Way and this is it: helping Blair balance work and family'. Likewise, 'although by nature Hillary Clinton is not a touchy-feely type of person', Cherie saw her as 'much warmer than her public persona might suggest'. Hillary had certainly gone out of her way to offer advice to Cherie about being a spouse of a national leader. 'You're not going to please everyone the whole time', she had told Cherie 'and you're certainly not going to please the press and therefore you should do what is right for you'.

Away from prying eyes, Cherie felt the president had been 'bloody stupid' over Lewinsky and muttered to herself, 'Oh Bill, how could you'. She admired Hillary's courage throughout and her ability to separate the political and personal dimensions. On the first, the Clintons were united that 'this had been politically motivated and stirred up by those who wanted to undermine the Democratic presidency'. As to the latter, understandably, Cherie found Hillary 'furious and hurt'. Although forthright in other areas, Cherie never raised the Lewinsky question with Bill: 'it wasn't me [who] he betrayed'.[8]

All this, of course, was playing out in the glare of the media. Blair and Clinton had a press conference to give on 6 February and the issue was bound to come up. The two leaders, Campbell, McCurry and Sandy Berger therefore went through the likely questions. As Campbell recalls, 'the breaking story [that day] was about a secretary being told to lie, he said he would deal with it, no need to bother Tony on the detail'. Clinton was nervous and cracked jokes about how many members of the press could truthfully claim to be faithful to their wives. Blair, as he so often did, took Campbell to one side. Unlike the 1996 visit, it was Blair who was now the dominant figure and the Englishman who could cut the president loose. Campbell went through the strategy once more: 'total support, big picture, important relationship between our two countries'. This chimed with Blair's reassurance over the telephone that he would do 'anything you want me to do', to which Clinton had replied that 'one or two things might make the difference'. The two left to face the baying press mob with Senior Advisor Rahm Emanuel's rejoinder: 'don't fuck it up'.[9]

Blair had been given a list of journalists to call on and, after 25 minutes or so, called Phillip Murphy from the Press Association. Murphy told Blair that, 'you could have come here and just talked about serious politics. But some people have been struck by the personal statement of warmth that you have given the president. Have you ever considered that that could be a politically risky strategy?' Blair went all in on his answer, as Campbell had advised: 'I've said it because I believed it and because I believe it is the right thing to do. I have worked with President Clinton now for some nine months as British Prime Minister. I have found him throughout someone I could trust, someone I could rely upon, someone I am proud to call not just a colleague but a friend'. And then, in a vindication of the Third Way: 'I happen to think – I don't know if it's my place to say it or not – that if you look at the American economy, you look at the respect in which America is held right round the world today, if you look at the standing and authority of the president, it's a pretty impressive record for anyone'.

Blair had gone out on a limb – as everyone present understood. One American Senator watching the event approached the British diplomat Simon McDonald, then with the Embassy in Washington. 'You know, Mr McDonald, in Washington everything is a trade', remarked this anonymous Senator. 'You do a favour for someone, he has to do one back for you. Your Prime Minister has just done the biggest public favour that any British PM has done for an American president ever. You can now ask for anything.' McDonald promptly returned back to the Embassy and the matter was relayed to London. A special committee was set up to debate Blair's 'ask' of the president but, after weeks of deliberation, it was decided not to push the matter.[10]

Clinton might have been in a giving mood. In the press conference he looked very much Blair's junior despite their age difference and the fact the Prime Minister had been in office for less than a year. He even made the obvious joke of saying 'no' to a question as to whether he appreciated Blair's effusive praise. But as the two retreated to the back after the questions were finished Clinton told Blair that 'I'm going to make sure you will always be proud of what you did out there. It was a noble thing to do'.[11] There was clearly a personal bond here. A week or so later Blair called Clinton to check in on the evolving situation in Iraq, but the two were interrupted by Clinton's barking dog. 'Taking care of Buddy are you?' asked Blair. 'Yes, he's got to go outside, I have a door right here.' 'Hillary', Clinton pointedly noted, 'is at another place working. We are not together'. That, just about, would not be true in the long run. With an eye to the future, however, Blair ended many of his calls to the president around this time with variations of 'love to Hillary'.

It was only on 15 August, after a long and sleepless night, that Bill told his wife the full truth about Monica. After providing his testimony to Ken Starr's Grand Jury investigation, Clinton then apologised formally before his Cabinet on 10 September. The reaction was a mixture of a stoic desire to get on with the job and outright condemnation of the president. Donna

Shalala told Clinton that it 'was important for leaders to be good people as well as have good policies', while Madeline Albright remarked that she was disappointed and he was wrong, 'but our only option was to go back to work'. Nobody resigned from the Cabinet, but the president was clearly in trouble. The most powerful man in the world spent over two months sleeping on a couch.[12]

Back in London the question was still what to do about it. Blair told Campbell that Clinton needed to focus on the Middle East, 'one because it was right and he could do it, but also because he needed something major to focus on to get away from the US obsession with his sex life'. Northern Ireland provided something of a valve, especially in light of the recent bombing in Omagh, but there was, Blair argued, 'a real vacuum in world leadership and *we* had to do something' – particularly as the Russian economy was then in freefall. When Clinton came to Belfast in early September, Alastair Campbell observed a 'shattered man' who could barely extract a word or two in response to his various attempts at conversation from his wife. When Joe Lieberman launched an attack on the president's morals, however, Blair's conclusion again was that 'the bottom line is he is a good president being killed by the 24-hour news cycle'. As such, 'we should be totally supportive'.[13]

Brown's America

When it came to Blair's obvious affinity with the Clintons, Jonathan Powell notes that 'one assumes that it must have rankled with Gordon quite a lot that he was the one who had discovered America first and he had introduced Tony to it'. Still, Brown had his own contacts and perspective on America. Writing in 2018, he noted that 'I met and knew Al Gore, Ted Kennedy (whom I often visited), Joe Biden and Dick Gephardt, but our contacts were often through Bob Shrum who later worked with us'. Certainly, Brown considered America a safe haven from the turmoil of being Chancellor. As such, in the summer of 1997, flush after the success of his first budget, he set up home for a month in Cape Cod, Massachusetts. Throughout his life, Brown's trips to the States had far exceeded Blair's in both number and intellectual importance and it was said by advisors that he would travel to the US with suitcases full of dense policy heavy books and head straight to Harvard Library, where he could catch up on his reading. Clinton, was not so far away in Martha's

Vineyard, but since Blair was the head of the British Government it would not be good form for his finance minister to pay the president an unofficial visit, however friendly. In the event, Brown spent two weeks with his future wife Sarah MacAuley devouring books, until his brother and his family joined the party for a further fortnight. The only major trips Brown took out of the holiday estate in which they were ensconced were to local bars which showed the European football and to Hyannis Port to stock up on even more literature.[14]

Brown's other major haunt was Washington DC. This was largely due to the presence of the IMF in his role as Chancellor, though he managed to catch up with Democratic colleagues where possible. Still, it was not all work. Whilst in the US capital Brown was more prone to let his hair down than at home. Damian McBride, his spin doctor, recalls the occasion when Team Brown gathered in the bar of a DC hotel at the same time as an international pilots' convention. McBride was suspicious of the number of women wearing figure-hugging dresses, which both Ed Balls and Ed Miliband wrote off as just the wives of the pilots. When Brown surfaced from his room, Balls told his boss that 'Damian's got something to tell you'. 'I know', Brown whispered, 'we've got to get out of here, this place is full of hookers'.[15] Fortunately no photographers were around to document the uncomfortable scene. As in Cape Cod, when in DC, Brown would seek out either books or places to watch football. Given it had multiple TV screens showing the football, Summers Restaurant in Arlington was a favourite and Brown enjoyed the chance to watch some Premiership action in an ordinary bar – a luxury hardly available in Central London to one of the most famous faces in the land.

In later years, when Brown grew impatient at Blair's unwillingness to stand down as per the broad understanding reached at Granita in 1994, he would bring US allies to London to bolster the seriousness of his work. Before big set-piece speeches such as Britain's annual budget, Bob Shrum would be flown over to sit in a room with New Labour aides such as Ed Balls, Spencer Livermore, Sue Nye and Michael Jacobs and debate how they would sell their latest policies. One witness recalls that 'Brown would bash away on a keyboard in his rather aggressive two-fingered way and the image would be displayed on to a huge Plasma TV where we all could watch. It was all in bold and capital letters because of his eye sight'. Brown's live speech crafting process was almost unique amongst his generation of frontline politician. As this former advisor notes, 'Gordon wrote speeches: that's how he thought and strategized. He was fascinated by speeches and would give books of speeches to senior aides as Christmas gifts'. The use of Shrum was still rather odd, however. Newer figures in the room would ask, 'what exactly is this guy contributing – he doesn't know the policy ins and outs and is largely contributing metaphor and structure at most'. They further noted, not unreasonably, that 'this is a rather extraordinary way to use Shrum's time: why not just give him a first go at it and then Gordon and we could correct the draft? But it was how Gordon worked'. Soon, however, most in the room worked out that 'his presence calmed Gordon – Bob Shrum was really important in doing that'.[16]

The Transnational Third Way

For many British politicians, visiting America or bringing over key Democrats was partly about opening up minds from the day-to-day grind of Westminster politics. The realities of government meant longer-term thinking and intellectualising of 'the project' was understandably tougher in office than it had been in opposition. Ever seeking to keep the Prime Minister up-to-date on the latest centrist thinking, Patrick Diamond sometimes mused about how much of his efforts actually got through. He recalls that 'there's two sides of the coin. I think the more optimistic interpretation is to say, [Blair] never sent any of us any messages saying 'please don't send me these papers, they're ridiculous' or anything like that. Generally speaking, we did quite a few events – some joint seminars with the *Renewal* journal, Policy Network and other think tanks and that wasn't just for us, but because Tony thought it important. He never lost the sense that there had to be a project and that needed to be intellectually rooted. However, he didn't have the time to be seriously engaged with it'. As another advisor notes, 'he'd give speeches saying "where are we going, what are we doing," and over time these speeches became progressively more boring. There was something about becoming stuck and being reliant on ideas that he'd first seriously thought about, say, ten years before'.[17]

In May 1998, Blair asked Giles Radice to join a group of intellectuals to advise him 'on the theoretical underpinning of Blairism' – a stance to which cynics whispered that it was typical of the man to place his own mind out to competitive tender. Radice had been, in the words of the Prime Minister himself, 'a Blairite before Blair' and the other names Blair mentioned: David Marquand and Tony Giddens were deeply entrenched in this politics. Giddens had pressed the case for mainstream politicians to go *Beyond Left and Right* well before his 1994 book of that name and, in September 1998, his work on *The Third Way: The Renewal of Social Democracy* attracted interest on both sides of the Atlantic. His view of the Third Way as 'a framework of thinking and policy-making that seeks to adapt social democracy to a world which has changed fundamentally over the past two or three decades' was of course catnip to New Labour and the New Democrats. Soon after the publication of *The Third Way*, Giddens would take part in a panel discussion at NYU with Hillary Clinton (during *le sommet surrealiste*), whilst he generally enjoyed easy access to members of the Clinton team. A profile of Giddens in the *New Yorker* had been read by many in the White House and on Capitol Hill and numerous New Democrat pens underlined Giddens' view that 'the radical center is an oxymoron only if you believe that the left and right still define all the worthwhile ideas and policies. I don't and I don't think Blair does'.[18]

Still, back at home, Giles Radice remained uneasy with the label 'Third Way' – since it implied an equidistance between 'Thatcherism and old-style social democracy, which is, of course nonsense'. Neil Kinnock had an 'instinctive reservation about the term, since it sounded like Mussolini'. But, Radice mused, by calling it the Third Way 'Blair gets it discussed in the Tory newspapers'. The PM liked such debate and particularly with world statesmen such as Clinton and Schroeder whom he viewed in such an intellectual light. But an arguable failing was in not seeing the project through at a deeper level – thus ensuring the Third Way had no 'substitutes bench' to call upon at crucial times. As Jonathan Powell recalls, 'Tony didn't see many Congressmen or Senators when he was PM in London. Not many of them would have gotten through the door – I used to see some of them. When he went to Washington he would see them in groups, including meeting Obama on a couple of occasions'. Perhaps this made it easier for the Democratic centre to dump Blair when Iraq turned sour.[19]

When it came to Chancellors and presidents, however, Britain's Prime Minister was all ears. In June 1999, Tony Blair and Gerhard Schroeder would issue their joint declaration on the Third Way. At the media launch at Millbank, Blair looked tired and Schroeder 'somewhat bored'.[20] Such, again, were the rigours of government. But, if it had been read by a left-leaning politician even ten years earlier, their document would have seemed like a radical departure. For Blair and Schroeder, 'public expenditure as a proportion of national income has more or less reached the limits of acceptability'. These 'constraints on "tax and spend" force radical modernisation of the public sector and reform of public services to achieve better value for money'. Likewise, 'the belief that the state should address damaging market failures all too often led to a disproportionate expansion of the government's reach and the bureaucracy that went with it'. Crucially, for the left, 'the promotion of social justice was sometimes confused with the imposition of equality of outcome. The result was a neglect of the importance of rewarding effort and responsibility and the association of social democracy with conformity and mediocrity rather than the celebration of creativity, diversity and excellence'. The Third Way's overriding aim – in London and Berlin – would be to give people the tools to empower themselves, rather than to seek to be in a constant state of servility to the big state.

This agenda was continued in Florence a few months later. In November 1999 the world's centre-left gathered in the beautiful Italian city to discuss 'Progressive Governance for the Twenty-first Century' – France's Lionel Jospin having vetoed the term 'the Third Way' since it didn't scan well domestically. Blair was tired – with stories about his wife Cherie's pregnancy having just hit the press (Schroeder joked that 'there is nothing you won't do to fill your damn newspapers'). For Labour spinner Lance Price, it was 'too big and too public for any serious discussion and with no side seminars to give the policy wonks a chance to exchange views properly'. Still, it gave the Blairs and the Clintons the chance to talk and Bill annoyed the rest of the leaders by not turning up to a breakfast he had requested which was supposed to gather them all together. Part of the reason was that he, Hillary and Chelsea had been up to nearly 2am drinking and chatting with the Blairs. As ever, Clinton 'hoovered up other people's stories and experiences, because they interested him, but also because he could use them'.[21]

In June 2000, a further summit was held in Berlin. For the Schroeder-hosted event the field was wider – 14 global leaders from France and South Africa to Brazil and New Zealand – though Blair was absent due to paternity leave after the birth of his son, Leo. 'Progressive Governance and the Third Way are pro-family', Clinton guffawed to journalists when asked about his friend's absence. The conference discussed the potential for technological advance liberating the ordinary citizen, the need for globalisation to lead to a higher standard of living for all without a race to the bottom and, at the behest of the Latin American contingent, greater regulation of the financial markets which had recently imperiled such

FIGURE 14 The Blairs and the Clintons were friends as well as intellectual soulmates. With Clinton's presidency winding down by the time of this picture in September 2000 (featuring the four-month old Leo Blair), he joked that 'after January I'm available for babysitting duties' (Courtesy: Clinton Presidential Library).

nations.[22] But the clock was ticking on the Clinton presidency and, in some ways, Berlin marked part of his farewell tour. Still, if America elected a second New Democrat, the show itself could go on a little longer.

Gore 2000

The e-mail subject line read 'WHAT A BUSINESS' and so it was. On 12 December 2000, the US Supreme Court had ruled that the vote certification carried out in Florida the previous month should stand, thus George W. Bush rather than Al Gore would become the 43rd President. It was in this context that David Miliband sat down to compose a message to Bruce Reed, Director of Clinton's Domestic Policy Council. Consoling a close political ally, Miliband remarked that Reed 'must have suffered badly in the last five weeks'. He went further in asserting that it had all been an 'awful business – they stole it!' For Miliband, the machinations over the previous weeks had been clear evidence that 'they don't actually like democracy on the right and hate the idea that their right to rule is being challenged'. In finally accepting the verdict, Gore had 'sounded good last night – big man vs small man'.

It is perhaps no surprise that New Labour was pulling hard for the continuity presidency of Gore. As Miliband wrote to Reed on 9 January 2001, a couple of weeks before Clinton left the White House, 'the new lot seem very depressing'. For sure, the 'small man' of George W Bush would go on to have some fairly big consequences for the globe and for New Labour in the UK. But little of this could have been predicted as America's new president took office. Bruce Reed, sad to be out of office but somewhat pleased to have some time off at last, told Miliband that he was 'glad to hear you've bounced back in the polls. We're counting on you to keep the Third Way alive'. With Blair's second landslide election victory in May 2001 this would be achieved. George W Bush even rang Blair after the result to enquire, 'Man, how did you do that?'[23]

But why wasn't it President Gore making that call? Throughout the campaign, the Blair and Clinton teams continually discussed its likely outcome. By October 1999, Clinton had identified that Bush had emerged as the major threat to Gore. That month, the president told Blair that he would 'have to figure out how to expose the fraud that Bush is the new Clinton, establishing a new Republican party like I made a new Democratic party. It's helping Bush but it is killing Al'. Bush's compassionate conservative agenda was causing problems for Gore who would have to position himself 'between Bush and Bradley' – the latter his main Democratic primary opponent.[24] In February 2000, Blair found the race 'interesting' while Clinton couldn't 'tell where it's going yet. It's got a few turns left in the road. We have got to see if Bush has anything inside him to pull himself back up and respond to McCain'. Clinton expected Gore to win, but his verdict was not without qualification, particularly once Bush sealed the nomination in March. Clinton told Blair that 'we have a big problem here. The cultural aversion of white, married, Protestants to voting Democratic is a real problem – and one we have to overcome. Bush is a skilled politician, but he is not ready to be president, maybe not ever, certainly not now. But they want it real bad and they've got lots of money and lots of media access and they are not freshly discredited'.[25]

During the spring of 2000, Clinton conceded to Blair that 'Al had not the best couple of months' and warned him that 'if he doesn't [win], then you will have to do a lot of heavy lifting' on issues like Russia during a Bush presidency. Through the early summer Bush began to open up a steady margin over Gore in the polls, though Third Way figures on both sides of the Atlantic continued to hope he could pull through. In July, Clinton told Alastair Campbell that if the election was about 'the economy stupid' then Gore would win. In August, Blair felt that, when it came to the slogans, Gore's 'with the people not the powerful' beat 'prosperity for a purpose' every time 'because Bush was not clear what the purpose was'. Yet by early October, after a trip to the States, Philip Gould had become a lot less upbeat about Gore's chances.[26]

Some No 10 staffers felt 'it was a mistake for Gore to distance himself from Clinton so openly. Clinton had been pretty successful economically and it was a bit like Gordon and Tony. You want to be careful if you're going to try and counterpose yourself to a popular predecessor'. Indeed, Clinton had added 21 million jobs during his tenure and the poverty rate, including for African Americans, reached an all-time low during the Clinton–Gore years. Some of this was good fortune (the global price of oil remaining low for much of the 1993–2001 period), but the tech boom which fuelled a significant chunk of the growth had undoubtedly been aided by wise government decision making. 'Of course', our No 10 source notes, the negative takes on Gore's differentiation strategy were 'very coloured by Clinton calling Tony and telling him this, so it wasn't necessarily a case of us reaching our own analysis'.

What was harder to manage, however, was the candidate himself. Jonathan Powell had seen him on the trail in 1992 and recalls, 'he is the most appalling wooden campaigner. It was very funny because on the plane he would be hysterical and make jokes the whole time. But as soon as he got off, he became too wooden and cautious'. Bill Galston, who was working for the campaign, likewise remembers that on the stump 'the Vice President would talk for thirty seconds about the record of the Clinton administration and then immediately pivot to the future. Doesn't he understand that in part he's running for Bill Clinton's third term?' Bush's homespun southern charm, together with his claim to represent a compassionate conservatism, moved into this territory.[27]

As the 7 November election neared, Gould was 'more and more worried' while Campbell began to prepare for a hammering as the press would likely 'present a Bush win a disaster for us'. Hillary's victory in the Senate race in New York provided a modicum of good news and Blair told Clinton that she 'did wonderful. Give her our love. She was just fantastic during the campaign. She was so strong and brave. I thought she was just great'. But for the most part New Labour watched the results come in with the same degree of utter confusion shared by the rest of the world. Whilst Number 10 aides had been working up memos looking to adopt the most successful elements of Gore's message in the autumn of 2000, such notes ended up in the shredder fairly quickly after election day.[28]

As the disputed ballot issue in Florida rumbled on, the Blair government was in the bizarre situation of having extended an invitation for Clinton to come and speak in the UK. As the right-leaning press on both sides of the Atlantic tried to bounce the verdict for Bush, Blair told Clinton that 'they are a lot more ruthless than our folks aren't they?' Clinton agreed, arguing that 'they hate us more than we hate them. It's all about power to them. They don't care as much about government, they just want the power'. Still, Clinton thought there might be a twist in the tale, telling Blair he 'wouldn't even be surprised to see the U.S. Supreme Court try to overturn the Florida Supreme Court'. In classic British understatement, Blair simply replied, 'blimey'. Elsewhere, freed from the niceties of office, Neil Kinnock wrote to his friend Jack Binns deploring the fact that the 'the Supreme Court can contain such a mixture of wisdom and stupidity'. He continued: 'if there's any reasonable doubt about whether a vote has been allocated in line with the intention of the voter, the assessment of that vote should be exhaustive – regardless of timetables and other bullshit'.[29] The vast majority of British voices interviewed for this work contend that Gore should have fought on, longer and harder.

But it would not come to pass. Whilst Clinton was in Britain, the verdict on *Bush v Gore* came out. A joint post-mortem therefore began. Campbell had previously lamented that 'they had been daft not to use Clinton properly' during the campaign, which his American communications counterparts agreed with. Clinton himself was tired, whilst Hillary was fighting to keep a brave face on things. Both felt Gore had blown it and were fairly indiscreet about it. Clinton told Campbell that 'his legacy was at risk', that Gore had 'lost by allowing the Republicans to neutralise the economy' and 'by allowing their basic message to move leftwards'. The president gave Blair 'a tip or two on how to make sure he got in with Bush' and the group then travelled to Warwick University where Clinton was slated to give a speech. Clinton's address at Warwick would highlight his attempt 'to try to develop a response to globalization that we all call by the shorthand term, the Third Way'. 'For us' – and here he clearly meant Blair – 'it's a very serious attempt to put a human face on the global economy and to direct the process of globalization in a way that benefits all people'. With the election of George W Bush, that agenda was truly in Blair's hands now.[30]

Blair alone

Without the New Democrats in power, could the Third Way survive? Certainly, there was still Schroeder in Germany and the soon-to-retire Wim Kok in the Netherlands. Yet, with the rise of Bush, Berlusconi and the victory of the right in the French legislative elections of 2002, it was now Blair around whom the progressive centre left was firmly gathered. As such, on 8 June 2002, Clinton and the DLC rolled back into town. At Hartwell House, a grandiose Buckinghamshire mansion, New Labour's powerbrokers and assorted figures from the New Democrats debated the meaning of the Third Way. Peter Mandelson had organised the event and though Charles Clarke and Alan Milburn could not make it (as Denis MacShane noted in his diary, 'you've got to give people some time off') the turnout was impressive. Blair and Brown both appeared (the latter insisted a big screen TV was set up in advance of his speech the previous day, so he could watch David Beckham's penalty secure a precious World Cup victory for England over Argentina).[31] Other Cabinet Ministers such as Patricia Hewitt and John Reid arrived eager to hear what the DLCers had to say; also present were both Miliband brothers and Douglas Alexander.

MacShane was a little sceptical. He found the affair 'crawling with American millionaires who pay for this kind of event and get proximity with the powerful in exchange for their dollars. It turns out to be a very right-wing crowd still obsessed with the Clinton victory of 1992 and his undoubted achievements in office. And still full of hate and anger that Al Gore lost the election and did so, in their view, by adopting left wing populist politics'. Indeed, should they stand a chance in 2004, the presentations suggested, 'the people the Americans have to attract back to vote democratic all seem to be very keen on capital punishment and, David Miliband says gently, "the swing vote"'.

Mandelson loved the setting and was in a 'most frisky' mood. He wanted to 'put the "glitz and glamour" back into Third Way politics and obviously adores being feted at this kind of millionaires outing'. For the coming figures, however, there was a danger. Douglas Alexander sarcastically turned to MacShane to enquire, 'whether the next meeting might take place "in a council house not in a country house"' He also used his own contribution to note that 'if you favour just well-off people and ignore the poor or the losers then you will lose your distinctive centre-left characteristics'. David Miliband agreed and framed the Third Way's 'trilemma – how to keep up high employment, fiscal responsibility and promote more equity in society'. Getting all three in sync was the challenge and Miliband 'called for more boldness in leadership so we start to think of ourselves as insurgents again, not as incumbents'. Ruth Kelly, likewise, talked of the need to 'redistribute assets and increase a material store of wealth', which MacShane saw best delivered through employee share ownership.

Later in the day, a coach whisked the participants to Ascott House, the country seat of the Rothschild family. Lynn Rothschild, wife of Sir Evelyn, had been a Democratic supporter for decades and had previously volunteered for Pat Moynihan. After a while, Blair and Clinton entered – Blair in an open necked shirt, Clinton more formally dressed in a blue shirt and red tie. MacShane found the president 'shorter than I thought, about my height when he shook my hand'. 'You look like you've lost some weight, Mr President'. 'I hope so', chuckled Clinton, 'but I need to lose fifteen more pounds'. The party then adjourned to one of the drawing rooms where both leaders answered questions as to where the Third Way could and should, go next.

During this event MacShane found 'Clinton so articulate, with never a word out of place and an extraordinary gift for making intellectual points but in homely language'. At the same time, 'Blair, by contrast, was very Blairish, but with lots of little stutters when he says, "right" or he stops and just says, "now" and then pauses as he continues his train of thinking. It almost became like a good Rory Bremner take-off'. The most pressing transatlantic question was Bush and Iraq. There, even amongst friends, Blair 'insisted on the importance of staying close to the United States and while Clinton was partly supportive, partly critical of decisions and policies initiated by Bush – there is a presidential solidarity after all – Blair was careful not to join in anything that could remotely be taken as criticism of Bush'.

The dinner that followed was a mixture of the kitsch and the controversial. It certainly spelt something of the end for a truly international Third Way. The Rothschild money that had helped finance the event had produced an odd set of merchandise, 'little baseball caps with a Stars and Stripes and a Union Jack on it'. Running his hand over his cap, MacShane 'looked at the French and German and Swedish and Dutchmen and just shrugged since they thought they were coming to a European-American event but there were gushing speeches from the people paying for the dinner saying that Blair was the Leader of the Free World and had given the United States complete support after 11 September'. For MacShane, ever the Europhile, 'I suppose it's the language one gets used to in the United States but it was all too extravagant and dollar laden for my liking and I'm not sure I enjoyed that part of it at all'. This would be true for many. Indeed, the 2002 gathering would prove something of a last hurrah, for events on the international stage would soon come to overshadow everything.

Notes

1 Campbell 2/510, 504.
2 See FLOTUS Press Release Binder ARC/CPL/FOIA 2011-0415-S; From/241.
3 MCI/Blumenthal.
4 Blumenthal/298; Al From to DLC Annual Conference October 27, 1997, ARC/CPL/FOIA 2006-0469-F; COR/Osborne.
5 Greenberg 2/216; Draper/88.
6 ARC/CPL/MDR 12 Feb 1998 and 19 April 2000 calls.
7 6 August 1998 Grand Jury Testimony via, e.g. *Washington Post*; Campbell 2/506.
8 Blair 2/244, 250 and 260.
9 Campbell 2/287; ARC/CPL/MDR, 27 January 1998 call.
10 COR/Macshane.
11 Campbell 2/288.
12 Clinton/809, 811.
13 Campbell 2/482–94.
14 COR/Powell; Pym and Kochan/113–22.
15 McBride/128.
16 COR/OTR.
17 COR/Diamond and COR/OTR.
18 Giddens 1/26; *New Yorker*, 6 October 1997.
19 Radice 1/416; COR/Kinnock and Powell.
20 Radice 1/443.
21 Campbell 3/165, 166; Price/163.

22 *LA Times*, 4 June 2000.

23 Blair 1/336.

24 ARC/CPL/MDR, 13 Oct 1999 call.

25 ARC/CPL/MDR, 8 Feb and 19 April 2000 calls.

26 ARC/CPL/MDR, 27 May 2000 call; Campbell 3, 374, 384, 416

27 COR/Powell; MCI/Galston.

28 Campbell 3, 446; ARC/CPL/MDR, 10 November 2000 call.

29 ARC/CPL/MDR, 23 November 2000; Kinnock to Binns, 15 December 2000, KNNK/1/9/19.

30 Campbell 3/446, 478, 479.

31 DMAC/8 June 2002; COR/From.

9 INTERVENTION AND IRAQ

Due to Tony Blair's close association with a New Democrat in Clinton and then a Republican president in George W Bush, his foreign policy and that of the Third Way per se, has opened up several debates. This final chapter, therefore, deals with the continuum of Third Way foreign policy stretching from Haiti in 1993 to the invasion of Iraq ten years later. Two points may, however, be made from the outset. First, foreign policy forms an exception to the general rule and, in diplomacy, the room for manoeuvre of a British Prime Minister is necessarily less than that of an American president. Not only does the president's charismatic authority as Commander-in-Chief give him greater leeway on military matters than the gridlock domestic reform can often generate in Congress, the sheer size of the American army allows the United States freedom to act unilaterally, should it wish. The British army was and remains simply of a different scale to American military might. As John Kerry put it in the 2004 presidential debates, 'I have nothing but respect for the British, Tony Blair and for what they've been willing to do [in Iraq]'. But 'you can't tell me that if the most troops any other country has on the ground is Great Britain, with 8,300 ... that we have a genuine coalition to get this job done'. There is an argument to be had about whether Iraq was in the British national interest, but the invasion would have happened come what may. The 130,000-sized American army which poured into Iraq saw to that.

Critics would later state that Iraq was 'not a blunder, not an error, not a mistake: whatever the law decides, this was – from any moral standpoint – one of the gravest crimes of our time'. The Chilcot inquiry would more soberly declare that Blair's Britain '*chose* to join the invasion of Iraq before the peaceful options for disarmament had been exhausted' and that 'military action at that time was not a last resort'. One senior American voice interviewed for this book asserts that 'Tony was manipulated. He felt that he should maintain the US relationship and that the alliance was essential. I know *for a fact*, from a close friend of mine, that the intelligence was distorted that was given to Tony'. Certainly, as Gordon Brown has asserted, the Americans were likely somewhat underhand in their dealings with their British allies. But even Iraq must be viewed in the round of Third Way foreign policy military interventions. And those began thousands of miles away from the Middle East.[1]

Haiti

In 1991, the first democratically elected president of Haiti, Jean-Bertrand Aristide, was deposed by a military coup. Soon after, people started fleeing Haiti on rickety boats, with one-third capsizing in the Caribbean. With Miami only 600 miles away, many Haitians wanted to seek asylum in the United States and this created a political problem for Clinton both before and after the 1992 election. Before November, Clinton staked out a position opposed to Bush's policy of intercepting boats and returning them to Haiti. As Sandy Berger later admitted, it was 'not a well-considered decision' and one partly down to the electoral calculation that 'there are a lot of Haitians in New York'.[2] In any event, after the victory, CIA operatives came to Berger with images of Haitians dismantling the roofs of their homes to construct makeshift boats. The CIA predicted there would be more than 150,000 boats in the water on 21 January 1993, the day after Clinton took the oath of office and that, consequently, tens of thousands would likely drown.

Clinton backtracked on his election commitment. But he did so with two provisos. The first was to step up the processing measures of those applying for asylum in Haiti, to determine the genuine political refugees over the many more attempted economic migrants. The second was, however, far more wide reaching. As Clinton put it to his aides, 'if we can't restore democracy to this little island 100 miles [sic] off our coast, what kind of a great power are we?' When Berger presented a plan along these lines that the president found unacceptable, he thundered that 'this is the same bullshit I heard in the campaign! You guys have to do better than this. This is just bullshit'.[3] Eventually, the Governors Island agreement was signed with Cedras and Francois – the leaders who had deposed Aristide – to restore democracy to the island, but soon the Haitian militia reneged on the deal. When the new regime blocked the entry of the US *Harlan County* to a Haitian port and, subsequently, began further oppressing its own people, it was clear something needed to be done. The US military began to prepare for a 25,000-strong troop invasion.

But then the White House received a phone call from Jimmy Carter. As Sandy Berger recalls, Carter said 'he was going to Haiti and taking Colin Powell and Sam Nunn with him. It was a sort of self-appointed delegation [but] he didn't realize that we had a military plan and Sunday at 4 o'clock those planes were leaving from North Carolina and heading with troops to Haiti'. 'Okay', the administration told Carter, 'you go down there, but you've got to be out by 12 o'clock on Sunday'. Carter would visit Haiti and extracted a vague agreement from Cedras to leave the country along the terms of the Governors Island agreement. Eventually, after much negotiation, including Cedras holding out for the US State Department to compensate him for the value of his house and boats before he would agree to leave for a third country, the militia gave in and the invasion was called off. Clinton had avoided a disaster, at least for now.

Anguish in Africa

Haiti was at least close to Florida. Clinton also faced two early instances where humanitarian intervention thousands of miles away in Africa was raised. The first was a hangover from the previous president in Somalia. During the transition, Bush enacted what one historian called 'the most remarkable action ever taken by a lame-duck president', which involved pledging American troops to the 28,000-strong multinational force which was looking to secure delivery lines of food to stop regional clan warfare leading to mass starvation. As Bush told the American public in December 1992, whilst he knew that 'the United States alone cannot right the world's wrongs' there were also some crises in the world that could not be resolved without American involvement. Likewise, 'American action is often necessary as a catalyst for broader involvement of the community of nations'. Sandy Berger remembers Brent Scowcroft briefing him that troops would be deployed to Somalia but 'it's not something you've got to worry about because they will be gone by Inauguration Day'.[4]

In reality, Somalia was a lawless state where brokering any kind of peace between the various factions was a virtual impossibility. The Clinton administration had hoped to 'muddle through' as David Jeremiah put it but, in many ways, it would form his Bay of Pigs – as Nancy Soderberg later conceded. The project had been farmed out to the military, where Colin Powell continually argued they had it under control. But on 5 October 1993, it became clear that this was not true. That day an American helicopter was shot down, 18 soldiers were killed and then their bodies were dragged through the streets. These events, later memorialised in the book (and film) *Black Hawk Down*, led to 'people wondering why we were doing this and why were Americans dying in some place that nobody had heard of'. Clinton would later tell Blair that Somalia had been a 'messy deal. I lost some American boys over there and one of them was dragged naked through the streets of Mogadishu. We made some mistakes there in what we *did* and did not do'. Back in 1993, Warren Christopher and Les Aspin were summoned to explain the events to Congress and with Aspin taking the lead he was 'absolutely massacred'. Senior senators such as Robert Byrd declared they were going to cut off funding for any continuation of American troops in the region and, although a 90-day phase-out period was eventually negotiated with the White House, the lessons here were salutary. It was, for Clinton, 'the lowest point in my presidency'. Aspin was forced out as Defence Secretary in February 1994.[5]

But what were the larger lessons? In May 1994, Clinton signed Presidential Defence Directive 25 which laid out the terms of future peace-keeping measures. The text was studied in its ambiguities, but some in the administration read it as 'circumscrib[ing] peace keeping operations and [to] not do them anymore'. As Sandy Berger noted, it could also be read as merely laying out the ground rules *for* intervention: that any intervention 'had to make sense on its merits' and 'politically it was going to be necessary to be able to show that this was serious and that we'd asked the right questions'.[6] Somalia had also raised the question of the right international vehicle for US participation in foreign affairs. Somalia had been a UN peacekeeping mission that had cost American lives; whether NATO would offer a better, more streamlined, leadership would remain a key question going into the late 1990s.

The immediate impression garnered, however, was that the Clinton administration then 'decided not to intervene military in Rwanda, even though there was a genocide, because we were so scared by Somalia'. This was not wholly true. As Berger pointed out, running through the options on Rwanda in the wake of PDD 25 saw 'a lot of them coming up zeroes'. As in Somalia, there were many sides in the Rwandan conflict that were difficult to unpick, at least early in 1994. For Warren Christopher, it was unclear whether the battle was between Hutus and Tutsis, an intra-Hutu conflict or just a general power grab from which it was best to stay out. A reliance on Francophone European powers had not produced much reliable intelligence in Rwanda and, for many in the Clinton administration, Burundi looked the more unstable of the central African states at the time. As such, because of the logistical difficulties in mounting any US peacekeeping operation, Tony Lake notes that 'the sad fact is the possibility of American intervention [in Rwanda] never came up'.[7]

After the Tutsi-dominated Rwandese Patriotic Front invaded the country (many of whose supporters had previously been exiled to Uganda) in 1990, an uneasy peace had been brokered in 1993. But after a plane carrying the Rwandese president was gunned down in April 1994, a Hutu-led genocide of the Tutsis broke out within a matter of hours. This saw an estimated 1 million people killed over the next few months. During this period, the US and British governments did virtually nothing. As then Defence Secretary Bill Perry recalls, after the events of Somalia, 'there would have been an explosion in Congress' had they tried to intervene militarily. Likewise, James Steinberg, then director of policy planning at the State department, points to the torture and murder of ten Belgian soldiers, posted as a nominal buffer force to keep both sides apart, as the potential outcome of any action. These were the procedural explanations for non-intervention, but Clinton would still travel to Kigali in 1998 to declare that the US should have done more to prevent the loss of life. Nancy Soderberg could not bring herself to watch the film *Hotel Rwanda* 'because I feel so bad'.[8]

Going in

Years later, Tony Blair arrived by helicopter to a sports stadium where he was due to meet local leaders to discuss the holding of a new and democratic election. As word had spread that Blair was about to arrive, crowds had grown and grown to a point where the police were getting worried. After the British Prime Minister conducted his official business and was set to leave, he was given 'a hero's welcome as warm and powerful' as any one observer had seen. A local man clasped Blair's hand and wouldn't let go, simply repeating 'thank you'. The throng was chanting his name: Tony! Tony! Tony! Children ran up to the visiting leader, handing him flowers. Many babies would later go on to be named 'Toni' or 'Tonibler' in honour of their liberator. After meeting British soldiers, Blair was led to the main town square where he gave an off-the-cuff address, relayed to the crowd through an interpreter. The cheering seemed to go on forever and the mood was triumphant.[9]

To some, the above account perhaps reads like an alternate history of the 2003 invasion of Iraq 'gone right' or, uncharitably, how Blair thought his victory parade in Baghdad might proceed. The more salient point remains that it was not some figment of the imagination. In July 1999, Tony Blair was given precisely this hero's welcome when arriving into Pristina, Kosovo. He had faced doubters both at home and abroad and had seemingly come through unscathed. It was Blair, rather than Clinton, who had forced the pace on the recent bombing campaign and events had proven him entirely correct. Whereas Blair's 'awakening on domestic policy took place over time' and he 'probably only found his voice on domestic reform in the last term', his 'awakening on foreign policy was abrupt'.[10]

Kosovo was only the latest chapter in the reordering of the Balkans that had occurred in the immediate post-Cold War period. In 1989, Slobodan Milosevic became President of Serbia, then a state of the communist republic of Yugoslavia. A committed free marketer, Milosevic was also a pan-Serb nationalist who encouraged Serbian communities across Yugoslavia, particularly in Croatia and Bosnia, to press their desire to be unified with their motherland. As Yugoslavia looked likely to collapse under the weight of its ethnic divisions, Milosevic sought to cut deals, first with the Slovenians and then the Croatians, which would allow Serbia to expand at the expense of Bosnia. Through his Presidency of Serbia, he further used the Yugoslav People's Army to put down nationalist sentiment elsewhere, all the while with his real aim in mind: an ethnically uniform Greater Serbian nation.

Between 1992 and 1995, a civil war in Bosnia, between the pro-Milosevic Serbs on the one hand and Bosnian and Croatian elements on the other, would cost over 100,000 lives. Joe Biden, who flew to meet Milosevic in April 1993 in an attempt to broker a peace, saw first-hand something of the mentality which caused this. As he later wrote, 'the Serbs had an overwhelming sense of being put upon by history. Their argument ran like this: we are the noble people, the Serbs who did so much for Europe and were always persecuted . . . Milosevic understood the power of the Serbs' victim mentality [and] fed it back to them in a constant self-fulfilling loop'. An agreement to end the conflict was eventually signed in

Dayton, Ohio, but only after Europe had seen its first post-1945 instance of ethnic cleansing (that of the Bosniaks – Bosnian Muslims) through massacres including, most famously, Srebrenica. As Biden later wrote, to that point, 'not a single European country was willing to extend itself to do something about the continuing slaughter of Muslims and Croats'. This included the Conservative government in the UK.[11]

Nor did the Dayton Accords provide anything but a temporary respite. Towards the end of 1998 Tony Blair received official intelligence reports and the testimony of Liberal Democrat leader Paddy Ashdown (who had visited the region), that Kosovo, still part of Serbia but largely of Albanian Muslim ethnicity, was about to erupt. By this stage the Serbs had already displaced hundreds of thousands of Kosovans and killed around 2,000. Blair then characterised the next few months as one where the international community tabled resolutions, 'statements were issued and daily declarations were made about the unacceptable nature of what Milosevic was doing, but the killing and cleansing carried on'.[12]

Blair saw the international community as seeking 'to pacify, but not to resolve' whereas he was 'totally and unyieldingly for resolution, not pacification'. After all, 'here were ordinary civilians being driven from their homes and turned into refugees, killed, raped, beaten up with savagery and often sadism, whole families humiliated or eliminated'. What was western morality if it was not prepared to act in the face of all that? As such, he became 'extraordinarily forward in advocating a military solution', even at the cost of 'putting the most colossal strain on my personal relationship with Bill Clinton'. Blair recognised that 'it was quite hard to describe the direct American interest in Kosovo' and that the American people generally felt 'it was Europe's problem'. In a private conversation back in 1993, Warren Christopher had 'used every argument a good lawyer' should to Joe Biden on non-intervention: 'air strikes are not our call. It's NATO's overall. Second, arming the Bosnians would only cause more killing. Third, this is a civil war'. Essentially, these still held five years later. Amongst the Europeans, Chirac, Schroeder and D'Alema were willing to commit to 'the necessary expressions of disgust' but demanded the west explicitly rule out committing ground troops. For Blair, this showed 'there was a limit to our seriousness of intent'.[13]

Even the meaningful use of air power in Kosovo demanded US involvement. Over January and February 1999 Blair and Clinton spoke regularly. To get Clinton to commit to bombing Blair tactically accepted the initial need to rule out ground troops – 'I thought it worth agreeing to. We could work out how to unravel it later'. An air-only mission at least offered what Clinton advisors called a 'thousand to one advantage on Milosevic', whereas, in a mountain campaign against the dug-in Serbs, 'there were bound to be [American] casualties'. It soon became clear, however, that *something* must be done. In March, Milosevic stepped up the cleansing of Kosovans, which tipped the White House's hand in favour of action. Clinton and his aides told each other that 'geez, this is bad . . . If we don't [act], he will just clean them out, kill a bunch of people and do bad things'. With Russia willing to veto any action whatsoever at UN Security Council level, the impetus would fall on NATO.[14]

Bombing thus began on 24 March and the main military targets were soon taken out. By mid-April Clinton told Blair that 'Americans are concerned but they're basically supporting what we are doing'.[15] This was a view more or less borne out by opinion polls (on 14 April, 61 to 34 were favour of Clinton's handling of Kosovo), but Blair wanted a little more than that. The issue with bombing, for Blair, was that 'the enemy is being damaged, but not being beaten'. As it ticked on and on, the 78-day long bombing campaign would test an American public now conditioned, as Sam Gejdenson, a Democratic Congressman from Connecticut argued, to want conflicts over quickly.[16]

A combination of left and right therefore began to move against the policy. Republicans like Mitch McConnell went after Clinton, calling the Kosovo affair 'horribly managed'. Others, like Pat Buchanan, put it more bluntly: 'who cares what flag flies over Pristina?' They were joined in this endeavour by the British hard left. Tony Benn favoured 'the use of force, but not by NATO' – in effect ruling out action by the back door, since who else was realistically going to act? Jeremy Corbyn continued to harangue the Defence Secretary George Robertson on greater UN involvement in the issue and the nature of NATO bombing. Robertson would occasionally snap back that it 'will be nice – and, gosh, will I welcome it! – when my honourable friend comes to the Chamber and denounces the violence perpetrated against women and children inside Kosovo'. Corbyn had, Robertson noted, 'a long record of campaigning against tyrants. Perhaps he will tell us how he would deal with *this* particular tyrant'.[17]

Blair was increasingly unhappy. The committee-based procedure NATO had for identifying targets was 'hopelessly, almost laughably, complicated' and the advice to the Prime Minister was that 'you can't win this by an air campaign alone'. Even if NATO targeting proved far more effective than previous western bombing campaigns, bombing was also difficult PR wise. Whilst the camps in Albania and Macedonia provided ample evidence of the plight of fleeing refugees, over 500 civilians were killed during the air campaign and not just Milosevic supporters. When NATO bombs landed on the Chinese Embassy in Belgrade on 7 May, there was a global media storm. But Blair remained resolute, telling Clinton that 'Milosevic can take the cameras to wherever he likes and point to these things. But in Kosovo this is a daily happening, as a result of deliberate policy, not as an accident'. The question was how to convince Clinton of a ground offensive which would likely involve at least 100,000 American soldiers and perhaps 50,000 British troops.[18]

There was a twofold strategy here: Blair the world statesman and Blair the 'behind the scenes' operator. As to the first, in a landmark speech on 22 April 1999, Blair took his argument stateside. Addressing the Chicago Economic Club, Blair told his American audience that 'we cannot let the evil of ethnic cleansing stand. We must not rest until it is reversed. We have learned twice before in this century that appeasement does not work. If we let an evil dictator range unchallenged, we will have to spill

FIGURE 15 Blair and Clinton appointed their nations' first female Foreign Secretary (Margaret Beckett) and Secretary of State (Madeleine Albright) respectively. Albright, pictured here, would prove a key ally to Blair when pressing for intervention in Kosovo (Courtesy: Clinton Presidential Library).

infinitely more blood and treasure to stop him later'. The Blair doctrine, at its core, was to argue that 'we live in a world where isolationism has ceased to have a reason to exist'. The world mattered: economically, politically and morally. As he argued, 'we cannot refuse to participate in global markets if we want to prosper. We cannot ignore new political ideas in other countries if we want to innovate. We cannot turn our backs on conflicts and the violation of human rights within other countries if we want still to be secure'. On the latter, he pointedly noted that 'armed force is sometimes the only means of dealing with dictators'.

Blair was partly helped here by the nature of his enemies. Tony Benn and Mitch McConnell aside, the libertarian Ron Paul, in a congressional speech denouncing the 'illegal' action on Kosovo, declared in early May that 'this war institutionalizes foreign control over our troops. Tony Blair now tells Bill Clinton how to fight a NATO war, while the U.S. taxpayers pay for it'. Even after the successful conclusion of the bombing, Paul would note that 'by Blair demanding more American bombs, money and the introduction of ground troops, many have become skeptical of his judgment'. For Paul, America had not been 'attacked and there has been no threat to our national security . . . it is illegal even according to NATO's treaty as well as the UN charter'. The latter points were precisely those to be later used on Iraq. Back in the spring of 1999, however, mainstream Republicans like John McCain (who had earlier opposed action in the region) wanted preparations for a ground campaign to begin for precisely the reasons Blair articulated. Global opinion shifted around the same time and Giles Radice confided in his diary that 'what is interesting is that the generation of '68 now in power, like Robin Cook and German Foreign Minister Joschka Fischer, back the war mainly because of the human rights issue'. It was the 'older pragmatists' like Denis Healey and Thatcher's foreign secretary Peter Carrington who were against.[19]

Sandy Berger would later claim that 'Tony Blair is given a lot of credit for Kosovo, but Blair did not convince Clinton'.[20] This is at least arguable. For one, Secretary of State Madeleine Albright disagrees and notes the gender dynamics then at play. Albright had herself been arguing to deploy ground troops before the winter set in. Since preparations for an invasion could take up to two months, a decision was coming ever nearer as spring ticked on. Clinton's military chiefs and his defence secretary Bill Cohen were dead against and, as Albright notes, 'when you have [them] telling you this is a lousy idea and you have this woman secretary of state on the other side, I think [the president] questioned it'. But when Blair came to the White House, he managed to persuade Clinton, not least by the simple mechanism of getting him out of the room. Albright recalls that after their meeting on Kosovo had dragged on, Blair remarked that 'I really need to use the facilities'. Clinton offered to show him where they were and, when the two were alone, Blair secured his agreement for a ground intervention. As Albright would note, 'it was a great way to get out of talking with all of us'. Certainly, in the gap between Blair's visit on 22 April and their teleconference on 29 April, Clinton had conceded the need to 'do joint planning on the ground force option'. In the event, other than securing locations after the withdrawal of Serbian troops, no armed action would be necessary. In mid-May, Clinton had been calling Joe Biden asking him 'what would you say to my halting the bombing?' By early June, Milosevic finally agreed to withdraw from Kosovo. In the face of resolute and decisive action, the other side blinked.[21]

Soon afterwards, Blair was enjoying a celebratory dinner with David Blunkett in Downing Street. Blair had served up a vegetarian spinach dip, which disappointed his Education Secretary, a self-proclaimed 'carnivore of the first order'. Within minutes Blair's 12-year-old son Nicky stopped by, ostensibly to get his dad's help with some homework. Blunkett was amused, but also told the child to 'give your dad a big hug because he has saved thousands of people's lives'. Nicky dutifully obliged. And it would not be the last moment of congratulation. Blair was famously mobbed as he visited the refugee camps, a reaction which also greeted Bill Clinton on his own visit. Even the *Guardian's* Polly Toynbee, hardly a reactionary neo-con, declared that 'it was right to break the United Nations' convenient illusion that tyranny within national borders is out of bounds to outside saviors' and noted that 'NATO did fight and win in an honorable cause – and might again'.[22]

Blair's triumph here was significant in many ways. As international relations scholar Adam Roberts has ably set out, Kosovo was 'the first sustained use of armed force by NATO ... in its 50-year existence'. It was 'the first time a major use of destructive armed force had been undertaken with the stated purpose of implementing UN Security Council resolutions but *without* Security Council authorization' and was 'the first major bombing campaign intended to bring a halt to crimes against humanity being committed by a state within its own borders'.[23] The diplomatic course matters here. UN Resolution 1199 in September 1998 had demanded Milosevic 'cease all action by the security forces affecting the civilian population' and had referred to 'further action' if it did not. A month later, Resolution 1203 accepted that NATO had a direct interest in

FIGURE 16 In Kosovo, Blair and Clinton took action to avoid a genocide. In June 1999, Clinton visited refugee camps, including here, near Skopje, Macedonia, where the plight of refugees from Milosevic was obvious (Courtesy: Clinton Presidential Library).

the Kosovan question. But there was no Security Council resolution authorising the bombing, principally because Russia would veto it.

In his actions on Kosovo, Blair had remade established precedent. As Lord Goldsmith, the Attorney General at the time of Iraq put it, 'in relation to Kosovo, there was essentially a new legal theory that was developed, which was that there could be military force used to avert a serious humanitarian crisis'. In Kosovo, 'United Nations authority was not present. Still the view was taken, by this country and by others, that military action was justified on this new basis and I think there was a sort of view in some places: well, we managed to, as it were, avoid the fact that there was a veto on that occasion'. The issue would resurface. Kosovo would embolden Blair to deploy British forces in the Sierra Leone civil war (leading Kofi Annan to declare 'at least they moved, they have done something') and, latterly, of course, when it came to a far wider conflict.[24]

The Iraqi Prelude

Iraq both made Bill Clinton and, in the eyes of some, would come to finish Tony Blair. After all, Congressional Democrats' unwillingness to support George HW Bush's conflict against Saddam had cleared the path for Clinton's run in 1991 and Blair's domestic support would drop fairly dramatically after the invasion of Iraq in 2003. The narrative here is simple and mesmerizing. Politicians from Barack Obama to Donald Trump have since made political capital out of varying degrees of opposition to the war. The symbolism of the heroes and villains of this story are now fairly ingrained in our psyche. Famously, on 15 February 2003, Jeremy Corbyn addressed a Hyde Park rally declaring he found it 'deeply distasteful that the British Prime Minister can use the medieval powers of the royal prerogative to send young men and women to die, to kill civilians and for Iraqis to die'. He asked why £3.5 billion was about to be spent on a war that 'nobody wants'. That same day 1 million citizens gathered on the streets of London to protest against the war, mirroring similarly impressive gatherings in Madrid and Rome. There was a significant caucus virulently against the conflict and for those who would lose loved ones as a result, such anger cannot be questioned.

The issue, however, is that this was clearly not a conflict that, as Corbyn put it, 'nobody wants'. British and American legislatures voted for the war and figures across the political spectrum backed the conflict, as we will see, for reasons more complex than just the much-vaunted and certainly never found weapons of mass destruction. As Coalition forces entered Baghdad in April 2003, two-thirds of the British public backed the war. It was not until February 2004 that YouGov showed a consistent margin of the British public thinking it had been 'wrong'. In the US, the turn in opinion came at the beginning of 2005 – months after George W Bush had been re-elected against an opponent, John Kerry, who had attempted to use ambivalence to the conflict to his advantage. When, in May 2005, it came to his own test at the ballot box, Tony Blair would go on to secure a comfortable, if reduced, 66-seat majority. Since then, both the British and American publics have suffered a collective amnesia. We must, therefore, return to the world of Blair and Clinton if we want to understand the policies of Blair and Bush.[25]

There were three strands to the Clinton agenda on Iraq: sanctions to undermine the stability of Saddam's regime, a UN-mandated decommissioning programme and limited military action in response to specific provocation. The first began with the Iraqi invasion of Kuwait in August 1990 and effectively isolated Iraq economically. Clinton introduced the Oil for Food Programme in 1995, allowing Iraq to sell oil on global markets in exchange for humanitarian goods like food and medicine, but anything that remotely resembled military arsenal was banned. US forces inspected and occasionally impounded ships entering Iraq. Concurrently, in 1991, the United Nations Special Commission (UNSCOM) was given the mandate to oversee Iraq's compliance with UN resolution 687 after its army had been removed from Kuwait. This resolution demanded Iraq destroy its stock of chemical and biological weapons and eliminate its nuclear programme.

Through the 1990s, however, Iraq failed to comply with the letter or even spirit of UNSCOM's remit. In December 1998, the head of UNSCOM, Richard Butler, wrote to Kofi Annan declaring that Iraq's 'disclosure statements have never been complete' and that, rather than carry out such activities with international observers, it had engaged in 'extensive, unilateral, secret destruction' of its weapon stocks and had 'also pursued a practice of concealment of proscribed items, including weapons'. In various ways, Iraqi bureaucrats repeatedly refused requests for information on its biological programmes. Since Saddam had used gas in his purge of the Kurds – over 50,000 had been deliberately killed during his genocide in 1987–88 – this was hardly a moot point.[26]

Blair and Clinton wanted action, but the left disagreed. In February 1998, Tam Dalyell wrote a letter to the Prime Minister expressing his dismay at a parliamentary vote authorising military action against Saddam Hussein's Iraqi regime. Having the 'dreadful feeling that [Blair had] been infected with a "touch of the Thatcher" attitude to war', Dalyell looked around for the cause of this supposedly overly muscular foreign policy. Part of this he felt was President Clinton looking for a 'potential diversion from his own personal problems' – the Monica Lewinsky affair. But much, as the hard left was wont to do, he ascribed to prominent American Jews. 'Given the gravity of what [Secretary of State Madeleine Albright] and [Secretary of Defense] William Cohen might contribute to, in the way of destruction [of Iraq], it is fair comment that they are Jewish and perceived ... by many in our country, not only of the ethnic community, to have their own agenda'.[27] Blair's reply has not survived the record.

Saddam, of course, was not the only threat. On 20 August 1998, US cruise missiles destroyed the Al-Shifa pharmaceuticals factory in North Sudan in retaliation for the Al-Qaeda sponsored attacks on US embassies in Nairobi and Dar es Salaam. The intelligence here was ambiguous at best, though George Galloway, as ever, was not one to live in ambiguities. 'To my *certain* knowledge', he told the House of Commons in January

2001, 'the Foreign and Commonwealth Office knew from the beginning that this murderous act, carried out by President Clinton on the eve of his mistress's court appearance, was based upon a bright shining lie'. The simultaneous attempt in August 1998 to bomb Al-Qaeda hideouts in Afghanistan had, Galloway contended, 'further alienated Muslim opinion, inflated the burgeoning reputation of Bin Laden and added a new twist to the hatred of the USA that exists in large parts of the third world'. Five years before the August 1998 raids, it is worth adding, Al-Qaeda trained operatives had placed a truck bomb underneath the North Tower of the World Trade Centre in New York, killing six people.[28]

To be sure, George W Bush was not the first US president to adopt a strategy of both trying to take out Al-Qaeda and removing Saddam in Iraq. In June 1993, Clinton authorised the firing of 23 tomahawk missiles against the headquarters of the Iraqi Intelligence Service, after an assassination attempt by Iraq against former President George HW Bush during his visit to Kuwait a couple of months earlier. Five years later, with decommissioning dragging on interminably, on 31 October 1998, Clinton signed into law the Iraq Liberation Act which mandated funds to be used for Iraqi opposition groups looking to overturn their dictator. Congressional support for the bill ranged from 'Morning Joe' Scarborough to Bernie Sanders. After announcing that regime change was the White House's formal policy henceforth, between 16 and 19 December 1998 Operation Desert Fox was launched against Iraq with the aim of degrading Saddam's ability to produce new weapons. As Galloway and Dalyell noted, this four-day bombing campaign wrapped up the same day the House of Representatives voted to impeach the president on the grounds of perjury (i.e. lying to the grand jury about Lewinsky) and obstructing justice (his pressuring or asking others to lie about Paula Jones). In February 1999, the Senate would vote along party lines to acquit Clinton.

Clinton got through impeachment, but he had not solved the Iraq question. Indeed, after Desert Fox, Saddam Hussein told his anti-aircraft gunners that they would receive $14,000 each if they managed to shoot down any Allied aircraft patrolling Iraq's northern or southern no-fly zones – vast stretches of the country where Iraq was forbidden, on British, French and American say-so, from flying military planes. From the US side, certainly, Desert Fox looked more like an attempt at regime change than simply degrading Iraq's capacity to produce WMD. As the US Army Intelligence analyst William Arkin noted, 35 of the 100 bombing targets had been air defence facilities, 49 were facilities of the regime's domestic oppression (secret police, transport facilities and palaces) and only 13 had any connection to chemical and biological weapons or even ballistic missiles. Therefore, as Americans prepared to elect a new president, Saddam was contained, uneasily, by a country now legislatively committed to his removal. The link between 9/11 and Saddam would be indirect at best, but the picture was more complex than a Republican establishment obsessed with his removal. Pointedly, in February 2001, seven months before the Twin Towers were attacked by Al-Qaeda, 52 per cent of Americans supported the invasion of Iraq on the basis of regime change alone.[29]

9/11

Many Labour politicians, like Anne Campbell, had been 'pretty dismayed at the results' of the 2000 US election. What really angered some members of the PLP, however, was the idea that although it would always be necessary to have a cordial relationship with the American president, Blair 'didn't', as Campbell recalls, 'have to be such *close friends* with Bush'. Jack Straw remembers likewise: 'we had a right-wing Republican administration in the States and, okay, a New Labour, but a left-wing Labour Party here, whose natural allies in the US were the Democrats and not the Republicans. There had been soft and cuddly Republican administrations, but this was not one of them. So, there was great anxiety about the intentions of the Bush administration'. Crucially, given Blair 'was slightly less left-wing than most members of the Cabinet, shall we say – had he decided himself to take a different view from the prevailing sentiment in the Cabinet?'[30]

The hanging chads of Florida, which had generated such controversy in November and December 2000 would, within months, assume a wider historical significance. The Texan Governor had won and less than eight months after he had taken the oath of office, America was attacked by Al-Qaeda. It would be Bush, not Clinton or Gore, who would lead the world's response to the barbarous acts which had directly killed 2,977 innocent people, including dozens of British citizens. Blair had to deal with that new reality. Even so, Madeline Albright would be 'very' surprised that Blair had gotten so close to Bush. 'I have to say that when Blair went to Camp David for that first trip with Bush and they started talking about sharing toothpaste or whatever, I couldn't believe it. I felt that he had betrayed Clinton. I talked to Clinton about it later. He said, of course he's going to be friends. It doesn't mean that *we're* not friends anymore ... But I was very surprised because I thought they were really kind of soul mates'.[31]

Events would take their course. On 11 September, Blair had been scheduled to give an address to the Trades Union Congress in Brighton. Just after 1.45 GMT, 8.45 Eastern, Alastair Campbell was called out of the hotel room where Blair and his team sat framing his speech for later that day. Campbell soon came back in, switched on the television and told Blair that he'd 'better see this'. There the Prime Minister sat watching the same images as millions around the globe, the 'Trade Center [looking] like someone had punched a huge hole in it, fire and smoke belching forth'. Then, fifteen minutes later, a second plane hit, 'this time captured graphically live on-screen'. After the brief shock, Blair suddenly became eerily calm. He ordered his thoughts: 'it was the worst terrorist attack in human history. It was not America alone who was the target, but all of us who shared the same values. We had to stand together'. Blair issued a brief statement to the TUC and then promptly returned to London.[32]

Patrick Diamond remembers understandable chaos in Whitehall as departments struggled to comprehend the developing picture. As the security services initially feared that there might be a similar attack on London, the No 10 evacuation plan swung into gear: 'if you were a very senior civil servant you got to go in the bunker with the Cabinet, if you were a very senior political official you got to go to a different part of the Cabinet Office and everyone else was told to get the No 3 bus home'. More substantively, over the next few weeks 'in terms of the work of Number 10 the focus just shifted. There had been a period for three months after the 2001 election when we had been trying to work out what the manifesto meant. [But our focus] completely changed overnight. Whereas you'd be seeing the Prime Minister regularly for a lot of meetings on, say, the Delivery Unit processes or strategic long-term work on health and education, 9/11 happened and it just all changed'.

The momentous nature of the day hit home wherever one was. Denis MacShane, then Minister of State at the Foreign Office, would see the second plane hit the towers on a big television screen at Changi airport in Singapore. MacShane had been in Australia at an event to celebrate the 100th anniversary of the Australian Federation and was making his way back to Britain. Thinking the second leg of his journey would be cancelled after the attacks, MacShane was surprised when his plane left for Heathrow with only an hour's delay. Though the flight was certainly a time to collect his thoughts on a tragic day, the journey was not without some jarring geopolitical commentary. The Australian pilot taking the foreign office delegation back to the UK greeted his passengers: 'Ladies and gentlemen, I understand some of you are nervous about us flying to London given the situation. Let me tell you: we will not be traversing over Afghanistan, Iraq, any of those places and I feel a lot safer up here than I fucking would do down there.'

Within days, Blair had marshalled European allies through a series of telephone calls. He spoke to Berlusconi, Chirac, Putin and Schroeder, all of whom pledged their solidarity to America. 'It is hard now to realise just how fearful people were at that time', he later recalled. 'The collective sense of solidarity was absolute.' Tens of thousands of Chinese would lay flowers and cards at the American Embassy in Beijing, Orthodox Churches across Russia said their prayers for the dead and, in France, *Le Monde* ran the headline: 'nous sommes tous *Américains*'. In this climate, the Prime Minister's lockstep support for the US was met with 67 per cent approval from British voters.[33]

Blair's thoughts were becoming clear, but he was not without counter-veiling voices. Jamie Rubin, former US State Department Spokesman under Clinton, caught Alastair Campbell's arm at the memorial service in London on 14 September. 'Be very careful of these people', he told the New

FIGURE 17 Here a sheepish Blair is hailed by, amongst others, Laura Bush and Rudy Giuliani, as he watches President Bush's congressional address after the 9/11 attacks (Courtesy: George W Bush Presidential Library).

Labour spin doctor, 'the right in America will use this as an excuse to do all sorts of things around the world'.[34] A day earlier, Neil Kinnock had visited Downing Street in a meeting arranged before the attacks. His view was that Bush was a 'vacuum' who 'on a good day . . . is therefore inadequate' and 'on a bad day he is filled by others who are better than adequate and can be worse than bad'. Bush's language of 'dead or alive', 'crusade' and getting the 'folks' responsible, Kinnock found particularly worrying.

The question, as Kinnock noted, was 'what is to be done?' The former leader had 'no doubt that the war horses will have to leave the stable. Indeed, I think they should'. But 'they'll only have the chance of having the necessary effect if the charge is very deliberate and as well targeted as possible'. Kinnock told Blair he should 'make Bush as obligated as possible and try everything to give maximum sustenance to Colin Powell' – a strategy Kinnock described as 'engage to influence'. Pointedly, he also told the Prime Minister that 'if people in the UK (not just the Labour Party) come to form the view that engagement continues but influence has dried up, support will ebb quickly'.

Kinnock's approach to Blair was both reassuring and steely. He told the Prime Minister that he had been 'been stunningly good in his reaction' to 9/11 – a statement to which Blair nodded gratefully. The Prime Minister then turned to the former leader.

"How do you think I ought to handle it, Neil?"

"Well, there is only one thing to do. That is to get as close to this guy as you possibly can – to exercise the maximum amount of influence. Left to his own devices he is absolutely bewildered and he's got some bad guys around him."

Blair chewed this over.

"Get close to him, make yourself valuable. And then give him the news that no one else will give him. He must understand that this is the action of a genuine friend."

Blair frowned, "I didn't expect that."

"Well, that's because *I'm* a genuine friend, Tone. Anybody can be friendly in good days, when the sun is shining. Real friendship comes in the bad days when it is pissing with rain and we've got some bad days coming."

Kinnock expanded on his own views in a memo of talking points for his wife, the MEP Glenys Kinnock, to consider in advance of her appearance on the radio programme *Any Questions*. This noted that 'plain justice requires that those responsible [for the attacks]and those who assist or shelter them, be found and punished. Force will be necessary for that'. To the question of 'How much force? The answer is "As much as it takes." There is no other answer that can credibly be given'. Alongside this agenda, for sure, there needed to be 'peacefare' too – destabilising arms trades on the one hand, 'unprecedented and sustained investment by the USA and others in economic, social and political development in poverty-stricken countries' on the other. But 'tough on terrorism, tough on the causes of terrorism' was now more or less the line from across the centre-left spectrum.

This mood was transatlantic – a fact obvious to even a Deputy Prime Minister who later called the Iraq War 'illegal'. Indeed, John Prescott was talking to a number of Democratic Senators soon after 9/11 and 'was absolutely surprised to find them talking about an aggressive attitude'. One of these was Chris Dodd, of whom Prescott asked, 'how can you be expressing this?' Dodd simply replied that Iraq was 'unfinished business. We have to sort it out'. Such a view was shared by Neil Kinnock, who, through John Major, had urged George HW Bush back in 1991 'to continue Desert Storm with the purpose of catching or killing Saddam Hussein'. As he later wrote, 'my view was that even if he couldn't be taken or finished it was essential to ensure that he fled in ignominy, lived in hiding and never came back'. Surveying the scene in the post-9/11 climate, Kinnock believed that, had the allies gone in in 1991, 'the liberation of Iraq would be celebrated in every souk and the defeat of a mass murderer would not be mourned as a triumph over Islam. After Desert Storm I put these issues to Major and Bush again. I understood their responses – 'disproportionate risk' etc – but I did not find either of them convincing. The awful stalemate of the last 10½ years has deepened my scepticism'.[35]

With such memories in mind, most Democrats fell lock step behind Bush the younger. Clinton's former security adviser Sandy Berger told reporters that the US response to the attacks would pale into insignificance compared to what had gone before. 'No single action will be sufficient', he said, 'we'll have to buckle down for the long effort'. As for Bill Clinton, he, like Denis MacShane, had been in Australia when New York and DC had been attacked, but promptly secured an US Air Force plane to fly him back to the States. Aside from a brief call to Condy Rice, it was Hillary who had kept him up to speed as he flew home. Two days after 9/11 Bill and Chelsea Clinton visited the relatives of those so cruelly affected by the events. He told them that, 'we need not to show fear and not to give in'.

'We need to prove that the people who did this are wrong. They have a view of the importance of life and the nature of politics and faith and human nature that is very different from ours.' As for his views on Bush, 'it's going to be difficult for him because you feel this as a human being and as a citizen, as well as a leader. The president will handle this just fine. He'll do a good job, as long as we stick with him.'[36]

Afghanistan

The immediate target was Afghanistan. On the evening of 11 September, a briefing paper had been prepared for the British Prime Minister, buttressed by a meeting Blair held with MI6, Foreign Office and other intelligence officials. Based on this, Blair had a telephone conversation with Bush which made clear that taking out Al-Qaeda meant intervention against the Taliban – and, by consequence, that Iraq was a second order problem at best. On 14 September, Blair told parliament that, when it came to the terrorists, 'the limits on the numbers that they kill and their methods of killing are not governed by any sense of morality. The limits are only practical and technical. We know that they would, if they could, go further and use chemical, biological, or even nuclear weapons of mass destruction'. He further noted that 'we know, also, that there are groups of people, occasionally states, who will trade the technology and capability of such weapons. It is time that this trade was exposed, disrupted and stamped out'.

The day after the attacks a UN resolution condemned those 'aiding, supporting or harboring the perpetrators' and authorising 'all necessary steps' to respond. George Robertson, Blair's former Defence Secretary and now Secretary General at NATO, invoked Article 5 of that organisation's charter – an attack on the United States was thus conceived as an attack on all members of the alliance. When the Taliban regime refused to extradite Bin Laden, the US began covertly smuggling special operative teams into Afghanistan with the aim of supporting the opposition Northern Alliance. On 7 October 2001, Operation Enduring Freedom, the invasion of Afghanistan by a coalition of the UK, US, Australia, Canada and Germany commenced. The war against the Taliban was swiftly won by December, though many Al-Qaeda agents managed to flee into neighbouring Pakistan.

On 29 January 2002, with the new interim leader of Afghanistan, Hamid Karzai, sitting in the balcony, George W Bush would declare in his first State of the Union that the recent campaign was not the end of the job. Naming North Korea, Iran and Iraq, he declared that 'states like these and their terrorist allies, constitute an axis of evil, arming to threaten the peace of the world'. He told his audience that he would 'not wait on events while dangers gather. I will not stand by as peril draws closer and closer. The United States of America will not permit the world's most dangerous regimes to threaten us with the world's most destructive weapons'. The 'axis' of which Bush spoke was beginning to plague Britain's leaders. Foreign Secretary Jack Straw wondered whether the 'inclusion of Iran in the "axis of evil" ... was negligent or wilful', but he was certain 'it was a disaster' and would 'strengthen those darker forces in Iran whose position depended on demonizing America and Israel'. Internal British Ministry of Defence memoranda pointedly referred to the speech as 'unclear and ... unfortunate'.[37]

The shifting kaleidoscope

A few months later, it seemed that Bill Clinton had gone rogue. On 1 October 2002, he had pitched up at the Labour Party conference in Blackpool, ahead of a speech he was to give which would eulogise his friend Tony Blair. That afternoon Clinton had talked with Alastair Campbell on the serious geopolitical challenges facing Britain in the wake of 9/11 and how the Prime Minister should handle the American political landscape with a war with Iraq looming ever more likely. This was the serious stuff. But when evening came the now ex-president could not be persuaded to retire to his suite and get an early night. Calling his security detail over, Clinton said he fancied going for an evening walk. And so, as the rain began to tumble down over Blackpool Pier and the wind crashed in from the Irish Sea, Bill Clinton, Campbell and another A-list guest at that year's conference, the latterly disgraced actor Kevin Spacey, took a stroll for a couple of miles through the town.

Clinton loved Blackpool, calling Hillary to tell her how much he was enjoying himself. He first wanted to play the local arcade machines, but they looked less inviting up-front. He then decided he wanted some fast food, 'nothing fancy' and, upon discovering almost everywhere was closed, the collective ended up in a nearby McDonald's. With his trademark Diet Coke in hand and scoffing down some chicken nuggets, the group began to discuss the Third Way and what Clinton could do to best help Blair in his speech the next day. Clinton, Campbell noticed, 'was like a man replenished, not because of the food but because he had been out with real people and got something out of it'. This 'was probably the biggest single difference between him and [Blair] . . . Bill was the one who most saw politics in terms of its outcome in people's lives'.[38]

After introducing himself to the conference the next day as 'Clinton, Bill, Arkansas CLP, *New* Labour', Clinton told the gathering that they should appreciate that Blair was in a unique position to influence the Bush administration to go down the UN route on Iraq – a strong resolution which demanded Saddam get rid of any weapons of mass destruction he was holding or face the consequences. Glancing over at Clare Short, the international development secretary who would prove so critical of New Labour's foreign interventions, Blair and Campbell both noted that she 'had looked like death warmed up after Bill's speech, presumably because it had been so fulsome about TB and his unique position'.[39]

A twin track of diplomacy was therefore before the British Prime Minister. On the one hand: to seek to avoid a conflict if at all possible. On the other: to simultaneously work up the strongest possible legal grounds for an invasion of Iraq should it become necessary. Two days after Clinton's conference speech, Peter Ricketts counselled on 3 October 2002 that he did not 'think the "Kosovo option" help[ed]' the government's legal case. After all, in 1999 the government had 'an alternative legal base, i.e. that action was necessary to prevent an overwhelming humanitarian catastrophe'. Blair did not demur from his point but argued that 'in Kosovo we had had to accept we could not get a UN resolution even though we wanted one because Russia had made it clear it would wield a political veto. So *we*, not the UNSC, made the judgment that the humanitarian catastrophe was overwhelming'. Thus, there *was* some leeway for individual member states to disregard a veto if it was 'a bad faith assessment'. Lord Goldsmith, as Attorney General, disagreed, arguing that 'there were only three potential bases for the use of force: self-defence, humanitarian crisis, [and] United Nations authority'.[40]

UN Resolution 1441 would be passed the following month. Passed unanimously, it gave Iraq 'a final opportunity to comply' with the disarmament provisions that had been put in place after the first Gulf War. Should Iraq fail to fully comply with weapons' inspections this would constitute 'a further material breach', though France and opponents of the conflict never saw anything within 1441 that suggested it would form justification for war on its own. At the time, many British politicians had little doubt the Iraqis had the weapons. Gordon Brown had several conversations with MI6 which left him with the impression 'that it was almost as if they could give me the street name and number where they were located'.[41]

This was curious since, simultaneously, the American Joint Chiefs of Staff and Defence Secretary Rumsfeld, were being told by their intelligence agencies that they could not 'confirm the identity of any Iraqi facilities that produce, test, fill, or store biological weapons'. Such information was not passed on to the British, or indeed the UN. One state department official would tell Joe Biden around this time: 'damn those guys across the river [at the Pentagon]. They're fucking nuts'. Despite such doubts, in October 2002 Bush declared for the first time that Iraq 'possesses and produces chemical and biological weapons' and was 'seeking nuclear weapons'.[42] UN weapons inspectors under Hans Blix then reported in February 2003 that they had found no WMDs, but asked for more time to complete their work.

The momentum towards war was growing and, as Blix later noted, the UK was to some degree a 'prisoner on that train'. But Blair still wanted his legal pretext. In January 2003, Blair was ascertaining whether he could 'revive the self defence argument as a legal basis' or if the UN Security Council, short of passing a second resolution giving a direct mandate for intervention, could at least 'make plain [Saddam had made] a breach' with the spirit of free and unfettered access for inspectors under 1441. His Attorney General had told him on 14 January that the latter route, at least, would afford the necessary legal cover. A month later, however, Goldsmith wrote again to Blair having reconsidered his view. Whilst the 'safest legal course would be to secure the adoption of a further Council decision ... which would authorize the use of force', Goldsmith now acknowledged that 'a reasonable case can be made' that 1441 revived previous UN resolutions 'to use force' given Saddam's lengthy lack of compliance. Part of this lay in the fact that 'UK forces have participated in military action ... under international law [that] was no more than reasonably arguable', not least Blair and Clinton's bombing of Iraq in 1998. Ideally, the UK and US should gain UN sign off that Saddam had not taken his 'final opportunity', but, if not, they might be able to construct a case. Numerous former aides of Blair would later remark that, on Iraq, his 'training as a barrister saw him try to support the case for war as best he could'.[43]

On 7 March, the UK, US and Spain published a draft second resolution declaring that Iraq had 'failed to comply with and cooperate fully in the implementation' of weapons inspections and 'will have failed to take the final opportunity afforded by resolution 1441 unless, on or before 17 March 2003, the Council concludes that Iraq has demonstrated full, unconditional, immediate and active cooperation in accordance with its disarmament obligations'. They now needed nine votes for the new resolution in the Security Council and for no permanent member – i.e. Russia, France or China – to veto it. So, who could help Blair get the numbers he needed? His old friend Bill Clinton.

The day after the second resolution text was published, Clinton arrived at Chequers to be met by a nervous Blair. 'Look, our only chance to work this out, short of war, is to try and get an extension of the UN resolution with a deadline', the Prime Minister remarked. He hoped that 'George will take what Blix says he needs, three weeks' – pushing the original final deadline then proposed some time into April. Clinton's role was to try and feel out enough Security Council members to vote for the measure – a favour he undertook with relish and assured Blair he would try and persuade Ricardo Lagos of Chile and Vicente Fox of Mexico. Lagos said he would back a measure but would want the support of Fox first. Eventually, on 13 March, the Chileans published their own draft resolution – backed by Mexico, Guinea, Cameroon, Angola and Pakistan – calling for a three-week deadline and then a further Security Council gathering (rather than an implicit authorisation for war). The Americans torpedoed the initiative which, given the French and Russian announcement that they would veto any authorisation of force, remained moot anyway. In the midst of international gridlock, on 20 March 2003, the invasion of Iraq began.

Blaming Blair

Less than three weeks later, standing outside 10 Downing Street on the evening of 9 April 2003, the BBC's Political Editor Andrew Marr cleared his throat. He was about to give his take on the day's events to anchor Huw Edwards, sitting in the BBC studio. And what a day it had been. With Coalition troops now in Baghdad, hundreds of Iraqis had taken to the streets and, in one defining image, pulled down a towering statue of their oppressor, Saddam Hussein and beat it with their shoes. Marr began his report with the usual notes of caution, but he could barely contain the manner in which the day had moved him: 'all the usual caveats apply, there could be some ghastly scenes in the future, there could be terrorist attacks, all sorts of things could go wrong, but frankly Huw the main mood is unbridled relief. I've been watching ministers walking around with faces like split watermelons'. He continued, 'Mr Blair is well aware that all his critics, out there in the party aren't going to thank him, because they are only human, for being right when they are wrong and he knows that there might be trouble ahead as I've said, but this gives him a new freedom, a new self-confidence'. Blair had, after all, 'confronted many critics, [and] I don't think anybody after this is going to be able to say of Tony Blair that he is someone who is driven by the drift of public opinion, or focus groups, or opinion polls'. The Prime Minister had 'said that they would be able to take Baghdad without a blood bath and that in the end the Iraqis would be celebrating and on both of those points he has been proven conclusively right and it would be entirely ungracious, even for his critics, not to acknowledge that tonight he stands as a larger man and a stronger Prime Minister as a result'.

When Blair was invited to give a speech to Congress in June 2003 such congratulations only drew louder. Thanking his hosts for having awarded him the Congressional Gold Medal Blair's soaring rhetoric involved telling Americans that 'You are not going to be alone, we will be with you in this fight for liberty' and 'what the president is doing in the Middle East is tough but right'. The reception this received from Democrats – when American voters, after all, still backed Iraq – is worth recording. Whilst Joe Biden called it 'remarkable', Chris Dodd believed Blair had 'captured the essence of what all of us would like to see in the coming weeks and months and years; that is, a joint coalition of peaceful, liberty-loving nations to address the scourge of terrorism'. Dianne Feinstein likewise declared her view that 'that speech, in my book, was a 10. I have never heard better. And I have never seen a course charted that is sounder, truer, or can redound in better benefits for freedom-loving people'.[44]

As Iraq descended into a tribal bloodbath thereafter, it is difficult to recapture such an atmosphere. But many on the left were swept up by this sense of emotion in early 2003. Prior to the invasion, Peter Jay, former Ambassador to Washington, had sent a letter to Blair telling him that he could only 'admire and applaud the outstanding courage and statesmanship which you are showing and have consistently shown in the face of the challenge which Saddam Hussein represents to all human decency'. Neil Kinnock was even more effusive in his views. On 1 April 2003, he wrote to Alastair Campbell telling him that his 'favourite game at the moment is envisaging what life would have been like if today's broadcasters, writers and pundits had been covering the Battle of France in 1940. Hitler would probably have lived to about 1978 and there would have been a few other sad consequences too'. Even as the prospect for finding weapons of mass destruction receded, on 2 June 2003 Kinnock wrote to Blair stating, 'as you may recall, I didn't set too much store by the WMD stuff. That was partly instinct, partly ignorance of the intelligence material, but mainly that I thought that removing Saddam was the pre-eminent justification for war'. His advice was clear: 'those who are saying "Where are the weapons that justified the conflict" MUST be told: 'Saddam Hussein was *the* weapon of mass destruction – not a millilitre of poison or a firing squad, or a torture chamber existed without his orders or his endorsement'. Indeed, 'he killed hundreds of thousands and caused early death for millions. *That* weapon of mass destruction existed and exists as a menace no longer'.[45]

This was a not ignoble position and, for all the later moralising, there were no black and white certainties here. Certainly, the combined allied planning for post-invasion Iraq would prove woefully inadequate. There were clearly egregious profits made by defence contractors with strong links to the US government. But the decision to remove Saddam was more nuanced. The major recent foreign policy legacies before March 2003 were inaction in Rwanda leading to genocide and concerted action in Kosovo stopping it. Leaving a dictator in power who had directly butchered a quarter of a million of his own people would be the consequence of doing nothing. For sure, attempts to recant on previous pro-war statements certainly did not play well. When Ed Miliband won the Labour leadership in 2010, he declared in his victory speech that the party had been 'wrong to take Britain to war and we need to be honest about that'. The conference hall broke into sustained applause, though, pointedly, such number did not include his brother. Turning to Harriet Harman, David Miliband spat 'You voted for it! Why are you clapping?'[46]

The American story was not dissimilar. In October 2002, Congress passed the Act giving George W Bush authorisation to 'use the Armed Forces ... as he determines to be necessary and appropriate in order to defend the National Security of the United States against the continuing threat posed by Iraq'. Twenty-nine of the then 50 Democratic Senators voted for the bill including Joe Biden, Hillary Clinton, Tom Daschle, John Edwards and John Kerry. In his biography, released prior to his 2008 presidential run, Biden declared that on Iraq: 'I made a mistake. I underestimated the influence of Vice President Cheney, Secretary of State

Rumsfeld and the rest of the neocons; I *vastly* underestimated their disingenuousness and incompetence.'[47] At the time, the first-term Senator Edwards had been counselled by Bob Shrum that he 'had to be for it'. He shouldn't 'want to look too liberal and out of the mainstream; he was, after all, the southern candidate and Clintonesque'.[48] Eventually, Edwards would be chosen as Kerry's running mate in 2004, only for extra-marital activities to curtail his own run for the presidency four years later.

Kerry himself was slightly different. He'd voted against the 1991 Gulf War and believed the new vote was being rushed to scare Democrats into supporting it before the 2002 midterms. And he saw no link between Iraq and 9/11. For Shrum, Kerry's best bet was to do 'whatever he thought was substantively right'. He had 'the freedom to do what he wanted' and Shrum felt 'it was impossible to predict the political fallout if we went to war'. However, Kerry's 2004 campaign manager, Jim Jordan, hammered him on the issue: 'go ahead and vote against it if you want, but you'll never be president of the United States'. Kerry would later claim that there was a difference between giving the president the *potential* authority to use force and backing him waging an actual war, but it was not one which counted much with the American electorate in 2004 and added to the general impression that he was a 'flip-flopper'. In London, Patrick Diamond recalls that 'in the foreign policy and defence establishment in Whitehall there was a real sense of hoping Kerry would not win. That wasn't deeply political, it was more "we don't want to manage a whole series of new relationships". And I think there was a sense that if Kerry had won this would have been seen as a repudiation of the Iraq War'. Another former British aide, somewhat playfully, sums up the 2004 presidential election as one between a candidate who 'wasn't serious' and another who 'wasn't sane'.[49]

Kerry emerged from the primaries as the nominee, but, from the outset, there wasn't the same Clintonian buzz. Kerry was a perfectly serviceable candidate, but he was not *the guy* to the extent that Bill Galston remembers of Clinton in 1990. As Galston has noted, 'I'm comparing that moment of unity and clarity to what happened, let's say, in 2003, 2004, where the New Democratic movement was all over the map. There were people working for [Joe] Lieberman, people working for [John] Kerry, people working for [John] Edwards. There were New Democrats flirting with Wes Clark. There was just total chaos. In 1990 [it was] Stalinist unity, but not because anybody was forcing us into it'.[50] This general impression made it across the Atlantic, too.

Sitting in a Washington DC bar after attending a meeting of the IMF, Gordon Brown watched the first Bush–Kerry debate. Although no fan of everything Bush was saying, Brown sat, 'rasping criticism at his good friend Kerry'. 'Look at what Bush is doing', he thundered, 'security, security, security. He's defining the election and, instead of challenging him on it, Kerry's going along with it. He'll never win on security'. As the debate went on, Brown went in ever harder, gasping, 'rubbish! You've lost man, you've lost'. On 2 November 2004, it would prove to be so. The race began as neck and neck and Jonathan Powell even received phone calls on election day from Kerry aides 'celebrating and working out what their jobs would be'. But it was not to be. By some 3 million votes, 12 states and 35 votes in the electoral college, George W Bush would, comfortably, be re-elected. Still, not everyone saw the cause of the defeat the same as Brown. For David Blunkett, 'I haven't forgotten how, when I was in Boston [at the Democratic Convention], the organisers dismissed the idea that they needed to reach out to people on the issues of security and stability'. Evidently, Kerry ended up somewhat betwixt and between.[51]

There was another future presidential candidate making her calculations through all of this. For *Fox News* analyst Bill O'Reilly, writing just after the conflict, the 'one big stealth winner in the Iraq War' was Senator Hillary Clinton. 'She simply disappeared after voting for military action last fall, dodging all direct questions about the war but making it clear she did not side with the peace movement. Say what you want about Hillary, she has no use for losers'. According to one senior British source, 'the Clintons were tactfully fed up and cheesed off – particularly Hillary – with what Blair was doing on Iraq, going along with it and risking his career'. In the autumn of 2002, however, Bill and Hillary had discussed the matter between them and had backed a rather different strategy. 'So, what should I do?' asked Hillary, leaning on her husband's political radar. 'Look, the case is balanced', argued Bill, 'but if you are serious about running for the White House then you – if you *really* want to be the first female president – have got to be stronger on foreign policy than any man'.[52] That meant voting for the war.

Blair had his deliberations, too. Charles Clarke notes that 'I think Tony was hurt by aspects of American Democratic opinion seeking to denigrate him once Iraq became unpopular and Obama – and indeed Trump – always based their foreign policy worldview on a repudiation of the war'. Such sorrow was also felt by his Chancellor. In October 2005, Brown wrote a warm message of congratulations to the economist JK Galbraith

– whom he had long admired – on the occasion of his 97th birthday. Galbraith thanked him for the wishes, but also noted that they came 'notwithstanding my most energetic recent effort, which has been to inquire: why the continuing support of our insanity in Iraq?' If Brown had time to reply before Galbraith's death six months later, it has not survived in the economist's archive.[53]

Still, the left was out of power in the US. Therefore, it is important to acknowledge Charles Clarke's belief that Blair's sense of 'honour' in not shirking the Iraq conflict 'bought him influence with the Bush camp at the time and was part of shifting the agenda on issues like Africa and Climate Change'. This is a view with much credence. As Nigel Sheinwald, foreign policy advisor under Blair, recalls, 'Blair was criticised throughout this period for being the poodle of America and having too collusive a relationship with George Bush, but he actually chose as the twin big agenda items of his G8 Presidency [in 2005] ... two issues which were very problematic from the American point of view'. The first was 'to try and build, after the American decision to back out of Kyoto, a new international consensus on climate change'. The second was 'to try and raise international aid-giving particularly to Africa' from the wealthiest nations on earth.[54]

On climate, Sheinwald notes, the American's chief complaint was that they 'should not be expected to do things that China and India and the emerging economies were not prepared to do'. In bringing in the G8 + 5 format for Gleneagles, Blair ensured that Brazil, India, China, South Africa and Mexico were at least round the table and a global dialogue on lowering emissions was possible. Meanwhile, the expansion of technological research and development, particularly through wind power, electronic cars and other technologies, if it could be done through the market, also began to arouse Bush's interest. Blair's advocacy enabled moderate Republicans like John McCain to press his more sceptical colleagues. In a 2005 Senate speech, McCain pointedly asked of climate sceptics, 'why is it that our best partner in Europe, Tony Blair, is so dedicated to the proposition that we need to act on this issue? I do not find him to be an irrational individual'.[55] Such an approach eventually bore fruit in the 2015 Paris Climate Accord, albeit later repealed by Trump.

On aid and debt relief, the gains were more immediate. As Sheinwald observes, Blair was able to tap 'into the constituency within the White House and on the right of American politics which was incredibly generous on AIDS and other development and health issues. Bush actually pushed

American policy in a direction of very, very much greater structure and generosity on those issues than had been seen before, even under Clinton'. In 1997, New Labour had created Britain's new Department for International Development which had emerged as a global thought leader on such issues and, after 2001, Blair recalled having to 'use a lot of my capital with [Bush] – which was nonetheless considerable – to get him to agree [on that] agenda and go with it'. The result was a comprehensive plan for Africa totaling $50 billion on aid, debt relief, malaria and Aids treatment and schemes to boost governance structures. As David Blunkett recounted on Gleneagles, 'Tony and Gordon have worked a miracle here. A small-population country off the edge of Europe and we have really driven the agenda on both world development and on climate change. There are times – and I've had them – when you think to yourself: "If I've done nothing else in my life, this was worthwhile" and for Tony and Gordon, this must surely be worthwhile'. In the aftermath of the event, Oxfam recorded that 'no previous G8 summit has done as much for development, particularly in Africa'. For the campaigners, the package meant, amongst other things, that 'millions of children who otherwise would be denied an education [will get] the chance to go to school and [it will] provide life-saving medicines for millions who would not otherwise have had them'. For all Iraq remains on the Third Way's ledger, this was hardly an insignificant legacy, either.[56]

Notes

1   Chilcot; Owen Jones, *Guardian*, 7 July 2016; COR/OTR.

2   Riley/195.

3   Riley/195.

4   *New York Times*, 5 December 1992; Riley/204.

5   Riley/204–7; ARC/CPL/MDR, 10 April 1999 call.

6   Riley/210.

7   Riley/210–12.

8   Riley/212–15.

9   Campbell 3/96.

10 Blair 1/223.

11 Biden, 263–64, 260.

12 Blair 1/226.

13 Blair 1/227–30; Biden, 273.

14 Blair 1/235; Riley/223; ARC/CPL/MDR, 23 March 1999 call.

15 FOIA 16 April 1999.

16 Gallup, 13–14 April 1999; Blair 1/236; *Hartford Courant*, 26 April 1999.

17 *Hartford Courant*, 26 April 1999, *The Post Star* (NY), 23 April 1999;
    LR/HOC/19 April 1999 vol 329, col 607, 26 May 1999 vol 332, col 370
    and 31 March 1999 vol 328, col 1217.

18 Blair 1/237; ARC/CPL/MDR, 8 May 1999.

19 H2778 Congressional Record – House 5 May 1999, h3744, 7 June 1999 and
    Radice D, 439.

20 Riley, 223.

21 Riley, 223–25; ARC/CPL/MDR, 29 April 1999; Biden/287.

22 Blunkett/126; *The Age (Melbourne)*, 8 June 1999.

23 Adam Roberts, 'NATO's "Humanitarian War" over Kosovo', *Survival*, Vol 41,
    No 3 (1999), 102–23, 102.

24 Goldsmith testimony, 27 January 2010, Chilcot; see www.wsws.org, 20 May
    2000.

25 YouGov Iraq Tracker. Available at: http://cdn.yougov.com/cumulus_
    uploads/document/raghpsamv0/YG-Archives-Pol-Trackers-Iraq-130313.
    pdf; Gallup polling at http://news.gallup.com/poll/1633/iraq.aspx.

26 Annan to UNSCOM, 15 December 1998. Available at: www.un.org/Depts/
    unscom/s98-1172.htm; *Guardian*, 11 September 2006.

27 Dalyell to Blair, [undated but February 1998], ARC/CAC/TADA/3/11/2.

28 LR/HOC/10 January 2001, vol 360, col 279.

29 *Washington Post*, 6 January 1999; Gallup, (n 25).

30 Straw to Chilcot, 2 February 2011.

31 MCI/Albright.

32 Blair 1/345.

33 Blair 1/351; IPSOS-MORI, 20–25 September 2001.

34 Campbell 4/11.

35 Prescott to Chilcot, 30 July 2010; Kinnock to Binns, 3 October 2001,
    ARC/CAC/KNNK/1/9/21.

36 *Democrat and Chronicle*, 12 September 2001; *Quad City Times*,
    14 September 2001.

37 Straw/444, 366.

38 Campbell 4/316.

39 Campbell 4/318.

40 Ricketts memo, 3 October 2002, Blair statement, 14 January 2011 and
    Goldsmith evidence, 27 January 2010, Chilcot.

41 Brown 1/250.

42 Brown 1/253–54; Biden/337.

43 Chilcot documents.

44 LR/CRS/17 July 2003, S9545.

45 Jay to Blair, 17 February 2003, ARC/PJAY/4/8/18; Kinnock to Campbell, 1 April 2003, ARC/KNNK 1/9/27; Kinnock to Blair, 2 June 2003, ARC/KNNK 1/9/24.

46 Harris/76.

47 Biden/342.

48 Biden/342 and Shrum/387.

49 Shrum/388; COR/Diamond; COR/OTR.

50 MCI/Galston.

51 McBride/132; COR/Powell; Blunkett/711.

52 *Democrat and Chronicle*, 14 April 2003; COR/OTR.

53 Galbraith to Brown, 20 October 2005, ARC/JFK/JKG/78.

54 COR/Clarke.

55 LR/CRS/21 June 2005, S6892.

56 ARC/CAC/ODHP, Sheinwald interview; Blair 1/555; Blunkett/798; Oxfam briefing note. Available at: www.oxfam.org/sites/www.oxfam.org/files/glen_0.pdf.

AFTERWORD

J

ust after 9pm on the evening of 8 November 2016, the truly bizarre looked like it was about to happen. Thirteen years after the Anglo-American invasion of Iraq, eight years after the financial meltdown of 2008 and long after anti-migrant rhetoric had been stoked by elements of the radical right, America was about to elect Donald J Trump as its forty-fifth president. The defeat was stunning, not least to the Democratic nominee Hillary Clinton, who just about managed to murmur, 'ok, ok' when she heard of the negative polling numbers coming in from Florida and North Carolina. Amidst the general melee, her husband looked deep in thought. For weeks, quietly, Bill had been telling friends that this Trump thing was no isolated affair. If the British could vote to leave the European Union, as they had that June, maybe the 'screw-it' vote in the west was larger than they had all thought. 'It's like Brexit', he mumbled. 'I guess it's real.'[1]

For Labour's moderates it had been 'real' for a good deal longer. As former minister Tom Harris has ably chronicled, the period after Tony Blair left Downing Street in June 2007 can justly be described as *Ten Years in the Death of the Labour Party*. A domino effect of bad decisions took Labour from three historic election victories to the brink of disaster. First, Gordon Brown would fail to call an election in October 2007 he could have won, albeit then going on to handle the global financial crisis the next year a good deal better. During the campaign he eventually did fight in 2010, the Prime Minister would then be caught on a *Sky News* microphone calling one elderly voter 'a bigoted woman' for having raised concerns about increased migration from Eastern Europe. Thereafter, under a vacillating leader of the centre-left, Ed Miliband ('Kinnock without the foreign policy balls' as one former Labour figure notes), the party would attempt to regain power on a '35 per cent strategy' which sought to add Labour's 2010 vote to enough Lib Dem voters disaffected by that party's decision to go into government with the Conservatives. In trying to appease both the *Guardian* and the *Financial Times*, it secured the unequivocal backing of neither and turned down some odd paths. It offered voters the opportunity of a gender-equal cabinet but could not fully commit to a living wage which would have helped millions of women. It spoke of unifying 'one nation' that, at the time, was made up of 'predators' and 'producers'. Unsurprisingly, this didn't work. The rise of UKIP and then Jeremy Corbyn were both, in part, reactions to this degree of mealy-mouthed form of opposition – not credible enough to persuade middle England, not radical enough to engage the disenfranchised. As one American voice argues, 'both Hillary and Ed thought power would be easier to win and presumably easier to use – had they won – than it was. But it's just not *that* easy'.

In the wake of Jeremy Corbyn winning the Labour leadership in September 2015, Bill Clinton spoke off-the-cuff at a Democratic fundraiser in Potomac, Maryland. While he went through a few of the old hits from 1992, his mind was clearly occupied by events across the Atlantic. Back in 2010, he argued, 'the British Labor Party disposed of its most [electable] leader, David Miliband, because they were mad at him for being part of Tony Blair's government in the Iraq War. And they moved to the left and put his brother in as leader because the British labor movement wanted it. When David Cameron thumped him in the election, they reached the interesting conclusion that they lost because they hadn't moved far left enough and so they went out and practically got a guy off the street to be the leader'.[2] For Clinton, 'when people feel they've been shafted and they don't expect anything to happen anyway, they just want the maddest person in the room to represent them. And that is perfectly psychologically understandable and predictable'.

The Donald Trump phenomenon has also weighed heavy. In April 2018, Blair noted that 'the really depressing thing about western politics at the moment is that the leadership of what I would call a strong progressive centre is just not there, it is lacking'. Into this vacuum emerged 'right-wing politics going into anti-immigration nationalism and left-wing politics going into sort of anti-business old forms of statism and neither are the answer to the problems of the future'. With his think tank, the Institute for Global Change, Blair has been keen to argue that 'globalisation is essentially a good thing, not a bad thing, but its risks have to be mitigated'.[3] Undeniably, what Liam Byrne calls 'the three I's' – immigration, inequality and Iraq – undermined faith in the ability of centre-left leaders to enact change for the better, in the UK and beyond. Moderates no longer command the major parties, let alone their countries.[4]

Still, the green shoots of recovery can be seen. In February 2019, moderate MPs across the British political spectrum including Chuka Umunna, Luciana Berger and Heidi Allen quit their parties to initially coalesce around an Independent Group of parliamentarians. Their opening statement of values – 'more prosperous communities' delivered through both 'the extension of opportunity' to individuals and a government with the 'responsibility to ensure the sound stewardship of taxpayer's money' – was positively Clintonian. Meanwhile, in the US, New Democracy, the think tank whose advisory board includes 'pragmatic elected leaders from all levels of government' such as New Orleans Mayor Mitch Landrieu and Congresswoman Stephanie Murphy, is doing some important thinking on the effects of globalisation. As they argue, 'this will mean 'big changes in public policy: pro-growth tax reform; lowering regulatory obstacles to innovation and entrepreneurship . . . an open and globally connected economy; and, a robust new system for upskilling workers that does not require four-year college degrees'.[5] Moderates contemplating taking such an agenda in the 2020 presidential race include Senators Cory Booker and Kirsten Gillibrand. Though such movements face challenges, the centre is not dead yet.

Some of this will require updated solutions – somewhat to the left of the Third Way economically and, perhaps, a bit to the right on migration. Whatever the travails seen in the years since, the moderate French President Emmanuel Macron has noted that the 2016 vote for 'Brexit is the expression of a need for protection . . . Protection from a society that advocated openness, without concerning itself with the industrial, economic and social destruction necessarily engendered by such openness when it takes place too quickly'. On globalisation, he has pointed to the 'tens of thousands of jobs' lost in his native Amiens and Bagnères during the 1980s and 1990s – textile regions where the mills became less competitive and people could more cheaply purchase clothes elsewhere – at that time from the Maghreb and, later from Eastern Europe, then China and now Vietnam'. His solution, rather like Blair and Clinton, is state financed, locally tailored re-training. And, when it comes to the banking world, Macron has declared that 'we have to be discriminating – by opposing finance for its own ends while encouraging finance that promotes investment'. Whatever the rigours of office, this has been a good intellectual starting point.[6] For sure, the basic insight that a centre-left government should encourage private-sector growth to then use the proceeds for socially progressive ends remains valuable.

In the 1990s the Third Way lived up to its mantra of opportunity, responsibility and community through significant increases in funding for public services, a willingness to use the forces of law and order at home and the military abroad, and improving life chances for millions. The left-wing trope that Blair-Clintonism was just a watered-down neoliberalism and that as a consequence somehow elections don't matter, has not just been proven wrong since the election of Trump, it was always ridiculous. It was in this light that an ageing Ted Kennedy, lion of the liberal left, cast his eye on the Anglo-American sphere in a Senate speech in 2006. Then he told his colleagues that 'Tony Blair said 7 years ago that he was going to end poverty in Britain by 2020'. Kennedy continued: 'there were 4 million [British] children living in poverty and he said, as a matter of national direction and vision, that he was going to eliminate poverty for children by 2020. This is what they have done. They will have a minimum wage of $9.80–$9.80 an hour this October. They have moved 1.8 million children out of poverty over the last 4 years'. Though there was work to do, the comparison with Bush was galling: 'The United States has refused to increase the minimum wage [since Clinton's 1997 increase] and we have put 1.4 million children into poverty. That is completely unacceptable'. So it was. But the point remains that the Third Way involved a series of deliberate choices to avoid such extremes.[7]

The period from January 1993 to May 2010 should not, therefore, only be defined by its low points. Nor should the received wisdom of the hard left be regarded as sacrosanct. Ed Miliband bet the house on the idea that, after Iraq, the British public were opposed to all forms of military intervention. He lost in 2015 – and aspects of Jeremy Corbyn's foreign policy would prove even more controversial thereafter. Yet, as moderate voices like Gemma Doyle and Stephen Doughty have noted, 'there are times when it is necessary for Britain to take military action to protect the lives of others. This is not imperialism – it is not the flexing of our military muscle for show. It is an unequivocal commitment to lessen the harm done to others. We did not act in Rwanda and we were too slow to act in the Balkans'. Charles Clarke has agreed, arguing that 'an internationally stable world order requires the main countries to accept again the responsibility of sustaining it'.[8] Whatever the difficulties of Iraq, there is a necessary debate surrounding a foreign policy which avoids nineteenth-century splendid isolation on the one hand and its updated version, President Trump's 'America First', on the other.

We may, then, have go back to the future. Back in early 1985, after Walter Mondale's catastrophic defeat against Ronald Reagan, the then Chair of the Michigan Democrats, Richard Wiener, wrote to Stan Greenberg. Greenberg, as we have seen, was vital in reconnecting the Democratic Party with areas that had politically moved to the right in the 1970s and 1980s. Thanking the pollster for his efforts on the campaign, Wiener told him that 'hopefully we can learn from what we did wrong – and resist the temptation to throw out what we did right'. Eventually, thanks to some hard thinking, a good deal of political bravery and no little skill, the centre-left got there, on both sides of the Atlantic – finally winning over the American rust belt and London commuter belt alike. As such, the argument of this book has been that the Third Way saw a good deal more positives than negatives. It broadly engaged with the needs of a changing electorate in opposition and acted in their interest when in power. Whatever the buffeting effects of the 24-hour news cycle, the precedent of the *March of the Moderates* should continue to inform our politics today.[9]

Notes

1 Jonathan Allen and Amie Parnes, *Shattered: Hillary Clinton's Doomed Campaign*, (New York, 2017), 379.

2 *UK Business Insider*, 8 November 2016.

3 *Guardian*, 10 April 2018.

4 COR/Bryne.

5 Available at: www.theindependent.group/values and http://www.newdemocracy.net/about/ (both accessed 21 Feb 2019).

6 Macron/46, 48, 207.

7 Senate speech, 21 June 2006.

8 COR/Clarke.

9 Wiener to Greenberg, 23 January 1985, ARC/BHL/DPM/43.

SELECT BIBLIOGRAPHY

This work has utilised three categories of material: archives, correspondence/ interviews with the author and published works. To save space, most sources are abbreviated in the references, e.g. Gould/28 indicates page 28 of Philip Gould's *The Unfinished Revolution*. Authors who have published more than one cited work are rendered as Campbell 2/28 and so on, with the different books denoted as below. An exception is made for those where an obvious year can be assigned, e.g. Labour Party (1981) for the proceedings of its 1981 annual conference. For published sources, the place of publication is London, unless stated.

Archival material (ARC)

United Kingdom

Bishopsgate Institute (BGI), London
Campaign for Labour Party Democracy (CLPD)

Churchill College, Cambridge (CAC)
Tam Dalyell (TADA)
Peter Jay (PJAY)
Neil Kinnock (KNNK)
John Newbigin (NEWB)
Oral Diplomatic History Programme (ODHP)
Nigel Spearing (SPRG)
Margaret Thatcher (THCR)

London School of Economics (LSE)
Andrew Faulds (FAULDS)
Peter Shore (SHORE)

National Archives, Kew, London (KEW)
Cabinet Papers (CAB)
Prime Minister's Papers (PREM)

People's History Museum, Manchester (PHM)
Michael Foot (MF)
Shadow Cabinet Minutes (SHADCAB)

Private Collection (PRIV)
Denis Macshane diaries (DMAC)

United States of America

Bentley Historical Library, Ann Arbor, Michigan (BHL)
John Engler (JENG)
Democratic Party (Michigan) (DPM)

Clinton Presidential Library, Little Rock, Arkansas (CPL)
Files indicated by their FOIA number, MDR for Mandatory Declassification
Reviews, or, in the case of the Rahm Emmanuel Files, (REF)

Ford Presidential Library, Ann Arbor, Michigan (FORD)
Max Friedersdorf (MFD)
John Marsh (JM)
Presidential Handwriting File (PHF)
Robert Teeter (RT)

Hoover Institution, Palo Alto, California (HOV)
Arnold Beichman (ABE)
Thomas Edsall (TED)
Firing Line Broadcast Records (FLBR)
Milton Friedman (MFR)
Charles Hill (HILL)
Richard Wirthlin (WIRT)

John F Kennedy Presidential Library, Boston (JFK)
John Kenneth Galbraith (JKG)

Library of Congress, Washington D.C. (LOC)
House Democratic Caucus (HDC)
Daniel Patrick Moynihan (MOY)

Princeton, New Jersey (PRN)
Jim Baker (BAKER)

Missouri History Museum, St Louis, Missouri (MHM)
Dick Gephardt (GEP)

South Dakota State University (SDS)
Tom Daschle (DAS)

State Historical Society, St Louis, Missouri (SHS)
Thomas Eagleton (TEL)

Correspondence and interviews with the author (COR – and then relevant surname)

Ed Balls, Sidney Blumenthal, Gordon Brown, Anne Campbell, Charles Clarke, Patrick Diamond, Al From, Dick Gephardt, Tony Giddens, Beverley Hughes, Michael Jacobs, Neil Kinnock, Jim Leach, Helen Liddell, Roger Liddle, Kirsty McNeill, Denis Macshane, Geoff Mulgan, Off-the-record testimony (OTR), David Osborne, Jonathan Powell, Margaret Prosser, Giles Radice, Chris Smith, David Steel, Jordan Tamagni.

Selected publications

Albright, Madeleine, *Madam Secretary: A Memoir*, (2003).
Baer, Kenneth, *Reinventing Democrats: The Politics of Liberalism from Reagan to Clinton*, (Kansas, 2000).
Balls, Ed, *Speaking Out: Lessons in Life and Politics*, (2016).
Benn, Tony, *Against the Tide: Diaries 1973–1976*, (1990).
Biden, Joseph, *Promises to Keep: On Life and Politics,* (New York, 2007).
Black, Ann 'Reports of Meetings', NEC and NPF via annblack.co.uk (1999–Present).
Blair, Tony, (1), *A Journey*, (2011).
Blair, Cherie, (2), *Speaking for Myself*, (2008).
Bloodworth, Jeffrey, *Losing the Center: The Decline of American Liberalism, 1968–1992*, (Lexington, 2013).
Blumenthal, Sidney, *The Clinton Wars*, (2003).
Blunkett, David, *The Blunkett Tapes: My Life in the Bear Pit*, (2006).
Brandreth, Giles, *Breaking the Code: Westminster Diaries*, (1999).
Brown, Gordon (1), *My Life, Our Times*, (2017).
Brown, Gordon (2), *Where There is Greed*, (Edinburgh, 1989).
Byrne, Liam, *Information Age Government: Delivering the Blair Revolution*, (1997).
Campbell, Alastair (1), *Vol 1: Prelude to Power, 1994–1997*, (2011).
Campbell, Alastair (2), *Vol 2: Power & The People, 1997–1999*, (2011).
Campbell, Alastair (3), *Vol 3: Power & Responsibility, 1999–2001*, (2011).
Campbell, Alastair (4), *Vol 4: The Burden of Power: Countdown to Iraq*, (2012).
Chilcot, John et al, *The Iraq Inquiry* (2011). Archived online at: http://webarchive.nationalarchives.gov.uk/20171123123237/http://www.iraqinquiry.org.uk/
Clinton, Bill, *My Life*, (2004).

Clinton, Bill and Al Gore, *Putting People First*, (New York, 1992).

Crine, Simon, *Reforming Welfare: American Lessons*, (1994).

Crosland, Anthony, *The Future of Socialism*, (1955).

Davis, Jonathan and Rohan McWilliam (eds), *Labour and the Left in the 1980s*, (Manchester, 2017).

Dionne, EJ, *They Only Look Dead*, (1996).

Falk, Gene, *The Earned Income Tax Credit (EITC): An Overview*, (Washington DC, 2014).

From, Al *The New Democrats and the Return to Power*, (New York, 2013).

Galston, William and Elaine Kamarck, *The Politics of Evasion: Democrats and the Presidency*, (Washington DC, 1989).

Giddens, Anthony (1), *The Third Way: The Renewal of Social Democracy*, (1998).

Giddens, Anthony (2), *The Third Way and Its Critics*, (2000).

Gore, Al and the National Performance Review, *From Red Tape to Results: The National Performance Review*, (Washington DC, 1993).

Gould, Philip, *The Unfinished Revolution: How Modernisers Saved the Labour Party*, (1998).

Greenberg, Stanley (1), *Middle Class Dreams: The Politics and Power of the New American Majority*, (New Haven and London, 1995).

Greenberg, Stanley (2), *Dispatches from the War Room*, (2009).

Greenspan, Alan, *The Age of Turbulence*, (New York, 2007).

Harman, Harriet, *A Woman's Work*, (2017).

Harris, Tom, *Ten Years in the Death of the Labour Party*, (2018).

Hasan, Medhi and Tom Macintyre, *Ed: The Milibands and the Making of a Labour Leader*, (2011).

Hayter, Dianne *Fightback! Labour's Traditional Right in the 1970s and 1980s*, (2005).

Hewitt, Patricia and Philip Gould, 'Labour and Clinton's New Democrats', *Renewal*, 1/1, (1993).

Hutton, Will, *The State We're In*, (1995).

Hyman, Peter, *1 Out of 10: From Downing Street Vision to Classroom Reality*, (2005).

Labour Party (1981–83), *Report of the Annual Conference*, (1981–83).

Levin, Robert E, *Bill Clinton: Inside Story*, (New York, 1992).

Macron, Emmanuel, *Revolution*, (English edn, 2017).

Mandelson, Peter, *The Third Man*, (2011).

Mandelson, Peter and Roger Liddle, *The Blair Revolution: Can New Labour Deliver?*, (1996).

Marquand, David, *The Unprincipled Society: New Demands and Old Politics*, (1998).

Mattinson, Deborah, *Talking to a Brick Wall*, (2010).

McBride, Damien, *Power Trip: A Decade of Policy, Plots and Spin*, (2013).

Morris, Dick, *Behind the Oval Office: Winning the Presidency in the Nineties*, (1997).

O'Hara, Glen, 'New Labour's Domestic Policies: Neoliberal, Social Democratic, or a Unique Blend?' *Tony Blair Institute for Global Change*. Available at: https://institute.global/news/new-labours-domestic-policies-neoliberal-social-democratic-or-unique-blend, (2018).

Osborne, David and Ted Gaebler, *Reinventing Government*, (Reading, MA, 1992).

Powell, Jonathan (1), *Great Hatred, Little Room: Making Peace in Northern Ireland*, (2008).

Powell, Jonathan (2), *The New Machiavelli: How to Wield Power in the Modern World*, (2010).

Price, Lance, *The Spin Doctor's Diary: Inside Number 10 With New Labour*, (2006).

Pye, Neil, 'Militant's Laboratory: Liverpool City Council's struggle with the Thatcher Government', in Jon Davis and Rohan McWilliam (eds), *Labour and the Left in the 1980s*, (Manchester, 2017), 151–71.

Pym, Hugh and Nick Kochan, *Gordon Brown: The First Year in Power*, (1998).

Radice, Giles (1), *Diaries 1980–2001: From Political Disaster to Electoral Triumph*, (2004).

Radice, Giles (2), *Labour's Path to Power: The New Revisionism*, (1989).

Radice, Giles (3), *Southern Discomfort*, (1992).

Reich, Robert (1), *The Work of Nations*, (New York, 1991).

Reich, Robert (2), *Locked in the Cabinet*, (New York, 1998).

Rentoul, John, *Tony Blair: Prime Minister*, (2001).

Richards, Steve, *Whatever It Takes*, (2010).

Riley, Russell L, (ed), *Inside the Clinton White House: An Oral History*, (Oxford, 2016).

Robinson, Emily, *The Language of Progressive Politics in Modern Britain*, (2017)

Saunders, Robert, *Yes to Europe! The 1975 Referendum and Seventies Britain*, (Cambridge, 2018)

Shrum, Robert, *No Excuses: Confessions of a Serial Campaigner*, (2007).

Stephanopoulos, George, *All Too Human: A Political Education*, (1999).

Straw, Jack, *Last Man Standing: Memoirs of a Political Survivor*, (2012).

Miller Center Interviews (MCI – and then relevant surname). Available at: www. millercenter.org
Madeleine Albright, Tony Blair, Sidney Blumenthal, William Galston, Elaine Kamarck, James Steinberg

Legislative records (LR)
House of Commons (HOC)
House of Lords (HOL)
Congressional Record – House of Representatives (CRH)
Congressional Record – Senate (CRS)

INDEX